# Artists and society in Germany 1850–1914

# Artists and society in Germany 1850–1914

ROBIN LENMAN

MANCHESTER UNIVERSITY PRESS
Manchester and New York
distributed exclusively in the USA by St. Martins Press

Published by Manchester University Press
Oxford Road, Manchester M13 9NR, UK
*and* Room 400, 175 Fifth Avenue, New York, NY 10010, USA

*Distributed exclusively in the USA by*
St. Martin's Press, Inc., 175 Fifth Avenue, New York,
NY 10010, USA

*Distributed exclusively in Canada by*
UBC Press, University of British Columbia, 6344 Memorial Road,
Vancouver, BC, Canada V6T 1Z2

*British Library Cataloging-in-Publication Data*
A catalogue record for this book is available from the British Library

*Library of Congress cataloguing-in-Publication Data*
Lenman, Robin.
Artists and society in Germany, 1850–1914/Robin Lenman.
p. cm.
ISBN 0-7190-3636-4 (c)
1. Painting, German. 2. Painting, Modern--19th Century--Germany.
3. Painting, Modern--20th century--Germany
4. Art and society--Germany. I. Title.
ND567.L46 1997
759.3 09 034--DC21

ISBN 0 7190 3636 4 hardback
First published 1997

01 00 99 98 97 10 9 8 7 6 5 4 3 2 1

Designed and typeset
by Vaughan Collinson Design

Printed in Great Britain
by Biddles Ltd, Guildford and King's Lynn

# CONTENTS

# LIST OF PLATES

# ACKNOWLEDGEMENTS

I am deeply indebted, for their tireless help over many years, to the staffs of the Prussian State Library, Berlin, the Bavarian State Archives, the Munich Municipal Archive, the Monacensia Department (especially Richard Lemp and Gaby Weber) of the Munich City Library, the Municipal Gallery and the Main-Fränkische Museum in Würzburg, the Art Archive of the Germanische Nationalmuseum, Nuremberg, the Western Art Library of the Ashmolean Museum, Oxford, the Warburg Institute and the Victoria & Albert Museum, London. I owe special gratitude to Richard Parker and his colleagues at the University of Warwick Library, and especially those in the Inter-Library Loans Section. Several periods of sabbatical leave from Warwick, and grants from the British Academy, the Wolfson Foundation and the Twenty-Seven Foundation were indispensable for both research and writing.

Friends and colleagues who gave stimulus and encouragement along the way include Volker Berghahn, Marion Deshmukh, Walter Grasskamp, Matthew Jefferies, Peter Jelavich, Ekkehard Mai, Maria Makela and Jim Obelkevich. The late James Joll gave me years of kindly encouragement, and my initial interest in German cultural history. Julia Mills created the map with speed and accuracy. I am grateful to the galleries and copyright-holders who granted permission to reproduce the illustrations; and most especially to Dr Martina Sitt at the Kunstmuseum Düsseldorf. The staff of the Warwick University branch of the National Westminster Bank sorted out complicated international payment problems.

The editorial staff of Manchester University Press handled the book's production with efficiency and good humour. The late Eva Heilmann's friendship and generosity were of inestimable value: without her, this book could never have been written. My daughter Sophie reminded me throughout that book-writing is not the only thing in life. To my wife Anita Ballin I owe unfailing love, help, and toleration of an ever-growing tide of books and papers threatening to engulf our home.

# ABBREVIATIONS

| | |
|---|---|
| ADKG | Allgemeine Deutsche Kunstgenossenschaft |
| BKrA/M | Bayerisches Kriegsarchiv, Munich |
| *BVKS/D* | *Berichte über die Verwaltung der königlichen Sammlungen für Kunst und Wissenschaft zu Dresden* |
| *DKB* | *Deutsches Kunstblatt* |
| GHA/M | Geheimes Hausarchiv, Munich |
| GHK | Gesellschaft Hamburgischer Kunstfreunde |
| GNMAbK/Nbg | Germanisches Nationalmuseum, Archiv für bildende Kunst, Nuremberg |
| GStA/M | Geheimes Staatsarchiv, Munich |
| HSA/M | Hauptstaatsarchiv, Munich, Allgemeine Abteilung |
| *JbGHK* | *Jahrbuch der Gesellschaft Hamburgischer Kunstfreunde* |
| *KChr* | *Die Kunstchronik* |
| *KfA* | *Die Kunst für Alle* |
| *KHB* | *Kgl. Museen zu Berlin: Kunsthandbuch für Deutschland* |
| *KM* | *Der Kunstmarkt* |
| *KuK* | *Kunst und Künstler* |
| *KVB* | *Kunstverein München, Jahresberichte* |
| MFM/W | Main–Fränkisches Museum, Würzburg |
| NKV | Neue Künstlervereinigung |
| NS | New Series |
| PRO/L | Public Record Office, London (Kew) |
| PStB. H/B | Preussische Staatsbibliothek, Handschriftenabteilung, Berlin |
| SAM/M | Staatsarchiv für München, Munich |
| *SBBayKdA* | *Stenographische Berichte über die Verhandlungen der Bayerischen Kammer der Abgeordneten* |
| *SBPrAH* | *Stenographische Berichte über die Verhandlungen des Preussischen Abgeordnetenhauses* |
| *SBRT* | *Stenographische Berichte über die Verhandlungen des Reichstages* |

| | |
|---|---|
| *SHKK* | *Statistisches Handbuch für Kunst und Kunstgewerbe im Deutschen Reich* |
| SPD | Sozialdemokratische Partei Deutschlands |
| StadtAM/M | Stadtarchiv München, Munich |
| StB. M/Mon | Stadtbibliothek, Munich, Monacensia-Abteilung |
| StGL/M | Städtische Galerie im Lenbachhaus, Munich |
| StG/W | Städtische Galerie, Würzburg |
| VBK | Verein Berliner Künstler |
| *ZBSL* | *Zeitschrift des Bayerischen Statistischen Landesamtes* |
| *ZfbK* | *Zeitschrift für bildende Kunst* |
| ZIK/M | Zentralinstitut für Kunstgeschichte, Munich |

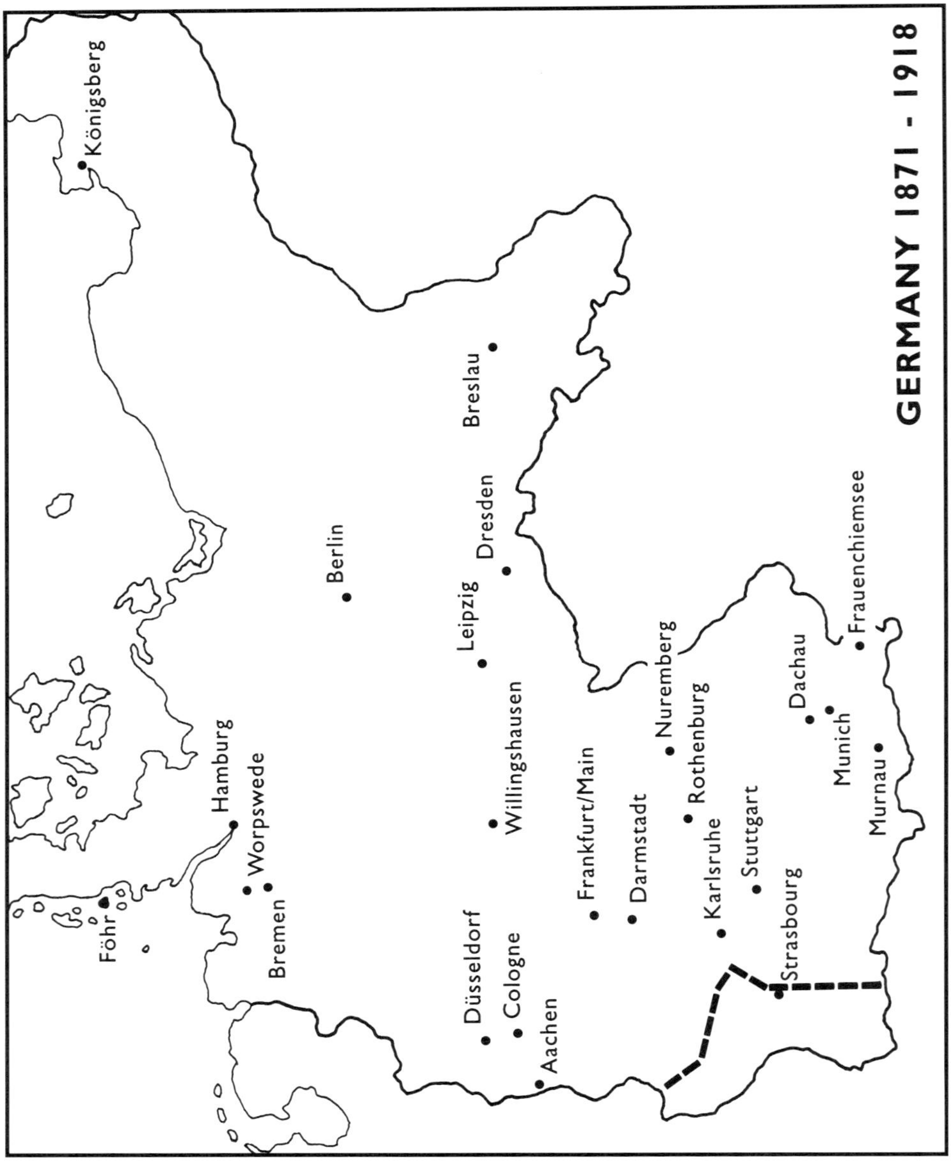
GERMANY 1871 - 1918
Königsberg
Breslau
Berlin
Dresden
Leipzig
Hamburg
Worpswede
Bremen
Föhr
Willingshausen
Düsseldorf
Cologne
Aachen
Frankfurt/Main
Darmstadt
Nuremberg
Rothenburg
Karlsruhe
Stuttgart
Strasbourg
Dachau
Munich
Murnau
Frauenchiemsee

# Introduction: painting and society in Germany 1850-1914

The period from the middle of the nineteenth century until the outbreak of the First World War witnessed, in the states which became part of the Second German Empire, a major increase in the production, exhibition, discussion, reproduction and sale of painted pictures. In particular there was considerable growth in the quantity of artists training and practising in the main German art centres; of pictures shown at salons organised by academies, art unions (*Kunstvereine*) and artists' societies; of dealers, their clients and business associates at home and abroad; of specialist art journals and articles on art in the ordinary press; of public art museums, the pictures they acquired and the visitors they attracted; and of money spent by private individuals, commercial organisations, municipalities and governments on two-dimensional painted images, whether movable (though sometimes huge) or in fixed, mural form. Other indicators could be extracted from the official and unofficial handbooks published from the 1880s onwards which offered overviews of an art world that, in all its aspects, was becoming ever larger and more complex.

Many of these developments had their origins well before 1850, and these will be discussed, where appropriate, in the course of this book. But the imperial period and the two decades preceding it were for various reasons especially important. In the first place, for example, although the market for contemporary art had begun to develop after the end of the Napoleonic Wars, stimulated by the picture-lotteries and touring exhibitions organised by the art unions, the pace of activity increased markedly from the 1850s and 1860s onwards, influenced by growing prosperity and economic integration, the proliferation of major art collectors and – later than in France or in Britain – the emergence of a dealer network. Secondly, however, the private function of painting as ornament, status symbol and store of value was widely regarded as subordinate to its public ones as an expression of national cultural vitality and – in conjunction with sculpture and architecture – as a propaganda medium. Here too, post-1850 developments had a strong impact on artists and debates about art. On the one hand, after the frustrations and reverses of 1848/49, political unification gradually became a serious possibility and, between 1866 and 1871, a reality. On the other, linked with the unification process, there was the enormous expansion of the German industrial economy that was to continue, with only occasional interruptions, throughout the imperial period. These developments did more than merely create more heroes to commemorate and more wealth to be spent on private and public art collections, although these consequences were important. They were also accompanied by a widespread sense that Germany had entered the circle of great powers with a certain cultural deficit – one art historian described her as 'the Cinderella of European history, ridiculed by all nations'[1] – and that there must be a renaissance of the arts and sciences that would both dignify the crass materialism of the so-called 'founding period' (*Gründerzeit*) and validate the new Empire's economic and political might. This attitude towards culture was clearly expressed in a 1915 obituary of the 'theatre duke' Georg II of Saxe-Meiningen: 'After the great task of national unification had been completed, he set out at the head of a great army of artists in order, in a series of great bloodless triumphs, to proclaim the glory of the nation before all peoples.'[2]

Yet although German achievements in the theatre and music, as well as in scholarship and the sciences, came to be universally acknowledged, the standing of the visual arts was much less certain. Painting had played a significant role, as in other developing nationalisms,[3] in promoting a sense of collective identity and in helping to construct a national (historical and mythological) past and landscape. Especially in the middle decades of the century German academies had considerably influenced the emergent national art of a swathe of countries from Scandinavia through eastern Europe to Greece; and of the United States, many of whose leading painters, from Emanuel Leutze to Frank Duveneck, spent fruitful years in centres like Düsseldorf and Munich. However, Germany's failure seriously to challenge the artistic hegemony of France, resented by nationalists since the eighteenth century, continued to cause deep frustration after 1871. This envenomed the debates surrounding the great international exhibitions of contemporary art, treated all too often as virility contests between opposing cultures; fuelled protests about the importation of French influences and French paintings; and underlay the controversies in the Wilhelmine period (1888-1918) about public patronage and the development of Germany's museums of modern art.

Germany's economic transformation, in less than three-quarters of a century, from backwardness to near-superpower status was accompanied by a vast social upheaval. Between 1871 and 1910, despite substantial emigration, the Empire's population increased by 58 per cent, from about forty to sixty-seven millions.[4] More significant was a fundamental change in the demographic balance of society, with a major shift of population from agriculture to industry, and rapid urbanisation. Whereas in 1871 only 4.8 per cent of Germans lived in cities of more than 100,000 inhabitants, by 1910 the figure was 21.3 per cent. Over the longer period 1850-1910 the population of Hamburg increased more than five times, from 175,000 to 931,000, Leipzig nearly elevenfold, from 63,000 to 679,000, and Essen nearly thirty-threefold, from 9,000 to 295,000. Berlin in 1840, on the eve of the vast economic upswing of the railway age, had had about one-third of a million inhabitants. Attracting immigrants from all over eastern and northern Germany, it grew to 826,000 by 1871, 1,889,000 by 1900 and 2,071,000 by 1910, becoming one of Europe's largest industrial centres and its most densely populated area.[5]

The impact of these changes on contemporaries was intensified by their rapidity, with a particularly hectic burst of urban growth in the 1890s; by the disruption caused by the creation of industrial and transport infrastructure, and housing, on an immense scale; and by the fact that many migrants to the new industrial cities were young single men, some of them Polish-speakers from Prussia's eastern provinces. Dreadful working-class living conditions and the fluctuations of the trade cycle also perpetuated demographic instability within cities and industrial regions as workers searched incessantly for better jobs and wages; indeed, before 1914 an estimated one-third of the urban population moved house every year.[6] Anxiety about issues of public health, order and morality was rife throughout the period but most acute in the 1890s, with a major cholera epidemic in Hamburg and a sustained moral panic, triggered by events in Berlin, about crime, prostitution and venereal disease. Finally there was also the perceived threat of revolution, linked to the growth of the industrial proletariat and the spread, despite Bismarck's Anti-Socialist Laws (1878-90), of Social Democracy. In the elections of 1912, indeed, the SPD became the largest party in the Reichstag, and in Berlin captured more than 75 per cent of the vote.[7] With hindsight, of course, this was a symptom of stabilisation rather than of imminent upheaval. But together with the disorientation caused by economic and demographic change, the physical transformation of the landscape, pollution, new technology and methods of work-organisation, industrial conflict and incipient changes in gender relations, this political development heightened the widespread feeling of crisis and uncertainty that accompanied Germany's spectacular – but very unevenly distributed – increase in prosperity since the middle of the nineteenth century.

This was the context for Emperor Wilhelm II's notorious pronouncement, on 18 December 1900, about art's duty to distract attention from the grimmer aspects of reality and encourage contemplation of the 'Ideal'.[8] (It remains probably one of the best-known facts about 'Wilhelmine' culture.) Such sentiments, doubtless shared by respectable citizens throughout the Empire, explain not only why artists who confronted poverty and social problems were tarred with the brush of 'subversion', but also why governments and municipalities since Unification had been spending large sums on propagandistic works of monumental art. These ranged from huge structures like the Kyffhäuser Monument sited in open country to the elaborate equestrian statues of 'Wilhelm [I] the Great' in Berlin and many other cities and the vast expanses of mural painting, mostly on historical or mythological themes, commissioned for public buildings all over the Empire. As we shall see, the post-1871 monumental art boom revived a whole branch of painting, kept a phalanx of history specialists in work until the turn of the century and beyond, and helped to prolong their dominant position at

German academies. Whatever effect these large and complex allegorical–symbolical–historical paintings may actually have had on the adult citizens and parties of schoolchildren exposed to them, their perceived significance as patriotic and monarchical propaganda can be measured not only by their cost but by the elaborate pageantry and speech-making marking their inauguration. This was especially conspicuous in relation to the decoration of Imperial Germany's many new and restored town halls, which was frequently financed by a mixture of State and local funds. In June 1882, for example, no fewer than four Prussian ministers arrived to celebrate the completion of Peter Janssen's mural-cycle for the Neo-Gothic *Rathaus* in Erfurt which had cost 60,000 marks (three-quarters of it found by the Government) and depicted scenes from the city's history between the age of Saint Boniface and the Wars of Liberation.[9] Sometimes such paintings testify eloquently, if obliquely, to the tense atmosphere in which they were created. In the municipal council chamber of the grim industrial city of Bochum, for example, Fritz Neuhaus's 1903 *Industry Salutes the Hohenzollerns*, funded by the Rhenish–Westphalian Art Union and local businessmen, depicted the paladins of Unification, and Wilhelm II, being hailed by a procession of miners and metalworkers (actually costumed employers and councillors), with a crowd of cheering onlookers (members of their families) and a chariot-borne figure of Industry (the wife of the District Administrator (*Landrat*)).[10]

An even larger segment of German art production might be crudely interpreted as a symbolic denial of the new urban and industrial reality, and in psycho-cultural terms, along with much of contemporary literature, as a kind of steadying sea-anchor for society on its plunge towards modernity. Two obvious examples were landscape painting and the 'timeless' small-town genre scenes painted by artists like Karl Spitzweg (1808-85) and his many imitators. More widespread, however, was the idealised depiction of rural life that dominated the market for paintings, prints and book-illustrations until well into the twentieth century. One of its most celebrated practitioners was the Dresden painter–illustrator Adrian Ludwig Richter (1803-84), whose chubby-cheeked village children, cute animals and picturesque cottages clustered around ancient churches found their way into countless middle-class homes. Though superficially more naturalistic, and identifiably linked to particular regions such as the Black Forest, Southern Bavaria and the Tyrol, the peasant pictures produced by all the major German schools from the middle decades of the nineteenth century onwards continued to evade the realities of country life: on the one hand, poverty, violence and the effects of work, weather and old age; and, on the other, the inroads of capitalism, mechanisation, urban dress and manners and other manifestations of 'progress'. Like contemporary ruralist fiction, such images of the countryside created for a largely urban public can be related to the vast change in attitudes towards nature taking place since the eighteenth century, and to the strident anti-urbanism of writers like Wilhelm Heinrich Riehl after 1850.[11] By 1900 this was reflected in the so-called 'homeland art' (*Heimatkunst*) movement that tended to move away from the mere prettification of peasants and their habitat towards a stylised monumentality with 'blood and soil' undertones. Actual town–country relations were increasingly complicated by the expectations, influenced by decades of nostalgic and escapist painting, of growing numbers of tourists, to which rural entrepreneurs, for good capitalist reasons, were eager to conform.

In his classic study of the nature and effects of modernity, *All That is Solid Melts into Air*, Marshall Berman summarised the characteristics of modernisation thus:

> the industrialisation of production, which . . . creates new human environments and destroys old ones, speeds up the whole tempo of life, generates new forms of corporate power and class struggle; immense demographic upheavals, severing millions of people from their ancestral habitats . . . ; rapid and often cataclysmic urban growth; systems of mass communication, dynamic in their development, enveloping and binding together the most diverse people and societies; increasingly powerful national states, bureaucratically structured and operated, constantly striving to expand their powers; mass social movements of people, and peoples, challenging their political and economic rulers, striving to gain some control over their lives; finally, bearing and driving all these people and institutions along, an ever-expanding, drastically fluctuating capitalist world market.[12]

At first sight this might stand as a convenient description of the transformations that took place in Germany as a whole between 1850 and 1914. In reality, of course, the most extreme changes were fairly localised, while many provincial communities altered little and, drained of their more enterprising inhabitants, became relatively more backward than before. On an imaginary late-nineteenth-century 'modernisation scale', one end would have corresponded to remote and still primitive villages in regions such as East Prussia or the Bavarian Forest. The other, increasingly perceived as the very capital of modernity (or 'Americanism': Walther Rathenau was to describe it in 1899 as 'Chicago on the Spree'),[13] would have been Berlin. This was more than a matter of size and population, since the raw statistics of the city's growth conceal the fact that its economy was dominated by some of Germany's most advanced high-technology enterprises – names like Agfa, AEG, Siemens, Schering – closely linked to the banks and related institutions that had made Berlin Central Europe's leading financial centre since the 1860s.[14] For most of the period Berlin was at or near the leading edge of innovation in all kinds of fields: public amenities, with electric street lighting (from 1882) and Germany's first underground railway; commerce, with state-of-the-art advertising, fast-food restaurants and fabulously opulent department stores;[15] and entertainment, with 'round-the-clock nightlife'[16] in pleasure-zones like the Friedrichstrasse, proliferating boulevard theatres, cabarets and music-halls and, by 1914, hundreds of cinemas. (The negative side, constantly highlighted in anti-urban polemics, included thousands of prostitutes, a criminal underworld, a high proportion of Germany's motor accidents,[17] and an ocean of barrack-like, overcrowded tenements in the Northern and Eastern suburbs). By the pre-war years, such descriptions of Berlin as 'a wonderful modern machine-hall, a gigantic electric motor' (Egon Friedell)[18] or 'a terrifyingly eerie city, ugly and magnificent' (Franz Marc)[19] had become almost obligatory commonplaces. But as early as 1860, those archetypal *flâneurs* Edmond and Jules de Goncourt had described their fleeting eye-contact with Berlin women in the streets as 'one-second novels' and registered the city's atmosphere of 'American' modernity.[20]

Berlin artists, like writers, responded to what they saw around them in many different ways.[21] Adolph Menzel, whose life (1815-1905) coincided with the city's transformation from the capital of a regional power into an imperial metropolis, and who turned increasingly from historical to contemporary subjects at the end of the 1850s, depicted innumerable aspects of its life, from court balls to building sites, with the extreme precision and coolness characteristic of his art. In more nostalgic vein, a whole branch of late-nineteenth-century Berlin painting recorded picturesque corners of the old city threatened with demolition and redevelopment. Between the 1870s and about 1910 those Berlin-based artists who were inspired by the city itself (others, including important members of the Secession, concerned themselves with the lakes, forests and green-belt suburbs of surrounding Brandenburg) can be divided into a minority, fascinated – though not necessarily throughout their careers – with its more troubling social aspects, and a larger group who sought to capture its ever-changing surface appearance in a spirit of aesthetic detachment. Prominent among the former was the young Max Klinger (1857–1920), whose early etching cycles of the 1870s and 1880s, in modes ranging from the melodramatic to the proto-surreal, depicted the new social spaces of cafés and skating-rinks and transmuted the 'human interest' stories peddled by the expanding boulevard press into harrowing images. Later, figures like Hans Baluschek (1870–1935), the printmaker Käthe Kollwitz (1867–1945) and Heinrich Zille (1858–1929) achieved notoriety with their unvarnished glimpses of working-class life. On the other side, such painters as Lesser Ury (1862-1937) and Franz Skarbina (1849-1910), after their own experiments in urban Naturalism, reacted in an impressionistic or Whistlerian way – like August Endell in his book *The Beauty of the Great City* of 1908[22] – to the purely visual stimulus of Berlin's ever-changing atmosphere, light-effects and human flux. This approach was galvanised by the arrival of radical newcomers from Dresden and other places around 1910, and French and Italian avant-garde influences. In the immediate pre-war years Expressionist images of the metropolis – sometimes interspersed with an idyllic ruralism – by artists like Ernst Ludwig Kirchner (1880-1938), Max Beckmann (1884–1950) and Franz Heckendorf (1888-1962) ranged from a more stylised and anti-naturalistic reprise of 'Impressionist' subjects such as shoppers and strollers in the elegant West End to images of stress and alienation. An extreme transition was made by the Breslau- and Paris-trained Ludwig Meidner (1884-1966). After quasi-documentary views of suburban building-sites and U-Bahn excavations, he painted the Schöneberg gasometer planted incongruously like a Martian spacecraft (1911) and then, after experiencing a religious crisis, the catastrophically exploding and capsizing forms of an urban apocalypse.[23]

Although the visual arts were constantly represented throughout the period, for political, economic and other reasons, as the property and concern of the entire nation, in reality different sections of society participated very unequally in their production and enjoyment. The working class not only had even less opportunity to enjoy fine art than other branches of high culture but, with exceptions which were either highly controversial or – as in the case of Neuhaus's Bochum mural – completely bogus, remained practically invisible to artists. The liberal–nationalist associations of much German art in the second half of the nineteenth century also made it unpalatable to many Catholics, increasingly estranged from the largely Protestant liberal movement since the 1850s and feeling beleaguered and persecuted in Bismarck's 'little German' (*kleindeutsch*) Empire. Women, finally, an even larger segment of the population, faced major obstacles in becoming professional artists and were assigned a decidedly subordinate role in the overall economy of art.

Before 1800 monarchs, princes and aristocrats had played a major, though by no means exclusive,[24] role in Central European patronage and art-collecting. Between the end of the Napoleonic Wars and 1914 royal patrons remained very important, from Ludwig I of Bavaria and Friedrich Wilhelm IV of Prussia in the early and middle decades of the nineteenth century to Prince Regent Luitpold of Bavaria and Grand Duke Ernst Ludwig of Hesse-Darmstadt under the Empire. In the grim conditions of October 1919 the Munich Art Union that, like similar societies in other capitals, had had numerous royal members, lamented that 'not even the most ideal democratic state form' could ever replace the support it had received from 'the Wittelsbach ruling house'.[25] Yet the Wittelsbachs had always been exceptional; and in relative terms, even in Bavaria, dynastic contributions to the visual arts (as to music and the theatre) had declined substantially as the market expanded, museums and monuments were funded increasingly by taxpayers and private benefactors, and the whole cultural environment became more pluralistic. In liberal–nationalist circles, moreover, art-creation had for long been regarded as much too important to be left to courts and dynasties. This belief – however much nostalgia might disguise the fact later on – had permeated the art union movement for most of the nineteenth century, and fuelled the campaigns in the 1840s and 1850s for a national gallery of modern art, and it was robustly expressed by Friedrich Pecht, Southern Germany's premier mainstream critic, in his 1888 survey of modern Munich art. Celebrating the Munich School's extraordinary fame and prosperity in the reign of Ludwig II (1864-86), he frankly rejoiced that the eccentric king had had virtually no influence on painting, and claimed that, since the sixteenth century, it had been 'the mark of all truly creative art movements in Germany that they had not been brought about by the favour of monarchs or other individual patrons but had developed, if not in open opposition to the ruling powers, then more or less ignored by them and freely out of the bosom of the nation'.[26]

Terms like *Nation* and *Volk* that were used repeatedly in this kind of context did not, of course, refer to the whole population, but to the middling stratum of society that was increasingly representing itself as Germany's principal culture-creating group and source of national values. Decades before Thomas Mann's famous dictum, enunciated in the First World War, that 'German culture [*Bildung*] is *bürgerlich*',[27] the image of a uniquely creative (and patriotic) *Bürgertum* had been vividly constructed in Gustav Freytag's huge novel of mercantile endeavour, *Debit and Credit* (*Soll und Haben*), first published in 1855, endlessly reprinted and still topping library popularity lists at the turn of the century.[28] The book's hero, Anton Wohlfahrt, is the poor but capable son of a lowly official who, after many adventures, finds fortune, love and fulfilment in a great trading company. In doing so he thwarts the evil machinations of various Jewish characters and joins in the struggle to promote German culture and interests in the 'Wild East' of the Polish–Silesian borderlands. Although Freytag's prime concern was the culture of commerce rather than of art, the book reads like a vast homily in which 'German' creativity is equated at every level with the virtues – self-discipline, thrift, perseverance, idealism and so on – of the Christian (but implicitly Protestant) middle class. These positive characteristics are set against stereotypical negative ones: 'Jewish' materialism and rapacity, 'Polish' turbulence and destructiveness. Particularly fascinating, however, is the contrast between the aristocratic characters, presented as ill-educated, feckless and incapable of maintaining their patrimony, and Wohlfahrt, who possesses not only 'bourgeois' qualities but also the 'knightly' ones of honour, loyalty and physical courage. At the end of the book, when he becomes betrothed to the merchant's sister, he is shown the firm's master ledger in a scene that must have reminded many readers of the discovery of the Holy Grail.[29] *Debit and Credit*'s underlying theme, therefore, articulated at times in almost religious language, is that of an aspiring new elite bidding for leadership by virtue of values that are both modern and historic.

Fiction, of course, is not sociology (although it may well be more influential), and by the 1850s the two overlapping but not synonymous terms *Bürgertum* and *Mittelstand* encompassed a reality so complex and heterogeneous that it has been described not as a class but as a 'post-corporate supra-local social formation' (Jürgen Kocka).[30] Its 'economic' component alone was becoming increasingly differentiated in terms of wealth, commercial sophistication and, no doubt, nuances of political and cultural outlook, as between merchants like Freytag's Herr Schröter – already quite an old-fashioned figure by the 1850s – in Breslau; modern industrialists such as Krupp in Essen; and the tens of thousands of retailers and other small businessmen active throughout the German states. Another important category was the 'cultural middle class' (*Bildungsbürgertum*), dominated in the early nineteenth century by graduate State officials, academics and secondary-school teachers, but later expanding to include the ever more numerous members of the 'free' professions, doctors, lawyers and journalists. Detailed local research would probably show that these two middle-ranking sections of society were in most places the main pillars of the expanding

German art market between the 1850s and the 1900s. They certainly dominated those crucial and ubiquitous institutions, the *Kunstvereine*. Of the seventy-five male members (there were also six women) of the Saxon Art Union in the administrative and manufacturing town of Bautzen in 1842, for example, twenty-nine, ranging from shopkeepers and publicans to merchants and industrialists, fitted the classification 'trade and industry', while thirty-one were officials, teachers, lawyers and a doctor.[31] A 1905 breakdown of the 4,180 non-artist members of the Munich Art Union revealed that 1,240 (almost 30 per cent) were teachers, academics or officials, while another 900 (21 per cent) had commercial occupations.[32]

Doubtless by this time, though less perhaps in Munich than in more heavily industrialised cities, the latter category included members of the new technical and managerial groups employed in Germany's increasingly modern economy. Probably less well represented in the art unions by the Wilhelmine period were the very rich – the number of millionaires in Prussia alone rose by nearly 60 per cent between 1895 and 1907[33] – who, if they were interested in art, probably patronised Germany's new commercial galleries, and fashionably modern artist-groups like the secessions. Also expanding, but at the opposite end of the middle-class spectrum, were the white-collar commercial and industrial employees created by the second industrial revolution. Their share of the workforce more than doubled, to 10.7 per cent, between 1882 and 1907, and their average earnings also rose substantially, in boom periods to near-professional levels.[34] No doubt many of these clerks and retail workers, sneeringly dismissed as philistines ('one great "Piefke family" ') by mandarins like the historian Friedrich Meinecke,[35] sought to imitate the leisure and cultural patterns of the old middle class. Some, however, especially the young, were clearly being drawn to the cinema and other branches of a modern commercial culture that was to reach full maturity in the 1920s.[36]

The relationship between the industrial working class and visual high culture between 1850 and 1914 was tenuous. Although academies offered bursaries and subsidised fees to students from relatively impoverished backgrounds, opportunities for workers' children to become artists were practically nil; even Zille, whose images of the Berlin proletariat have a compelling authenticity, was a Saxon artisan's son. (He knew real poverty, however, and his family's first Berlin lodgings were in a cellar.)[37] In fact workers' access – albeit passive – to other branches of mainstream culture increased considerably after 1890 via the numerous libraries and associations affiliated to the SPD and the trade unions; membership of Berlin's popular dramatic society, the *Neue Freie Volksbühne*, for example, had reached 48,000 by 1910.[38] (Still, less than a quarter of the working class belonged to the labour movement in 1914, and 'working-class culture' as a whole was highly diverse, localised and to a considerable extent rooted in the pre-industrial past.)[39] But enjoyment of fine art was more problematical. By the Wilhelmine period skilled men living in company housing may well have been able to decorate their homes with the low-cost lithographs promoted by bourgeois reform groups and the SPD, and the budget reproductions published by firms like Hanfstaengl and Bruckmann in Munich and Seemann in Leipzig. But the vast majority of those other workers who had households at all – in 1893 a quarter of Ruhr miners were lodgers[40] – probably met their aesthetic needs with the crude devotional and topical prints mass-produced in Germany and abroad and peddled to tenement-dwellers (as, formerly, to villagers) along with trinkets and pulp novels.[41] Art unions were effectively closed to workers for reasons both social and financial: in 1907, for example, some 80 per cent of working-class incomes were spent on basic necessities.[42] Museums not only had inconvenient opening hours but were also intimidating places, decorated with arcane symbolism and policed by guardians on the look-out for inappropriate dress or behaviour. (There appears to have been no German equivalent of London's Whitechapel Gallery, where selected Royal Academy pictures were exhibited for respectable working people.)[43]

Considerations of cost and atmosphere probably also excluded workers from the commercial panoramas that flourished in Germany in the last three decades of the nineteenth century.[44] These were vast painted scenes, in the 1870s and 1880s often of Franco-Prussian battles, mounted on the interior walls of special – and standardised, so that the paintings could be sent on tour – circular buildings, and viewed from raised central platforms. Although realised by teams of academically-trained artists, this was essentially a commercial medium, requiring large amounts of capital and with admission charges to match: 1.50 Marks (or 50 pfennigs on Sundays), for example, to view Louis Braun's panorama of the Battle of Mars-la-Tour in Hamburg in 1893.[45] (Berlin panorama patrons included aristocratic socialites like Baroness Hildegard von Spitzemberg[46] and, in fiction, Theodor Fontane's Effi Briest and her *Landrat* husband.) The nearest popular equivalent was the fairground panorama, created by specialist firms and often similar in subject-matter, but simply a painted backdrop in a booth viewed through rows of binocular lenses.[47] Much more attractive by 1914, however, was the cinema, with dozens of primitive *Kintopps* springing up in the working-class districts of big cities. The noisome atmosphere of these establishments – in 1909 Alfred Döblin described Berlin audiences of petting couples, tubercular children, unwashed workmen and prostitutes[48] – and their lurid programmes inevitably alarmed both the bourgeois establishment and the cultural theorists of the SPD. But their extreme cheapness, the opportunities they offered for passive escapism and their links with pulp fiction made them an irresistible distraction from the grim conditions of urban-industrial life.

Finally, if one slices the cake of German society vertically rather than horizontally, it is clear that, as in France and Britain, the position of women in relation to art was very different from that of men. It is true, as we shall see, that there was a sizeable and growing minority of female professional painters by the Wilhelmine period. However, women were excluded from the leading State academies; the institutions of the art world – art criticism, art unions, the leading artists' societies, exhibition juries, commercial galleries, museum acquisition committees, and so on – were overwhelmingly dominated by men; and women's artistic activity was hampered by a highly developed 'culture of separate spheres'. In these conditions, famous and/or commercially very successful female artists were likely to be almost as rare as, in Linda Nochlin's phrase, 'Eskimo tennis players'.[49] The obstacles facing women as painters were, of course, simply one aspect of their position in society generally.[50] Although a radical emancipation movement flourished just before and during the revolutions of 1848/49, it subsided again in the reactionary 1850s, and for the rest of the nineteenth century opposition to the extension of women's political, educational and economic rights remained massive. A key component of this situation was the bourgeois cult of domesticity, which required the full-time presence of a woman to supervise servants, rear children and generally maintain the home as 'the best protector of our virtues'.[51] This was enshrined in the 1900 Imperial Civil Code which, although improving women's legal status in some respects, affirmed male supremacy within the family and allowed a wife to pursue gainful employment outside the home only with her husband's consent.[52]

By this time, nevertheless (and probably fuelling the *fin-de-siècle* cult in art and literature of the voracious and unpredictable 'New Woman'), conditions were changing. In the first place, there was growing pressure to broaden employment opportunities for middle-class women, at least until marriage.[53] Secondly, women were gaining access to higher education. The epoch-making decision of Heidelberg University in 1901 to admit them to all faculties was followed by other universities, with the Prussian ones bringing up the rear in 1908; and by the winter semester of 1913/14 6.3 per cent of all university students in Germany were women.[54] Yet in general German society remained heavily dominated by patriarchal values. Women who flouted sexual and social convention – like Franziska von Reventlow, painter, novelist, bohemian and unmarried mother[55] – were completely ostracised. The principal reform organisation, the General German Women's Association, was cautious in its demands and continued to propagate conservative notions about women's aptitudes and social role. The ambivalence of liberally-minded men was perhaps epitomised by the Berlin physicist Max Planck, who admitted women to his lectures in 1897 but still maintained that 'Nature herself assigned to women the role of mother and housewife, and that to ignore natural laws is to invite great damage which will in this case be inflicted upon coming generations.'[56] Fascinating in this context was an 1895 handbook aimed at well-brought-up girls on the threshold of adulthood, *From the Girls' School into Life*.[57] An introductory essay entitled 'Then and Now' not only contrasted the enforced idleness of early-nineteenth-century women with contemporary work opportunities, but positively stressed the need for women to create security for themselves in the event of non-marriage or widowhood; and other contributions described a substantial range of occupations, from nursing and commerce to the arts. By far the longest piece, however, written in the form of letters to a young woman from her grandmother, detailed a woman's domestic duties. Although lip-service was paid to the reader's desire to become a doctor, the responsibilities described were so multitudinous and time-consuming as to have made any serious professional activity impossible.

The frequently heard comment, in the two or three decades before the First World War, that art centres like Munich and Karlsruhe, and popular painting locations like the Dachau *Moos*, were crowded with female artists, had some basis in statistical fact: in Munich, for example, the number of professionals rose from 48 to about 220 (with another 159 elsewhere in Southern Bavaria) between 1886 and 1907.[58] Amateurs (headed by Emperor Wilhelm II's mother Victoria) were much more numerous, and probably included many women capable of selling pictures privately or through the art unions. Among the professionals, alongside such canonical figures as Paula Modersohn-Becker (1876-1907), Gabriele Münter (1877-1962) and Käthe Kollwitz, were some who, though subsequently neglected, achieved substantial success in the market-place. One was the German–Swedish landscapist Jeanna Bauck (1840-1926), who won prizes at exhibitions in Germany and abroad and was eventually represented in galleries in Stockholm and Trieste. She was well enough known to be cited as a role model for aspiring female professionals in the 1895 handbook cited above, and was also praised by the young Paula Becker as an inspiring teacher.[59] Another artist who deserves to be better known was the Munich doctor's daughter Albertina (Tini) Rupprecht (1867-1956) who, though mainly self-taught, was well established by her late twenties and eventually became one of Central Europe's most highly-remunerated society portraitists. Working in pastel, and with a predominantly royal and aristocratic clientele – though with the occasional press baron or American millionairess thrown in – she earned well over a million marks by 1914 and had to decline far more commissions than she could execute.[60] At a more modest level, but certainly as successful as many of their male colleagues, were such figures as the flower-painters Marie Nyl and Olga Weiss, the landscapists Tina Blau-Lang, Marie Starke and Emmy Lischke and the child-portraitist Lucia van Gelder.

The fact remains, however, that, as in London and Paris,[61] women played a far less prominent role in the art world than men. Among the hundreds of exhibitors at the Berlin Academy's important centenary salon in 1886 there were only forty-three women, of whom twelve were based in Austria, Belgium or Holland.[62] A three-volume album of Munich painters in their studios published in 1889 included only four females, one of them Rupprecht, among ninety-seven males.[63] In the Wilhelmine period elite groups such as the Berlin and Munich secessions and the German Artists' League (*Deutscher Künstlerbund*) counted only a tiny proportion of women among their exhibitors and members; in 1911, the more conservative Munich Secession had no local female members at all.[64] Women also seem to have been totally excluded, except as the guests of artist-husbands, from clubs like the Düsseldorf Paint-Box and the Munich Allotria, and more generally from the social life of art communities. In particular it was impossible for a respectable woman to associate with the waitresses, seamstresses and models – routinely treated as prostitutes by the authorities, at least in

Munich[65] – who were the regular companions of unmarried painters and students at the masques, drinking sessions and studio festivals that made up the artist's calendar. Yet these involved more than just pleasure and relaxation. As in other countries, such badges of professional status as decorations, museum purchases and membership of key committees and juries were often brokered by means of networking and lobbying under the guise of sociability.[66] Moreover, artistic success usually required, in addition to talent and hard work, assertiveness and business sense, the relentless cultivation of social contacts and considerable showmanship; Anton von Werner in Berlin and the Munich 'painter-princes' Lenbach, Kaulbach and Stuck were classic examples. Here women were fundamentally handicapped by the culture of separate spheres, and by the admonition, inculcated practically from birth, to keep a low profile on every possible (non-domestic) occasion.[67]

But they also faced other obstacles. Although, as we shall see later, private tuition for women was quite an industry in Germany, female students were unable to participate fully in State academy courses until after the First World War. This was all the more disadvantageous in that academic training was not only more prestigious and cheaper than private instruction, but probably more likely to provide valuable professional contacts. Once launched, female professionals found themselves largely confined to 'minor' subjects such as children, small animals or flowers: there were no German equivalents of Elizabeth Butler, Henrietta Ward, Suzanne Valadon or Rosa Bonheur. And they also evidently found it more difficult than men to persuade dealers to handle their work.[68] Underpinning this segregation and discrimination was an ideology of (male) genius and creativity that, personified by old masters like Dürer and modern ones such as Arnold Böcklin and Hans Thoma, was increasingly stridently articulated in the second half of the nineteenth century. Its implications for women were spelled out frankly by Jacob von Falke in the fourth (1882) edition of his best-selling handbook on interior decoration. 'Everything truly great and beautiful in fine art,' he wrote, 'and that still today delights our wondering gaze, was created by the strong sex, not the fair one.' Women, by contrast, found their natural creative outlet in the charming, the delicate, the small-scale; those few who matched male virtuosity usually did so at the cost of their feminine role in home and society.[69] Both for Falke and for other theorists, most especially the founding father of German museum education, Alfred Lichtwark, women's proper function in relation to art was simply an aspect of their broader 'natural' role as nurturers and home-makers. 'Woman,' continued Falke, 'by encouraging what is beautiful in the home and by cultivating her own taste and that of her family and those around her, collaborates in the education of the nation, and the culture of humanity.'[70] Finally, of course, although some women, Bauck and Rupprecht for example, remained single and independent, there were the constraints imposed by marriage and motherhood. One can only speculate how women like Charlotte Berend Corinth, Frieda Putz, Alice Trübner, Cella Thoma, Maria Marc or Paula Modersohn-Becker might have developed if they had married men who were not artists, or not married at all. But the emotional and conventional

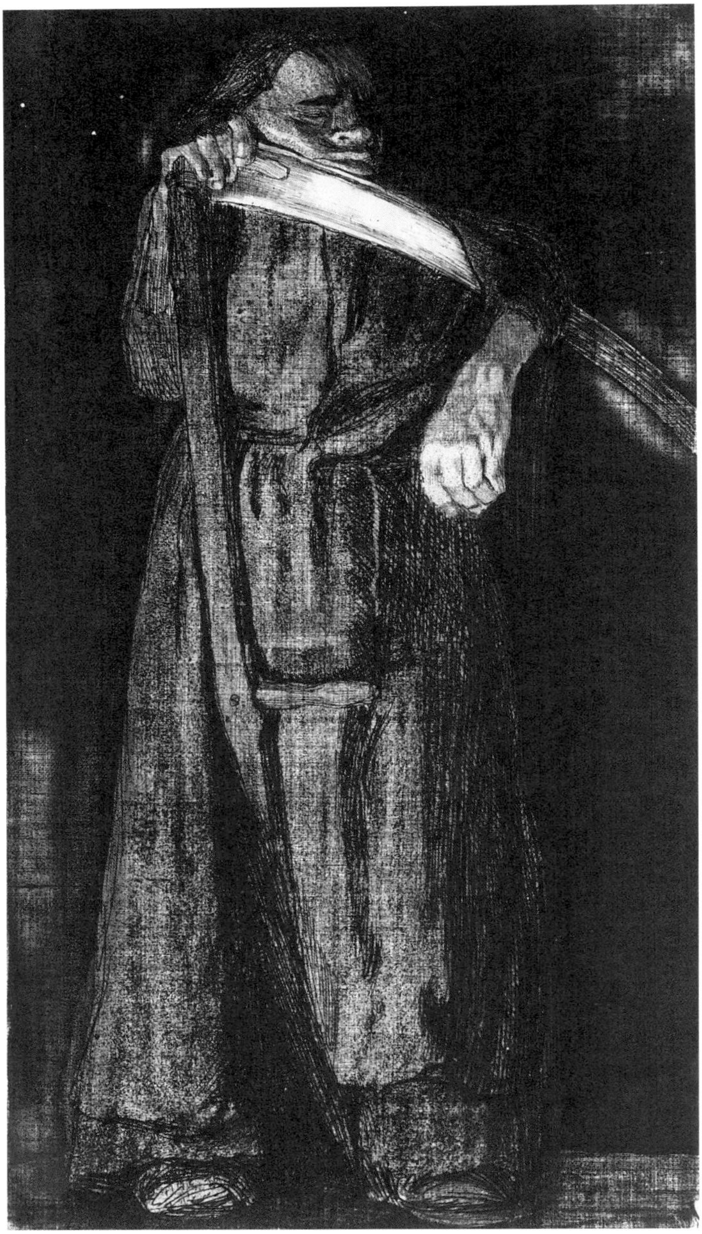

Plate 1 Kathe Kollwitz, *Woman with Scythe*, 1905, etching and aquatint, 36.7 x 19.8 cm. This etching is closely related to an image in the famous *Peasants' War* print cycle created by Kollwitz between 1902 and 1908, and was perhaps inspired by the fearsome 'Black Anna' she had read about in Heinrich Zimmermann's history of the uprising.

pressure on women to subordinate their own aspirations to a husband's career, especially if he were both an artist and his wife's former teacher, was enormous and in most cases clearly irresistible.

Unlike the working class, which was rendered semi-invisible by contemporary artistic taboos, women were depicted in tens of thousands of images. These ranged from portraits and historical and genre scenes to – increasingly from about 1890 onwards – nudes, often but not always in biblical, mythological or Orientalist settings. With the notable exception of Modersohn-Becker's series of nudes, and the nude self-portraits she painted in 1906, these last were created solely by men, and thus inevitably reflected male fantasies, fears and erotic predilections. The artistic hedonism of the *fin-de-siècle*, fuelled by Nietzschean ideas of instinctual self-fulfilment[71] and welcomed by sensualists like Max Klinger (for whom, as for Renoir, the depiction of the female body was a kind of sexual act),[72] as a long-overdue relief from decades of buttoned-up historicism, became the preserve of male Secessionists, Expressionists and contributors to racy magazines like *Jugend*. As in other countries, the prolonged exclusion of women from mainstream art training reflected not only economic protectionism but determination to keep the artist's special relationship with the naked human body as a male monopoly.[73] However, if women were overwhelmingly depicted as domesticated and/or, at whatever level, sexually available (even the Salomes, Judiths and vampire–females created by male artists were titillating as well as threatening), one powerful alternative perspective was offered by Käthe Kollwitz. Raised in a radical family, allowed as an adolescent to roam the docks and poorer districts of her native Königsberg, then married to a (highly supportive) doctor in Northern Berlin, she was one of the few German artists of either sex to devote herself consistently to working-class themes.[74] And her female subjects were rendered either as unpicturesquely battered, bereaved or ill or, especially in her illustrative and historical print cycles, as rebellious and out of control, goading their lumbering menfolk to violence or, as in the terrifyingly malevolent *Woman with Scythe* of 1905 (Plate 1), themselves preparing for bloody homicide. Though professionally well established by 1914, however, and able to reach a large public through papers like *Simplicissimus*, Kollwitz remained, in terms of her social and artistic vision, an isolated figure and a source of misgiving even to some of her strongest admirers.[75]

# 1
# History, art and nation

## NATIONAL SYMBOLS

Early on the morning of 14 August 1880 work began on the last pinnacle of Cologne Cathedral's south tower, as its stone finial was lifted and fixed in place. The massive piece of masonry, weighing some five tons, had to be hauled straight up the 157-metre edifice: a tricky, dangerous operation personally supervised from atop the vast scaffolding by Richard Voigtel, Director of the Cathedral building works for the past quarter of a century. At last, when the task of cementing and polishing was done, the Prussian flag was unfurled from the north tower – completed a few weeks earlier – and the flag of Germany from its twin. It was 9.53 a.m. Six hundred and thirty-two years, less one day, had passed since the Cathedral's original foundation-stone had been laid in 1248; three and a half centuries since the original building works had been suspended; and nearly thirty-eight years since King Friedrich Wilhelm IV of Prussia, at a new stone-laying ceremony on 4 September 1842, had restarted the gigantic project. Now the building itself, until the completion of the Eiffel Tower in 1889 the tallest structure on earth, was finished. (It would be much longer before windows, frescoes and sculptural decorations were all in place.) In the square below and the surrounding streets flags were hung out, and in the dense crowd of onlookers tears of joy were freely shed.[1]

It had been an extraordinary saga. The choir had been completed in 1322, and by 1410 the south tower had reached a height of more than 58 metres. But interruptions had become longer and more frequent, and in 1560 work had stopped entirely, although by this time the incomplete shell was one of the largest buildings in Europe, bigger even than the finished cathedral of Amiens. Services were held in the choir until the arrival in 1794 of the French revolutionary armies, which requisitioned the building as a forage store. It was during this most dismal period of its history, when the city itself (until 1814) was part of France, that the unfinished cathedral topped by its medieval crane became a symbol for Romantic nationalists, and during the Wars of Liberation against Napoleon schemes to complete it began to germinate. Their most energetic supporters were the writer Friedrich Schlegel and the Cologne scholar and art-collector Sulpiz Boisserée and his brother Melchior. By November 1814, when the Rhenish publicist Joseph Görres, briefed by Sulpiz, appealed in the *Rheinische Merkur* for the completion of the Cathedral as 'a thank-offering for liberation from French oppression', not only Goethe but Prussia's reforming statesmen Stein and Hardenberg and the architect Karl Friedrich Schinkel had been won over. But most important in the long term, as Cologne had become a Prussian city, was the enthusiasm of the romantically-minded Crown Prince Friedrich Wilhelm. After years of halting progress under his parsimonious father, Friedrich Wilhelm III, the prince's accession to the throne in June 1840 marked a turning-point. In 1841 the Cathedral Building Association (*Dombauverein*) was formed, soon with many branches throughout Germany, and in September 1842 Friedrich Wilhelm IV laid the foundation-stone of the façade of the south transept and pledged to complete the whole building. Although funding remained a problem, grants from the Prussian State were soon outdone by contributions from other German princes and from the *Dombauverein* network, and the creation of a cathedral lottery in 1864 decisively accelerated the work.

Each phase of construction from September 1842 onwards was marked by an elaborate festival. On 15 August 1848, the cathedral's 600th anniversary, the nave with five stained-glass windows donated by King Ludwig I of Bavaria was dedicated in the presence of Friedrich Wilhelm IV, 'Imperial Regent' Archduke Johann of Austria and deputies from the Frankfurt National Assembly, with heady invocations of national freedom and harmony between monarchs and people. (This euphoria soon evaporated, and in riots later that year parts of the cathedral scaffolding were used for barricades.) Friedrich Wilhelm returned in 1852 and again, for the last time, in 1855, and there were further celebrations in 1863 and 1867. But these events were outshone by the two-day completion festival held on 15 and 16 October 1880. On the morning of the fifteenth – the birthday of Friedrich Wilhelm IV, who had died in 1861 – Emperor Wilhelm I and Empress Augusta, Crown Prince Friedrich and his wife Victoria and other royal guests, after worshipping in the Protestant Frauenkirche, attended a formal act of celebration at the cathedral, during which a casket containing a history of the building, coins, medals and other artefacts was inserted into the finial of the south tower. As the last stone was cemented into place bells pealed and cannon thundered, and the vast throng of spectators sang 'Now thank we all our God.' That evening there were torchlight processions, fireworks and electric floodlighting of the cathedral and surrounding buildings. The next day the emperor watched a vast municipal pageant designed by a team of historical painters from neighbouring Düsseldorf in which about 1,000 people in period costumes, 400 horses and 8 floats symbolically re-created Cologne's history from the thirteenth century. The last of these bore a huge figure of Germania holding a laurel-wreath above a model of the cathedral, and was followed by detachments from all the armies of the German Empire marching to the strains of *The Watch on the Rhine*. The festival ended with a banquet in the city's fifteenth-century ceremonial hall, the Gürzenich, and yet more fireworks and illuminations.[2]

From every point of view Cologne Cathedral was an extraordinary creation: in size, cost, splendour and stylistic harmony, and because of the technical ingenuity and political will required for its completion. But it was also remarkable for the diversity of its symbolic associations – for romantic conservatives and radical democrats, liberal nationalists and countless ordinary Catholics and Protestants – and for the debates surrounding it from the Napoleonic period onwards. The art historian Karl von Lützow wrote in September 1880: 'What we older ones marvelled at in our childhood as a gigantic fragment, whose sometime completion we looked upon as a beautiful dream; what for us was a sad symbol of our people's vanished and annihilated greatness, now stands physically before our eyes in glorious consummation: a far-seeing monument to national unity and power regained.'[3] For many nineteenth-century Germans Cologne Cathedral was the supreme national monument in a period in which, not only in Germany but also in other European countries and the Americas,[4] more monuments were created than at any other time in modern history. Notable German examples included the Valhalla (1830-42) and the Hall of Liberation (1842-63) overlooking the Danube in Bavaria; the Hermann Monument (1835-75) in the Teutoburg Forest near Detmold; the National Monument (1877-83) above the Rhine near Rüdesheim that marked the foundation of the Empire; and the Kyffhäuser Monument (1890-96) in Thuringia. The great tower commemorating Napoleon's defeat at the Battle of the Nations near Leipzig, inaugurated in 1913, was the largest and, at six million marks, the most expensive monument in Europe. Equally significant, in addition to these huge, elaborate and costly structures sited in open country, were many smaller urban monuments to cultural figures: Luther in Wittenberg (1821), Gutenberg in Mainz (1837), Schiller in Stuttgart (1839), Dürer in Nuremberg (1840), and many others. Between 1800 and 1883 the number of commemorative statues of all kinds – dynastic, military and cultural – in Germany grew from 18 to about 800;[5] to which were added, between the 1890s and 1914, some 500 'Bismarck towers' erected on hilltops throughout the Reich.[6]

The major monuments were by no means uniformly sponsored or funded. The Valhalla and Hall of Liberation were created by Ludwig I, the vast equestrian statue of Wilhelm I at the confluence of the Rhine and Mosel in Coblenz by the Prussian State, the Kyffhäuser Monument by Germany's huge ex-servicemen's organisation.[7] But other projects were financed by a mixture of private, State and royal contributions, and the Bismarck towers mostly by local associations and student groups. Mixed funding from both 'above' and 'below' fostered symbolic tension between monuments' dynastic–authoritarian meanings on the one hand, and national and democratic ones on the other. (Their negative messages were less ambiguous: francophobia, anti-ultramontanism and, increasingly, anti-Socialism). There can be little doubt, however, about their emotional impact on contemporaries. When the monument to Hermann the Cheruscan's victory over the Romans in AD 9 – a huge copper statue of the hero, brandishing a sword manufactured by Krupp – was at last inaugurated on 16 August

1875, the event was attended by Wilhelm I (saluted as 'Arminius Wilhelmus'), many of his fellow-princes, veterans' and students' groups and ordinary patriots from all over Germany, Austria and even the United States. Karl Woermann, the Düsseldorf Academy's resident art historian, had looked forward to the day since boyhood, and half a century later recalled it as one of the great experiences of his life.[8]

The idea of the cathedral-as-monument, symbolising national and democratic rather than monarchical aspirations, was prevalent in early-nineteenth-century Germany, and made visible both in the paintings of Schinkel and Caspar David Friedrich and in the schemes of Schinkel and others to commemorate the heroes of liberation.[9] The nationalist revolutionary Karl Ludwig Sand even envisioned a new capital to be named *Aller Teutschen* with its parliament in 'a great Christian cathedral'.[10] By this time, too, the most appropriate-seeming style for such structures was Gothic. Dismissed by Renaissance writers like Giorgio Vasari as weird and barbaric, it had been rediscovered in the late eighteenth century and increasingly revalued in comparison with the Baroque and Rococo styles favoured by Germany's francophile courts. Goethe, visiting Strasbourg Cathedral in April 1770, and half-expecting to find a cluttered monstrosity, was overwhelmed by the building's harmony and majesty and inspired to write a famous essay *On German Architecture*. In this, he not only celebrated one of the cathedral's principal creators, Erwin von Steinbach, as a genius of the German Middle Ages but also, following a long tradition, claimed Gothic as quintessentially German, and much more of a national style than anything created by the Italians or the French.[11] Even in 1880, when Gothic's mainly French origins were recognised, Lützow – quoting a fellow art historian, Karl Schnaase – could still describe Cologne Cathedral's medieval architecture as 'the marvellously developed flower beside the only half-opened bud' of French Gothic.[12] The style was also entwined with the national nature-symbolism to be found in such diverse places as Friedrich's forest-paintings, Grimm's *Fairy-Tales* and the oak-leaves on the Iron Cross. (At the end of the century Bismarck would present delegations of admiring students with oak-saplings from the Sachsenwald to be planted as monuments to unity.)[13] In 1790, standing in the choir of Cologne Cathedral, the scientist and revolutionary Georg Forster compared its soaring pillars to 'the trees of an ancient forest'.[14] Eight years later, visiting the mainly Gothic church of St Sebaldus in Nuremberg, the nationalist writer Ernst Moritz Arndt imagined himself in 'a wood of sacred pines through whose crowns faint light pierces from the radiant heavens'.[15] Such sylvan images linked cathedrals to the ancient habitat of Rome's Germanic conquerors and, again and again, implicitly contrasted the nature-rootedness of German art with the 'civilised' artificiality of Latin (*welsch*) culture.

Anti-French symbolism was stridently in evidence in October 1880, when the military march-past and the striking of the cathedral's huge 'Emperor Bell', cast from the iron of captured guns, suggested yet another celebration of victory over Napoleon III. For the Hohenzollerns the dynastic and power-political dimensions of the project had always been crucial. During Wilhelm I's reign, association with it stood to benefit

Prussia's claim to leadership of a united Germany, and in 1867 the king even considered being crowned in the cathedral.[16] But under Wilhelm's two predecessors the main priority had been to integrate the newly-acquired Rhine Province into the Prussian Kingdom. The Great Powers' assignment of the disparate territories along the Rhine to Prussia after Napoleon's defeat, mainly as a barrier to future French expansion, was widely regarded as both artificial – the new and old territories were not even contiguous – and economically and culturally undesirable. Prussian conservatives resented being 'pulled westwards' by this new responsibility, disliked the Rhineland's French-implanted legal institutions, and would have preferred more Saxon territory instead. Urban, educated Rhinelanders regarded Prussia's agrarian heartland as underdeveloped and its social structure as barbarically feudal, and feared the imposition of absolutism and militarism. Although the strength of opposition to the new order after 1815, in the Rhineland or elsewhere in the German Confederation, should not be overestimated, some major figures, including Görres, who was forced into exile in 1819, became increasingly frustrated with Friedrich Wilhelm III's refusal to grant a constitution. And it was tempting, in these circumstances, for Rhinelanders to prefer a German to a Prussian identity, and the memory of the Holy Roman Empire to the reality of the Hohenzollern monarchy.[17]

Prussia's political strategy, as in Silesia in the previous century, was rapidly to impose the higher military and administrative structures while leaving some scope for autonomy at municipal level. But cultural initiatives were also important, especially the creation of Bonn University in 1818 and the refounding of the moribund Düsseldorf Academy the following year. Considerably more resources were devoted to culture after the accession of Friedrich Wilhelm IV. In 1843 the liberal art historian Franz Kugler was given official responsibility for artistic matters throughout the kingdom, and the architect and writer Ferdinand von Quast became conservator of Prussian monuments.[18] Three years earlier, the State had opened the way for the restoration of the historic Imperial Hall in Aachen, another symbol-laden and politically sensitive project that, in all its architectural and decorative stages, was to drag on for more than sixty years.[19] But the completion of Cologne Cathedral was exceptionally important: as a paternalistic monarch's token of harmony with his subjects and in the 1840s especially, as critics were quick to point out,[20] as a substitute for such real concessions as press freedom and a constitution. The 1842 celebrations, moreover, had followed a serious war scare in 1840. Best remembered today as the inspiration for Hoffmann von Fallersleben's *Deutschlandlied*, it was a political watershed that had brought renewed French claims on the Rhineland, a fierce resurgence (after passions had earlier waned) of anti-French feeling in Germany, and a shift within German liberalism from cosmopolitanism to nationalism.[21] Finally, also, it had enhanced the cathedral's aura as a symbolic bridgehead for Prussia, widely perceived as the prime defender of German soil, on the west bank of the Rhine.

On his arrival at the cathedral on the morning of 15 October 1880 Wilhelm I was formally greeted by a Catholic suffragan bishop, and in his speech duly emphasised that no earthly enterprise could succeed without God's help.[22] Yet there was no congratulatory message from Pope Leo XIII, and the fact that Cologne Cathedral was one of the world's largest Catholic churches and the seat of a great archdiocese was little stressed. Indeed, of all the major Cathedral festivals held since 1842, only one – for the dedication of the nave in 1863 – had been predominantly ecclesiastical in character, and the 1880 occasion could well have been mistaken for a tribute to the late Friedrich Wilhelm IV with nationalist trimmings. Archbishop Melchers was in exile, having earlier appeared on police wanted notices like a common criminal, and was forbidden to return for the celebrations, while the demolition of his palace and other functional buildings strongly suggested, as some Catholics had long feared, the appropriation of the cathedral as a secular monument. Even the Papal flag was banned.

The reason for this situation, stranger still in view of the decades of dedicated Catholic support for the project, was the bitter struggle between Church and State, the aptly-named *Kulturkampf*, being waged in Prussia and other states of the Empire, and the train of events preceding it.[23] After 1815 Church–State relations had been smooth enough, with the latter, especially after the Prussian Concordat of 1821, wielding extensive powers of control through generally compliant bishops. In the background was the still-persisting Romantic ideal of a Christian nationalism inspired by the Middle Ages and transcending confessional divisions. But conditions changed from the 1830s onwards, under the influence of a Europe-wide revival of popular Catholic piety, and the Prussian hierarchy's efforts to harness the movement in order to increase the Church's independence. Especially in the Rhineland, where four-fifths of the population was Catholic, this nourished official fears that religious discontent and political separatism might fuse, as they already had, with French support, in the Low Countries. Friedrich Wilhelm IV's speech of September 1842 in Cologne in fact came at the end of seven years of strife over mixed marriages and other issues, with serious popular disturbances and the imprisonment of Archbishop Droste-Vischering. The latter's presence on this occasion was therefore an important gesture of reconciliation.[24] Yet liberal anti-clericalism, and inter-confessional tension generally, was growing, not least on artistic matters. In 1842 Karl Friedrich Lessing's huge painting *Hus at the Council of Constance*, showing the doomed Czech reformer disputing with fanatical prelates, aroused fierce controversy, particularly as Lessing (1808-80) was one of the king's most favoured artists.[25] The previous year, 'Protestant' allusions in one of the proposed frescoes for the Aachen Imperial Hall had brought protests from the local clergy.[26] Church–State relations improved in the 1850s on the basis of common conservatism after the 1848 revolutions, but worsened again in the sixties with Catholic Austria's exclusion from Germany and the creation of the Prussian-dominated 'little German' Empire. Post-1871 nationalism remained imbued with anti-Catholicism, as the Lutheran hymns and *kulturkämpferisch* sermon at the Hermann Monument's inauguration amply demonstrated (Hermann had been an anti-papal symbol since the time of Ulrich von Hutten);[27] and Rhenish Catholics soon found their educational and ecclesiastical freedoms attacked not only by Bismarck but, in the name of 'civilisation', by their former liberal allies. Even after the *Kulturkampf*'s formal termination in the 1880s, the opposition between progress-orientated liberalism and Catholic traditionalism remained a fundamental feature of German political and cultural life. In some places – for example Hildesheim, where anti-ultramontanism was symbolically expressed in the new city hall frescoes – the bitterness was still perceptible in the 1920s.[28]

Paradoxically, considering its medieval origins, Cologne Cathedral could also be seen as a symbol of modernity.[29] The floodlighting of the entire structure in October 1880, made possible largely by the development of the Siemens dynamo, was one spectacular aspect of this. (In 1909 an electric bell-ringing mechanism was to be installed which substituted press-button technology for the strength of fifty-three men). But the whole construction process owed a vast debt to modern technical progress. Both Voigtel and his predecessor Ernst Friedrich Zwirner were creative engineers who, in the manner of their French contemporary Eugène Viollet-le-Duc, viewed their task not as the restoration of an ancient monument but as the construction of a living building for which the use of up-to-date techniques and materials was wholly appropriate. The entire roof-framework of the new nave was an iron skeleton weighing over 180 tons, and the original wooden rafters of the choir were also eventually replaced with iron struts. The 63-metre ridge turret, weighing 214 tons and supported inside the roof on tubular legs, was one of the largest all-iron structures of its time. Cast zinc and Portland cement were employed wherever necessary. Serial production of many components, the use of steam-driven stone-hoists and other specially designed machines made building operations faster, safer and cheaper. The scaffolding, nearly 160 metres high around the towers and able to withstand enormous weights and wind pressures, was a technical triumph in its own right, much admired by visiting American skyscraper-builders. Practically and symbolically, too, the cathedral was closely linked to the railway, a prime factor in the Rhineland's economy since the late 1830s and by mid-century the main driving force of the German industrial revolution. Trains transported stone and manufactured components for the cathedral, and on his last visit in 1855 Friedrich Wilhelm IV not only celebrated the completion of the south transept façade but also laid the foundation-stone of Cologne's first fixed bridge across the Rhine, a combination of iron lattice-work and crenellated stone towers constructed exactly on the cathedral's main axis.[30] By 1880, when Prussia nationalised the Rhenish railways, the completed cathedral looked down on one of Germany's most important junctions. By 1894 it was flanked by a huge new station which, with its 255-metre-long iron and glass roof canopy, neo-Renaissance façade and tall tower housing the imperial suite was, like the *Dom* itself, a complex symbol of dynastic authority, national self-confidence, and progress.[31]

Monarchs, certainly, had dominated the October 1880 celebrations: Emperor Wilhelm I (increasingly, since the failed attempts on his life in 1878, the object of a 'Wilhelm the Great' cult) and, in spirit, his late brother Friedrich Wilhelm IV. But, as the elaborate costumed procession on the second day made clear, the cathedral's long history was closely bound up with the history both of Cologne itself and of cities generally. For it was true not only that modern – i.e. urban – technology and economic prosperity had made the final, nineteenth-century phase of the project possible, but also that medieval cathedral-building had been an urban phenomenon, dependent on a degree of financial, mathematical and organisational sophistication inconceivable in the feudal and agrarian society outside the towns.[32] Such considerations prompted Cologne's civic leaders not only to spend some 140,000 marks on the 1880 pageant but to commemorate it in permanent visual form. As with Emperor Franz Josef's silver wedding celebrations in Vienna in April 1879, organised by the painter Hans Makart and clearly a model for the Cologne occasion,[33] the procession was comprehensively recorded in albums of photographs and chromolithographs. But two years later Wilhelm Camphausen and the other Düsseldorf artists who had designed it were commissioned to paint murals in the Gürzenich depicting some of the historic events it had recalled. The result was a monumental link between the city's and the nation's history comparable to the repainted Hall of Emperors in the Frankfurt City Hall, the Römer, and the ongoing restoration work in Aachen. And, like their contemporaries in Nuremberg, in a painting depicting the arrival of the imperial regalia in March 1424,[34] Cologne's city fathers incorporated portraits of themselves and their families in the pictures: symbolic affirmation of the unity of past events and present aspirations.

The latter were considerable. In the 1880s Cologne and other large cities were still strongholds of liberalism, and widely regarded as test-beds for enlightened social and cultural policies. The middle decades of the century had been for the most part a period of urban prosperity and expansion during which, within the framework of the Prussian Municipal Ordinance of 1808, and similar measures in other states, city governments had embarked on a wide range of tasks in the fields of public health, education and general culture. The German Constitution of 1871, which allowed only limited parliamentary influence on national government while forcing liberals to compete with new mass parties at the polls, increased the significance of cities, with their restricted franchises, as arenas for middle-class political and cultural activity; indeed, the National Liberal Party justified political inequality in exactly these terms.[35] In 1880, with a population of almost 145,000 (by 1914 it would reach 635,000), Cologne was about to begin a new phase of rapid growth beyond its old fortifications, and four and a half decades of massive spending on public buildings, cultural institutions and the municipalisation of key utilities.[36] For much of this period, thanks to the Prussian three-class voting system, the process was controlled by a National Liberal elite mainly representative of Protestant or Jewish big business and the professions, and despite the growth of an industrial proletariat and the fact that the overwhelming majority of the city's population – 82 per cent in 1880 – were Catholics. After the turn of the century, it is true, important gains were made by Social Democracy and political Catholicism, and in 1906 the Catholic Centre Party finally achieved a majority in the Cologne municipal assembly.[37] (Five years later in Munich the liberals and their Socialist and Centrist opponents were almost exactly balanced.)[38] Yet still in the decade before 1914 German cities, with their soaring budgets, expanding bureaucracies and powerful, highly-qualified mayors, could present themselves, and be admired by foreigners, as models of enlightenment and purposefulness. Indeed in 1911 one writer, pointing to their collective annual expenditure on education and culture alone of more than 250,000,000 marks – almost twice the budget of the German Navy – described them as 'standard-bearers of spiritual, economic and social progress to the benefit of the whole Fatherland'.[39] Pride in such achievements, though also fear of new forces from below, and a sense of isolation in a society still dominated by traditional (military, aristocratic, agrarian) elites, all helped to shape the urban, liberal *Bürgertum*'s perception of its own historical origins and role; and its interpretation, via images and pageantry as well as print, of the remote past.

## VISIONS OF THE PAST

Cologne in 1880 had few resident painters, and it was obvious for two reasons, apart from proximity, that artists would be summoned from Düsseldorf to design the cathedral pageant. In the first place, Düsseldorf was one of Germany's major art-production centres, with a large artist population and an artists' club, the Paint-Box (*Malkasten*), famous for its imaginative festivals.[40] Secondly, its Academy had long been identified with history-painting in the grand manner, and Camphausen and his colleagues belonged to a group of specialists who executed commissions all over northern Germany in the late nineteenth century. But by 1880, in any case, it would have been unthinkable for such an occasion not to have included the kind of artist-directed costume pageant which actually took place.

Since the early nineteenth century such spectacles had been created increasingly often both by artists for their own festivals and, with their collaboration, to celebrate major national events. Four mid-century examples from Frankfurt-on-Main illustrate the trend:[41] the first National Choral Festival in 1838, dedicated to Mozart as 'Germany's greatest composer'; the 400th anniversary of Gutenberg's invention of printing in 1840; the Schiller Festival – one of many held throughout Germany – of 1859; and the first German National Shooting Festival in 1862. All these events attracted crowds of participants from far and wide: an estimated 30,000 people joined the Gutenberg procession, and 12,000 took part in the marksmen's historical pageant. National, democratic, and to a degree anti-monarchical symbols were prominent on each occasion, including the flying of German flags, figures of Germania, and vast processions reminiscent of recent radical movements in Belgium and Switzerland, not to mention Germany. Swiss connections were especially interesting: 1,100 alpine marksmen came to Frankfurt in 1862; three years earlier the Schiller festivities had included a performance of *William Tell*; and at the dedication of the Frankfurt Schiller monument 30,000 onlookers had raised their hands against tyranny in the Rütli Oath. In 1838, 1840 and 1859 emotional tributes were paid to commoners instead of to monarchs or warlords, and Wilhelm Lindenschmit's cycle of decorative battle-paintings for the 1862 *Schützenfest* showed kings and generals on the margins while the heroic centre space was occupied by common soldiers.[42]

Under the Empire such oppositional overtones seem to have evaporated. At the 1880 Cologne celebrations the monarch was the guest of honour, and negative sentiments were directed at the Catholic Church (officially marginalised) and the French (off-stage). Such was the pattern for many other post-1871 pageants marking the opening of exhibitions and museums, the dedication of monuments and the anniversaries of dynasties, cities and associations, with tributes to the Hohenzollerns and symbols of imperialism displacing those of freedom and democracy. Thus only a tiny Swiss contingent appeared for the seventeenth Shooting Festival in Frankfurt in 1912, Tell's presence was confined to chocolate advertisements, and the fraternal and libertarian practice of marksmanship was overshadowed by a show of military armaments. The obligatory francophobic note was struck by a procession of Tyroleans costumed as anti-Napoleonic guerillas.[43] These were striking changes that, as far as the middle-class sponsors of such pageants were concerned, suggest (like many a town-hall mural cycle)[44] a sense of historic partnership between emperors and citizenry, as well as strong affirmation of Germany's assertiveness abroad.[45] In the last analysis, however, the differences between the earlier and the later festivals were probably less significant than what linked them over many decades: the public's enduring fascination with the past, and the value attached to re-created history as a means, with whatever emphasis, of articulating collective concerns in the present.

The past was as central a component of national identity in Germany as in other emerging nations,[46] but with the difference that nineteenth-century German scholars were among the pioneers of history as an academic discipline, and in fields like classical studies and the history of art achieved a position of world leadership. Although this development was well advanced in the eighteenth century, the Napoleonic occupation vastly stimulated interest in remote and supposedly more glorious times; thus in 1810, for example, G. A. H. Stenzel began his *History of Germany under the Frankish Emperors* in order 'to tell the subjugated nation how faithful and fearless its fathers had been'.[47] Prussia's catastrophic defeat in 1806 led directly to Wilhelm von Humboldt's transformation of Prussian universities from bureaucrats' training-schools into power-houses of scholarly research. Later, in 1823, the desire both to advance knowledge and to reveal past German greatness led Baron vom Stein to found that great corpus of critically edited source-material, the *Monumenta Germaniae Historica*. In the same year appeared the first volume of Friedrich von Raumer's widely-read *History of the Hohenstaufens and their Time*, which helped to kindle an enduring interest in the high Middle Ages and above all, at both an academic-historical and a popular-mythological level, in the figure of Emperor Friedrich Barbarossa. Another landmark was Leopold von Ranke's *History of Germany in the Age of the Reformation* (1839-47), a richly-textured account of the late fifteenth and early sixteenth centuries as a period of both imperial decline and national rebirth, in its town-centred cultural and economic aspects prefiguring Ranke's own time. Common to both works was the 'historist' assumption that, although historical writing should be source-based and rigorously objective, seeking to explain the past in its own terms, historians had an obligation to educate public opinion and contribute to the debates of the present. This they did with such gusto that by the imperial period they occupied a position of extraordinary cultural importance, as 'bestowers of identity, explicators, interpreters, fashioners of the future'.[48]

The rising status of historians, the growth of an educated middle class fascinated by the past, and the sense that the nineteenth century was itself a period of momentous historical change – indeed, an age of revolution – explains why historical argument and analogy deeply permeated political discourse. The classic example was the 'German question' debate of the 1850s and 1860s, when the narrower political controversy (initially over whether to support Austria against French-backed Italian nationalism) became entwined with an academic–historical one between *kleindeutsch*-Protestant-'Borussian' historians such as Johann Gustav Droysen and Heinrich von Sybel, determined to construct a centuries-old Prussian mission to lead and unite Germany, and a *grossdeutsch*-Catholic-universalist school led by Julius von Ficker, who looked back to the broader, more diverse entity of the medieval Empire. Overlapping with this debate, and continuing fiercely after 1871, was another about the historical relationship between Germany and Rome. Not only Raumer and Ranke but the next generation of predominantly liberal–nationalist academic historians postulated an organic connection between Protestantism and nationalism, arguing that the Papacy had hindered German aspirations since the Middle Ages, and that individualism and modern civilisation were born in the Reformation. Catholics, of course, dissented. But mainstream history's growing institutionalisation in universities,[49] at which Catholics were under-represented, made it easy to marginalise their views.

Press comments in 1880 that Church–State strife had accompanied both the commencement and the completion of Cologne Cathedral doubtless reminded many readers of the struggles between the thirteenth-century Hohenstaufen emperors and the Papacy, given that familiarity with major historical events was more widespread in the late nineteenth century than ever before. This knowledge was disseminated partly by academic historians since, despite growing specialisation, Ranke and other leading figures also addressed their lay contemporaries via public lectures and the press, and from the 1850s the historical essay became a significant branch of history-writing.[50] Nineteenth-century legal training, the background of most officials, also included an important historical element.[51] Yet Germans' perception of the past is likely to have been influenced at least as strongly by popular media such as historical novels and plays,[52] and as scholarship stripped away fable and romance, fiction fleshed out heroes according to present needs and interests. The last Hohenstaufen emperor, Conradin, executed in Naples in 1268 after Italian, French and Papal intrigues, inspired sixty-six novels and plays between 1800 and 1900 alone, their tone strongly influenced by current attitudes to France and Rome.[53] On another level, the growing army of archivists, school history teachers and members of historical associations, and the founding of historical museums, also helped to bring the past to life.[54] But images, too, were vital; in the nineteenth century, popular history was above all painted history and its offshoots book-illustration, stage design and pageantry.

Modern German history-painting, *Historienmalerei* - a term that also embraced biblical and mythological subjects – had begun with the 'historical idealism' of the Catholic Rhinelander Peter Cornelius (1783-1867) and his followers.[55] Successively Director of the Düsseldorf, Munich and Berlin academies, Cornelius designed mythological and religious frescoes for the Bavarian and Prussian kings in a style that combined classical linearity with Romantic expressiveness. Earlier he had belonged to the Nazarene colony in Rome whose members hoped to promote a patriotic and spiritual rebirth in liberated Germany through the revitalisation of religious painting in the spirit of the early Italian Renaissance. In November 1814 Cornelius had written to Joseph Görres, just before the latter's appeal for the completion of Cologne Cathedral, advocating a fresco revival as the basis for a new national art. Such paintings, he argued, on 'the walls of tall cathedrals, of quiet chapels and lonely monasteries, of town– and market-halls', would bring alive the great figures of national history and myth and herald a Christian and national reawakening.[56] (The collective production of frescoes, moreover, would revive the community of the medieval workshop, on which Cornelius was later to model his teaching.) In 1819 the artist was commissioned to paint mythological frescoes for Crown Prince Ludwig of Bavaria's new museum of classical sculpture in Munich, the Glyptothek, and, despite his appointment in Düsseldorf soon afterwards, he continued to spend much of his time in Munich, where he became Academy Director in 1825. After quarrelling with his patron (by now King Ludwig I), he left for Berlin in 1840 and spent the rest of his life planning frescoes for a projected Hohenzollern family tomb.

In elite circles Cornelius at the height of his powers had a legendary reputation, and his influence persisted at the more conservative academies for decades. Berlin's new National Gallery, opened in 1876, was specially designed to accommodate his cartoons, to which actual frescoes, transferred from the Casa Bartholdy in Rome, were added later.[57] Like other historical idealists, notably Julius Schnorr von Carolsfeld and Wilhelm Kaulbach, he also created memorable book illustrations. Yet he never became popular as a painter, and certainly failed to achieve the impact anticipated in his letter to Görres. Technical shortcomings were partly to blame: Cornelius was no Raphael. But, believing that art's supreme function was to communicate ideas, he also crammed his paintings with classical and scriptural allusions – he referred to the Glyptothek frescoes as his 'philosophical dissertation'[58] – and distrusted colour as a sensuous distraction from thought: as a later critic wrote, his cartoons should have been executed in marble rather than in paint.[59] In this, he and his fellow-idealists were reacting against the dominant Rococo style of the previous century, which they regarded as frivolous and un-German. But the result was an esoteric and bloodless art that alienated an increasingly colour-hungry public and ultimately also Ludwig I, who dismissed Cornelius with the classic *mot,* 'a painter must be able to paint'.[60]

When Cornelius died in 1867 he was remote from the main artistic currents of the time. His pupil Kaulbach, creator of abstruse 'world-historical' canvases and frescoes and Director of the Munich Academy from 1849, was also an isolated figure with more foreign than German admirers. More significant was Alfred Rethel (1816-59), whose major achievement, in addition to powerful woodcuts, was the cycle of historical frescoes in the Aachen Imperial Hall.[61] Their execution was delayed by debates about the building's restoration (indeed, about the direction of the whole project), and then overshadowed by the upheavals of 1848/49 and by Rethel's illness: he was finally declared insane in 1853, leaving the work to be completed by his colleague Joseph Kehren. But Rethel's conception marked an important transitional stage between Cornelius's 'airborne idealism',[62] with its floating angels and heroes in timeless draperies, and the positivistic naturalism of the mid-century. While his Aachen kings and emperors have an epic presence appropriate to their setting, they are also palpably earthborne and convincingly medieval, due partly to Rethel's study of the *Monumenta Germaniae Historica* and contemporary costume manuals. It was this latter tendency, but pushed to lengths of theatricality and illusionism already apparent in Kehren's continuation of the Aachen frescoes, that was increasingly capturing the public's imagination.

Early examples of the historical colourism that was to dominate both large- and small-scale painting in Germany for the rest of the century came from Düsseldorf, where Academy training had taken a more naturalistic turn after Cornelius's departure.[63] Theodor Hildebrandt's *Murder of the Princes in the Tower* of 1835 rendered fabrics, costumes and the deadly bolster with almost *trompe l'oeil* fidelity. Lessing's sombre scenes from the life of Hus were hailed both as marvels of characterisation and empathy, 'history as it actually was, an image of the time, true to nature',[64] and as supremely accessible: 'We never need any commentaries for his pictures, they are comprehensible in themselves to anyone with the least understanding of visual language.'[65] One source of inspiration for such work was Paris, where Paul Delaroche had been painting richly-coloured historical dramas since the 1820s. Another was Antwerp, where the Belgian independence movement had encouraged artists to paint episodes from the Low Countries' earlier struggles for freedom. Stylistically, they cultivated a juicy old-master colourism reminiscent of Van Dyck and, especially, Rubens, increasingly celebrated as a national hero as 1840, the 200th anniversary of his death, approached.[66] An epoch-making stimulus to German historical painting was the extensive tour of two new Belgian *grandes machines*, Louis Gallait's *Abdication of Karl V in 1555* and Édouard de Bièfve's *Compromise of the Netherlands Nobility in 1566*, between 1842 and 1844.[67] Although the two huge pictures – 'veritable stage-spectacles of history-painting, as broad and high as a theatre curtain!' according to Carl Gustav Carus in Dresden[68] – now seem wooden and obscure, their impact on contemporaries was remarkable. Even Lessing was completely upstaged. In the conditions of the early 1840s the Belgian paintings had radical implications: artistically, since most German academies were dominated by neo-Nazarene idealists, and politically in relation to growing nationalism and the tensions preceding the March 1848 revolutions. For liberally-minded Germans who read historical novels and treatises (including works like Franz Kugler's illustrated *History of Frederick the Great*, which began to appear in 1840), and hoped for political emancipation and progress towards national unity, idealism *à la* Cornelius was not only visually uninspiring and unlifelike, but subservient to the autocratic aims of monarchs like Ludwig I and Friedrich Wilhelm IV. By contrast, the Belgian pictures were dramatic, packed with authentic-seeming detail, and related to events with which history-conscious nationalists, especially Protestant northeners, could identify: the spread of the Reformation, the decline of the medieval Empire and the rise of dynamic successor-states like Prussia. Finally, it was also significant that in many places the pictures were exhibited by art unions: products of the bourgeois association movement developing since the previous century and, like other cultural societies, a focus for political feelings that could find no other legitimate outlet.[69]

In 1843 both the aesthetic and the political issues were spelled out by the young Jakob Burckhardt, for whom the Belgian pictures were far superior to anything being done in Germany. Only oil painting, not fresco, he claimed, could satisfy the contemporary demand for psychological depth. And great historical painting not only presupposed the existence of a national history, but the possibility of *participating* in history and public life.[70] Burckhardt's friend and teacher Kugler, defending him against a furious conservative reaction, rejected the view that the significance of historical events should be conveyed by poetic idealisation and the elimination of mundane detail. Citing Ranke, the exponent of history 'as it really was', he supported Gallait's depiction of Karl V as sick and exhausted (rather than in a pose of sublime resignation) and argued that both pictures' poetry lay in their energy and their subject-matter: 'the Netherlanders' glorious struggle for freedom'. 'Aristocratic' art in Germany – i.e. the work of Cornelius and his followers – was esoteric and elitist, outside the mainstream of national life. What was needed was something both accessible and concerned with progressive themes, and thus democratic: 'Only where a powerful common feeling prevails among the people,' he concluded, 'where the latter has a national existence, do artistic images acquire that conquering vitality which is irresistible to our senses'; and it was the awakening of national consciousness, a sense of common identity, in Germany that explained the Belgian pictures' reception.[71]

From the 1840s onwards, despite a long rearguard action against what Schnorr described as the 'reality swindle',[72] German history-painting developed unstoppably in the direction of rich colourism, theatrical composition and ultra-positivistic detail. There were American contributions too: Emanuel Leutze's *Washington Crossing the Delaware*, the first version of which was completed in Düsseldorf in 1850, also combined patriotic verve with near-photographic illusionism.[73] But the great sensation of the fifties was Karl Theodor Piloty's 1855 *Seni by the Corpse of Wallenstein* (Plate 2) that, not long before the nationwide celebrations of 1859, centred on an incident vividly described in Schiller's *History of the Thirty Years' War* and dramatised in one of his most famous plays.[74] As a student, Piloty (1826-86) had been powerfully

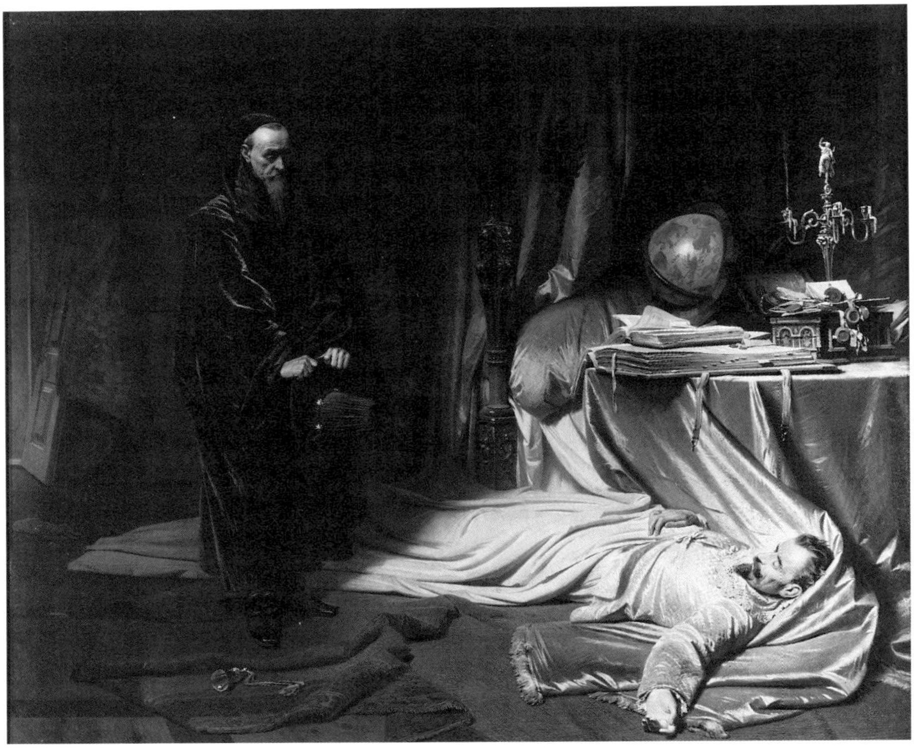

PLATE 2 Karl Theodor Piloty, *Seni by the Corpse of Wallenstein*, 1855, oil on canvas, 312 x 364 cm. The picture has been compared not only with French and Belgian historical paintings but also with contemporary murder scenes depicted in papers like the *Leipziger Illustrierte Zeitung*, although Piloty has toned down the mess and general ghastliness of the spectacle in the interest (still) of epic solemnity. Ludwig I's prompt purchase of the work illustrates his determination to make the latest developments available to Munich artists. Few if any of Piloty's many later works equalled *Seni* in dramatic power or impact on the public.

impressed by the Belgians – he eventually copied Gallait's *Abdication* – and was later influenced by Delaroche in Paris. *Seni*, which shows the fatally ambitious warlord's astrologer contemplating his master's corpse amid the debris of assassination, invited the viewer both to read the clues of a crime scene and, in established nineteenth-century fashion, to ponder the workings of destiny. (Other examples of the formula featured Julius Caesar, Lady Jane Grey, the martyred Dutch patriots Egmont and Horn, and Charles I of England, in similarly macabre circumstances.) But it was Piloty's skill at simulating the texture of fabrics and surfaces, and symbolic touches like the snuffed, still-smoking candle, that captivated the public. His approach was later summed up by the British critic Beavington Atkinson: 'History, as here painted, is a drama, not to say a melodrama; the artist usually seizes the strongest situation in his story, and the climax is enhanced by striking accessories, realistic details, decisive light and colour, to the highest pitch of sensational intensity.'[75] Ludwig I bought the picture for his new gallery of contemporary art, the Neue Pinakothek, and in 1856 the 30-year-old Piloty joined the Munich Academy faculty, and soon achieved international fame as a teacher. Ironically, however, his reputation as a painter was declining well before he succeeded Kaulbach as Director in 1874, and it was his pupil Makart, who combined lush colour handling with exceptional gusto in painting the nude, who in the 1860s and 1870s took historical colourism practically to its limits. His huge *Entry of Karl V into Antwerp* (Plate 6), based loosely on an eye witness account of the event by Albrecht Dürer, centred on a group of barely-clad maidens, exquisitely painted and – in this sense doubly titillating – supposedly modelled on the painter's Viennese acquaintances. When first shown in the Austrian capital in 1878 it attracted 40,000 visitors in five days.[76]

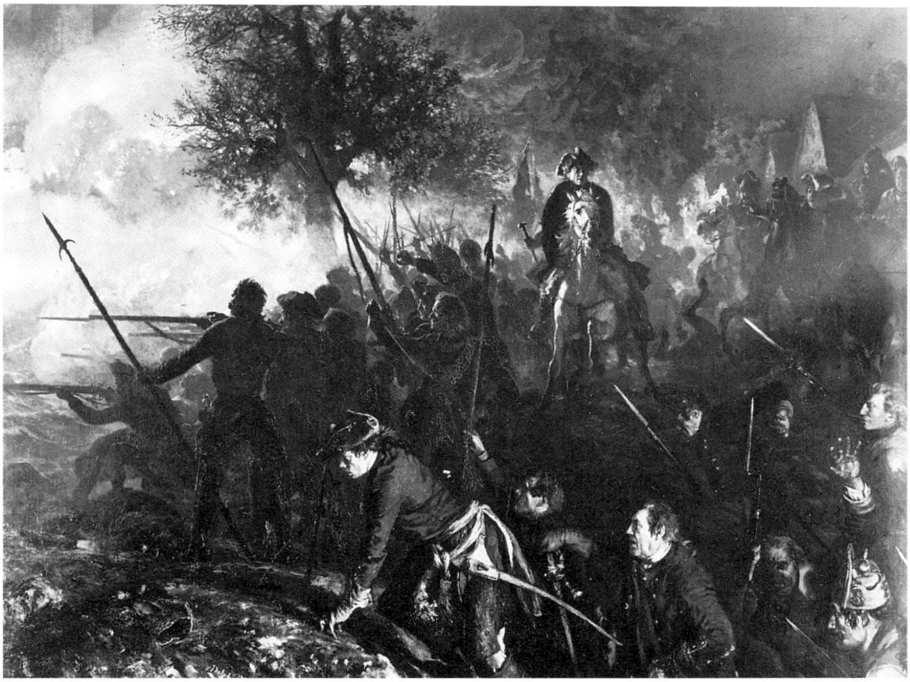

PLATE 3 Adolph Menzel, *Frederick the Great and his Men at the Battle of Hochkirch*, 1856 oil on canvas, 295 x 378 cm (destroyed). Menzel had worked on the picture intermittently since 1850, possibly influenced in his choice of subject by Prussia's diplomatic humiliation by Austria at Olmütz that year. Concerned as ever to capture realistic lighting effects, he arranged with the local night watchman to be woken in the event of a fire in the neighbourhood. Critical reception was mixed, but comments such as 'in his hands the workaday quality of the chronicle fails to transform itself into the Sunday of History' typified 'idealistic' rejection of his approach.

The year after *Seni*'s completion, 1856, saw the exhibition in Berlin of Adolph Menzel's very different *Frederick the Great and his Men at the Battle of Hochkirch* (Plate 3), that depicted a disastrous Prussian defeat in the Seven Years' War.[77] Whereas *Seni* is a theatrically lit, static composition inviting contemplation of an event already past, Menzel's picture (now destroyed) was a snapshot of violent, confused nocturnal action, with the Prussian King appearing off-centre towards the murky background, and in the foreground, partly cropped by the frame, realistically observed soldiers scrambling up an embankment under fire. The painting was acclaimed by Menzel's colleagues and bought – reluctantly, given the subject-matter – by Friedrich Wilhelm IV. Menzel by this time was emerging as the leading historical painter of northern Germany, on the way to extraordinary fame and wealth. He was, however, an enigmatic figure hard to categorise psychologically, artistically or as an interpreter of Prusso–German history.

He had established himself in the field with 376 wood engravings for Kugler's *History of Frederick the Great*, which presented a 'pre-March [1848] liberal' view of the king as not simply a warlord but an enlightened monarch concerned about his people's welfare.[78] Drawing on a vast range of visual sources, including popular prints and the work of the eighteenth-century painter and etcher Daniel Chodowiecki, Menzel showed Frederick both in his public and 'historical' aspect and in more intimate moments, making music or reading, and in the despondency of defeat and the torpor of old age. He also vividly depicted the day-to-day reality of military campaigns, and the cruelty of war for soldiers and civilians alike. (Later, as an observer of the Austro–Prussian conflict of 1866, he experienced at first hand the 'horror, misery and stench' of history in the making.)[79] His characteristically exhaustive study of Frederick and his times for this project carried him on to other major publications, and a cycle of Fridererician paintings that developed themes from the Kugler illustrations. One of the earliest, *The Flute Concerto at Sans Souci* of 1852, eventually became one of nineteenth-century Germany's most celebrated historical images.[80]

At the time they were created, in the 1840s and 1850s, Menzel's sympathetic but un-monumental and un-idealised – or, as Kugler put it, 'daguerrotypical'[81] – depictions of Frederick's life were attacked as well as praised. Max Schasler, the leading Berlin critic of the mid-century, who continued to define historical art in terms of sublime remoteness from common reality,[82] found it unacceptable for a Prussian king to be shown with muddy boots,[83] and dismissed works like *The Flute Concerto* as trivial costume genre. But later, when the Borussian–Hohenzollern mission to unite Germany seemed complete, Menzel became an almost legendary figure, his paintings bought by the State and he himself distinguished with the title of 'Excellency' and – on the same day as Bismarck! – the *Pour le Mérite*.[84] At Berlin exhibitions in the 1880s his latest works would be displayed, roped off, on special easels.[85] On his death in 1905 Wilhelm II personally oversaw the planning of his funeral and followed the cortège on foot. *Hochkirch*, originally consigned to an obscure corner of the Berlin Palace, but now perceived as (somehow) presaging the victory at Sedan, was hung above the emperor's desk. Yet Menzel never accepted the role of court painter or dynastic propagandist, stayed aloof from the academic establishment, and on political issues – such as official discouragement of Prussian artists' participation in the 1889 Paris Exhibition – took a robustly independent line. Unsentimental and dismissive of 'vision stuff',[86] he was driven to capture the appearance of concrete reality. His historical pictures were only part of a vast *œuvre* embracing everything that caught his interest or challenged his skill: Berlin building workers, boatmen, drinkers in beer-gardens, zoo animals, Zulu dancers, severed horse-heads and casts on his studio wall. At a time when the art scene was dominated by the oil painting, much of his total output and nearly all his late work was done in other media and, like his experimental early oils, remained unexhibited until late in his life or after his death. These images, like Menzel's vivid letters, reveal a

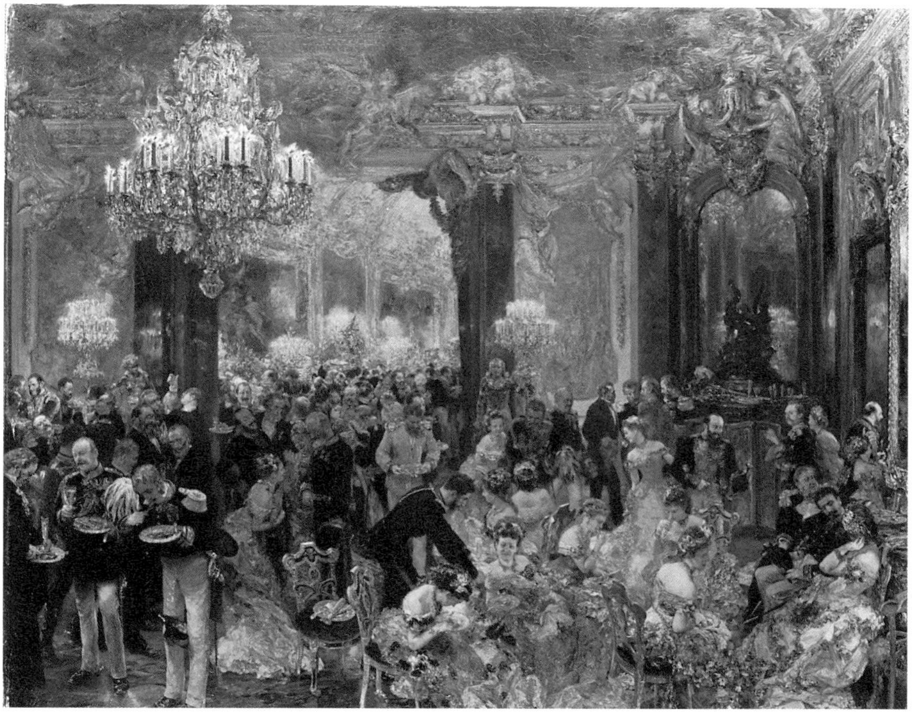

PLATE 4 Adolph Menzel, *Supper at the Ball*, 1878, oil on canvas, 71 x 90 cm. This shows one of the winter balls held at the Berlin Palace attended by hundreds of officers, diplomats, academics and other notables, and notorious for their overcrowding and uncomfortable eating conditions. Menzel had plenty of opportunity to observe such occasions, but the settings in this and similar pictures relate only loosely to Andreas Schlüter's ornate palace interiors, and known individuals are not depicted. Contemporaries marvelled at the painting's virtuoso light effects; later, though, Karl Scheffler cited such works as examples of the increasingly myopic painter's obsession with visual minutiae, and linked it to his rejection of Impressionism. Degas liked the picture enough to copy it in 1885, though in an 'impressionistic' manner which omitted most of the detail.

fascination with human peculiarities and oddly-juxtaposed objects and, during a lifetime in which petroleum, gas and electricity revolutionised illumination,[87] with light-effects of every kind. Paradoxically, his passion for technical challenges (he built a special 'set' to experiment with candlelight for *The Flute Concerto*, and later claimed 'I only painted it because of the chandelier . . .')[88] conveys a sense of emotional detachment from his subject-matter. This was accentuated, possibly, by post-1848 political disillusionment and by the diminutive artist's position as an outsider, even a figure of fun, in a society dominated by stalwart military men. But it may explain the impishly subversive, disconcerting details scattered through his work: a soldier's hand wiping blood off a sword with laurel leaves; a grotesque youth baiting a dog as Wilhelm I sets off for war; a general, his hat between his knees, awkwardly forking food in the unidealised setting of a court ball. (Empress Augusta's reaction to *Supper at the Ball* (Plate 4) was 'Are we really so ugly'?)[89] This mentality, as well as technical mastery and phenomenal powers of observation, distinguishes Menzel's best work from the waxwork staginess of run-of-the mill history-painting.

Historical colourism developed within a certain institutional framework. Both Piloty's *Seni* and Menzel's *Hochkirch* were, as we have seen, bought by monarchs, neither of whom, despite a shared enthusiasm for Cornelius, was exclusively committed to idealism. Both painters subsequently received important royal and public commissions. But each had effectively launched himself, and Menzel embarked on *Hochkirch* because of an urge, after years of illustration work, to do a large-format painting; he had little hope, he wrote later, of selling such a negative subject.[90] Although such independence was typical of Menzel, most of whose pictures found buyers only after completion, risk-taking of this kind hardly made economic sense. One safety-net for the historical painter was offered by the art union movement, which not only created a market for 'cabinet-sized' genre and landscape pictures, but sponsored the monumental frescoes and oil paintings that many of its supporters regarded as the highest form of patriotic art. In 1837 Kugler passionately advocated the preservation and creation of monuments not only by monarchs but also by 'the people' (*das Volk*) – by whom, of course, he meant educated men of property – via art unions. 'Art's greatest moral power', he wrote,

> resides in the creation of monuments, whether of architecture, sculpture or painting . . . Monuments are the great letters with which history impresses itself on the hearts of the people from generation to generation. A people without monuments is a people without a history, without a home. A people without monuments offers little guarantee of all those virtues that stem from love of the Fatherland.[91]

Already by this time large sums were being spent on works of epic size and content. The Rhenish–Westphalian Art Union, founded in 1829 largely to support the Düsseldorf School, assigned a quarter of its income to monumental projects ranging from church murals to the paintings in the Frankfurt Römer and Rethel's Aachen frescoes.[92] By 1914 it had contributed to over 150 decorative works in churches, as well as municipal murals (including those in the Cologne Gürzenich), monumental sculptures, outsize easel paintings, and even theatre curtains, in places as remote as Königsberg and Tilsit. Still, although major figures like Lessing and Menzel had art unions vying for their work, this level of commitment was clearly exceptional. Complaints that, in general, too little was being done, led eventually to the formation in 1854 of the Historical Art League (*Verbindung für historische Kunst* (VHK)), a national organisation with a mainly corporate membership that included art unions, royal houses and official bodies like the Prussian Ministry of Education.[93] It set out to buy or commission one or more major easel paintings every year, exhibit them on tour and distribute them to members by lottery. (Menzel's *Meeting of Friedrich II and Joseph II at Neisse*, for example, commissioned by the League in 1855, was won by Grand Duke Karl Alexander of Saxe–Weimar.)[94] Although leading advocates of historical art like Schasler regarded its efforts as a poor substitute for State patronage[95] – also a major issue of the fifties, as we shall see – the VHK persevered in its task for half a century or more.

Another important creation, at a convention at Bingen on the Rhine in September 1856, was the first national artists' organisation, the General German Art Guild (*Allgemeine Deutsche Kunstgenossenschaft* (ADKG)), mainly on the initiative of a group from the Düsseldorf Paint-Box.[96] Its purpose was both to promote *grossdeutsch* cultural nationalism and, more practically, to improve artists' status, economic well-being, and bargaining power on key issues like copyright. But it also set out to sponsor regular national salons, beginning with the National Historical German Art Exhibition held in Munich in 1858.[97] Hung in the Bavarian capital's new glass and iron exhibition building, the Glaspalast, the nearly 1,750 items on display comprised recent work from all the main German-speaking art centres, and a historical section going back to the late-eighteenth-century rebel against Rococo, Asmus Jakob Carstens; Philipp Otto Runge; and Friedrich. Though the show included hundreds of landscape and genre pieces it was inevitably dominated by history-painting, from cartoons by Cornelius, Kaulbach and Rethel to Lessing's *Hussite Sermon*, Piloty's *Seni* and Menzel's *Hochkirch*. Unprecedented in scope, and drawing crowds of German and foreign visitors, it was hailed as an epoch-making event that for the first time gave modern German art a history,[98] and revealed 'art's national language'.[99] Its financial success enabled Munich artists to found a branch of the ADKG that, within a few years, had taken over the organisation of the city's salons from the Academy. Paradoxically, too, considering the movement's Rhenish origins, it highlighted Munich's increasing pre-eminence as Düsseldorf stagnated. Subsequently the ADKG itself, although it outlasted the Empire, was overshadowed by developments at local level, and its influence declined as the art world became increasingly fragmented. In 1903 its position as artists' principal national organisation was formally challenged by the foundation of the rival Artists' League (*Künstlerbund*) representing the more modern and internationally-orientated societies – the secessions – formed in German art centres during the previous decade.

In the 1860s, although 'minor' branches of art such as genre and landscape painting were finding their way into academic curricula, reflecting their popularity with the public at large, training remained dominated by history-painting, the emphasis on either linear idealism or illusionistic colourism varying from one institution to another.[100] 'German artists have the receipt [recipe] for this kind of thing', commented Atkinson in 1869: 'history they can turn out of hand by the acre or the mile, according to academic rule taught by professors'.[101] But by this time both patronage and inspiration were flagging, and would probably have continued to do so had it not been for the Franco–Prussian War and the propaganda needs of the new Empire. Berlin's leading history-painters were called up summarily to prepare for Wilhelm I's triumphal return to his capital on 16 June 1871. Menzel produced life-size pictures of Bismarck and Moltke for the façade of the Academy.[102] In only a week, the young Anton von Werner painted a banner-like allegory, *Struggle and Victory*, measuring twenty feet by eighteen, to be suspended with four other such *velaria* across the emperor's route.[103] In Munich and other capitals painters were mobilised to similar effect.[104] Subsequently, governments spent heavily on more permanent monumental works: Prussia, for example, paid out over 2.6 million marks between 1889 and 1902 alone,[105] stimulating a revival in which Düsseldorf specialists such as Wilhelm Camphausen, Peter Janssen and Hermann Wislicenus were particularly prominent.

But Imperial Germany's premier history-painter was unquestionably Werner (1843-1915), Director of the Berlin Academy's art schools from 1875, artist by appointment to the Hohenzollerns, and a formidable figure in Berlin cultural politics until the First World War.[106] Behind his success was stupendous industry and an exceptional combination of professional and social skills. But his career, like those of history-painters generally, was decisively shaped by the Franco–Prussian conflict. In the late 1860s, influenced probably by the continuing Church–State tensions in Germany, he had favoured medieval subjects like *Conradin in Prison* and *The Abduction of Emperor Heinrich IV by Archbishop Anno of Cologne*.[107] But on the outbreak of war in 1870 the Grand Duke of Baden's influence gained him access to the military and political elite at Crown Prince Friedrich of Prussia's headquarters near Paris, and the contacts he made there won him innumerable subsequent commissions. He also made hundreds of on-the-spot studies that fuelled his output for decades thereafter. Back in Berlin, he maintained cordial relations with Wilhelm I, Bismarck, the Crown Prince and his wife Victoria and their son, the later Emperor Wilhelm II. Though the *bête noire* of anti-academic and above all French-influenced painters, whom he denounced as exponents of 'modern anarchism and terrorism in art',[108] Werner was a not wholly unsympathetic figure: an energetic Academy reformer and campaigner for artists' rights, no sycophant, and an opponent of anti-Semitism. In his memoirs he wryly acknowledged his 'Ivan the Terrible' reputation among the younger generation.[109] His

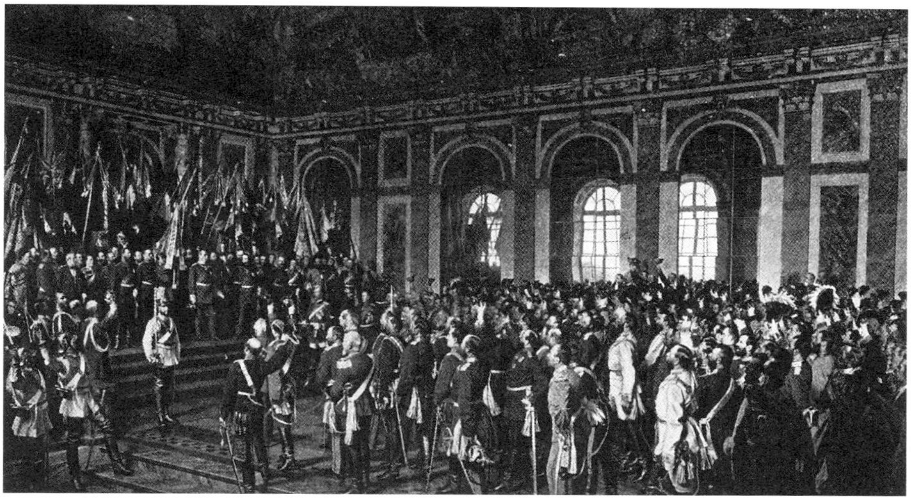

PLATE 5 Anton von Werner, *The Proclamation of the German Empire* (first version), 1877, oil on canvas, *c.* 430 x 800 cm (destroyed). Werner was summoned back to Versailles from Karlsruhe to witness the occasion on 18 January 1871, and the painting included a self-portrait of the artist at bottom right. It was commissioned by Grand Duke Friedrich of Baden, who persuaded his fellow monarchs to share the cost (60,000 marks), and presented to Emperor Wilhelm I on his 80th birthday on 22 March 1877. Together with Hohenzollern portraits and Menzel's *Coronation of Wilhelm I in Königsberg* it hung in the main gallery of the Berlin Palace, in a massive gilt frame decorated with the donors' coats of arms. More famous later versions were differently composed, giving more prominence to Bismarck and Moltke, but losing the original's glimpses of Le Brun's ceiling-decorations in the Galerie des Glaces, Werner's ironical allusion to earlier French triumphs.

style as a history-painter was 'naturalistic idealism':[110] the theatrical arrangement of masses of colourful minutiae to convey a sense of both historic glamour and actuality. His celebrated set-piece, *The Proclamation of the German Empire* (Plate 5), transformed a sober, hurried and frigid occasion – at which Werner had just managed to be present – into a glittering spectacle whose details changed from one version to the next.[111] He also led the team of painters that created Berlin's huge panorama of the Battle of Sedan, reviving himself with steaks and champagne when heatstroke interrupted his punishing location-schedule.[112] The staginess and ultra-illusionism of his pictures, suggestive of both press illustration and waxwork, naturally repelled the francophile avant-garde, and sometimes irritated even conservatives like Adolf Rosenberg, doyen of Berlin critics.[113] For a later generation of Germans, such as Paula Modersohn-Becker, he remained a byword for art-as-*trompe-l'œil*-highlights-on-boots.[114] In fact, as his studies and book illustrations reveal, Werner was a man of much more varied talents. But ambition and the treadmill of commissions tied him to the re-creation of historic or merely grandiose occasions, his images endlessly multiplied as prints, schoolbook illustrations and even wall-hangings until his death in 1915.

On the eve of war in 1870, Werner had been working on murals for a *Gymnasium* in Kiel and his last, 1913 version of the *Proclamation* was also done as a mural, at a school in his native Frankfurt-on-Oder. The purpose of historical art in such settings was obvious. 'From the walls of school halls', wrote Rosenberg in 1883, 'the heroic figures of classical antiquity will look down on boys and youths, the deeds of history will speak to them and fire them to emulation.'[115] (Ironically, two of the 1871 *velaria*, Otto Knille's *Oath at the Altar of the Fatherland* and August von Heyden's *Peace*, ended up in the school attended by Hans Baluschek, 'subversive' painter of the Berlin proletariat.)[116] But during his long career Werner also created wall-paintings for many other public buildings, from city halls to the Berlin Arsenal. From Cornelius's time onwards, in fact, exterior and interior murals, executed *al fresco* or in oils, were a prime vehicle for historical art and an integral element of historicist architecture. They flourished especially in the Rhineland, thanks to the efforts of Wilhelm von Schadow, Cornelius's successor at the Düsseldorf Academy, and of the Rhenish–Westphalian Art Union that he helped to found. Crown Prince Friedrich Wilhelm's ancient castle of Stolzenfels near Koblenz was rebuilt with extensive murals by Düsseldorf artists, and other princes vied with each other to restore or re-create their own medieval buildings.[117] In the middle of the century Moritz von Schwind decorated both the historic Wartburg near Eisenach for Karl Alexander of Saxe–Weimar, and Maximilian II of Bavaria's restored castle at Hohenschwangau. Maximilian's son, Ludwig II, who visited the Wartburg in 1867, commissioned yet more murals for his pastiche-medieval fortress of Neuschwanstein.[118] Indeed, the Bavarian Wittelsbachs from Ludwig I onwards probably outdid every other dynasty, and visitors to their capital marvelled at the expanses of painting all around: ' . . . every wall in Munich', reported Courbet in November 1869, 'is covered with frescoes like wallpaper, full of red, blue, green, yellow, pink robes, silk stockings, top-boots, doublets. Here's a king taking an oath, there's a king abdicating, the next is a king signing a treaty etc. etc.'[119]

After 1870 there was a sustained mural boom, stimulated by State spending, commercial expansion and technical advances. In the restored Imperial Palace at Goslar, where the Reichstag convened in 1871, Hermann Wislicenus painted a huge cycle celebrating the deeds of emperors from 'Red-Beard' Friedrich I in the twelfth century to 'White-Beard' Wilhelm I in the present.[120] By 1914 new imperial buildings like the Reichstag in Berlin and the Reich Appeal Court in Leipzig, and lawcourts, ministries, university buildings and schools throughout the Empire, had created acres of wall-space and lucrative opportunities for artists. Another particularly important field was the decoration of Germany's new town and city halls, about 200 of which were built between 1850 and 1914. A brochure commemorating the inauguration of the new Cassel city hall in 1909 spelled out the significance of the modern *Rathaus* as 'a palladium of municipal liberty, a stately monument to the reinvigorated middle class, a worthy symbol of its importance, rooted in self-administration, its power and its rights'.[121] Many of the buildings constructed or restored in the last three decades of the nineteenth century incorporated large-scale historical murals, which often presented emperors and burghers as allies, since the Middle Ages, in the fulfilment of a German national destiny. The role of cities, as here represented, was not only economic and cultural but military, in resisting such anti-national elements as feudal princes and Catholic bishops. Thus in the Hanoverian city of Hildesheim, whose National Liberal elite had euphorically welcomed annexation by Prussia in 1866, Hermann Prell's *Rathaus* murals juxtaposed extensive Arminian/Wilhelmine imagery and other imperial symbolism with a classic 'entry' set-piece showing the return of Mayor Brandis, in full knightly harness, after defeating the Duke of Brunswick at Bleckenstedt in 1493.[122] (Similarly the murals in the Cologne Gürzenich, following the programme of the 1880 cathedral pageant, included a re-creation of the Battle of Worringen in 1288, at which the archbishop's troops had been bloodily routed by the citizens and their allies.) Although the decorative projects in cities like Hildesheim and Erfurt were exceptionally elaborate and costly, many more modest ones provided useful work for painters. In Bavaria, for example, with the provision of regular State funds for monumental art from 1872 onwards, the embellishment of small- and medium-sized town halls became a valuable monopoly for Munich's history specialists, plied with commissions by a patronage machine run by State officials, local notables and their own colleagues.[123] By 1900 historicism was giving way to more abstract, sometimes *Jugendstil*-influenced decorative schemes. Thus in the magnificent neo-Baroque Dresden city hall (1905-10) most of the decoration budget – no less than 17 per cent of the building's cost – was spent on luxurious panelling, plasterwork and other embellishments rather than on subject-painting.[124] Wilhelmine muralists, however, from veterans like Werner to the young men of the Munich *Scholle* group, were comfortably compensated by commissions to decorate private villas, and by commercial work in settings ranging from inner-city cafés, beer-halls and banks to the saloons of ocean liners.

In mural painting legend was at least as popular as history, and the boundary between them fluid. This was true above all in the case of Emperor Friedrich I Barbarossa, who had spent much of his turbulent reign restoring imperial authority and resisting the claims of Rome, only to be drowned on crusade in 1190. The centuries-old Barbarossa legend reached its definitive popular–nationalist form in a famous poem by Friedrich Rückert in 1817, and the image of Friedrich awaiting Germany's rebirth in his cave under the Kyffhäuser Mountain in Thuringia lived on regardless of scholarly demystification of the historical emperor.[125] In the nineteenth century the story inspired paintings by Schnorr, Kaulbach, Lessing, Leutze and countless others in settings ranging from the Frankfurt Römer to businessmen's homes. In 1871 the Albrecht Dürer Association in Nuremberg, effectively Germany's oldest art union, presented an engraving of Barbarossa by Rudolf Geissler to its members. In the cutaway manner familiar from fairy-story illustrations (Geissler's usual specialism) it showed Friedrich and his retinue awaking in their cavern, while above ground, beyond a group of triumphant modern soldiers, appeared the ancient symbols of Franco–German conflict: Strasbourg Cathedral, Heidelberg Castle and the Rhine.[126] The Barbarossa legend, like the story of Hermann, also fed the cult of

Emperor Wilhelm I 'The Great', variously represented in book illustrations, Wislicenus's Goslar frescoes and, most spectacularly, in the colossal sculptures of the Kyffhäuser Monument.[127] The chauvinism generated by the latter's inauguration in 1896 in the presence of Wilhelm II, and the accompanying torrent of celebratory verses with their Rückert-derived paraphernalia of eagles, anthropomorphic (ultra-montane?) ravens, dwarves and treacherous Latin foes, anticipated the fable's role in twentieth-century imperialist ideology.

The medieval epic poem *The Song of the Nibelungs* (*Nibelungenlied*), rediscovered in 1757, underwent a similar transformation.[128] During the Wars of Liberation Siegfried and the *Song*'s other heroes became popular symbols of resistance to the French, acquiring in the process quasi-Christian associations of martyrdom and redemption. For Romantic medievalists like Friedrich Schlegel and the Boisserée brothers, the *Song* belonged to the same national cultural patrimony as Cologne Cathedral – described, indeed, by Heinrich Heine as a 'stone *Nibelungenlied*'[129] – and early German art. Though appropriated for a time by conservative monarchs like Ludwig I and Friedrich Wilhelm IV, who relished its theme of feudal loyalty, the translated saga eventually became a central component of nationalist mythology, widely disseminated and ultimately linked with the cult of Wagner's *Ring*. In the Wilhelmine period both the *Song* and the *Ring* acquired increasingly authoritarian and militaristic connotations that persisted in the twentieth century ('Nibelung loyalty' between the embattled Central Powers; the 'stab in the back' in 1918) until the final bars of *Twilight of the Gods* broadcast after the announcement of Hitler's death on 30 April 1945. Over the entire period from 1800 to 1945 probably only the Bible inspired German artists more often, the visual representations of the story extending from Schnorr's frescoes in the Munich Palace and the illustrations of Cornelius and Rethel to Fritz Lang's epic films.

## THE ARTIST AS HERO

In September 1858, a few months after the opening of the National Art Exhibition, Munich artists celebrated seven centuries of the city's history with a spectacular pageant.[130] About 2,000 people dressed in costumes from the mid-twelfth century – partly inspired by Schnorr's *Nibelung* frescoes – to the nineteenth processed from the Isartorplatz to the Palace and paid tribute to King Maximilian II and the Wittelsbachs. The event had taken months to prepare, with the dedicated collaboration of history-painters, Academy students and the stage-designer of the court theatre, and a mass of weapons and accoutrements assembled by the city fathers. Although the creation of fancy-dress 'living pictures' was a regular and enjoyable part of artists' social life – indeed, of social life generally[131] – these elaborate spectacles were much more significant: both as works of art in their own right (the 1858 procession was likened to 'an unrolled, magnificent and artistically finished painting'),[132] and as symbols of artists' collective identity and national role. Their precursors were the patriotic celebrations organised by the German artists' colony in Rome in 1813 and 1818. The guest of honour on the second of these occasions was Crown Prince Ludwig of Bavaria, who later invited many of those present to join in the artistic and architectural transformation of Munich. There, in the 1820s and 1830s many masques and pageants were held, including six sizeable festivals in 1835 alone. In February 1840 the inauguration of the Dürer monument in Nuremberg was celebrated in the capital by a pageant featuring artists and citizens costumed as the painter himself together with Hans Sachs, Emperor Maximilian I and a host of knights, mercenaries, courtiers, patricians, master-singers and craftsmen: a spectacle later immortalised in Gottfried Keller's autobiographical novel *Der Grüne Heinrich*.[133] In Düsseldorf too, artists devised fantastic masques, particularly during Karl Immermann's directorship of the municipal theatre in the 1830s. After 1848 the Paint-Box mounted a succession of festivals culminating in an elaborate tribute to Emperor Wilhelm I in 1877, by which time Wilhelm Camphausen's fame as a versifier and masque-producer made him a natural choice to design the Cologne pageant three years later. Munich, meanwhile, had surpassed itself the previous year by marking the opening of the National Applied Art Exhibition with another *Dürerzeit* spectacular: a re-creation, with thousands of extras, of Karl V's entry into Augsburg for the 1530 Reichstag.[134] Ten years later in Berlin replicas of the Temple of Zeus at Olympia and the Pergamon Altar, and an exuberant Pergamon festival simultaneously celebrated Heinrich Schliemann's State-funded excavations, the opening of the Berlin Academy's centenary salon and, in effect, the city's arrival in the major league of German art centres.[135]

The relationship between artists' festivals and history-painting was obvious and dynamic. Triumphs, entries and progresses were staple subjects for pictures, while festival costume drawings and commemorative albums of prints, then photographs, created an image-bank for painters; as did, for both purposes, the growing number of historical costume manuals. A classic example of cross-fertilisation was the activity of Makart. As a pupil of Piloty in the 1860s he witnessed both large-scale pageants and the Fasching masques mounted by the Munich artists' clubs, and later organised his own fancy-dress studio parties to mark the completion of pictures like the Venetian melodrama *Caterina Cornaro* in 1873.[136] His 1878 *Entry of Karl V into Antwerp* (Plate 6) was inspired not only by Dürer's diary but by the Munich pageant of 1876 and the lavish commemoration of Rubens's 300th birthday in Antwerp itself the following year, in which Makart and many other painters participated.[137] The picture's huge success brought the artist not only a Vienna Academy professorship but the job of designing the procession in honour of Emperor Franz Josef's silver wedding in the spring of 1879. This in turn, with its fantastic floats and (once again) Renaissance costumes inspired by Dürer and Holbein, was a triumph for Makart which led to further commissions for historical paintings.

Meanwhile, artists' status was rising. In 1782 it was reported that the standing of Munich painters was so low that every official considered himself half princely by comparison.[138] Yet less than a century later a successful artist was not only accepted

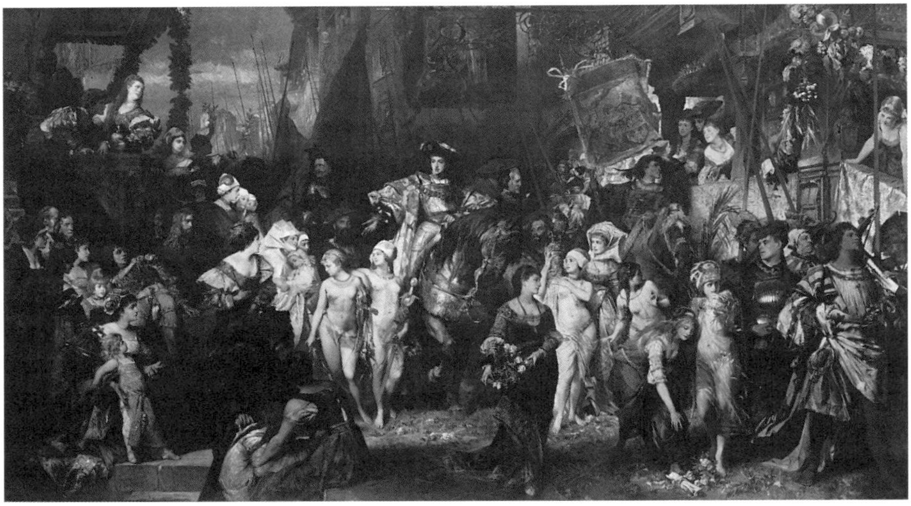

PLATE 6 Hans Makart, *Entry of Karl V into Antwerp*, 1878, oil on canvas,520 x 952 cm. This huge picture re-creates part of the procession witnessed by Dürer in August 1520 and described - though without reference to the undress of the women – in his diary. Influences included Titian's portrait of Karl V in the Prado, Dürer's self-portrait of 1500 in the Alte Pinakothek, and the spectacular commemoration of Rubens's 300th birthday in Antwerp in 1877 in which Makart had participated. Dürer appears towards the left of the picture and the painter himself on foot behind the emperor; the lady strewing roses is Hanna Klinkosch, later Princess Liechtenstein. Typically for Makart's work, the picture aroused fierce moral and aesthetic controversy.

but lionised in fashionable society. As one commentator put it in the 1870s, 'We are glad to be seen with him at the theatre or on the promenade, pass round his sketches and album-leaves at our salon . . . He may lead off with our wife or daughter at our dances, . . . in short, this darling of the gods is bound to us with a hundred ties, an ingredient of our social life without which we could scarcely exist.'[139] Late-nineteenth-century celebrities like the portraitist Franz Lenbach in Munich, Makart in Vienna and Werner in Berlin owned elegant mansions, entertained royalty and ministers and were welcome at court; Menzel was entitled to a general's salute from the palace guard; and the Munich sculptor and Academy Director Ferdinand von Miller entered the Bavarian House of Peers. Artists' festivals both documented and hastened this change of condition. In small cities like mid-century Düsseldorf and Munich they were talking-points for months, while even in Vienna and Berlin they raised the profile of art communities. Illustrated newspapers projected artists' increasingly glamorous image nation-wide. The centrepiece of the 1840 Munich festival had been Maximilian I's grant of a coat of arms to Dürer: a symbol of the artist's transition from medieval artisan to Renaissance *gentiluomo*. At the Vienna procession in

1879 Makart, on a white Lippizaner and in a costume that reminded many onlookers of Karl V, drew more applause than the emperor himself.

If Munich painters were understandably gratified by the participation in their festivals of Ludwig I, the poet-king, as 'one of you',[140] it was also true that by the 1850s German artists' status owed less to royal favour than to their constant self-identification with national destiny. Their pageants symbolically represented the nation as an unbroken chain of generations stretching back through time, and history as progress towards national self-fulfilment. Their organisations, from the Paint-Box, founded amid patriotic euphoria in the summer of 1848, to the ADKG, presented themselves as both vanguard and microcosm of the coming nation: as the latter's leaders proclaimed in 1857, 'In German art at least we want to found national unity, the unity which the Fatherland cannot yet offer us.'[141] The belief that artistic and national identity were linked inspired the 1858 Munich Exhibition: 'Oh take it not amiss', delegates to the accompanying artists' congress were told, 'that we cling hotly to the idea that our art is a national art. For . . . only on the basis of the nation does the tree of art grow deep roots, broad branches, a lofty crown.'[142] Close to the conception of artists' special relationship with the nation was the Romantic cult of genius, of the artist as a divinely gifted being in touch with God through nature and communicating eternal truths to the world.[143] Artists were to the rest of mankind, commented Friedrich Schlegel in 1800, what human beings were to the rest of creation.[144] Four years earlier, in a famous rebuff to a Prussian minister (who had modestly requested some return for a State grant), Carstens had stirringly asserted the artist's independence:

> I belong not to the Berlin Academy but to Humanity, which has a right to demand of me the highest possible development of my talents . . . My abilities were entrusted to me by God. I must be a faithful steward so that when He says: 'Give a reckoning of thy stewardship', I shall not need to say: 'Lord, the talent with which you entrusted me I have buried in Berlin.'[145]

Though often vitiated by market realities, such ideals remained potent throughout the nineteenth century and beyond and, with nationalism, infused the cults surrounding Schiller, Beethoven and eventually Wagner. These in turn, like the quasi-sacralisation of classical music, the concept since Schinkel of the museum-as-temple, and the quest for the 'total work of art' (*Gesamtkunstwerk*), were aspects of a complex of neo-Romantic culture-worship that continued to mutate and grow as prosperity and materialism increased and organised religion declined.[146]

As far as painters were concerned, the idea of the artist as super-being went back to the Renaissance, and especially to Vasari: 'One can claim without fear of contradiction', he wrote in *Lives of the Painters*, 'that artists as outstandingly gifted as Raphael are not simply men but . . . mortal gods.'[147] This image of Raphael as demi-god reappeared in the seminal writings of Ludwig Tieck and Wilhelm Heinrich Wackenroder in the 1790s and later influenced the Nazarenes, for whom Raphael, painter of

Christian subjects in a style of sublimely purified naturalism, was the positive counterpole to the frivolity and spiritual emptiness of late-eighteenth-century art. But before studying Vasari, Tieck and Wackenroder had been inspired by a visit to Nuremberg in 1792.[148] There they 'discovered' Albrecht Dürer as the founding father of post-medieval German art, and proof (as Wackenroder later put it in his *Heartfelt Effusions of an Art-Loving Monk*) that 'true art could grow up not only under Italian skies, among majestic cupolas and Corinthian columns, but also among pointed arches, intricately-ornamented buildings and Gothic towers'.[149] The same passage included a celebrated dream-image, often to be depicted by nineteenth-century artists, in which Raphael and Dürer, the two great geniuses on the threshold of the modern age, appeared hand in hand contemplating each other's works in an imaginary gallery. But it was Dürer who was to have by far the more potent influence on the image of the artist in nineteenth-century Germany.[150] One reason was that, through his fame as a printmaker, he had been the first German artist to achieve an international reputation: commendation enough for nationalists, given the provincial status of German art in the eighteenth century and the perceived dominance of French and even British influences in the nineteenth. Significant too, given the widespread view that a national art must be popularly accessible,[151] was the breadth of Dürer's appeal: not only to imperial and princely patrons and Nuremberg patricians, but also to a much wider public since, although images like *Melancholia* were complex and enigmatic, most of his prints with their vernacular captions could be easily grasped. Thirdly, Dürer's genius spanned both the poles between which German art developed in the nineteenth and early twentieth centuries: naturalism on the one hand and, on the other, fascination with the visionary and fantastic, with myths, dreams and a spiritual reality for which nature, in the Romantic terminology of Wackenroder and Carus,[152] was a mere hieroglyph. Both elements were fundamental to Dürer's art, which ranged from theoretically based anatomical exercises, incisive portraits, and such masterpieces of naturalistic observation as *The Hare* and *The Large Piece of Turf*, to the cosmic visions of the *Apocalypse* cycle pulsating with supernatural energy.

One other key component of Dürer's appeal was his religious orientation. Although he died a Catholic, his diaries revealed sympathy for Luther,[153] and the atmosphere in which he and his Humanist friends lived was conducive to the development of Protestant attitudes. Indeed, Nuremberg espoused Protestantism not long after the artist's death, the first imperial city to do so. In the nineteenth century, given the Reformation's perceived role in the development of culture and national consciousness, this was highly significant. Alfred Woltmann, the biographer of Dürer's near-contemporary Hans Holbein the Younger, described it as the Germans' great national achievement, just as the Renaissance had been that of the Italians.[154] Both Woltmann writing about early-modern Augsburg - Holbein's birthplace – and Moriz Thausing, Dürer's first major biographer, describing Nuremberg,[155] emphasized the cities' struggles with the Catholic hierarchy and the development within their walls of Hussitism and other dissident movements. Against this background, Dürer appeared as a forebear of modern liberal culture, free from two of the great constraining influences of the Middle Ages, the guilds (restricted in Nuremberg) and Catholic dogmatism. In an essay written in 1875, just before the appearance of Thausing's biography, the founder of the Vienna Art Museum, Rudolph von Eitelberger, memorably likened Dürer to 'a high mountainous divide, whose foot stretched far into the forests of the Middle Ages, and whose far-shining peak was illuminated by the rising sun of the Renaissance'.[156] Notwithstanding the importance of Catholic artists like Cornelius, Wilhelm von Schadow and most of the Nazarenes, and of Catholic patrons like Ludwig I of Bavaria, nineteenth-century German art now seems to have been largely attuned to the taste and aspirations of urban middle-class Protestants (whether practising or not): nationally-minded and broadly rationalistic people who were mainly interested in secular subjects, or historico–critical treatment of religious ones. From the middle of the century onwards both historical and religious painting was dominated by Protestants, men like Lessing, Eduard von Gebhardt and Fritz von Uhde, whose works, though often detested by Catholics, were praised by critics, favoured by exhibition juries and bought by museums. Just as liberal politicians regarded Catholicism as inimical to modern civilisation, and art historians such as Woltmann and Thausing, writing at the height of the *Kulturkampf*, attacked the obscurantism of the medieval Church, nationalist critics like Friedrich Pecht, editor of *Die Kunst für Alle*, consigned contemporary Catholic painting to a kind of ghetto.[157] Long after the end of the *Kulturkampf*, especially at individual–state level where most cultural conflicts were fought out, debates about official patronage, freedom of expression and related issues remained deeply permeated by confessional differences.

Although elite appreciation of Dürer had remained alive since the sixteenth century, the modern Dürer cult, stimulated by the writings of Tieck and Wackenroder in the 1790s, developed after the Napoleonic Wars. In April 1828, encouraged by Ludwig I and led by Academy-Director Cornelius, Munich artists organised a celebration in Nuremberg of the 300th anniversary of the master's death, to which artists from all over German-speaking Europe were invited.[158] The event had strong nationalist as well as artistic overtones. Indeed, alluding to Jena students' boisterous commemoration, in October 1817, of both the Reformation and the Battle of Leipzig, Cornelius described it as 'our Wartburg festival'.[159] Many participants, defying the repressive Carlsbad Decrees, appeared in the flamboyant '*altdeutsch*' costume sported by patriots since the Wars of Liberation. However, King Ludwig's involvement added a conservative ballast. His ambitious monumental projects, though conceived in the name of '*Teutschland*', were meant to promote a dynasty-centred small-state patriotism within the framework of the German Confederation.[160] (A related consideration in 1828 was Bavarian political integration, since Nuremberg and Franconia had been under Wittelsbach rule only since 1806.) For the festival itself, Cornelius's students painted banners with scenes from Dürer's life, with an allegorical centrepiece showing him and Raphael wreath-crowned before the throne of Art. After a procession early on the morning of 6 April to the artist's grave, emotional tributes were paid, amid snow-flurries, to Dürer as the father of modern German art. The next day, on the Nuremberg Milk Market – renamed the Albrecht-Dürer-Platz - the foundation was laid for a statue to be made by Christian Rauch. As one of those present, Sulpiz Boisserée, remarked, it would be 'the first monument erected in Germany to honour artistic merit'.[161] Significant also was the religious aura surrounding the commemoration, with Nuremberg presented as the goal of a pilgrimage, Dürer's house and grave as shrines, and he himself as a kind of artists' patron saint. The master's Christ-like self-portrait of 1500, which had been removed to Munich by Ludwig I after hanging for centuries in the Nuremberg City Hall, inspired Rauch's statue and the banners painted by Cornelius's students, and remained the basis for most nineteenth-century Dürer-images.[162] Such associations further reinforced the cult of artists as semi-divine beings mediating between God and humanity.

While Dürer festivals became an annual spring event for artists in many places, the next major occasion was the great Munich pageant in 1840 marking the completion of Rauch's statue in Nuremberg. Then, after a period of comparative quiet, the Dürer cult revived strongly in the 1870s, beginning with the 400th anniversary of his birth on 21 May 1871, an event celebrated with nationalistic fervour in cities across Germany.[163] Improved reproduction of Dürer's works, the appearance of a modern edition of his writings and Thausing's biography all helped to focus him more clearly in the public's mind. Notable too, however, had been an 1866 tribute by the Berlin art historian (and later art critic of the prestigious *Deutsche Rundschau*) Hermann Grimm, a brilliant public lecturer and one of the leading academic popularisers of his time.[164] A fervent admirer of Bismarck, Grimm also viewed the history of culture as the history of exceptional individuals ('self-made men') who to a unique degree had embodied the spirit of their times. It was an approach well suited to a period in which heroic statesmen, soldiers and industrialists seemed to be creating miracles for Germany; and Grimm's Dürer lecture, though vague about the artist's works, presented him in appropriately mythic terms, emphasising his craft origins, incipient Protestantism and contribution to German national identity. 'Those who do not know him,' he declared, 'lack part of the knowledge of our history; but for those who do know him the name Dürer, whenever it is pronounced, sounds like "Germany, Germany".'[165] (At the turn of the century, when Dürer was fast becoming an icon of cultural chauvinism, the art historian Richard Muther felt constrained to re-emphasise his cosmopolitanism. The greatness of 'the most German of all Germans', he wrote in *The History of Painting*, lay in his unprecedented openness to what was best in Europe: 'What he says is German. Yet the cultivated language in which he expresses it he owes to the South.)'[166]

## A NINETEENTH-CENTURY RENAISSANCE

Especially after 1871 the symbolic importance of Dürer himself merged increasingly with that of a whole epoch. Gothic had captivated Germany's first Romantic nationalists, and medievalism in various forms – neo-Gothic architecture, the Nibelung and

Barbarossa cults, the historical novels and ballads of Viktor von Scheffel, the mythic idealisation of medieval towns – remained an important strand in nineteenth-century culture. The imperial 'power architecture' of public buildings such as parliaments, ministries and lawcourts drew on Italian and French Renaissance, neo-Baroque and later also neo-Romanesque models. But the dominant domestic style of the Bismarckian and early Wilhelmine period was *altdeutsch* or German Renaissance: elastically defined to embrace regional variants from Augsburg to Danzig between the late fifteenth century and the Thirty Years War, and claiming kinship with non-German artists such as Rubens and Rembrandt. Whether describing municipal self-government, economic enterprise or bourgeois lifestyles, art historians such as Eitelberger, Woltmann, Thausing and the author of the magisterial *History of the German Renaissance*, Wilhelm Lübke, constantly presented the *Dürerzeit* as the precursor of the *Gründerzeit*. A spectacular early manifestation of the *altdeutsch* cult was the hugely successful 1876 Munich exhibition dedicated to 'Our Fathers' Works' – Berliners joked about 'Every man his own Fugger'[167] – which boosted demand for historicist furniture, ornaments and fittings. The 'Karl V' procession that preceded it, the Rubens celebrations in Antwerp the following year and the 1879 Makart pageant in Vienna, all in broadly the same style, further swelled the stock of images on which artists, designers and festival organisers could draw. (It was no coincidence that the burghers of Cologne celebrated the completion of their Gothic cathedral by having themselves painted in *Dürerzeit* costumes.) Contemporary publications were also important: for example the lavishly illustrated part-work on the architecture and applied art of different German cities issued by Seemann in Leipzig from 1871,[168] and the source-book *The Treasury of Renaissance Forms* (*Der Formenschatz der Renaissance*) edited by the Munich publicist, cultural entrepreneur and liberal patriot Georg Hirth, one of the 1876 exhibition's most energetic backers.[169]

Aptly, the Seemann series was edited by a Nuremberg-based writer, and its first ten parts were devoted to Dürer's native city. Since the end of the Thirty Years War Nuremberg had stagnated economically and demographically, hemmed in by predatory neighbours and ruled by a conservative oligarchy. Eighteenth-century travellers and guide-book authors disparaged its dilapidated and gloomy buildings, and Mozart dismissed it as an 'ugly city'.[170] But the writings of Tieck and Wackenroder and other Romantic medievalists, and then the impact of the Napoleonic Wars – the patriot Johann Philipp Palm, martyred by the French, was a Nuremberg bookseller – eventually transformed its image into that of a miraculously-preserved gem of late-medieval German culture. Its former status as a free imperial city, and the repository for nearly four centuries of the imperial regalia, further enhanced its lustre, and by the middle of the nineteenth century Nuremberg was widely regarded as a kind of spiritual capital or 'German Rome'; in 1848, indeed, there were proposals to make it the German seat of government. In 1853 the Germanic National Museum was opened, an archive and treasure-house of German culture which, with financial support from Bavaria and, after 1871, the Reich, became one of the country's few national cultural institutions.[171] The Renaissance cult and the popularity of Wagner's *Mastersingers of Nuremberg*, premiered in 1868, added further to the city's symbolic status in the new Empire, as a south German – but predominantly Protestant – counterpart to Cologne and its cathedral on the Rhine. As in Cologne's case, however, the cult of historic Nuremberg reached its height as population growth – from 83,633 to 360,000 between 1871 and 1914[172] – and industrialisation began to transform it. Redevelopment in the 1870s, with the demolition of ancient towers and fortifications, was compared by Thausing to the destructiveness of the Paris Commune.[173] Although most of the old city, with its refurbished Dürer House and medieval fortress, remained intact until the air raids of the Second World War, its atmosphere had changed, and the search by artists and tourists for relics of the *Dürerzeit* shifted to other, smaller places.

Thausing's glowing description, in his biography of Dürer, of early-modern Nuremberg's moderate and benevolent patrician government – Woltmann had described Augsburg in similar terms – and its enlightened innovations in public hygiene, security and poor relief, doubtless glossed over the harsh social realities of Dürer's time.[174] And it played down the patriciate's growing aristocratic pretensions, with families like the Tuchers and Stromers acquiring castles and a semi-feudal lifestyle. But it spoke to the heart of a public inclined to see urban culture- and welfare-creating institutions as a sphere peculiarly its own, all the more so as bourgeois–liberal hegemony in the cities was perceived as being increasingly under threat. (Bavaria's first Socialist Reichstag deputy was elected in Nuremberg in 1881.)[175] Moreover the whole symbolic complex Dürer–Renaissance–Nuremberg, which reached its full extent in the new Empire's formative years, had become a metaphor for middle-class cultural aspirations. In 1866 Wilhelm Lübke inaugurated the new *Zeitschrift für bildende Kunst* with a programmatic essay emphasising art's collective roots: 'For beauty may be the creative act of the individual master; but his whole people works with him in its production, and the artist is only the gifted genius who frees from the marble, or conjures with colours on to the canvas the beauty that is, as it were, latent in the whole spirit of the nation.'[176] Like other writers before him, above all Gustav Freytag, Lübke also explicitly identified this culture-bearing *Volk* with the middle stratum of society, the *Bürgertum*. Taking architecture as his example, he asked 'What was it in the last century if not the handmaiden of a degenerate aristocracy, providing the coquettishly decorated stage for its debauched life, showy festivals and dissipating pastimes?' But now, he continued, all this had changed. Whereas in the eighteenth century castles and pavilions had sprung up like mushrooms from a swamp of frivolity, contemporary architecture expressed a way of life that, 'in manly labour and the earnest grasp of material and spiritual ends has cast the main thrust of development back into the natural centre, into the *Bürgerstand*'.[177] The germ of this situation lay not in the nineteenth century but, as Lübke was to argue elsewhere, in the sixteenth, the seedtime of modern German culture. Ten years later, in the essay on the German Renaissance already cited, Rudolph von Eitelberger asserted:

> this artistic movement was above all at home in the towns, and the bourgeois trades there became the real bearers of the Renaissance . . . These bourgeois trades lent the Renaissance in the German Empire a quite definite character, which distinguishes the German Renaissance fundamentally from the Italian one and the French one. The French Renaissance bears altogether the character of a princely, noble, aristocratic, rather frivolous society, the Italian Renaissance predominantly a purely artistic, ideal type; the German Renaissance is largely a mixture of art and craft, bourgeois-solid and full of character.[178]

The idea of a peculiarly German 'mixture of art and craft' was important. Their separation, symbolised institutionally by the distinction between academies and design schools, was a subject of continual debate that overlapped with other contentious issues such as art's social function and the growth of an 'artistic proletariat'. Academies' historical links with French absolutism and cultural hegemony made it all the more emotive. Many Germans therefore looked back nostalgically to the Renaissance as a time before the establishment of a hierarchy of the arts, and to Dürer as – in Thausing's words – 'very much a representative of that art which knows no boundary against craft'.[179] In the 1870s the yearning for 'solidity' and artistic wholeness became strongly focused on the historicist domestic interior. Dürer's famous engraving of Saint Jerome and his lion ensconced in a sixteenth-century Humanist's study, later described by Muther as 'the most moving interior in the history of German art', and the classic expression of 'German joy in domesticity',[180] also captivated a public that saw the opaque windows, heavy drapes and sheltering alcoves of *altdeutsch* décor as an aesthetically harmonious refuge from the modern 'struggle for existence'. This image hovered before one visitor to the 1876 exhibition as he described panelled spaces subtly evocative of the German forest. In the *altdeutsch* rooms created by Anton Pössenbacher and Gabriel Seidl there were cries of 'How wonderfully cosy, how poetic', while young couples could be seen 'who in this unfeeling time let themselves be spiritually warmed and made to feel at home by the rich mellow tone of their surroundings'.[181] It was important, too, that by this time modern advances like collapsible panelling, electroplating and synthetic materials were bringing such décor within reach of a broad and increasingly mobile middle-class public.

Hirth, in his seminal book *The German Renaissance Room*, first published in 1877, also expanded on the wider psychological and ideological associations of the *Dürerzeit*, in particular presenting the *altdeutsch* interior not only as a sheltering nest for the German family but as a quasi-theatrical space for fantasy: for modern civilised man, he argued, as essential a shield against the blows of fate as insurance against fire or poverty.[182] Such notions were related to a much broader cult of make-believe ranging from Ludwig II of Bavaria's buildings and private stage performances to the late-nineteenth-century photographer's studio with its painted backdrops, props and costumes; and, of course, to historical masques and pageants. But Hirth also enunciated an *altdeutsch* 'colour code' that privileged warm and sombre hues, especially autumnal reds, old golds and browns, as quintessentially German and indeed 'natural'. 'In taking the warm and luscious tones of the German autumnal landscape at wine-harvest time', he wrote, 'we satisfy both our hearts and eyes.'[183] This had important implications for taste in painting. 'With a few good old portraits of the sixteenth or seventeenth century,' wrote Jakob von Falke in his famous design manual, 'a room can be pretty superbly decorated.'[184] Seventeenth-century Dutch genre paintings, with their meticulous workmanship, subdued tones and intimate subject-matter, also matched the *Dürerzeit* ethos; hence their rising popularity and prices. For those unable to afford old masters a passable alternative was the comparable – and often Dutch-influenced – work of contemporary salon artists, Munich painters like Wilhelm Diez and Franz Defregger, for example, who with their scores of pupils and imitators dominated an important section of the market from the 1870s until the 1920s.[185] But the supremacy of *altdeutsch*-inspired visual conventions also hindered the acceptance of other types of art, above all the 'open-air painting' (*plein-airisme* or *Freilichtmalerei*) of the early 1880s

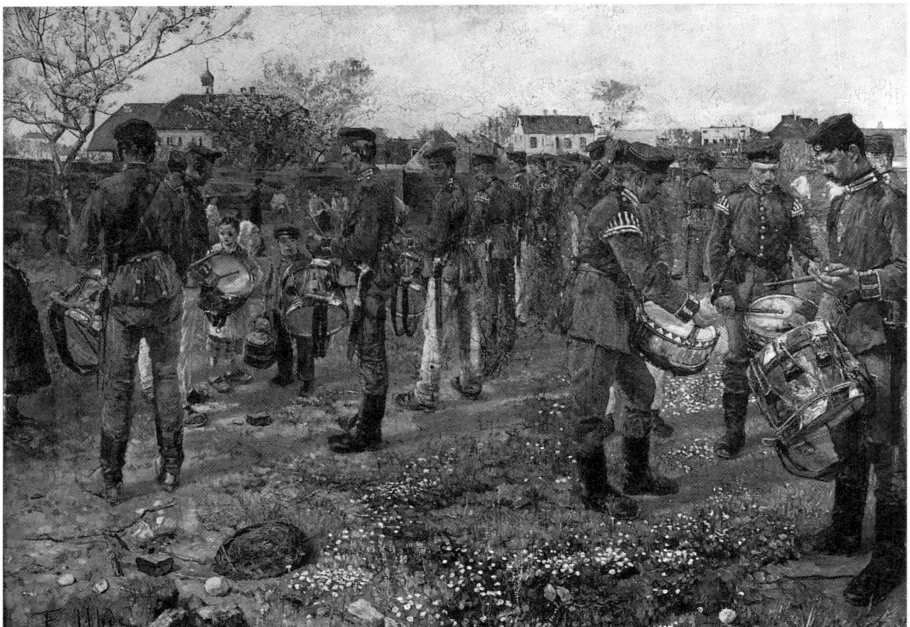

PLATE 7 Fritz von Uhde, *Bavarian Drummers*, 1883, oil on canvas, 72 x 95 cm. Uhde turned to full-time painting in 1878, after some years as an army officer. Contact with Liebermann in Munich in the early 1880s encouraged him to move from conventionally dark-toned anecdotal subjects to lighter interior and outdoor scenes, some of them set in Holland. Soon afterwards he turned increasingly to religious pictures with strong social undertones. In the 1890s he became a leading figure in the Munich Secession.

associated with such figures as Fritz von Uhde (1848-1911), whose *Bavarian Drummers* of 1883 (Plate 7), a picture of bandsmen in light blue uniforms practising on a spring day, undoubtedly struck many contemporaries not only as banal but as garish and even unnatural.

Another obstacle to the acceptance of this kind of painting was its perceived Frenchness at a time of intense political and cultural francophobia. Reviewing the 1883 Munich International Exhibition, Adolf Rosenberg lumped Uhde and his fellow-*plein-airiste* Max Liebermann (1847-1935) together with French participants such as Jules Bastien-Lepage; a demonstratively hostile gesture notwithstanding Rosenberg's grudging recognition of their talent. 'In the pictures of these light-enthusiasts', he wrote, 'all the figures look as though their heads, hands and clothes were sprinkled with flour.'[186] Hostility to France had infused German nationalism since the eighteenth century and been fanned to white heat during the Wars of Liberation; Friedrich Jahn's cry that teaching one's daughter French was tantamount to sending her whoring expressed it in its most rabid form.[187] Although cultural francophobia subsided after 1815, at least in relation to the visual arts, political hostility revived during the international crisis of 1840 and, more lastingly, that of 1859; gave Bismarck a powerful antidote to south German anti-Prussianism in the last phase of Unification; and remained intense after 1871. If the pageantry marking Cologne Cathedral's completion in 1880 had been a further manifestation of anti-French triumphalism, other national monuments, from the huge *Germania* above Rüdesheim to the cyclopean Leipzig *Völkerschlachtdenkmal* – proto-Fritz Lang out of Richard Wagner – were inaugurated in an atmosphere of still more strident francophobia. By the late nineteenth century a wide-ranging discourse of Frenchness versus Germanness had evolved that (echoing Görres in the Napoleonic Wars) contrasted 'French' frivolity, shallowness and superficial virtuosity in every sphere with 'German' depth, spirituality and thoroughness.[188] It was comprehensively invoked in 1872 by Lübke who, in an extraordinary lecture, compared the two nations' cultural development since the Middle Ages and set an agenda for the future: 'Now that we have established our relationship with the French thoroughly and, let us hope, finally in the field of politics and war,' he declared, 'the task of measuring our culture with the French one faces us all the more urgently.'[189] Two years later, requesting funds for the new Munich Academy building, Ferdinand von Miller warned the Bavarian Parliament that, despite German victory, 'This hereditary foe persists in making war on us by another, perhaps even more damaging means. French taste, formed by art, and the French sense of beauty, have subjugated the whole world, including us Germans.'[190] (Appropriately, much of the money was eventually found from Bavaria's share of the French war indemnity.) Prominent at the 1876 Munich exhibition were Werner's decorative designs for the Berlin Victory Column, and the event was hailed as a reaffirmation of cultural independence after centuries of French domination. Its overall purpose, wrote the architect Joseph von Schmaedel, was to promote an artistic rebirth that would raise Germany's international cultural standing to the same level as her political one, while the historical section would reveal that 'artistically highly endowed neighbouring peoples, which were pleased to call the Germans "barbarians", did not scorn to praise our masters' products as pearls of their own national art'.[191]

Yet it was soon clear that visions of German cultural supremacy over the 'hereditary foe' were, as far as the visual arts were concerned, an illusion. Even in material terms, French recovery after the disasters of 1871 was unexpectedly rapid. But the cultural policies of the Third Republic, especially the reorganisation of the academic training system and the success of the private schools that developed alongside it, soon made Paris's artistic reputation more brilliant than ever. For anyone who doubted it, the World Exhibition of 1889, celebrating the centenary of the French Revolution, was a powerful assertion of French artistic hegemony, as well as a demonstration of Gallic achievements in science and technology. Dominated by Eiffel's 300-metre tower – almost twice the height of Cologne Cathedral – it was visited by nearly thirty-two million people, including 150,000 from the United States. 'Paris is to the artist', wrote the American painter Edwin Lord Weeks the following year, 'what Wall Street is to the broker, the centre of all life.'[192] This view was not confined to Americans, and 1889 confirmed an already established trend by which foreign art students and art buyers, who had earlier flocked to German centres, were increasingly drawn to Paris. (Germans too, despite continuing French hostility, were also making the pilgrimage in significant numbers.)[193] This situation inflamed the chauvinism of Berlin's cultural establishment, and in January 1896, twenty-five years after the founding of the Empire, both Werner and Academy President Hermann Ende made violently francophobic speeches denouncing the 'arch-enemy' and exhorting German artists to express the ideal sentiments of their own nation.[194] This was the background for the looming controversy in Berlin and elsewhere over foreign, but above all French, art and German museums.

## MUSEUMS AND NATIONAL ART

Museum development and the formation of national consciousness in nineteenth-century Germany were closely linked.[195] Many of the 200 or so institutions in existence by the First World War were historical or antiquarian in character, and varied greatly in scope and importance, from major foundations like the Germanic National Museum in Nuremberg, which drew visitors and donors from all over the country, to hole-in-corner establishments in the remote provinces. But pride of place in the contemporary debates about museums' content, organisation and cultural role was occupied by the galleries of fine art founded by monarchs, art unions, private individuals and municipalities in the century after 1815.

It was in this period, in Germany and in other developed countries on both sides of the Atlantic, that the conception and physical shape of the modern specialised museum evolved, in contrast to the jumbled 'curiosity cabinets' or *Wunderkammer* of before 1800. At the same time, dynastic collections ceased to be monarchs' private chattels or treasure-reserves – Friedrich Wilhelm I of Prussia had traded statues for regiments of dragoons[196] – and became inalienable national property. In several German states, in fact, key modern principles were finding acceptance before the end of the eighteenth century: for example, bureaucratic gallery administration (Bavaria under Elector Max IV Joseph),[197] public accessibility (the Palatinate under Elector Johann Wilhelm, Hesse–Cassel under Elector Friedrich II),[198] and, though as yet in theory only, the idea of the purpose-built and systematically organised museum limited to painting and sculpture (Prussia under Friedrich Wilhelm III).[199] But for several reasons the impact of the French Revolution and the Napoleonic Wars vastly accelerated development. To begin with, the new *Musée Nationale* in the Louvre, opened in August 1793, was the first gallery of nationalised dynastic art, and under Napoleon became a unique showcase for masterpieces seized from all over Europe. Secondly, in Germany, the secularisation of ecclesiastical property in 1803, under pressure from the French, brought a flood of works of art on to the market; indeed, into the street. In 'Holy Cologne', for example, where sixty-three out of eighty-three churches were closed after secularisation, and piles of pictures and altarpieces were carted away on barrows, the Boisserée brothers were able to acquire practically for a song the nucleus of their celebrated collection of old Cologne, Rhenish and Flemish paintings.[200] (The eventual display of such works, many of them altar panels in 'stripped' museum-piece form, symbolised culture's new autonomous role, detached from its earlier – religious or dynastic – functional context.)[201] Finally, the return of looted works from France after 1815–Altdorfer's *Battle on the Issus*, for example, owned by the Wittelsbachs, had hung in Napoleon's bathroom at Saint-Cloud[202] – enhanced their aura as national treasures, and Berliners' enthusiastic response to an exhibition of repatriated Hohenzollern pictures gave new impetus to plans for a museum.[203] But Schinkel's Altes Museum, completed at great cost at a time of financial stringency, was also linked to two other consequences of the Napoleonic Wars: Berlin's new status as the capital of a major power and the perception of art as a medium of *Bildung* within the post-1806 strategy, already mentioned, of creating an educated, patriotic citizenry as the basis for a revitalised State. It was thus no accident that Wilhelm von Humboldt, the architect of Prussian educational reform, was closely involved with Schinkel's project at almost every stage. A comparable desire for stability and cohesion clearly influenced museum-formation in two other states greatly enlarged by the wars: Hesse–Darmstadt, where in 1820 Grand Duke Ludewig I made parts of the dynastic collection available to the public[204] and, above all, Bavaria, where King Ludwig I's classical Glyptothek (1830) was followed by the completion of an old-master gallery, the Alte Pinakothek, in 1836 and the Neue Pinakothek in 1853.[205]

Ludwig I as crown prince, king and ex-king (he was made to abdicate, in colourful circumstances, in favour of his son Maximilian in 1848) was until his death in 1868 one of nineteenth-century Europe's greatest art-collectors and museum-creators, if not the greatest. Although he acquired many other important old masters, his most outstanding coup was the purchase in 1827 of the Boisserée Collection, by this time practically a national institution, for 240,000 *Gulden*.[206] Other German princes, including King Friedrich Wilhelm IV and Emperor Wilhelm II, had also made major contributions to Germany's great galleries by 1914. Well before the middle of the nineteenth century, however, many private individuals and organisations were helping to shape museum development. The Frankfurt banker Johann Heinrich Städel (1728-1816), for example, bequeathed nearly 500 paintings and most of his remaining wealth for the creation of a gallery and drawing school, the Städel Institute.[207] Similar to Städel in his strong sense of national and local patriotism and civic obligation, was the Cologne scholar and university rector Ferdinand Franz Wallraff (1748-1824). His much more heterogeneous collection, described by Goethe as a 'chaos', comprised not only thousands of paintings, prints and engravings but a mass of books, artefacts and antiquities going back to Cologne's Roman origins. Like the Boisserée brothers he was spurred to action by the French invasion, and set about rescuing as many precious objects as possible from looting or destruction, including Rubens' *Stigmatisation of Saint Francis* from the city's doomed Capucin monastery. Wallraff's holdings were eventually bequeathed to the city, and housed in a purpose-built museum, funded by the leather-merchant J. H. Richartz, that opened in 1863.[208] By 1900, swelled by many more benefactions, both the Städel Institute and the Wallraff-Richartz Museum had developed into major galleries of old and modern art.

Private initiative of a somewhat different kind was responsible for the foundation of art-union collections, many of which became the basis for municipal galleries. By the turn of the century such institutions existed in Aachen, Bremen, Brunswick, Kiel, Königsberg, Rostock, Stettin and Wiesbaden, to name only some of the principal ones.[209] One of the earliest and most important foundations was the gallery opened by the Hamburg Art Union in March 1850.[210] Steadily enlarged both by the society and by private individuals, it became the basis for the Hamburg Kunsthalle, eventually located in a handsome building paid for by a mixture of private and municipal funds, inaugurated in 1869 and later greatly extended. In 1886, an important year in German museum history, its first art-historically trained director, Alfred Lichtwark was appointed, who in a term of office lasting until 1914 was to transform its assortment of some 900 pictures into one of Germany's great galleries. Another outstanding product of civic pride and generosity was the Leipzig Art Museum, founded by the Art Union in 1848, enlarged by the bequest of the merchant Heinrich Schletter's modern collection in 1853, and occupying its own premises five years later.[211] By the beginning of the twentieth century, housed in a magnificent neo-Renaissance building, it was one of the Empire's best-endowed civic galleries, boasting not only Italian and north European old masters but a large collection of modern painting and sculpture, including major works by Leipzig's most celebrated living artist, Max Klinger.

In 1826 the Director of the Nuremberg Art School, Albert Christoph Reindel, looking ahead to the approaching Dürer anniversary, had appealed to German artists to contribute paintings and sculpture for a national collection to be housed in the castle.[212]

Although this scheme came to nothing, the idea of a national gallery of contemporary German art as a symbol of cultural unity attracted increasing support over the next two decades.[213] In 1848 Düsseldorf artists petitioned the Frankfurt Parliament to create one, and in Prussia during the revolutionary period there were demands from artists in all the main teaching centres, Düsseldorf, Berlin and Königsberg, for regular State spending on both a modern gallery and monumental commissions, thus shifting the emphasis of 'patronage from above' decisively from dynasty to nation. These hopes, too, were frustrated, but in the 1850s artistic nationalism continued to gather strength, encouraged by new national organisations such as the VHK and the ADKG, and events like the 1858 Munich Exhibition. Demands for a national gallery persisted, with suggested locations including Munich, with its existing modern collection in the Neue Pinakothek; Nuremberg, with its Germanic Museum; and the Wartburg, offered by the Grand Duke of Saxe–Weimar. But eventually the decisive step took place in Berlin, where the replacement as Regent in 1858 of the incapacitated Friedrich Wilhelm IV by his brother Wilhelm, and the beginning of the initially liberal 'New Era', renewed interest in the whole issue, with more petitions for State action and funds. Given the new Government's aim to assert Prussian primacy in Germany by a policy of 'moral conquests',[214] and the apparent imminence of initiatives elsewhere, this would probably soon have resulted in the creation of a national gallery in any case. But the prospect of an actual collection materialised when, in March 1859, the Berlin banker and art-lover Joachim Wagener – for whom Caspar David Friedrich had painted *Moonrise over the Sea* in 1822[215] – bequeathed 262 pictures to the State for the purpose. Housed at first in the Berlin Academy after Wagener's death at the beginning of 1861, the gallery was eventually transferred to an imposing new classical building, completed in 1876, on Berlin's 'Museum Island'. Notwithstanding its title, however, the dedication 'To German Art' over its portal, and the fact that between 1871 and 1896 its director was a Reich official, the National Gallery was and remained a Prussian institution. Indeed, filled initially with history- and battle-paintings by Werner, Camphausen and their colleagues, it mainly resembled a Prussian hall of fame.[216]

While governments had been involved for much longer in the funding of academies and museum construction, it was not until the second half of the nineteenth century, and at an uneven pace from state to state, that taxpayers' money began to be used on a significant scale to buy and commission works of art, a role hitherto played by monarchs, art unions and private individuals. But after 1871 such expenditure increased considerably, albeit on an individual–state basis. (Reich spending on art between 1871 and 1918 was mainly confined to *ad hoc* contributions to the cost of major monuments, and of paintings and sculpture for national buildings such as the Reichstag and the Imperial Court of Appeal.)[217] In Prussia an annual art allocation of 25,000 Thalers (75,000 marks) was placed in the budget in 1862, and by 1873 had risen to 300,000 marks a year, together with the income from various private foundations, although these funds were used not only for National Gallery acquisitions but for monumental painting and sculptural commissions throughout the kingdom. In Saxony until 1873 acquisitions for the Royal Gallery were paid for from an assortment of funds administered by the Dresden Academy. But in that year an annual State allocation of 25,500 marks was created, and increased to 48,000 marks in 1874. At the same time part of Saxony's share of the French war indemnity was used to increase reserves by 450,000 marks and create a capital fund of 300,000 marks for the purchase of contemporary art.[218] Apart from the funding of monumental projects, development was slower in Bavaria, where the growth of the modern collection in the Neue Pinakothek continued to be paid for entirely by ex-King Ludwig I. But Ludwig's death in 1868 was an important turning-point, since his grandson Ludwig II had little interest in art except as an adjunct to his building projects, and these increasingly overstretched the Crown's finances.[219] By Ludwig II's death in 1886 and the beginning of his uncle Luitpold's regency, there was also growing pressure on Government to support the Munich salons, as competition from other centres, especially Berlin, intensified. As a result, a capital fund of 440,000 marks was created (in 1888) and a regular budget allocation established, rising from 20,000 marks in 1886 to 100,000 marks in 1890, and devoted almost entirely to modern purchases.[220] Parallel, finally, to increased State funding of modern public galleries was the increasing professionalisation of museum management; not only the systematic arrangement of the collections, the elimination of misattributed or inferior works and the compilation of modern scholarly catalogues, but the replacement in key positions of elderly artists by art historians. In addition to Lichtwark in Hamburg, notable appointees in the modern field included Max Jordan, who left the Leipzig Art Museum for the Berlin National Gallery in 1874, and Karl Woermann, who succeeded the veteran history-painter Julius Hübner as Director of the Dresden Royal Gallery in 1882.

In the last three decades of the century public acquisition of modern pictures followed a definite pattern. Firstly, there was a great deal of it, and sometimes at high prices. Secondly, especially in Munich where maintaining the appeal of the international salons was a major policy objective, modern purchases included a sprinkling of foreign art. But everywhere the main emphasis was on work by German or German-based artists, with a bias in favour of those resident in the state concerned. Thirdly, the spending of available funds was usually a matter, not for gallery directors alone, but for committees: the National Art Commission (*Landeskunstkommission* (LKK)) in Prussia, formed in 1862;[221] in Bavaria a raft of committees established in 1875 and restructured in 1907;[222] and in Saxony two bodies, the General Commission for the spending of public monies, and the Academic Council, which controlled the income from various private foundations, and to which even the Director of the Royal Gallery did not automatically belong.[223] All these committees were heavily dominated by local artists, whose self-interested and nepotistic tendencies, as we shall see later, presented gallery directors with a major problem. They were also conservative. On his arrival in Dresden, Woermann found that the art establishment's definition of modernity meant the historical colourism of the Piloty school. Thus although at the Munich

International Exhibition of 1883 he badly wanted to buy the Saxon-born Fritz von Uhde's *Bavarian Drummers*, he was stubbornly opposed by the General Commission and the picture was not acquired for another twenty-four years.[224] Yet the enormous sum of 50,000 marks was spent on one of Defregger's historical *grandes machines*, plus another 24,000 marks on a picture by the Düsseldorf landscapist Andreas Achenbach.[225] (Sculpture was a less exposed area, and Woermann's colleague Georg Treu was able to buy two major works by Rodin for the State in 1894, six years before the artist's breakthrough in France.)[226]

The question of what great modern galleries should contain, and who should decide it, was also ever-present during Max Jordan's directorship of the Berlin National Gallery.[227] But despite occasional clashes, for example over his enthusiasm for Arnold Böcklin well before the Swiss painter 'arrived' in the 1890s, Jordan had a reasonable working relationship with the LKK: hence his acquisition, among other items, of Max Liebermann's *Flax-Scourers in Laren* in 1887. The situation became much more difficult, however, after his replacement by Hugo von Tschudi in 1896.[228] Hitherto, Tschudi had not been professionally concerned with modern art at all. Later, like Jordan, he became a devotee of Menzel, and one of his undisputed achievements as director was to acquire, partly with funds donated by Wilhelm II, a number of the artist's major early works. But for some years Tschudi had been close to Liebermann, the modernist critic and art historian Julius Meier-Graefe, and Berlin's growing community of francophile and pro-Impressionist collectors and dealers, and soon after his appointment he set out to bring modern French art into the National Gallery.

French works had not been excluded from German galleries in the early and mid-nineteenth century. Two of the Hamburg Kunsthalle's first pictures had been Regnault's *Genius of France* and a version of Delaroche's *Cromwell Contemplating the Corpse of Charles I*,[229] and French paintings had featured prominently in the eventually public collections of Schletter in Leipzig and Wagener in Berlin. But the atmosphere of the 1890s, as we have seen, was very different; and the official principle that the National Gallery was 'exclusively designated for sculptural and painted works of German artists of our century'[230] was defended not only by the LKK, dominated by conservatives like Werner, but also by a monarch for whom Paris was 'the greatest whore-house in the world',[231] and whose dislike for *plein-airisme* and its German practitioners was often and stridently expressed. Tschudi, on the other hand, held the (then) provocative view that modern French art was not only superior to that of other countries but of truly paradigmatic significance. 'For the painting of the nineteenth century,' he asserted later, 'France is the classic soil, like Italy for the Renaissance and Holland for the painting of the seventeenth century. There is scarcely a problem of modern art that was not addressed and brought to its ultimate solution in France. A wealth of stimuli flows from here to all civilised countries.'[232] Thus for any collection of international scope and standing (Tschudi's controversial definition of a national gallery) French works were indispensable. Prices, too, were rising. Both to circumvent the LKK's certain opposition, therefore, and because of the National Gallery's by now relatively modest share of the art budget, the director followed the example of Wilhelm von Bode in the old master field and solicited gifts of money and works of art from Berlin's wealthy private collectors. As early as December 1896 he was able to mount an exhibition of twenty German and thirty-four foreign accessions, among the latter works by Courbet, Manet, Monet and Degas which, shown beside Cornelius's bloodless cartoons, caused a sensation. So too did Tschudi's subsequent rehanging of the whole gallery, that eliminated much of the original Wagener bequest and many of the more recent 'patriotic' canvases, and gave pride of place to works like Manet's *In the Conservatory*, Monet's *View of Vétheuil-sur-Seine*, Cézanne's *Mill on the Couleuvre near Pontoise*, and pictures by the German Realists Leibl and Trübner.

But there was an inevitable conservative backlash, doubtless all the fiercer because many of Tschudi's donors were French dealers and Jewish businessmen. In March 1898 his policy was attacked in the Prussian Parliament – gift-horses were all very well, complained one deputy from rural Oldenburg, but if they were half-knackered, one did not show them in public[233] – and in 1899 his gallery changes were partially reversed on Wilhelm II's orders. More seriously, all acquisitions, including gifts, were made subject to royal approval. Given the strength of conservative opposition, Tschudi's open support for the Berlin Secession (founded in May 1898), and his steadfast refusal to defer to the emperor's opinions, it seems amazing that he should have remained actively in post until the spring of 1908. That he did so and, though with much more difficulty, continued to acquire French works, was because of his good relations with important political figures, including Chancellor Bülow; and because the emperor's interest in art, as in everything else, was intermittent. Having organised successful major exhibitions devoted to Menzel (1905) and, in collaboration with Lichtwark, to German art from 1775 to 1875 (1906), Tschudi induced Wilhelm to approve a further package of Impressionists and in 1907 again reorganised the gallery. But his position remained insecure and early the next year became impossible after an open confrontation with the emperor, whose irritation with him had turned to uncontrolled antagonism,[234] and what were later aptly described in France as '*mesquines cabales*' against him.[235] Bode, Director-General of Prussian Museums since 1906, had long been working against him behind the scenes. After a year's leave Tschudi resigned and accepted the post of Director of the Bavarian State Galleries in July 1909. However, his departure from Berlin was a pyrrhic victory for his opponents. Rumours that Werner (who had served as acting director during Tschudi's absence, and schemed to reverse his policies) would succeed him proved unfounded, and the new director was another distinguished art historian, Ludwig Justi. Although more diplomatic than Tschudi, and more cautious over acquisitions, he successfully pushed through organisational reforms that made him practically independent of the LKK. Still more remarkably, he not only secured 100,000 marks of the annual art budget specifically for the National Gallery, but in 1911 obtained an extra regular allocation of 40,000 marks specifically for foreign purchases.[236]

Tschudi's career in Munich, meanwhile, had been spectacular but brief, since he was already seriously ill by 1909, and died in November 1911. In that time he not only completely rehung the old masters in the Alte Pinakothek but set about opening the Neue Pinakothek to modern French art. Here too he met formidable obstacles. Not only did political conditions in Bavaria make it impossible to increase State funds, but Munich's leading artists were at least as determined as their Berlin colleagues to defend 'their' share of both cash and gallery space. Thanks to his loyal circle of collectors and dealers, however, Tschudi still managed to assemble a handsome body of acquisitions and promised funds, the so-called Tschudi Donation, that was formally accepted after his death. This included, in addition to earlier paintings by Géricault, Delacroix, Daumier and Courbet and other items, Manet's *Breakfast in the Studio* and *Monet Painting on his Boat at Argenteuil*, Monet's *Bridge at Argenteuil*, Van Gogh's *Vase of Sunflowers*, two major Gauguins, three Renoirs, and a Rodin bust of Gustav Mahler.[237]

Hugo von Tschudi's significance in the history of Germany's museums can be measured in several ways: by the importance of the galleries he headed, the strength of his commitment to modern French art, the quality of the works he obtained, and the symbolic importance contemporaries attached to his conflicts with Wilhelm II and with other conservatives in both Berlin and Munich. Within months of his appointment in Berlin he had acquired the first pictures by Manet, Monet and Degas to enter a German museum, and the first Cézanne to hang in any public gallery.[238] But other German institutions were soon moving in a similar direction. The Städel Institute was given its first Impressionist painting, a Sisley landscape, in 1899, and over the next fifteen years acquired half a dozen others, including an important Monet, *Le Déjeuner* of 1868, in 1910.[239] Lichtwark in Hamburg probably never viewed the Impressionists with the same passion as did his friends Tschudi and Liebermann, and remained ever mindful of his public's conservatism.[240] But he increasingly appreciated the importance of modern French art, and a Monet still life presented to the Kunsthalle in 1897 was the first of several Impressionist acquisitions, culminating in the purchase of Renoir's large *Riders in the Bois de Boulogne* (1873) at the Rouart sale in 1912.[241] The following summer, six months before his death, Lichtwark invited Vuillard and Bonnard to Hamburg, where they executed a group of superb local portraits and landscapes.[242] In conservative Dresden, finally, the Royal Gallery did not obtain its first Impressionist painting, a small Monet landscape, until 1909. Five years earlier, however, Woermann had achieved a major coup by outbidding the Louvre and the Art Institute of Chicago for Courbet's *Stone-Breakers*.[243]

These developments, and the continuing climate of francophobia before 1914, formed the background for one of Wilhelmine Germany's most famous demonstrations of cultural chauvinism: Carl Vinnen's *German Artists' Protest*, published by the conservative firm of Eugen Diederichs in Jena in 1911.[244] Vinnen was a landscapist associated with the north German artists' colony of Worpswede, popular with nationalists since the turn of the century for an atmospheric ruralism verging on *Heimatkunst*. The *Protest* originated as a pamphlet inspired by Gustav Pauli's acquisition of Van Gogh's *Poppy-Field* (1890) for the Kunsthalle in Vinnen's native Bremen.

But other events, including the controversial purchase of Manet's *Execution of the Emperor Maximilian* by the Mannheim Gallery,[245] led him to seek a nation-wide audience. His message, in language reminiscent of the 1870s ('A nation can only attain the height of its powers through artists of its own flesh and blood'), was xenophobic and protectionist: Germany was importing far too much foreign art; unscrupulous dealers were palming off second-rate French works to museums at exorbitant prices; a clique of mostly Berlin-based critics, aesthetes and snobs was bamboozling the public and encouraging young artists to ruin their talents by aping Parisian fashions. Even more interesting than this polemic were the endorsements of 118 artists appended to it. Vinnen belonged to both the Munich and Berlin Secessions, and was clearly anxious to get this progressive section of the art world on his side. Though backed by only eleven Berliners, the *Protest* was supported by no fewer than fifty-seven artists based in Munich or other parts of southern Bavaria, including many prominent Secessionists: ironic considering that, as we shall see later, one of the society's original aims had been to revitalise Munich art by increasing its exposure to international trends. Although current economic anxieties were one reason for this, another was hostility to Tschudi, who certainly regarded himself as one of the polemic's principal targets.[246] It was therefore appropriate that two of his sympathisers among the Munich avant-garde, Franz Marc and Vassily Kandinsky, who had earlier been attacked by the (once progressive) Berlin critic Hans Rosenhagen in terms anticipating Vinnen,[247] should have been instrumental in organising a counterblast. This was first published as *Fighting for Art* (*Im Kampf um die Kunst*) at the end of 1911, and included essays by many of those most closely involved with modern art in Germany: nine gallery-directors (including Pauli and Lichtwark), forty-eight artists ranging from the leaders of the Berlin Secession to Expressionists, and a bevy of writers, academics and dealers.

In the short term at least, Vinnen's campaign achieved little. Indeed, his own ambivalence towards French art was easily demonstrated. As a member of the Bremen Kunsthalle's purchasing committee a few years earlier, he had actually approved the purchase of Monet's *Portrait of Camille in a Striped Dress* (1866) for 50,000 marks.[248] And, like dozens of other German artists over the previous forty years, he and many of his supporters had spent time in Paris. Between 1911 and 1914 German galleries continued to acquire Impressionist and Post-Impressionist works, and private collectors' enthusiasm for modern French art, already well established by the turn of the century, persisted even through the First World War. But the signs of an ever-fiercer backlash were unmistakable. In the third, revised edition of Adolf Rosenberg's *Handbook of Art History*, published in 1921, Hans Rosenhagen abandoned the earlier practice of beginning the nineteenth-century section with a discussion of developments in France. Such an arrangement, he declared in the preface, had been not only unpatriotic but in substance misconceived, since French and German art differed so fundamentally that it was completely inappropriate to attribute any kind of normative status to the former. 'The strength of German art', he continued, 'lies admittedly not in externals but in strength of feeling. This has always distinguished it, whether one thinks of Dürer and Grünewald, of Mozart or Beethoven, of Goethe or Mörike.' Germans should at last pay due tribute to their own painting, as they had to Wagner's music.[249] Such sentiments, which of course were hardly new, were central to the movement of cultural reaction that developed during the Weimar period and which, propagated officially after 1933, was to isolate Germany completely from the international art world.

## THE ECLIPSE OF HISTORY-PAINTING

In the mean time, the reorientation of public art-buying in the two decades before 1914 had coincided with a decline in the status of history-painting. State-funded mural production, it is true, continued until the war, to the advantage of long-established specialists like Werner and younger ones such as Arthur Kampf (1864-1950). At the other extreme, cabinet- or sub-cabinet-format historical genre, which quarried the past for picturesque anecdotes, also remained popular: part of the much larger category of narrative art that, though increasingly dismissed by pundits, still dominated much of the market into the 1920s and beyond. But the day of the historical *grande machine* was over. The idea, that in the 1870s would have been ridiculed by all but a few avant-garde artists and writers, that a bundle of asparagus painted by Manet might be artistically more significant, and museum-worthy, than the downfall of Napoleon III painted by Werner, was by no means universally accepted in Germany – or anywhere else – by 1914. But Tschudi articulated it (without naming names) in a major speech at the Berlin Academy in 1899,[250] and for the Empire's growing cohort of modern gallery directors it became an article of faith. Werner, who saw his life's work thus marginalised, reacted in his 1913 memoirs with bitterness and sarcasm: obviously, in the light of subsequent advances, the years from 1860 to 1890 had been a desolate period for German art: 'It's incredible how blind and crazy one can be!'[251] The last of his subject-paintings to enter the Berlin National Gallery – *In Quarters Before Paris* (Plate 8), another reminiscence of 1870 – had been acquired nearly twenty years earlier. (Showing campaign-weary Prussians singing *Lieder* to insulate themselves from the frivolous – but exquisite – surroundings of a requisitioned château, the picture now looks like an unconscious tribute to French culture.)[252] Other 'patriotic' canvases bought since the 1860s were being transferred by Justi to the military museum in the Berlin Arsenal; and for outsize narrative paintings all over Germany, relegation to such specialist establishments or to the provinces was becoming the only alternative to the oblivion of the depot. For those as yet unsold the prospects were bleaker still. Indeed, in 1910 August Dieffenbacher's enormous *In the Stone Age: Cave-Bears Attacking a Funeral* was rejected by the Bavarian State even as a gift.[253]

It was not only the changing of the guard at German museums, and directors' independence from traditionally-minded committees, that was draining the life-blood

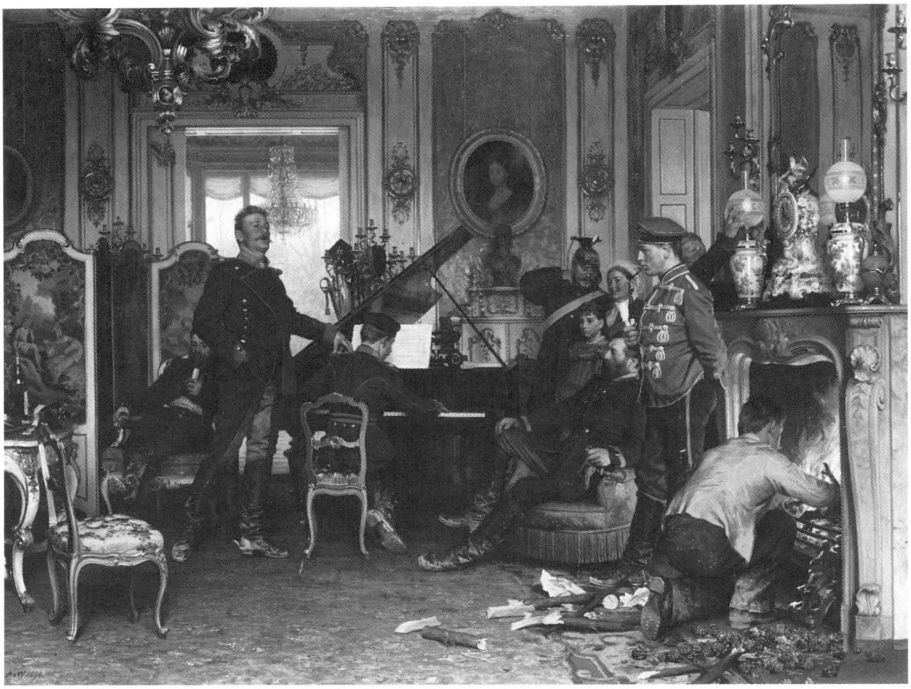

PLATE 8 Anton von Werner, *In Quarters before Paris*, 1894, oil on canvas, 120 x 158 cm. Finely executed in Werner's best illusionistic manner, the picture recalls an event he had witnessed and sketched on 24 October 1870, just after the beginning of the siege of Paris, at the opulent Château de Brunoy. Symbolically, the physical warmth of the fire is deftly balanced by the spiritual radiance of the song (Schumann's 'Das Meer erglänzte weit hinaus'), which moves both the soldiers and the French caretaker's wife and daughter. The picture was a great success and was bought by the Berlin National Gallery for 16,000 marks.

of historical painting. After 1900 even the Historical Art League, which had done much to sustain it since the heyday of Piloty and Menzel, was turning to other subjects and media: in 1907, for example, it commissioned Käthe Kollwitz's remarkable print cycle *The Peasants' War*.[254] That other vehicle of large-scale painted illusionism, the commercial panorama, was also in decline.[255] This did not mean that interest in historical spectacles as such was diminishing. In 1909, the 1900th anniversary of the Battle of the Teutoburg Forest, crowds flocked to see the Hermann procession near Detmold with its 900 Ancient Germans on foot and on horseback, and a Valhalla float manned by mead-swilling fallen heroes.[256] In 1913 a three-part feature film about Queen Luise of Prussia was released,[257] one of the first of a long line of cinema epics that was to continue into the 1940s. But painted history was being more and more undermined by shifts in artistic taste – from the narrative to the decorative, the monumental to the private, illusionism to impressionism – that in turn were related

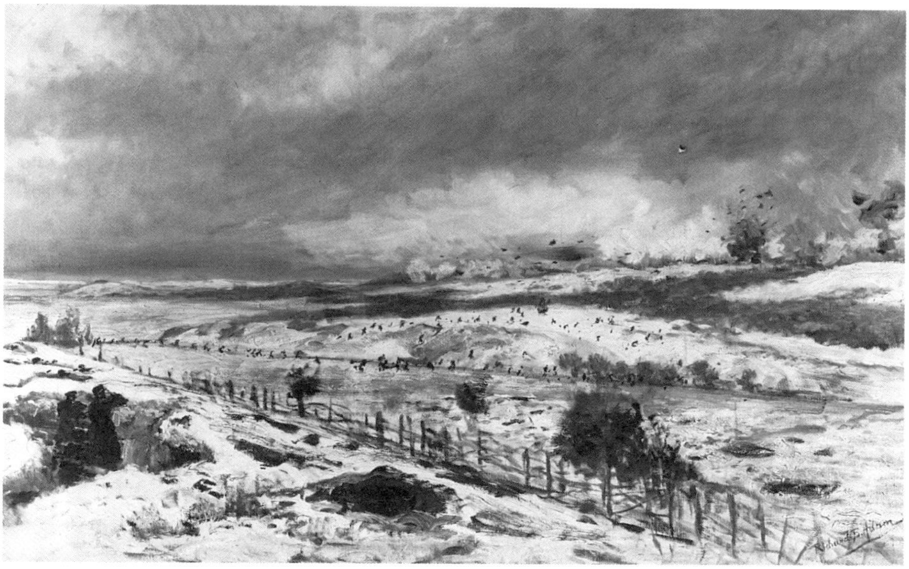

PLATE 9 Richard Benno Adam, *Crossing the Bug*, 1915, oil on canvas, 74.5 x 116.5 cm. Later Adam withdrew from the fighting and produced both conventional portraits of personalities like Crown Prince Wilhelm of Prussia and re-creations of 1870-like episodes from the early stages of the war which suited his skill as an equestrian painter.

to wider changes in society. The penchant of some of Germany's richest collectors for French Impressionism and Post-Impressionism was only part of the story. Quantitatively much more significant was the demand for what might be described as 'international *plein-airisme*' or, more broadly, the 'international *juste milieu*':[258] art that offered salon-goers from Berlin to Paris, and Pittsburgh to San Francisco, visually pleasing and unproblematical images of airy interiors, serene landscapes and healthy sun-dappled nudes.

The trend away from historical illusionism was not reversed by the outbreak of the First World War. Late in 1915 Richard Benno Adam, serving as a war artist on the Eastern Front, was commissioned to paint the crossing of the River Bug by Austrian forces. Adam was the youngest of a dynasty of Munich history- and animal-painters who had re-created European battles with meticulous fidelity for more than a century.[259] Now, in the best traditions of official art, he was given every assistance, including a detachment of soldiers, in reconstructing the action. Yet the result (Plate 9), completed in December 1915, departed almost totally from earlier conventions. Two observers in the left foreground, dwarfed by a vast wintry landscape, peer out towards a distant line of speck-like figures strung out between the frozen river and a horizon dissolving into cloud and smoke. There are no close-ups of hand-to-hand combat, artfully composed groups of dead and wounded, strong men overcome by grief or commanders directing the action. Indeed, the painting is still more impressionistic and impersonal than some of Adam's preliminary sketches. It and many similar officially-sponsored images, more strikingly perhaps even than artists' anguished or painterly-neutral private responses to the war, demonstrate art's much altered relationship with 'great times'.

# 2
# Movements

## THE RISE OF THE SMALL-SCALE PAINTING

In 1839 the poet, playwright and chronicler of the Düsseldorf School Friedrich von Uechtritz commented on a suddenly vast demand for pictures in Germany: 'The roads are thronged by a veritable picture-migration. In every town of any size exhibitions are organised, art unions have been formed, paintings are scattered to the four winds for the price of a trifling annual lottery subscription, art– and booksellers publish lavish volumes with steel engravings and penny magazines with woodcuts, and they sell like hot cakes.'[1] Alongside the huge quantity of illustrated books, reproductions and prints of all kinds being disseminated in the German states, painting production was becoming a flood. Already in 1836 the Berlin Academy's biennial salon had included 1,633 works,[2] and the size and frequency of such shows increased steadily, without counting dealers' exhibitions and the touring shows put on by the art unions. Despite fluctuations caused by political events and the trade cycle, this upward trend continued. In 1910 a well-informed commentator estimated that in one recent year about 40,000 canvases had been offered for sale in Munich alone,[3] and an average of more than 850 works were being submitted to the Art Union every month.[4] There was a matching increase of artist-numbers. Compared with 556 members – most of them painters – of the Munich Artists' Guild (*Künstlergenossenschaft*) in 1868,[5] there were almost 2,500 full-time professionals living in the Bavarian capital or elsewhere in southern Bavaria by 1907, and nearly 2,800 in and around Berlin.[6]

Diversity was the hallmark of nineteenth-century painting everywhere, with a strong post-Romantic emphasis on originality and individualism. But in Germany, as we shall see, it was accentuated by the existence of several major art-production centres with far from identical traditions. Academy training, although a unifying influence to some extent, also varied in emphasis from place to place. Moreover, many artists had non-existent or tenuous links with academies, and throughout the century between the Wars of Liberation and 1914 there were strong undercurrents of anti-academic feeling. Artists' own organisations, which developed partly in opposition to the academies, became fragmented in the face of economic pressures and new influences from abroad, and the founding of the Munich Secession in 1892 was symptomatic of an accelerating process of disintegration in the art world. Nevertheless, it is possible to sketch in the main outlines of German art production – including the work of some important foreigners – in the century after 1815.

The most prominent branch of nineteenth-century art, as we have seen, was large-scale history-painting. Vast sums were spent on it; historical, mythological and biblical *grandes machines* dominated the salons, attracted crowds of viewers on tour, were copiously discussed in the art and general press and widely reproduced, and history specialists frequently headed the academies. It has also been emphasised that much of the money devoted to historical art – both murals and easel paintings – came from the art unions, either directly or via the Historical Art League; that they as well as academies hosted the Belgian pictures on their celebrated tour; and that they regarded the promotion of patriotic monumental art as one of their principal functions. Yet by the 1820s and 1830s, as Uechtritz's remarks show, the *Kunstvereine*, like similar organisations in other countries, were also creating a market for smaller, cheaper and more intimate works of art suitable for the ordinary home.

The precursors of the art unions were eighteenth-century artists' and connoisseurs' clubs and so-called 'patriotic societies' in cities like Hamburg that undertook various projects from the creation of communal baths to the encouragement of education and the arts. The first society dedicated primarily to the promotion of art was founded in Nuremberg in 1792 by a painter, a doctor and an art dealer.[7] But the main thrust of the movement took place in the two decades or so after 1815, when many of the most important unions were founded: for example Munich (1823), Hamburg (1825), Stuttgart (1827), Saxony (1828), Rhineland–Westphalia (1829), Karlsruhe and Frankfurt (1830) and Königsberg (1832). New societies continued to proliferate throughout the nineteenth century, either as branches of the Saxon or Rhenish–Westphalian organisations or autonomously, and the *Statistical Handbook for Fine and Applied Art in the German Empire* for 1880 listed forty-nine associations ranging in size from 5,400 members in Munich to forty-seven in the town of Gera (Reuss).[8] By 1911 there were eighty-four art unions nationwide, with a total membership of about 85,000.[9]

Their aims were both patriotic and cultural: to promote national consciousness and civilised values through art. If one means of doing this was the creation of public art collections, another, fundamental from the outset, was the organisation of exhibitions and the encouragement of private art collecting. As important as the spread of individual art unions was increasing collaboration between them, and especially the formation of regional exhibition circuits, of which there were at least six by 1880, from the East German Art Federation (Bromberg, Memel, Thorn, Tilsit) along the Russian frontier to the Rhenish Federation (Darmstadt, Heidelberg, Freiburg, Mainz, Mannheim, Karlsruhe) in the south-west. This process of integration was facilitated by the relaxation of legal restrictions and, above all, by the railways, which by the early 1840s were transporting not only the vast canvases of Gallait and Bièfve in their fifteen-hundredweight frames, but wagon-loads of humbler works to the remote provinces and to neighbouring countries. The impact of this on individual careers is well illustrated by the case of the Munich painter Karl Spitzweg, who between 1837 and 1866 made 115 out of 206 recorded sales through twenty-five societies as far apart as Bergen and Trieste, Strasbourg and Königsberg.[10]

By the 1880s, for various reasons, the art unions' collective heyday was drawing to a close. By the 1900s denigrating them had become something of a sport: Josef Ruederer in 1907, for example, depicted the Munich *Kunstverein* primarily as a meeting-place and gossip centre: 'A few pictures hang around the walls,' he added, 'but they don't give any trouble.'[11] Yet the movement proved to be remarkably durable and in some places, for example Hanover, membership expanded vigorously after 1900. If some societies lapsed into provincialism and stagnation, this was not universal, and even the conservative Württemberg Art Union had held substantial Impressionist and Post-Impressionist shows by 1914.[12] The pre-war avant-gardes took the *Kunstvereine* very seriously in their efforts to gain a foothold in the market, and in 1911 the Barmen Art Union enabled Franz Marc to make his first exhibition sales outside Munich.[13] But in general by this time the societies were serving mainly as outlets for beginners, semi-professionals and artists at the lower end of the market.

The art unions' oppositional and anti-academic aspect, even at the outset, should not be overstated. Although their ethos was bourgeois–nationalist, their membership, like that of other cultural associations, was not exclusively middle-class, and in royal capitals like Dresden, Munich and Stuttgart extended from tradespeople to diplomats, aristocrats and monarchs. The Württemberg Art Union was founded in 1827 by establishment figures close to the court, and for ten years devoted a fifth of its spending to work by the veteran history-painter Eberhard Wächter;[14] the situation in Karlsruhe was similar.[15] Düsseldorf Academy-Director Wilhelm von Schadow was, as we have seen, one of the founders of the Rhenish–Westphalian Art Union. Both Cornelius and his patron Ludwig I soon joined the Munich *Kunstverein*. But it was true nevertheless that the art unions – particularly the Munich one – became increasingly identified with genre, landscape and other 'specialisms' rejected or ignored by the academic establishment. (Cornelius dismissed naturalistic landscape as 'a kind of moss or creeper on the great trunk of art',[16] while the Düsseldorf Academy did not appoint its first genre teacher until 1874.) The societies' aim to extend private art-ownership obviously meant encouraging small-scale work, and by the 1850s this was dominating the market more and more. Reviewing the 1858 Munich Exhibition, the art historian Anton Springer noted that alongside the latest historical *grandes machines* about an eighth of the paintings on show were genre pieces and more than a quarter landscapes. Many people, he thought, would liken this development to the advance of light music 'swamping our sense of sound', and explain it 'by the ease with which these pictures can be hung in our living-rooms between plant-stands and knicknack shelves and made to fit in with the existing décor'. He insisted, however, 'that landscape and genre painting are completely equal in worth to the other branches of art'.[17]

In Germany as in other Western countries the nineteenth century was *the* great era of landscape painting, perceived as a kind of magic window out of an increasingly grim industrialising world. In the early decades of the century German work can be divided into 'ideal' landscapes, often set in Italy and constructed according to well-established academic rules, and more naturalistic, Dutch-influenced pictures inspired by places closer at hand. (The deceptively lifelike, visionary images of the Dresden Romantics Friedrich and Carus were different again: Friedrich's pictures were likened by his Norwegian colleague Dahl to 'dream images from an unknown world'.)[18] But by the 1840s and 1850s the crisp and sober Biedermeier landscape was giving way to the more juicily-painted, self-consciously lyrical 'atmospheric landscape' (*Stimmungslandschaft*) inspired by regions like the wild and vaporous south Bavarian plateau. Modes and formats varied. The canvases of Eduard Schleich the Elder (1812–74) were often large and dramatic, deploying clouds, sunbursts and distant mountains to convey the illusion of almost limitless space. Adolf Lier (1826–82) and his followers, influenced more strongly than Schleich by the Barbizon School, favoured more intimate, apparently random slices of nature: forest clearings, moorland pools, or farmyards hemmed in by sheds and hayricks. In Düsseldorf in the 1830s Lessing moved from a sombre late-Romantic style with bandits, monks and Walter Scott castles to a preoccupation with colour, light and atmosphere for their own sake.[19] He also abandoned the tourist-infested Rhine Valley for the thickly forested volcanic mountains of the Eifel, where in 1841 he depicted himself and his friend Johann Wilhelm Schirmer gazing out from the shade of a tree into a vast deserted landscape shimmering in the midday heat. Schirmer (1802–66), too, developed what would later be termed a *plein-airiste* approach, both in the Eifel and on trips to the Normandy coast, and painted small-scale, botanically accurate vegetation studies of Düreresque beauty and precision.[20] Like Menzel's landscapes and Berlin views of the 1840s, most of this work was done for private and experimental purposes, and for decades official Düsseldorf landscape-painting was dominated by the hugely popular work of the brothers Andreas and Oswald Achenbach: highly finished, studio-painted, and with deft infusions of late-Romantic melancholy. But Schirmer had become a landscape teacher at the Academy in 1834, and twenty years later, when he became director of the new Academy in Karlsruhe, left many of his early open-air pieces behind as study material. Some of them clearly anticipate the 'Secessionist' style of Uhde, Liebermann, Gotthard Kuehl (1850–1915) and Lovis Corinth (1858–1925), whose loose spontaneous brushwork, bright palette and French-inspired commitment to outdoor work became the dominant landscape mode towards the turn of the century.

By contrast, Schirmer's dark-toned exhibition pieces of the 1850s reveal an obvious debt to the Dutch painters of the seventeenth century, above all Jakob van Ruisdael.[21] Other landscapists like the Achenbach brothers, and specialists in animal-painting and still life, demonstrated (in externals at least) similar influences. But admiration for the Dutch was especially important in the field of genre, naturalistic and small-scale anecdotal scenes in everyday, often rural, settings that were turned out in vast quantities in the nineteenth and early twentieth centuries. There were also other influences, particularly from Britain, and David Wilkie's trenchant mini-melodrama *The Reading of the Will* (1820) in the Neue Pinakothek, became famous far beyond Munich. But Dutch models were much more widely available. The royal galleries of Berlin, Dresden and Munich contained pictures by all the major masters, and the Frankfurt Städel Institute and the Wallraff–Richartz Museum in Cologne soon acquired their own important holdings. Düsseldorf was only a steamer-trip away from the great collections in Holland itself. The Dutch old masters and the best of their German imitators were popular because of their fine craftsmanship and, no doubt, because of the values they seemed to embody of order, harmony and discreet well-being. It is true that, writing in the 1900s about Dutch art and culture in general, Richard Muther used loaded phrases like 'replete placidity', 'cosy provincialism' and 'almost soporific excellence'.[22] Yet in the context of contemporary social and economic change such qualities were arguably at a premium. And, as already suggested, Dutch and Dutch-inspired works were well suited to late-nineteenth-century *Dürerzeit* décor. In Muther's words, their 'shadowy, subdued twilight' matched 'dusky, brown-panelled rooms with little bottle-glass windows', while the ordered, secure interiors of a Pieter de Hooch seemed to him as quintessentially Germanic as Dürer's *Saint Jerome*.[23]

Dutch influence, however, was uneven. Although artists like Ostade and Brouwer were well represented in German galleries, their scenes of coarse peasants carousing in primitive taverns were scarcely imitated, and German genre combined ethnographic fidelity and illusionistic detail with a strong tendency to prettify and sentimentalise. This was certainly true of Germany's first big genre success, Rudolf Jordan's 1834 *Marriage Proposal on Heligoland*, an image of cheery North Sea fisherfolk that was reproduced not only in prints but on crockery, pipe-bowls and other objects and inspired a popular song and even a play.[24] (Via Joachim Wagener, the painting eventually entered the Berlin National Gallery.) In the mid-1840s, admittedly, some Düsseldorf artists created harrowing pictures, Karl Wilhelm Hübner's *Silesian Weavers* of 1844, for example, a scene of capitalist oppression that in Engels's opinion 'made enthusiasm for socialist ideas acceptable'.[25] But such works were exceptions in a flood of generally bland and escapist images, and even the former softened the reality of poverty and degradation. Especially influential in the late nineteenth century, as wealth increased, were painters like Gerard ter Borch, famous for their Spanish elegance and superb rendering of fabrics and ornaments. The Munich-based Arthur von Ramberg's subtly erotic *After the Meal* (1870) (Plate 10), showing two seventeenth-century cavaliers and a lady making music in an opulently appointed room, probably owed a good deal to ter Borch's work in the Alte Pinakothek.

Genre subjects varied considerably, from military, monastic and period pieces to the exotic scenes, like Polish horse-markets and Jewish festivals, and wolves chasing travellers across snowy wastes, favoured by the many Russian, east and south European painters active in German art centres. In a class by itself, though widely imitated after

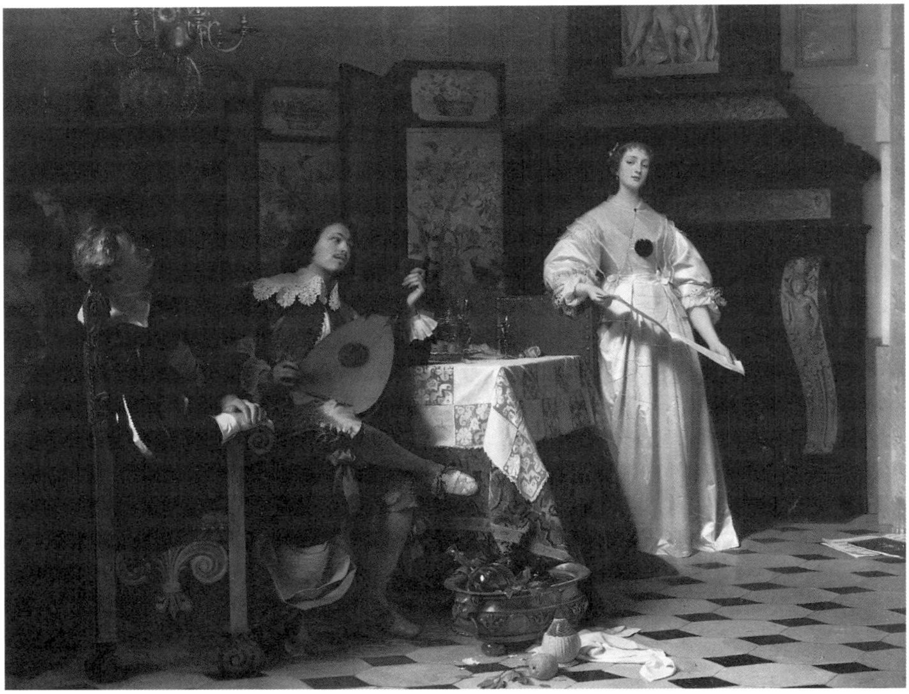

PLATE 10 Arthur von Ramberg, *After the Meal*, 1870, oil on canvas, 79.7 x 102.3 cm. While executed with great skill and refinement, both Ramberg's work and that of followers such as Albert von Keller generally lacked the allegorical undertones of their 17th-century Dutch models. Ramberg, a Munich Academy professor from 1866, was a versatile figure who also painted vast historical canvases and, as a friend of Gustave Courbet, hosted the latter on his visit to Munich in 1869.

the artist's death in 1885, was the time-warp romanticism (rustic hermits and small-town bigwigs and eccentrics) of Karl Spitzweg. But probably most popular of all were the peasant subjects associated with celebrities like Ludwig Knaus (1829-1910), Benjamin Vautier (1829-98) and Franz Defregger (1835-1921).[26] All three had hugely successful careers that in the cases of Knaus and Defregger continued long after the genre boom had passed its peak. Knaus and Vautier, who favoured Hessian and Black Forest scenes, made their names in the 1840s and 1850s as narrative colourism became established. Defregger, the son of a South Tyrolean farmer, was a pupil of Piloty who succeeded equally with outsize Tyrolean history-paintings and small-format, finely observed interiors and peasant portrait heads: pleasing and accessible subjects that brought him wealth and fame soon after his début in the late 1860s. In a *Gartenlaube* article marking Defregger's fiftieth birthday in 1885, Friedrich Pecht described a handsome, Dürer-like figure ('the Homer of the German peasantry') who owed his international appeal to his 'depictions of the simplest purely human situations, repeated all over the world and so understood everywhere'. 'Apparently so narrowly bounded in time and place,' he added, 'the world into which the master leads us is in fact a completely ideal one':[27] a comment that, with others about Defregger's 'chaste sensibility', 'inner cleanliness' and 'artistic optimism',[28] implicitly attacked contemporary Realism and Naturalism. Although some artists, such as Wilhelm Diez, gave their rustic characters a certain earthy vitality, Defregger was an unashamed prettifier of peasant models, and the fine-featured, sprucely clad figures complete with spotless baby in *The Visit* of 1875 (Plate 11) seem custom-made for a public sentimental about the family and apprehensive about the socially, even biologically degrading effects of city living. The popularity of peasant genre was dynamically related to that of rustic literature from Jeremias Gotthelf and Berthold Auerbach to Ludwig Ganghofer, with Vautier and many other artists active as illustrators, and writers like Ganghofer creating stories around popular paintings. Munich and Düsseldorf genre, disseminated via touring exhibitions, prints and family journals, also helped to open up the wilder parts of the countryside to tourism. This in turn encouraged country-dwellers to conform to urban images of their dress and customs and, at a deeper level, to humour urban notions about a timeless, pure and 'natural' rural world.[29]

In the first four decades of the nineteenth century probably more portraits were painted in German-speaking Europe than ever before or since, with some artists creating thousands of images in the course of a career. Though urban markets were the richest, portraitists also toured the provinces: Karl Friedrich Stelzner, for example, spent years working the farming communities of Schleswig-Holstein before starting a fashionable practice in Berlin and finally taking up portrait photography in Hamburg.[30] The product varied widely, from the traditional royal and aristocratic 'parade' portrait to the Biedermeier family group in its domestic setting, the no-frills peasant likeness and the miniature. But the 1840s and 1850s brought a major transition. In the first place, the rise of historical colourism, which influenced every branch of painting as well as fashion and interior design, encouraged increasingly elaborate costumes and *mise-en-scène*. Still more important was the spread of photography, although it was probably not until the advent of the wet-plate process and the *carte-de-visite*, which reached Germany at the end of the 1850s, that the bulk of the middle- and lower-middle-class painted-portrait market was eliminated.[31] Like Stelzner, many artists moved into photography, some scraping a living simply from retouching or colouring. But the growth of a mass photo-portrait industry from the mid-century onwards, and ambivalent attitudes towards machine-mediated images, tended to increase the opportunities for elite portrait painters. Outstandingly successful in the last three decades of the century was Franz Lenbach in Munich, whose clientele included Bismarck – for whom he created a practically definitive image – Moltke, Emperor Wilhelm I, Pope Leo XIII and a galaxy of scientists, explorers and captains of industry, as well as many less celebrated (rich) people.[32] After Lenbach's death in 1904 Munich remained an important centre of world-class portraiture, with leading figures like Franz Stuck,[33] Fritz August Kaulbach[34] and, probably out-earning them both, Tini Rupprecht.[35] For

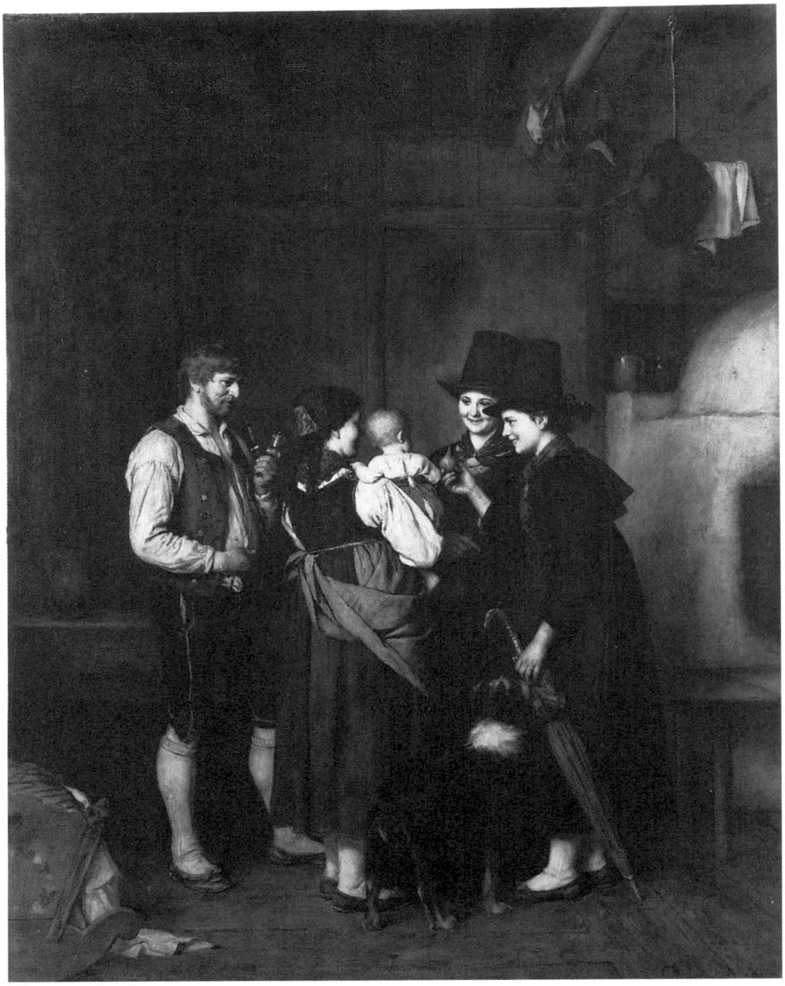

PLATE 11 Franz Defregger, *The Visit*, 1875, oil on canvas, 93 x 72 cm. An example of the finely crafted, pleasingly sentimentalised work which made Defregger for decades one of Germany's most popular artists and a highly successful exporter, especially to the United States. Scores of other painters, even if their main interests lay elsewhere, made a good living with similar subjects in this period.

the less affluent, second-rank practitioners offered a similar but more affordable product. At the same time in Hamburg Alfred Lichtwark promoted local portraiture as part of a broad campaign to improve public taste,[36] while Berlin's vast wealth enabled modern artists such as Liebermann and Corinth to put its prominent citizens lucratively 'under oil'.[37] Both in the capital and elsewhere the Norwegian Edvard Munch was also active as a roving portraitist in the 1900s, some clients having to support weeks of morose and alcoholic inactivity until a sudden burst of creative energy delivered images of themselves and occasionally their entire families.[38]

## GRADATIONS OF REALITY

If one way of ordering German art of the nineteenth and early twentieth centuries is to divide large-scale monumental from small-scale 'domestic' work, it is also useful to distinguish images that were non– or anti-naturalistic (pictures of hovering angels or blue horses) from those concerned with 'the accurate representation of the visible appearance of nature'.[39] Both modes were strongly in evidence during the period and, of course, had pedigrees reaching back to Dürer. Anti-naturalism in the visual arts waxed and waned in Germany between the 1800s and 1914. Cornelius and his followers created mythological and allegorical figures and sometimes ignored both the colours and the physical laws – e.g. gravity – of the visible world. Late-nineteenth-century neo-idealists such as Anselm Feuerbach, Hans Marées, Arnold Böcklin and, in much of his work, Max Klinger painted imaginary worlds peopled by fantastic beings in dream-like, hyper-real colours. The pre-war avant-gardes distorted reality in order to express subjective emotional states or, renewing an earlier Romantic tradition, looked through it to a spiritual realm beyond. Still, the bulk of German artistic output fell into the general category of naturalism, which can be roughly subdivided into early-nineteenth-century or Biedermeier naturalism, narrative colourism, and the various branches of Realism. (In the last three decades of the century, however, as we shall see, the German term *Naturalismus* acquired a narrower, pejorative meaning.)

The phrase 'Biedermeier naturalism' describes most of the non-monumental art produced in Austria, the German states and Denmark between about 1810 and the mid-1830s.[40] Its hallmarks were crisp and factual rendition of contemporary views and people in dry bright colours with a minimum of sentimentalisation or story-telling. Examples are the portraits of Ferdinand Georg Waldmüller in Vienna, Wilhelm Kobell's Bavarian landscapes and Eduard Gärtner's Berlin views. Such work was closely associated with the art unions and the growth of a middle-class buying public and tended, as we have seen, to be dismissed by Cornelius and his fellow-idealists as mundane and trivial. However, Biedermeier painting had significant links with the academic establishment. Particularly important was the role of Wilhelm Schadow (1789-1862), who succeeded Cornelius as Director of the Düsseldorf Academy in 1826, stayed until 1859, and became one of Germany's most influential teachers. A former member, like Cornelius, of the Nazarene colony in Rome, Schadow was at heart an idealist who regarded monumental religious painting as the supreme art form. In his Roman period he had worked on the Casa Bartholdy frescoes, and in Düsseldorf he tried hard to find similar commissions for his pupils. But he soon realised that there was much too little work of this kind, even after the foundation of the Rhenish–Westphalian Art Union, to support the numbers of newly trained artists entering the market. Whereas Cornelius had treated the Academy as a fresco school, Schadow emphasised oil painting, and his own finely executed portraits earned him a – by the standards of the time – considerable reputation as a colourist. Above all, he insisted on thorough study of nature and anatomy. 'Pictures, like human beings,' he wrote in 1831, 'are embodied spirits; hence their creator must know exactly how a body is put together.'[41] Schadow's later years at Düsseldorf were overshadowed by conflict with the growing numbers of much more realistically-inclined artists outside the Academy, and he became an increasingly isolated and anachronistic figure, struggling with vast unfinishable allegories. Still, the bridge he had built between academic training and popular painting was a major contribution to the Düsseldorf School's enormous fame and success in the middle decades of the century.

The colourists of the 1830s onwards, whether based in Düsseldorf or elsewhere, used richer, juicier pigments than their Biedermeier forebears, were much more interested in narrative, and cultivated an ostensibly extreme fidelity to observed or reconstructed (historical) reality. In the second half of the century Knaus, Vautier and Defregger filled their portfolios with authentic peasant studies, the monk–painter Eduard Grützner frequented the beer-brewing Benedictines of Andechs by the Ammersee, and period specialists filled their studios with costume manuals and old engravings, weapons, suits of armour and other picturesque bric-à-brac. But the result was always a softer, prettier version of reality attuned to the taste of a sentimental public. Lenbach's and Kaulbach's sitters appeared younger, better-looking and more commanding than their photographs reveal them to have been. Though Vautier occasionally depicted conflict and tragedy, he painted many more pictures of happy children and peasant couples, never showed people at work and even adjusted Black Forest costume to fit his own aesthetic preferences.[42] The 'chaste sensibility' of Defregger's sought-after Tyrolean portrait heads was achieved by deliberate manipulation. As one admiring biographer noted about a photograph of the artist at work in his Munich studio,

> The girl sitting on the dais before the painter is admittedly anything but attractive. If she is a child of the Tyrol then she has certainly lost much of her ethnic character and even more of her high spirits through hard work in the big city. Defregger has made good this loss in his picture, and from a being grown dull and unfeeling has created a thoughtful, sensitive Tyrolean girl.[43]

> Obviously I don't deliberately choose ugly models, yet I find those sweetly beautiful conventional heads that are the staple wares of ordinary art dealers more repulsive than anything else. It was my sole endeavour from the beginning, and will remain so in the future, to concern myself with those subtleties which nature alone offers; and I see in this the only path worthy of art.[44]

These words of Wilhelm Leibl (1844–1900) indicate the gulf between painters like Defregger and the Realists of the 1860s and 1870s. Leibl (whose father, incidentally, was Music Director of Cologne Cathedral, and had composed the cantata celebrating Friedrich Wilhelm IV's historic visit in September 1842) spent much of the 1860s learning to paint historical set-pieces at the Munich Academy. But his daringly unconventional portrait of Mina Gedon, the pregnant wife of a friend (Plate 12), was enthusiastically praised by Courbet at the Munich International Exhibition of 1869[45] and, after a brief but successful stay in Paris just before the Franco–Prussian War, he became the dominant member of a small but important group of like-minded painters. (After 1873, frustrated by lack of recognition, he spent more and more time in the country.) Also in Munich at this time, and in contact with the 'Leibl Circle', were a number of Americans around Frank Duveneck working in a Realist manner which they later transplanted to the United States.[46] Meanwhile, in May 1872, the 24-year-old Berliner Max Liebermann exhibited *Women Plucking Geese*,[47] the first of many paintings of people doing hard repetitive work in humble, often Dutch, surroundings (Plate 13). In 1875 Menzel, who had been painting impressionistic townscapes and interiors in private for the previous twenty years, completed his famous exhibition piece of a Silesian rolling-mill, the most elaborate of several pictures of manual labour done in his mature years, and one of the nineteenth century's most powerful industrial paintings.[48]

German Realism was strongly influenced by the French;[49] hence, largely, its unpopularity in the francophobic climate after 1870. Its subject-matter, as in France, was often lower-class and rural, showing poor people unsentimentally with the blemishes caused by age, harsh conditions and work. Leibl's 1876/77 double portrait (later, misleadingly, labelled *The Ill-Matched Couple*) of a toothless Ammersee fisherman and a buxom young peasant woman treats the figures almost like a still life, devoting as much attention to the man's stubble and wrinkles and the grime under the girl's fingernails as to their costumes and surroundings.[50] Liebermann's cottage and orphanage children are depicted, without cuteness or moralising, as participants in an economic process. The same refusal to elicit hackneyed responses characterised Realist landscape. Johann Sperl (1840–1914), Leibl's friend and companion, painted the alpine foothills under grey skies in the bone-chilling rawness of winter and early spring, and both painters scorned the artificial environment of the studio. 'If you don't get pictures done in the open,' Leibl told a beginner, 'and don't fancy wind, weather, cold and damp, then leave [outdoor painting] alone.'[51] Liebermann rendered dunes and potato-fields in dull, earthy colours with no concern for poetic effect. Realist portraiture aimed at psychological truth without idealisation or the distracting clutter of contemporary décor. Mina Gedon poses against a featureless dark background, elegantly dressed but obviously pregnant and, like Whistler's Cicely Alexander, visibly fatigued and out of temper. Seven years later Fritz Kaulbach portrayed Mina and her son in the late-medieval costume of the 1876 Munich artists' festival, against a backdrop of cloth of gold. Exquisitely painted for maximum decorative effect, and combining the fancy-dress

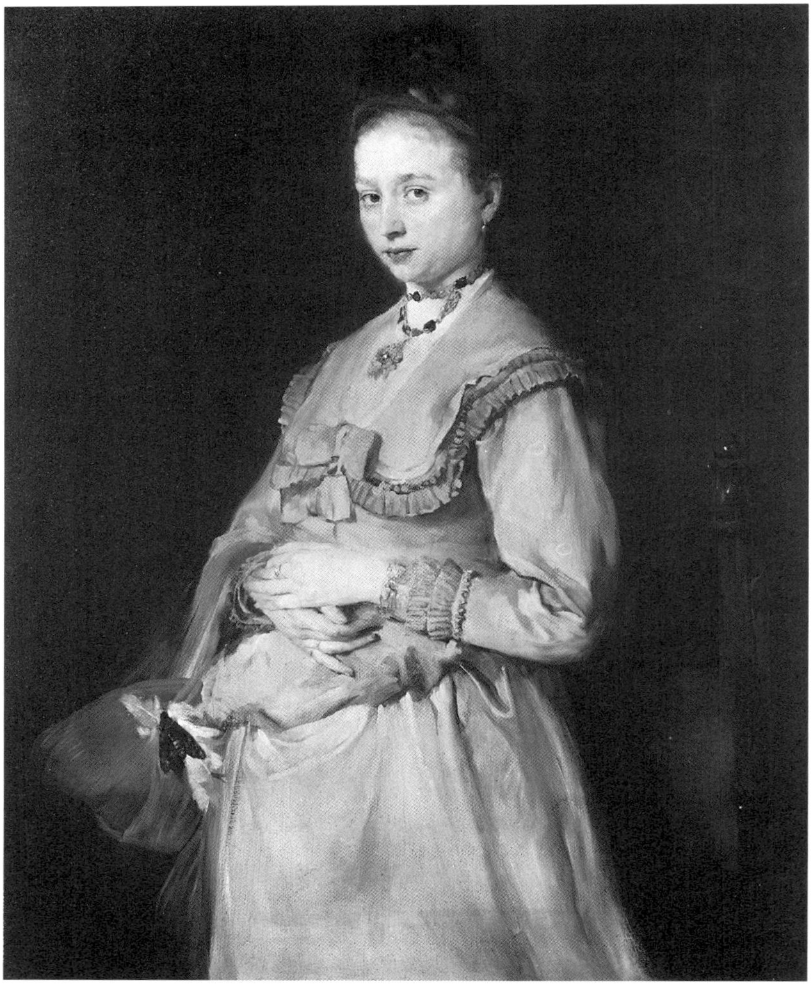

PLATE 12 Wilhelm Leibl, *Mina Gedon*, 1868/69, oil on canvas, 119.5 x 95.7 cm. One of the great portraits of the nineteenth century, the picture was painted slowly and in an atmosphere of nervous tension which caused the 20-year-old sitter great discomfort; after three months her husband abruptly terminated the ordeal. The picture achieved much greater success in Paris than in Munich, won a gold medal at the 1870 Salon and was bought by a French collector. It was not acquired by the Neue Pinakothek until 1913.

historicism rejected by the Realists with Kaulbach's talent for flattery, this image of her pleased the sitter far more.

In technical terms, the Realists reacted against the smooth glassy finish, comprehensive detail and translucent glazes of colour applied layer by layer that characterised conventional painting. Ramberg's *After the Meal*, painted soon after *Mina Gedon*, is a

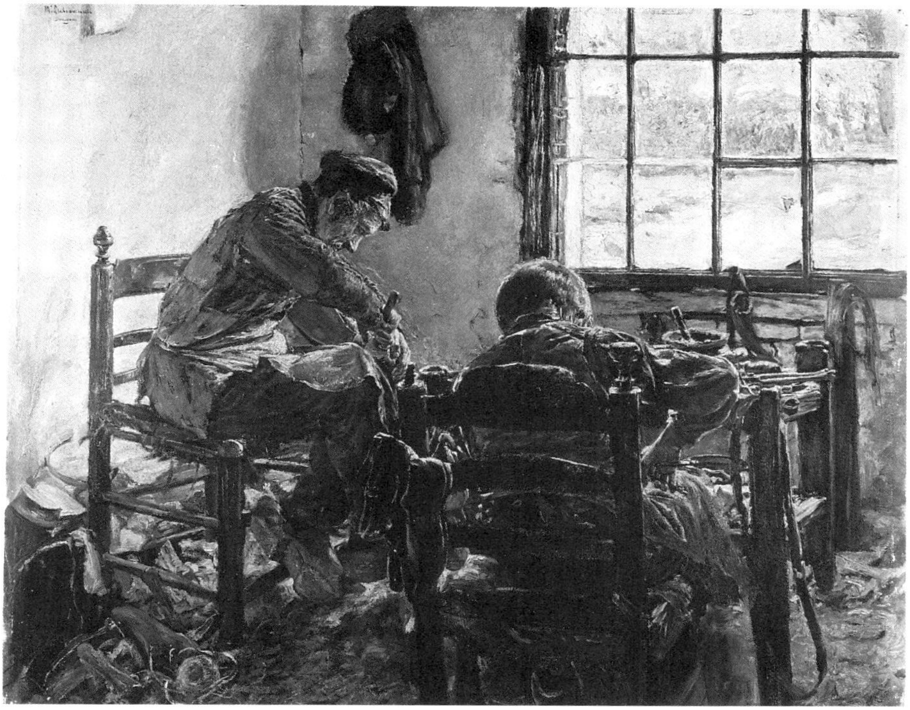

PLATE 13 Max Liebermann, *Cobbler's Workshop*, 1881/82, oil on canvas, 64 x 79.5 cm. Painted in the Dutch village of Dongen and in Munich, this was one of many unsentimental images of artisan or proto-industrial work in contemporary Holland. The reason for their negative impact on admirers of painters like Ramberg and Defregger is readily apparent. This picture's first owner was the French collector and friend of Manet, Jean-Baptiste Faure. Its purchase by the Berlin National Gallery in 1899, the year after the foundation of the Berlin Secession, exemplified the boldness of Hugo von Tschudi; although it was the third of Liebermann's major 'work' paintings to be acquired.

fine example of the latter, rendering the costumes, the foreground still life of fruit and bottles, the screen, the table-cloth and the chimney-piece reliefs with stupendous fidelity while suppressing all traces of actual brushwork. Realists, by contrast, often worked *alla prima* without glazes or underpainting, and textured the picture surface with robust visible brush-strokes. Often, as in the portraits of the Leibl Circle and the Munich Americans, this was combined with rigorously selective emphasis on facial features and hands while other areas were merely suggested. But in Leibl's Holbeinesque *Three Women in Church*, painted in the village of Berbling between 1878 and 1881 (Plate 14), every detail, from the lettering of the devotional books and the grain of the pews to skin blemishes, braid and intricate flower embroideries, is re-created with the assiduity of a lace-maker. Influenced perhaps despite himself by the villagers' awe as the painting developed, Leibl wrote to his mother in July 1879: 'Upon those capable of feeling,

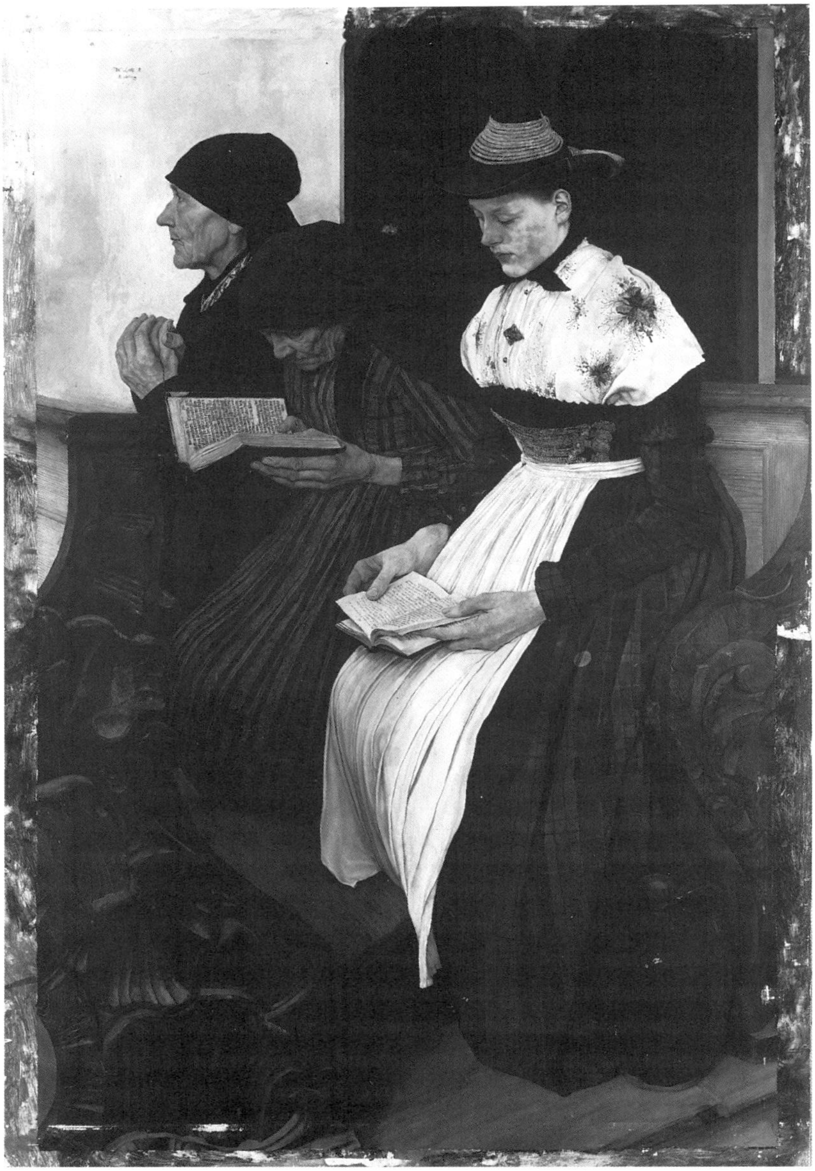

PLATE 14 Wilhelm Leibl, *Three Women in Church*, 1878-81, oil on canvas, 113 x 77 cm. Generally regarded as Leibl's masterpiece, this picture was a huge success in Paris and Vienna but, as usual, less so in Munich, where anecdotal genre still reigned supreme. The young woman wears minutely rendered local (Miesbach) costume; the old woman beside her reads an Ash Wednesday prayer from an identifiable devotional text. Böcklin dismissed the picture as 'the work of a galley slave', but Van Gogh was profoundly moved by a reproduction he saw of it in April 1883. A colour print of the painting hangs in the Berbling church today.

the picture should make the same impression as I received in my youth in [Cologne] Cathedral during High Mass, when our blessed father was conducting; and the solemn tones of the most moving church music, made by past masters of the art within those venerable walls, thrilled me to the core and evoked an indescribable sense of devotion.'[52] But the work became increasingly burdensome, and over four gruelling summers Leibl faced difficulties ranging from compositional problems to cold, damp, eyestrain, the opposition of the local priest and the illnesses of the models. Although the result was superb, the toll it took on the artist prevented him from completing anything so ambitious again.

When *Three Women* was shown in Munich for three days in March 1882, some 3,000 people came to see it, some from as far away as Amsterdam. Subsequently it was acclaimed in Paris and Vienna, and at the Munich International Exhibition of 1883 even Pecht, one of Leibl's long-standing detractors, could scarce forbear to cheer. Yet painters like Leibl continued to face great hostility. For years both he and Liebermann achieved much greater recognition, and found more buyers, in France than in Germany. Leibl, who had received a tempting offer from the Paris dealer Goupil during his 1870 visit,[53] attracted little commercial interest back in Munich and at times experienced real hardship. Sperl, who had earned a comfortable living painting rosy-cheeked peasant children and courting couples, was reduced to near-starvation when he turned to Realism.[54] Compared with Defregger's idealisation, or the fairy-tale purity of Ludwig Richter's rustic scenes, Realists seemed obsessed with squalor: 'the lyric of ugliness and the poetry of filth', as one writer characterised Menzel's art in 1870.[55] Their rejection of humorous or dramatic narrative perplexed the public and irritated the critics. Liebermann's *Carpenter's Workshop* was castigated for showing no trace of broom or washbowl and depicting a 'degraded family which probably never in its life forked out for a change of shirts'.[56] In similar vein, the Protestant liberal Pecht attacked Leibl's Berbling women for their supposed bigotry and vanity.[57] The picture would have been more popular, thought Leibl's fellow-Realist Wilhelm Trübner, if it had been called 'Three Women Praying For Their Relatives Away at War'.[58] At a time of confessional and social tension, conservative responses had an unmistakable political edge, just as in France in the 1850s and 1860s, when painters of humble subjects were automatically denounced as subversives. In fact, none of the leading German Realists was politically as radical as Courbet and the Parisian 'Realists of the first hour'. Leibl, a friend of the right-wing culture-critic Julius Langbehn, directed his resentments against the art establishment, not the social order. Menzel's 'pre-March' liberal reformism faded into sardonic detachment, and Liebermann, though an anti-monarchist and anti-Bismarckian '1848-er', was hardly a socialist revolutionary.[59] In the contemporary political climate, however, in which Bismarck could attempt the State suppression of Social Democracy, artists who refused to idealise reality could expect both critical and commercial penalties.

Yet the boundary between Realism and 'salon' art was more fluid than conservative criticism might suggest. Two major Munich Academy teachers of the late nineteenth century, Wilhelm Diez (1829-1907) and Ludwig Löfftz (1845-1910), had close links with the Realists, cultivated similar styles and showed the same preference for casually selected low-life models.[60] Defregger admired Leibl's *Ill-Matched Couple* enough to own and copy it – though in a characteristically prettier manner.[61] But most significant were his and other mainstream artists' 'private' pictures. These paintings, frequently interiors or small landscapes, were not studies for salon pieces but autonomous works done for recreation or experiment, 'Realist' in their spontaneous execution and lack of narrative, yet not intended for exhibition or sale. But their status eventually rose as both museums and private buyers became increasingly interested in sketches, studies and 'minor' media. The 1906 Century of German Art (1775-1875) Exhibition that, together with the previous year's Menzel memorial show, marked German Realism's belated official triumph, included not only *Three Women in Church, Women Plucking Geese* and other classic works, but also many comparable private paintings retrieved from the studios and attics of Defregger, Diez and their contemporaries.[62]

In the last third of the nineteenth century the term 'Naturalism' was used negatively, and often interchangeably with 'Realism', to denote anything German conservatives disliked: for example Pál Szinyei-Merse's *Picnic* of 1873, bourgeois-idyllic in subject-matter but painted in disconcertingly bright colours;[63] Leibl's *Three Women* ('the most extreme achievement of relentless Naturalism [in Munich]' according to Pecht);[64] and the paintings by Edvard Munch that scandalised the Berlin establishment in 1892.[65] It was also applied to controversial New Testament scenes by Liebermann, Klinger and Uhde, mythological fantasies like Max Slevogt's *Danaë*-as-prostitute, and such uncomfortably topical allegories as Böcklin's *Cholera*. But in retrospect Naturalism can be more precisely and neutrally defined as the urban 'wing' of Realism which concentrated, especially in the late 1880s and 1890s, on the new industrial cityscape and proletariat. (Johann Peter Hasenclever's *Workers before the City Council* of 1850, praised by Marx and probably the first German painting of modern class conflict, was a striking precursor.)[66] One of the starkest examples was the huge *Last Statement* painted in 1886 by the 22-year-old Düsseldorf student Arthur Kampf (Plate 15).[67] A scene of almost unsurpassable bleakness and squalor, it shows a large, almost bare attic room, harshly lit from above, in which a workman fatally injured in a knife fight – witnessed by the painter – is being questioned by a policeman silhouetted in the foreground. Two clog-shod male onlookers and the victim's wife complete the main group, which is balanced on the far right by a gaggle of fascinated, horrified neighbours peering through a doorway. The rendering of the figures, with bent postures, coarse, swollen hands – obligatory hallmark of the Naturalist proletarian – and the policeman's red, protruding ears, seems to label them as a race apart. This and the picture's monumental size (285 x 362 cm) and unmistakable echoes of Christ's Deposition were evidently calculated for maximum shock effect, and it would be interesting to know why, with the encouragement of his teacher Janssen, the artist embarked on it. At all events, both for him and for Düsseldorf, it was an exceptionally harrowing image. In 1888 Kampf recorded a rather different class of fatality, Emperor Wilhelm I

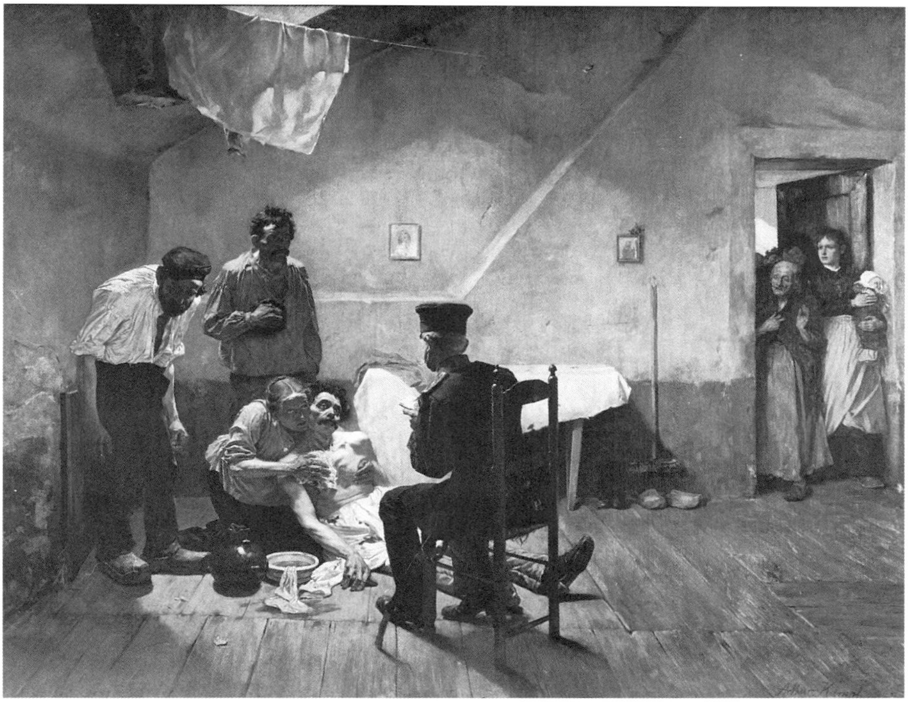

PLATE 15 Arthur Kampf, *The Last Statement*, 1886, oil on canvas, 285 x 362 cm. The reproduction hardly conveys the power of the huge and stark original, which seems all the more extraordinary in view of the Düsseldorf Academy's otherwise conventional output in the 1880s and Kampf's subsequent career.

lying in state in the Protestant cathedral in Berlin, and sold the finished picture to the Bavarian Government. Later, he succeeded Werner not only as Germany's leading historical painter but as director of the Berlin Academy's art school, and remained active well into the Third Reich. Naturalism was strongest and lasted longest in Berlin where, as well as French and Scandinavian influences, there were important links with the literary Naturalists – or 'Zola-ists' – of the *Freie Bühne* and the Friedrichshagen writers' colony, with their emphasis on 'scientific' observation of urban man in his bleak *milieu*.[68] The best-known visual artists were, as we have seen, Lesser Ury and Franz Skarbina, and in the 1890s also Hans Baluschek and Käthe Kollwitz, both of whom depicted Berlin working-class life from first-hand knowledge.[69]

In the post-Bismarckian 1890s, as the SPD continued to grow and conservatives campaigned for harsher laws against immorality and subversion, these artists were inevitably vilified by critics and baited by the art establishment and the emperor.[70] Even the Socialists regarded their work with more perplexity than enthusiasm.[71] In these circumstances the temptation, sooner or later, to compromise was difficult to resist. Kollwitz, it is true, the daughter of a Social Democrat and with strong Socialist views of her own, continued to create powerful images of misery and revolt throughout the Wilhelmine period. But Skarbina, who lost his Academy post in the wake of the Munch affair and was still painting desolate cityscapes in the mid-nineties, seems to have been back in official favour after 1900. Kampf by this time was well advanced on a conventional career. Perhaps the most complex figure was Baluschek. The son of a railway engineer, he had grown up in the social melting-pot of Berlin-Kreuzberg and later at school in Stralsund had encountered Socialist and Naturalist literature. Back in Berlin as an artist in the 1890s, he became a friend of the ultra-Naturalist writer Arno Holz and painted pasty undernourished workers' children and women pushing prams of coal through snowy streets. He also concentrated increasingly on the sidings and shunting-yards of Berlin's vast railway system, using a mixture of crayon and gouache to render human and mechanical detail with hyper-real precision. Before 1900 he sold few paintings and lived mainly from illustration and commercial work. Afterwards, as a member of the Berlin Secession, he became increasingly successful, albeit by cultivating a more detached, machine-centred techno-romanticism, and although he continued to paint unsentimental scenes of working-class and petty-bourgeois life, this fascination with machines for their own sake continued to grow. Doubtless it explains why, in the pre-war years, industrialists commissioned him to paint pictures of their plant,[72] meticulous technological portraits in which – compared especially with Menzel's famous image – men appear simply as diminutive attendants of huge steel-presses and dynamos.

*Plein-airisme* was also widely and negatively defined as Naturalism. Hostile responses to the French and German examples on show at the Munich International Exhibition of 1883 have already been mentioned, and Karl Woermann wrote later that if he had brought Uhde's *Drummers* or Bastien-Lepage's *Beggar* back to Dresden instead of Defregger's *Scythe-Smithy on the Eve of the Tyrolean Rising*, he would probably have been stoned.[73] Although, as we have seen, artists like Schirmer and Lessing had sometimes painted out of doors in the 1830s and 1840s, the more public and controversial *plein-airisme* of Uhde, Liebermann and other future Secessionists in the late 1870s and 1880s owed a large debt to Bastien-Lepage, whose images of poor children and peasants working in the fields were acclaimed both at the Paris salons and, by some critics, at Munich in 1883 and 1888.[74] After Bastien's death in 1884 *plein-airisme*'s development was maintained by his (and Liebermann's) friend Dagnan-Bouveret and by a number of other French painters, some of whom concentrated on scenes of urban working-class life. Until well into the 1890s these artists, most of whom continued to show at the Salon, probably had a much greater impact on non-academic art in Germany (and many other countries) than the institutionally marginal and artistically more radical Impressionists.

Working out of doors presented obvious problems, and it seems unlikely that most German *plein-airiste* pictures were painted literally from start to finish in the open air; as in France and England, glass-house garden studios were probably a practical compromise. But core characteristics of *plein-airisme* were the abandonment of soupy studio tones in favour of a lighter palette; anti-historicism and anti-anecdotalism; and determination to capture the effects of light and atmosphere as the eye registered them rather than as they were 'known' to be. This in turn accelerated the retreat begun by the Realists from conventional finish and, in some of their work, from illusionistic detail. In Germany at least as much as in other countries – see the Whistler–Ruskin trial of 1878[75] – such practice was widely perceived as an affront to ethically and aesthetically fundamental criteria of value in art. Conservatives also regarded the *plein-airiste* image as a machine– (or, more specifically, camera–)like reproduction of reality without the quintessentially human, transforming operation of spirit or intellect (*Geist*), manifested in scrupulously delineated form. Thus in 1879 Woermann tried to reassure his Düsseldorf Academy colleagues that 'Painting has learned once again that light, air and colour are elements in the appearance of things which are not only no less *true* but also no less *spiritual* than forms.'[76] But the barrage of opposition continued throughout the 1880s, and in the 1890s was intensified by Wilhelm II, who promised the Berlin *plein-airistes* a 'hard life'.[77] Nevertheless, partly thanks to Hugo von Tschudi and his allies, *plein-airiste* German Secessionism and French Impressionism were capturing an increasing share of the market by the turn of the century.

## BRUSH AND CAMERA

It seems highly likely that the Naturalist paintings of Bastien-Lepage were created with the aid of photography. In the case of Dagnan-Bouveret, Jules-Alexis Muenier, Emile Friant and others it is certain; indeed, they have been described as 'photo-realists'.[78] In Germany Carl Bantzer (1857-1941) used numerous photographic studies of costumed Schwalmthal peasants for his ambitious *Communion in a Hessian Village Church*, painted between 1889 and 1892 (Plate 16),[79] and by this time even the ultra-purist Leibl was making some use of the camera.[80] Although the extent to which other artists such as Uhde and Liebermann may also have done so remains a matter of speculation, hostile critics were quick to condemn Realist and Naturalist painting as 'photographic' and therefore soulless. Such responses reflected the new medium's rapid adoption and development in Germany.

Daguerre's process had been described in the *Kölnische Zeitung* within three days of its official announcement in Paris on 19 August 1839, and Louis Sachse had created daguerrotype views of Berlin before the year was out.[81] Within two years the first 'heliographic' studios had been opened, by Hermann Biow in Hamburg and Johann Baptist Isenring in Munich, and by 1860 there were ninety-four commercial establishments in Berlin alone.[82] Munich, where Carl August Steinheil and Franz Kobell had fixed photographic images on paper in the summer of 1839, soon emerged as a major photographic centre, associated with leading nineteenth-century practitioners such as Georg Böttger, Franz Hanfstaengl and Joseph Albert.[83] This was due both to the city's established optical and precision-instrument industry and to royal encouragement.

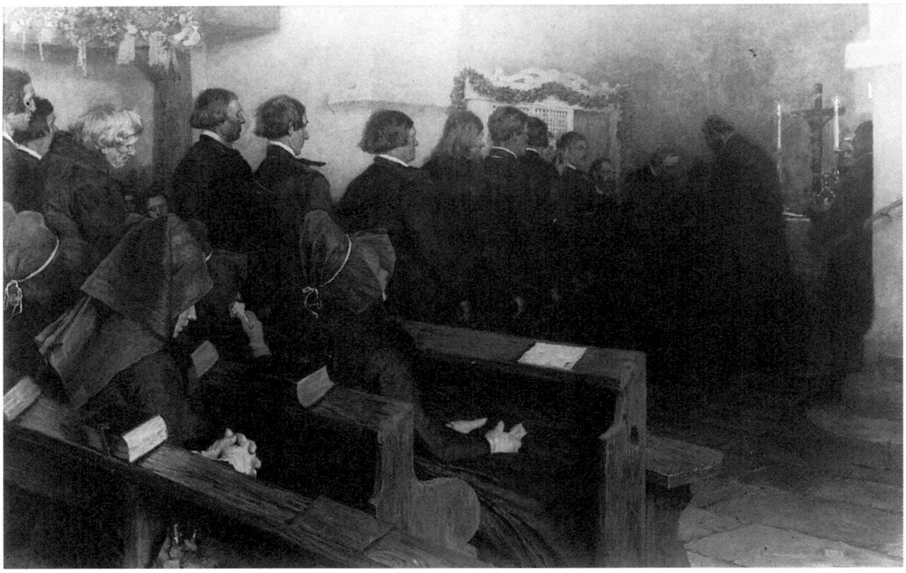

PLATE 16 Carl Bantzer, *Communion in a Hessian Village Church*, 1889-92, oil on canvas, 161 x 251 cm. Bantzer worked on the picture both on location and in Dresden, and troublesome compositional problems were solved only after the construction of the church 'set' on the Schwertzell estate near Willingshausen. Twenty-four models were used, who had to be kept warm in winter with hot bricks, schnapps and portable stoves. The painting was widely exhibited and bought by the Berlin National Gallery in 1899. Many oil and pencil studies and photographs, preserved in the Marburg State Archive and elsewhere, document the development of the work.

Particularly important was the role of Ludwig II, who not only dabbled in photography himself, but gave Albert hundreds of commissions to photograph works of art, the Palace of Versailles, and Ludwig's own buildings as they took shape.[84] By the time Germany's first publicly subsidised photographic school opened in the Bavarian capital in 1900 there were some ninety male and female professionals in the city. (They included Sophia Goudstikker, the façade of whose famous Elvira Studio, later destroyed by the Nazis, was decorated with August Endell's wave-like abstract forms in cyclamen-coloured stucco.)[85]

Photography's aesthetic aspirations also developed rapidly. Several of the pioneers had begun as painters (Stelzner, Isenring) or lithographers (Biow, Hanfstaengl, Sachse), and at least half the daguerrotypists practising in Berlin, Munich and Hamburg between the first days and the early 1860s had fine art backgrounds.[86] Already by the mid-sixties international photography exhibitions were being held in Berlin, and photographs were featuring prominently in the Munich Art Union's shows. In the 1890s a pictorialist amateur movement emerged whose practitioners, like their counterparts abroad, tended to equate 'artistic' with 'similar to painting', and there were close parallels in all the main specialisms, from landscape to portraiture.[87]

The secessions hosted photography exhibitions and in 1899 the Dresden Gallery's Graphic Cabinet began accepting photographs donated by leading German and foreign amateurs.[88] Particularly important was Hamburg, partly through links with England (Julia Margaret Cameron's work was exhibited in the city in 1898)[89] but also because of support from Lichtwark, who welcomed photography as yet another type of taste-improving amateur activity. In 1893 the Kunsthalle hosted an ambitious show that inaugurated an annual series of autumn photo-salons.[90] In 1913, finally, the Saxon State appointed the co-founder of the New York Photo-Secession, Frank Eugene, as professor of pictorialist photography at the Leipzig Academy of Graphic Art and Book Design. However, the choice of a man who had originally trained in Munich as a painter, and who extensively manipulated his images to create 'artistic' effects, reflected continuing ambivalence towards photography as an independent medium.[91]

Steinheil's reaction to the first photographs' amazing sharpness had been to remark on their potential usefulness to artists,[92] and their subsequent interest in the camera, both for recreation and as a tool, is well documented.[93] Pictures of posed models taken by the Polish Realist Aleksander Gierymski show that Munich-trained artists were using it as a compositional aid by the mid-1870s.[94] Later, not only Bantzer but also Max Slevogt, Franz Stuck, Heinrich Zille and Ernst Ludwig Kirchner worked extensively with photographs. High-speed and micro-photographs were among the sources for Hermann Obrist's abstract designs,[95] the young Paul Klee experimented with *clichés-verre*,[96] and Kandinsky's first abstract paintings have been linked to snapshots of alpine snow-patterns.[97] But the camera's most obvious application was in portraiture, and in the late nineteenth century probably the most systematic user of photography for this purpose in the world was Lenbach in Munich.[98] His surviving photo-archive contains about 13,000 images, most of them evidently taken under his own direction by professional photographers, particularly Karl Hahn, who sometimes accompanied the painter on location shoots of Bismarck in Varzin and Friedrichsruh. Although his portraits were far from being 'painted photographs', the camera enabled him to reduce sittings and offer a range of poses from which clients could choose for final working-up: part of a dynamic process of self-presentation in an increasingly achievement-orientated and individualistic society.[99] As, also, many portraits of celebrities like Wilhelm I and II, Bismarck and Moltke were commissioned by third parties for town halls, boardrooms or officers' messes, Lenbach's 'image bank', which eventually contained more than 250 studies of Bismarck and about 140 of Moltke, obviated the need for mere replicas.

Even for the experienced Lenbach, however, working from monocular, monochrome photographs was by no means easy. Fritz Kaulbach, who was probably pushed towards photography by the burden of directing the Munich Academy in the late 1880s, had great difficulty, even in collaboration with Hahn, in obtaining usable images for major commissions such as his 1903 portrait of the Tsarina.[100] There were also deeply-rooted aesthetic and ethical objections. The view that optical aids to drawing and composition were unworthy of the 'true' artist went back to Vasari and Dürer, and was fortified in the nineteenth century by ambivalent attitudes towards machines and industrial culture.[101] In this atmosphere even Lenbach and his admirers rarely referred publicly to his use of the camera, although it had long been known to colleagues, was lampooned by satirists,[102] and was clearly acceptable to most clients. (In 1902 the portraitist Franz Pernat was denied an honorary professorship partly on the grounds that 'one doesn't know for certain how much of a role photography plays in his portraits'.)[103] Other artists' reticence was striking. In a highly detailed later account of the creation of *Communion in a Hessian Village Church*, Bantzer was completely silent about his photographs.[104] In 1897, when the art historian Karl Voll complained to Slevogt about painters' reliance on the camera, he had no idea that his friend was already well versed in the practice.[105] More surprising, in view of his dedication to 'scientific' Naturalism, was Zille's virtual silence about the snapshots he used for his Berlin drawings and lithographs.[106] On the other side, the anti-naturalistic visionary artists of the late nineteenth century vehemently rejected the kind of work that exploited or aped photography to reproduce the 'skin' of reality. Karl Stauffer-Bern, who used the camera, occasionally without his sitters' knowledge, for a series of brilliant portrait etchings in the mid-1880s, soon rejected the practice as a symptom of artistic decadence. He wrote: 'To implant in the eagle that calls itself a man a photographic box instead of eyes and to expect it to fly towards heaven with this machine is simply ridiculous.'[107] Munch, though a keen photographer himself, famously concurred: 'The camera can't compete with painting as long as you can't take it with you to heaven or to hell.'[108]

## SPIRIT AND FLESH

Although also classifiable as peasant genre, Bantzer's *Hessian Communion*, which went to the Berlin National Gallery, demonstrates the importance of religious subjects in the late nineteenth century. Liebermann, Corinth, Slevogt and especially Uhde all painted major religious works, and although many contemporaries believed they were living in an age of unbelief, interest in religious art – broadly defined – remained strong.[109] In the early 1870s, more than a decade after Schadow's departure, the Düsseldorf Academy was still a major centre of religious painting, with most faculty members devoting at least some time to it.[110] The 1883 Munich International Exhibition included an entire room of biblical scenes,[111] and many salon set-pieces were expensively acquired by museums. Even beyond this there was clearly a vast public for religious or crypto-religious images of all kinds. Bruno Piglhein's panorama of the Crucifixion, which opened in Munich in June 1886, attracted huge crowds.[112] Ten thousand reproductions of Uhde's *Suffer the Little Children to Come unto Me* had been sold within a year of the picture's completion in 1884,[113] and quality religious prints – quite apart from popular chromo-lithographs, products of a much larger and older industry – were a mainstay of art publishing throughout the period; in 1914 the Munich firm of Hanfstaengl alone offered 500 religious items, mostly by modern artists.[114]

Stylistically, religious art veered between neo-Nazarene idealism – weakly individualised 'timeless' figures with flowing robes and dinner-plate haloes – and more realistic approaches that combined psychological insight with lifelike Orientalist or period *mise-en-scène*. The latter upset traditionalists by seeming to demystify sacred events in a spirit of materialism and scientism.[115] Thus the pioneer of German religious naturalism, Eduard von Gebhardt (1838-1925), was attacked in the 1860s and 1870s for modelling disciples and saints on the grim-looking peasants of his native Estonia.[116] Although Gebhardt's brand of naturalism, which was softened by his pictures' late-medieval settings, was widely accepted by 1900, some idealisation remained obligatory, especially in the treatment of Christ, who usually continued to resemble the dignified bearded figure of the Oberammergau Passion Play. In general, Protestants (who included Gebhardt and Uhde) tended to be more adventurous than Catholics, both as artists and patrons. Corinth's starkly unidealised *Crucifixion* of 1897, with himself as one of the thieves, was enthusiastically accepted as a gift by the Protestant church in Bad Tölz,[117] and Adolf Hölzel (1853-1934) received his only formal ecclesiastical commission for the new Protestant garrison church in Ulm.[118] There were, however, some unorthodox Catholic artists, such as the painter–monk Didier Lenz at Beuron, Jan Verkade, and the Christian Expressionist Carl Caspar (1879-1956).[119]

Cheek-by-jowl with Crucifixions, Resurrections and other traditional subjects, late-nineteenth-century salons included many pictures inspired by the contemporary craze for spiritualism and the occult; particularly in Munich, an important centre of paranormal research associated with Carl du Prel and Albert von Schrenck-Notzing.[120] Painters there with occult interests included Albert von Keller (1844-1920), a drawing for whose *Raising of Jairus' Daughter* (1886) showed Christ as a mesmerist literally conjuring the girl back to life,[121] and the recluse and mystic Gabriel Max (1840-1915) who, like Keller, frequently painted female martyrs and nubile young women in states of religious ecstasy. (Bastien-Lepage's strange *Joan of Arc* of 1879, which combined a meticulously lifelike depiction of a peasant girl in an orchard with hovering angelic figures, reflected parallel tastes in France.) Many contemporaries accepted such images as expressions of genuine spirituality. In May 1885, for example, the Bavarian Prime Minister Johann von Lutz explained to Ludwig II the State's proposal to pay 12,000 marks for Max's painting of the stigmatic Katharina Emmerich. 'The artist with his strong inclination towards mysticism', he wrote, 'wanted to express the idea, contrary to the materialistic notions of our time, that spirit is not a product of matter but an autonomous factor, and that indeed it can exert formative power on matter and gain ascendancy over it.'[122] Works by important artists like Keller and Max were only the tip of the iceberg, and the popularity of such subjects a century ago is indicated by the success of now forgotten figures like Alfred Seifert, whose cloying studies of entranced females were reproduced on a vast scale and drew fanmail from far and wide.[123]

Biblical pictures were frequently controversial. Menzel's painting of a self-confident young Jesus disputing with priests in the Temple caused a stir as early as 1852,[124] but this was mild compared with the furore surrounding Liebermann's late-seventies treatment of the subject, set in what seemed to be a contemporary Dutch synagogue. When first shown at the 1879 Munich International Exhibition it unleashed a storm of anti-Semitic abuse – the Jesus figure, actually modelled on an Italian child, was attacked as too 'Jewish' – was rehung in a side room and subsequently vilified in an unedifying parliamentary debate. The episode, coinciding with a general upsurge of anti-Semitism, deterred Liebermann from painting more than a handful of biblical subjects thereafter.[125] Later the picture was acquired by Uhde, who in the 1880s and 1890s became famous for his paintings of Christ in humble contemporary surroundings. One was *Christ with the Disciples at Emmaus* (1884-85), set in an inn so dilapidated that daylight shows through chinks in the walls. At a table cluttered with the remains of a meal, two scruffy low-life characters stare in perplexity at Jesus, who appears as a kind of wandering preacher with pinched, unprepossessing features, watery eyes and chapped 'proletarian' hands. In the background an old woman works and a man delves in a cupboard, both oblivious to the meaning of the event, which takes place in an atmosphere of squalor and eerie melancholy. Conservative rejection of such images (not to mention the full-frontal nudity of Max Klinger's 1891 *Crucifixion*)[126] was predictable, and critics repeatedly likened Uhde's downtrodden-looking New Testament figures to disaffected proletarians and Socialist agitators.[127] After 1900, though still a critical minefield, religious subjects continued to excite artists of many different tendencies, from Corinth to the Expressionists; Hölzel, after Realist beginnings in the late 1880s and 1890s, moved towards an increasingly spare decorative style and, by 1914, completely abstract expressions of spiritual experience.[128]

In the foreground of Corinth's *Deposition* of 1895 a bare-breasted Mary Magdalene is shown clasping the body of Christ: even in death, and in stark contrast with the Christ-figure in Uhde's *Emmaus*, a strikingly handsome and virile presence. The image's sexual resonance can hardly have been lost on contemporaries and, more generally, there were palpable links between religious/spiritualistic and erotic art in Imperial Germany. The ecstatic virgins, nubile flagellants and stripped martyrs painted by Keller, Max and their imitators had obvious sado-masochistic and necrophiliac undertones, quite apart from the overlaps between salon biblical painting and that most voyeuristic branch of nineteenth-century art, Orientalism. (By contrast, naturalistic contemporary nudes were rare in German painting before about 1890.) One of the most erotically-charged subjects of the *fin-de-siècle* was the dance. Keller repeatedly painted Madeleine Guipet, whose famous 'hypnotic' performances were the subject of a treatise by Schrenck-Notzing,[129] and she and other international stars – Saharet, Dolorosa, also Loië Fuller and Isadora Duncan – were depicted so often that they became part of the core iconography of *Jugendstil*. The dance theme was an offshoot of the much older Salome cult in art, literature and music.[130] Revived by Jakob Grimm and Heinrich Heine before 1850, it was later elaborated with increasing psycho-erotic verve by Moreau and Flaubert in France, Wilde and Beardsley in England. Wilde's version especially had such an impact in central Europe that the writer's posthumous debts were paid off largely out of German royalties, both from

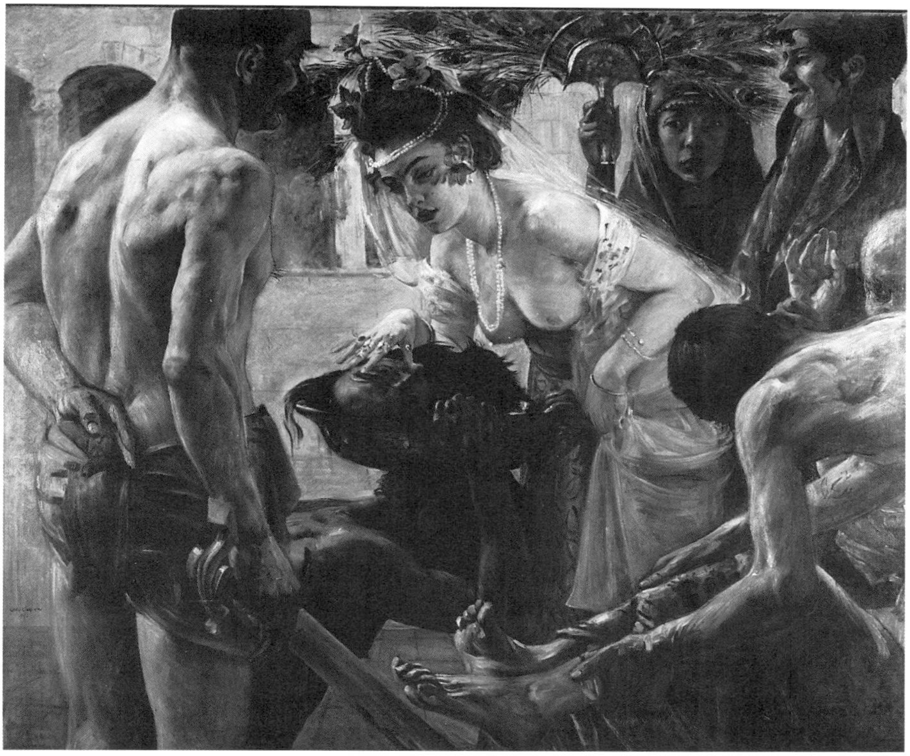

PLATE 17 Lovis Corinth, *Salome*, 1900, oil on canvas, 127 x 147 cm. This was Corinth's second version of the subject, which was a huge success at the Berlin Secession's second exhibition in 1900 and received a full-page reproduction in *Die Kunst*. The executioner bears a certain resemblance to Corinth himself.

the play and Richard Strauss's opera.[131] The story inspired pictures by Böcklin, Stuck, Lenbach, Slevogt, Klimt and many other artists, and also Klinger's polychrome bust of Salome as a kind of sadistic priestess with *two* severed heads. Corinth, who in 1902 designed the costumes for Max Reinhardt's production of Wilde's play, had earlier made his Berlin début with a painting of Salome, shown as a voluptuous young woman with exotic flowers in her hair and a cruel and sensual expression heightened by dramatic make-up (Plate 17).[132] As Saint John's headless corpse is lugged away she bends over the charger, pressing open the Baptist's left eyelid with a bejewelled finger but – a detail that considerably taxed the artist – unable to look directly at the face. Hearty sensualist though he was, Corinth also had an eye for the farcical, and in 1897 had painted a satirical *Temptation of Saint Anthony* that assembled all the currently fashionable vampire-females: Salome, Delilah, Judith and Eve, as well as Franz Stuck's *Sin*, a provocative nude entwined with an anaconda-sized serpent that had been the sensation of the Munich Secession's first show in 1893.[133]

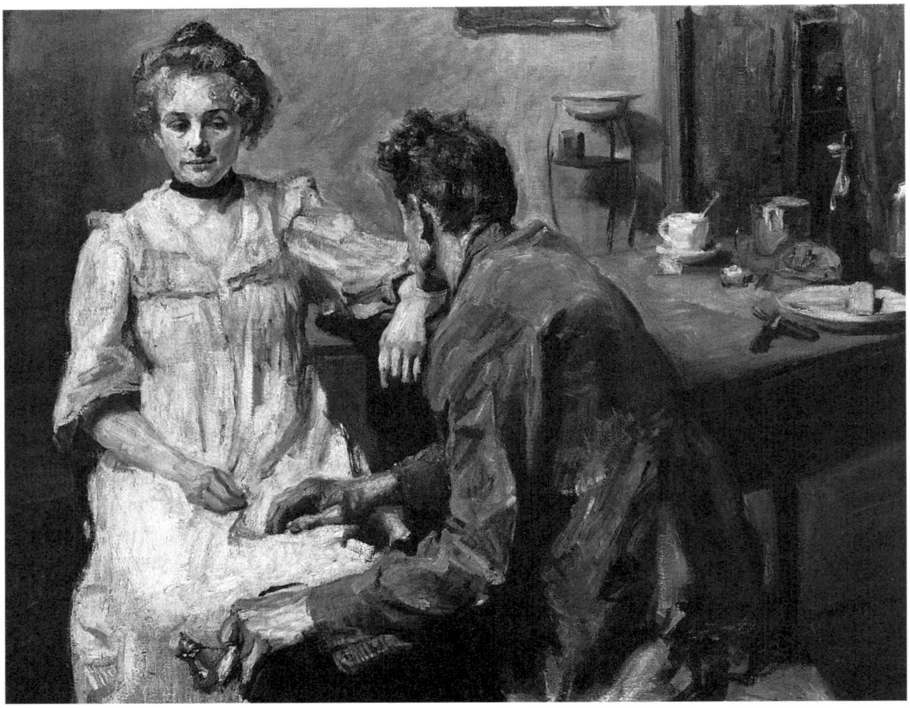

PLATE 18 Max Slevogt, *Leisure*, 1900/01, oil on canvas, 126 x 155 cm. This was the last major work painted by Slevogt before his departure for Berlin in 1901. The tentative, ambiguous body-language of the figures (modelled on the painter's janitor and his wife) reflects Slevogt's own uncertainty, as his letters reveal, about the situation he wanted to depict, but conveys rather well the mixed emotional responses of what appears to be a long-established couple. *Leisure* was bought by the State for the fairly low price of 6,000 Marks and then apparently 'skied' in the Neue Pinakothek.

Ridicule notwithstanding, however, Stuck and many other artists returned constantly to the vampire/*femme fatale* theme and, with fresh stimulus from Strindberg, Munch and Wedekind, and perhaps with anxieties about the 'New Woman' in the background, it lived on in art, literature and eventually the cinema.

Naturalists' very different treatment of sexuality as an aspect of contemporary life was epitomised by two paintings by Max Slevogt (1868-1932). *Danaë* (1895) shows the King of Argos' daughter as a coarse-featured prostitute lying asleep while her procuress catches the shower of gold in her apron. Slevogt was intrigued by the technical challenge of the model's radically foreshortened placement in the picture, but also by prostitution as a burning contemporary issue; hence, particularly, the scandal caused by the picture at the 1899 Munich Secession exhibition.[134] More subtly provocative was *Leisure* (1900-01) (Plate 18), a scene of lower-class conjugal intimacy which was intended to show that, as Slevogt elliptically put it, 'even the poorest have the right to something from the table of life'.[135] Here the wife's tired, half-resigned response to her husband's advance, his slab-like hand on her thigh and general unattractiveness, place the picture – like Slevogt's nudes of the same period, complete with cellulite and suspender-marks – in the forbidden zone of mundane and unaesthetic sexuality, far removed from the elegant eroticism of Ramberg's *After the Meal* and the harem– and boudoir-images of the salons. But *Leisure* was probably one of the last examples of full-blown Naturalist painting in Germany. After the turn of the century the scene was dominated by the kind of escapist 'soft' eroticism and decorative nudity associated with artists like Leo Putz (1869-1940), whose mythological and Rococo fantasies and carefree, appetising bathers, many of them reproduced in the Munich magazine *Jugend*, echoed the luxury advertising of an increasingly affluent and secular consumer society.[136] (Serious erotic art, created by Corinth, Kubin, Kirchner and others, remained largely confined to the more intimate graphic media.)

## ART OF THE INNER EYE

The idea of God's omnipresence in nature, and of the artist as celebrant and visionary, was rooted in German Protestantism and propagated at the turn of the eighteenth and nineteenth centuries by Christian pantheists like the pastor–poet Ludwig Theobul Kosegarten, now best known for his association with the two great visionary painters of the Romantic period, Philipp Otto Runge and Caspar David Friedrich.[137] In his mystical writings and paintings Runge evolved an abstruse symbolism in which colours, light and natural objects, especially plants and flowers, gave intimations of cosmic harmony. Friedrich wrote: 'It is not the faithful representation of air, water, rocks and trees which is the task of the artist, but the reflection of his soul and emotion in these objects . . . The artist should not only paint what he sees before him, but what he sees within him.'[138] His landscapes, lonely monks and wanderers, ships at anchor or nearing harbour symbolise his Christian (and patriotic) convictions and were conceived as visual metaphors, or hieroglyphs, for humanity's journey towards salvation.

Runge died in 1810 at the age of 33, already an isolated figure. Friedrich lived until 1840 but spent his last years in obscurity, and both painters' work was practically forgotten for many decades. Indeed, as late as 1891 Friedrich's *View of Greifswald in Moonlight* was auctioned for a mere 38 marks.[139] Neither the Biedermeier naturalists nor the historical colourists who followed them had visionary inclinations, and it was only in the atmospheric landscape, in diluted form, that Romantic nature-mysticism persisted into the middle of the century. But in the 1850s and 1860s an anti-naturalist, anti-materialist reaction set in which gathered strength in the post-Unification period. Its three principal exponents were Hans Thoma (1839-1924), Arnold Böcklin (1827-1901) and Max Klinger, each of whom turned away from naturalism to create haunting images of the 'inner eye'. All were more or less outsiders and spent years away from the main German art-production centres, in Frankfurt, Italy and Leipzig respectively. All were championed initially by a small band of devotees reacting against both salon narrative art and *plein-airisme*. And all, not least Böcklin, were hailed as quintessentially German. Klinger, the youngest and most versatile, was becoming established in the 1880s when Thoma and Böcklin were still marginal figures, and it was not until the 1890s that all were widely recognised. Their breakthrough was part of the upheaval in the visual arts that produced the secessions, Symbolism and *Jugendstil*. But it also owed much to the upsurge of cultural nationalism epitomised by best-selling tracts like Julius Langbehn's *Rembrandt as Educator* (1890) that encouraged even cosmopolitans like Woermann to view the three as 'German masters of independent vision and sensibility who wrenched themselves completely free of the tow-rope of the French and so were not understood by the latter and their one-sided admirers'.[140] At a time when virtuosity was commonly equated with superficiality, 'routine' and 'Frenchness', even their technical failings were widely condoned.

After Realist beginnings in Paris and Munich in the late 1860s and early 1870s, Hans Thoma moved in 1877 to Frankfurt where he worked in comparative isolation until called to Karlsruhe as an Academy professor and Director of the Kunsthalle in 1899.[141] By this time he had adopted a more monumental style and become increasingly interested in religious subjects. Links with Bayreuth, including a commission to design costumes for the *Ring*, brought him into contact with Wagner's son-in-law, and the Director of the Städel Institute, Henry Thode, whose writings and lectures helped to make him a figurehead of the cultural New Right. Probably Thoma's continuing lack of critical success, especially in modernist Berlin, also pushed him in this direction, and after 1900 nationalist writers like Thode and Ferdinand Avenarius, and organisations like the Dürer League, identified him with anti-modernist, intuitive, and 'rooted' – i.e. anti-cosmopolitan and anti-urban – 'homeland art'.[142] It was above all on his increasingly visionary landscapes, widely reproduced after the turn of the century, that his reputation came to rest. Unlike the enclosed corners of nature favoured by the Realists, they captured great vistas of the Taunus Mountains or Thoma's native Black Forest, often – echoing Romantics like Friedrich and Schwind – including foreground figures seen from behind whose presence invites the viewer to reverie. Typical of countless lyrical responses to his work was the art historian Friedrich Haack's description of *Laufenburg* (Plate 19), an image of two sun-drenched historic towns facing each other across the Rhine frontier between Baden and Switzerland:

> The greenish river roars in a mighty curve over a rocky bar and churns up a mass of foaming white waves. [And these river rapids are to be vandalised by a hydroelectric plant!!] . . . The charms of nature and of the ancient townscape that tempt us in our homeland to joyous wandering have been condensed into a picture. The picture sings and sounds like an authentic German folk-song.143

In the Prussian Parliament, where attacks on Tschudi were becoming an annual ritual, a deputy described Thoma in 1900 as 'not only one of the most important but also one

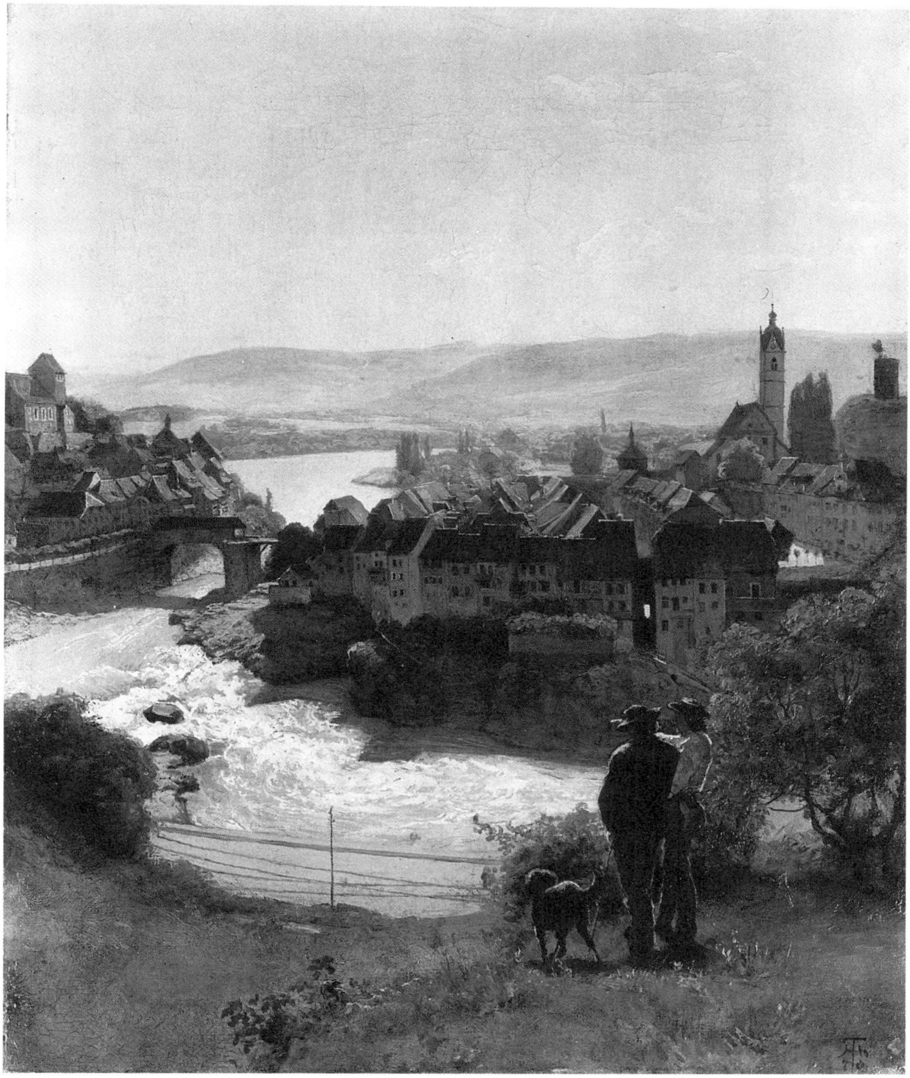

PLATE 19 Hans Thoma, *The Rhine at Laufenburg*, 1870, oil on canvas, 56 x 46cm. This was part of a commission to paint four towns on the upper Rhine which gave the still little-known painter a useful financial boost in 1870.

of the most national of all German artists, who grasps the German essence most profoundly and has depicted it with the greatest purity'.[144]

Böcklin's influence on painters, writers and composers well into the twentieth century would be hard to overstate.[145] Though periods of his life were spent in Switzerland, Munich and Weimar he was devoted to Italy, and for a time was closely associated with the 'German Romans' Anselm Feuerbach, Hans von Marées and the sculptor Adolf Hildebrand. An indomitable individualist, Böcklin pursued his own artistic vision despite critical hostility, economic hardship and friction with patrons. Though his *Pan in the Reeds* was bought by Ludwig I of Bavaria as early as 1859, he remained isolated for decades longer, attacked for technical shortcomings, bizarre subject-matter and – against the background of 'brown sauce' historicism – the extraordinary vividness of his palette. But in the 1880s his reputation and prices rose and in the 1890s he became a kind of living monument to artistic genius. His seventieth birthday was celebrated with elaborate festivities in Basle and Berlin, major exhibitions, and panegyrics in journals from the scholarly *Zeitschrift für bildende Kunst* to the *Gartenlaube* and *Jugend*. By 1900 Böcklin motifs were being appropriated by advertisers and reproductions of his work (lucratively monopolised by Bruckmann in Munich) were becoming an indispensable accessory for the bourgeois home.[146] As with Thoma, not everyone shared this enthusiasm. In 1905 Julius Meier-Graefe, Germany's leading pro-Impressionist writer, attacked the Böcklin cult in a famous polemic as a sinister phenomenon, and the painter himself as a kind of evil magician whose atavistic myth-conjuring threatened to block art's 'true' path to ever more perfect rendition of visible reality.[147] Nevertheless, Böcklin remained a towering figure, and the cult surrounding him (like, for example, the contemporary youth movement) was clearly part of a broader reaction against a perceived socio-cultural malaise. 'The feeling for nature, the yearning that speaks from his pictures,' wrote the art historian Emil Heilbut, 'is that of modern human beings who live in great cities.'[148] In his exotic landscapes, with villas half-hidden in cypress-groves, antique deities, and satyrs peeping from the undergrowth, repressed nature and pagan myth seemed to reassert themselves against civilisation and history.[149] Painted from memory in colours of dream-like intensity, they substituted a timeless mythic zone for contemporary Baedeker Italy and the modern world. If the visionary aspect of Böcklin's art, which attracted anti-materialists like Kandinsky,[150] suggested a spiritual harmony transcending the tensions of contemporary culture, the idea of his images as a trap-door into the folk-soul, which appealed to the mass psychologist Wilhelm Wundt,[151] was given a nationalist twist by Avenarius: 'Our everyday consciousness', he wrote, ' . . . knows no more of our soul than we can see in a murky flood . . . Thus our entire past dwells in our unconscious. And more: the heritage of our fathers.' With Böcklin, he went on, 'the old myth-creating force broke out again from the darkest depths of the Indo-Germanic race'.[152]

Doubtless another reason for the impact of Böcklin's pictures was their ability, like cinematic special effects, to give bizarre and impossible beings the illusion of reality: his sea-gods, it was said, smelled of fish (Plate 20).[153] There was also their enigmatic, reverie-inducing quality and openness to many meanings. The celebrated *Isle of the Dead*, painted in five versions between 1880 and 1886, one of which hung later in Hitler's Berlin Chancellery, shows a muffled figure and a coffin being rowed towards a cypress-shaded island with funerary vaults cut into its cliffs; eerie stillness pervades the scene. To the widowed friend who had asked for a picture on the theme of bereavement, Böcklin wrote: 'You will be able to dream yourself into the world of dark

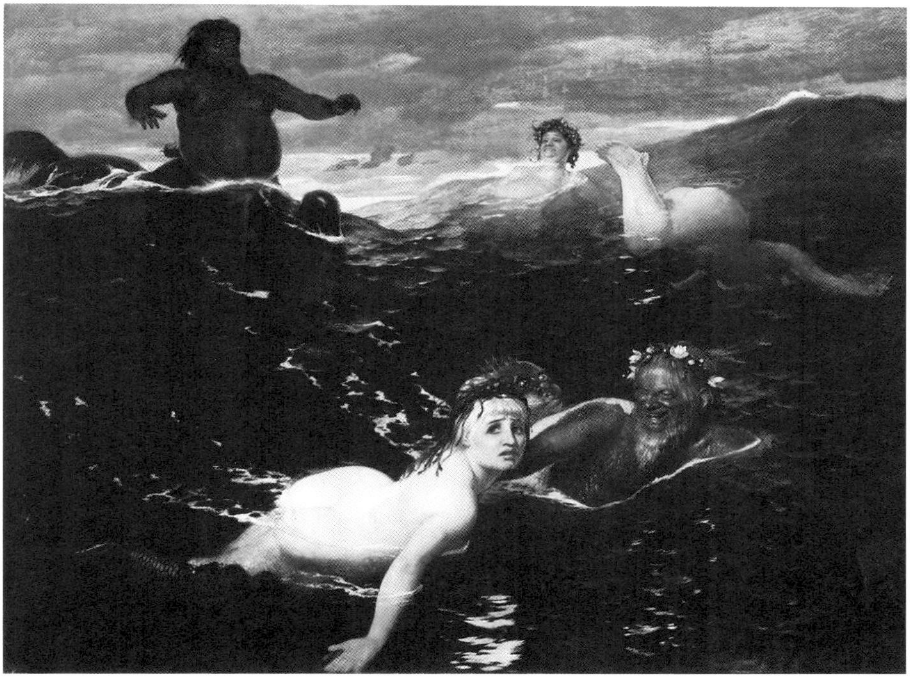

PLATE 20 Arnold Böcklin, *In the Play of the Waves*, 1883, oil on canvas, 180.3 x 237.5 cm. One of Böcklin's many pictures of mythical sea-creatures, but more humorous than most. It was inspired apparently by a bathing expedition off the island of Ischia with the family of a friend, the marine zoologist Anton Dohrn, who appears in the foreground. Presented to the Bavarian State in 1888, the painting predictably outraged Catholic politicians and morality campaigners, but delighted Munich's younger artists and café hedonists.

shadows until you believe you can feel the soft and gentle breeze that ripples the sea, so that you shrink from interrupting the silence with any audible sound . . . '.[154] (Theodor Fontane, however, who was immune to such incantation, described the pictures as 'even more boring than everyday life in Potsdam'.)[155] Later, the young male Böcklin-enthusiasts of the nineties hailed his paintings of nymphs and satyrs, mermaids and tritons disporting themselves as affirmations of guilt-free hedonism, and the painter himself as an ally against censorship and Victorianism. But ultimately Böcklin probably owed most of his charisma to his image, strongly projected in his self-portraits, as an embattled genius indifferent to fashion and contemptuous of critics and other philistines: in Nietzsche's words, a Zarathustra-like, 'path-breaking painter' who had created his own mythology and values out of nothing.[156]

Klinger's rise to fame was much more rapid. While still in his twenties he had work bought by the Berlin National Gallery and attracted the attention of the eminent Danish critic Georg Brandes.[157] In 1877 he had made his Berlin début with a disturbing picture, *The Red Wall*, that showed a solitary walker, apparently a clerk or shop assistant, on the desolate outskirts of Berlin about to be savagely assaulted by four toughs. He continued in this proto-Naturalist vein with the etching cycle *Dramas*, a series of harrowing, partly imaginary, partly press-inspired contemporary episodes: *crime passionel* in the suburbs, suicide and prostitution, insurrectionary violence and State repression. In one stark image the artist juxtaposed the working-class tragedy of a battered mother hauled from the river after drowning her child with an art exhibition in the background (Plate 21): high culture divorced from social reality. But Klinger's longer-term response to contemporary problems was a retreat into symbolism. As a student he had become an admirer of Böcklin, later he etched *The Isle of the Dead*, and his Mediterranean landscapes peopled by mythical beings revealed an obvious affinity with the older Swiss painter. (So too did the underlying pessimism and melancholy, and eroticism, of many of his images.) His graphic fantasies, from the early proto-Surrealist *Glove* sequence to his last major cycle, *Tent* (1915), contain arbitrary, eclectic symbols that he himself found difficult to elucidate,[158] but that doubtless gave serious-minded contemporaries the feeling that they were grappling with the meaning of life. Like Böcklin and, later, the Surrealists, Klinger also sought to create highly subjective or 'automatic' images of the kind experienced in dreams or induced by music, and demanding a wholly intuitive response; and it was this non-prescriptiveness that probably explains their appeal. Like music, wrote an early Klingerite, the Dresden Gallery official Max Lehrs, this kind of art owed its fascination to the fact 'that it whispers this in the ear of one person, that to another; that all love listening to it and each believes that he completely grasps its sublime mystery'.[159]

Klinger aimed not only to bring music closer to the visual arts but also to achieve a synthesis of the latter. From the mid-1880s onwards he embarked on polychrome sculpture, creating portrait busts, Cassandra and Salome figures and monuments to Beethoven and Brahms, and using coloured materials – paint, amber for eye-pupils, and different types of marble – under the influence of discoveries about ancient art. (He also considered setting light-bulbs into marble to enhance its luminosity.)[160] His desire to overcome what he perceived as the fragmentation of contemporary culture between antique and modern traditions, paganism and Christianity, inspired monumental projects such as *Christ on Olympus* of 1897.[161] One of the nineteenth century's oddest images, it shows Jesus, followed by the four Virtues carrying the Cross, confronting a perplexed Zeus and astonished attendant deities, while in a lower panel nude bodies writhe in turmoil. The huge wood and marble frame incorporated two sculptures, a classical frieze and vertical supports carved to look like palm-stems. For years Klinger and a devoted patron, the Trieste architect Alexander Hummel,[162] hoped to unite this picture with the equally monumental *Judgement of Paris* and the 1890 *Crucifixion* in one shrine-like setting. This conception of the 'total work of art' went back in its modern form at least to Runge, who had intended his visionary *Times of Day* cycle to be hung in comparable surroundings and viewed to the accompaniment of music and poetry.[163] But it gained much wider currency from the 1860s onwards,

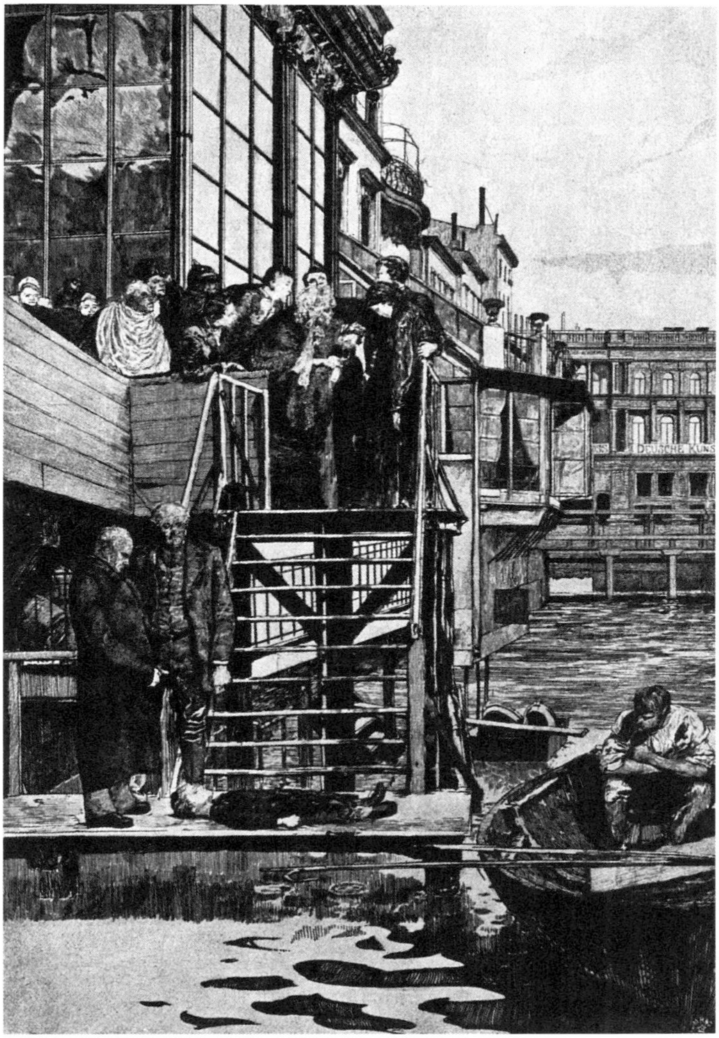

PLATE 21 Max Klinger, *The Mother*, etching from the cycle *Dramas*, 1883. One of a series of three pictures inspired by an 1881 court case, it is set in a part of old Berlin near the Royal Palace much frequented by Klinger as a student but later demolished to make way for the 'Wilhelm the Great' Monument. Klinger was strongly influenced by Zola at this time and considered dedicating the cycle to him rather than to his own teacher Karl Gussow.

realised in such different guises as Wagner's music-dramas, Ludwig II's and Gottfried Semper's buildings, the villas decorated by Böcklin, Klinger and other painters and, in scaled-down form, even the décor of the bourgeois salon. Although attempts to house Klinger's large paintings all together in Dresden, Vienna or Hanover failed, his elaborate Beethoven monument – late-nineteenth-century genius-worship frozen in coloured marble – became the centrepiece of one, albeit temporary, *Gesamtkunstwerk*: the Vienna Secession's fourteenth exhibition in 1902, which incorporated both Klinger's enthroned statue and Gustav Klimt's *Beethoven Frieze* in a setting that combined painting, sculpture and architecture.[164]

This event, which attracted some 40,000 visitors, was the high point of Klinger's career. Most of his major works were completed by the early 1900s, and by 1914 even Lehrs admitted that interest in him was flagging.[165] After his death in 1920 it plummeted. Moreover, even at the height of his powers, Klinger's imagination often outsoared his technical skill, although his shaky anatomy and perspective implant the nightmarish, horror-comic quality of some of his images still deeper in the mind. As his French admirer and friend Jules Laforgue noted, it was impossible to fit him into any neat category: like Füssli, Blake and Böcklin he was a visionary outsider, a '*sauvage insaisissable*'.[166] He was also to play a central role in the revival of German graphic art, and his fascination with the nocturnal workings of the mind later influenced such artists as Kubin, De Chirico and Ernst. Finally, both the creation and reception of his mature works might be seen as symptomatic of contemporary anxiety about social and cultural disharmony: between warring classes and disparate traditions, and between materialism and spirituality. The latter especially preoccupied the avant-garde groups that emerged in Germany in the last two decades of Klinger's life.

Pre-1914 visionary art in Germany culminated in Expressionism: shorthand for a many-faceted anti-naturalistic movement that attempted to give visual form both to inner psychic states and to intimations of a transcendent spiritual reality.[167] Before the war its two principal groupings were the Bridge (*Brücke*) painters in Dresden and later Berlin, and the more cosmopolitan circle around Kandinsky (1866-1944) and Marc (1880-1916) in Bavaria. Also important were more independent figures such as August Macke (1887-1914) in Bonn, Adolf Hölzel in Stuttgart and Paula Modersohn-Becker in Worpswede.

It would be easy to overstate what these artists had in common, since they differed widely in age and background and responded in highly individual ways to influences ranging from early-nineteenth-century German Romanticism to contemporary avant-garde movements in Paris and Russia, and the 'primitive' art of Russian and Bavarian peasants, and of Africa and Polynesia. Kandinsky's early paintings owed much to Munich *Jugendstil*, and the Arcadian nudes of Heckel and Kirchner to post-*Jugendstil* Secessionism. While the pre-war Berlin Expressionists, responding to their hectic environment, tended towards a 'modernistic' dissonance, the Blue Rider artists, in the more tranquil surroundings of rural Bavaria, mostly articulated visions of cosmic harmony. Although visual distortion as an expression of psychic turmoil went back to Grünewald and Dürer, more recent influences on this aspect of Expressionism included Van Gogh and Munch, both of whom were well known in Germany by the 1900s.[168] The latter, his friend Stanislas Przybyszewski had written in a perceptive 1894 essay,

> seeks to render psychic phenomena directly with colour. He paints with the vision of a personality stripped bare, who has averted his eyes from the world of appearances and turned them inwards. His landscapes are beheld in the soul . . .
>
> Munch is the naturalist par excellence of spiritual phenomena, just as someone like Liebermann is the most thoroughgoing naturalist of the external world.[169]

Munch in his turn was indebted to Klinger and Böcklin, and these artists – Böcklin was described by Kandinsky as 'a seeker of the interior in the exterior'[170] – had their own direct impact on the post-1900 avant-gardes.

One of their most important common characteristics was rejection of naturalism as an aspect of nineteenth-century positivist materialism; hence, too, their rejection of Impressionism and *plein-airisme* as movements concerned merely with the surface of reality. 'The whole of French art', generalised Jawlensky, 'is nature beautifully, extremely beautifully, observed; but all in all that is too little: one has to create one's own nature, Van Gogh.'[171] This was one of several points of contact between the Munich avant-garde and Tschudi (to whose memory the *Blue Rider Almanac* was dedicated), who felt increasingly that the Impressionists had taken naturalism almost to its limits, and since the turn of the century had been drawn more and more to Van Gogh, whose works he introduced to both the National Gallery and the Neue Pinakothek.[172] His sensitivity to purely formal picture-elements was indicated by his response to a Courbet in a friend's collection: 'No story, no interesting theme, not even atmosphere, nothing but a carpet of richly-nuanced green tones. The depiction of a secluded pond in the woods, surrounded by tall oaks, seems merely the pretext for this symphony in green.'[173] In 1905 Hölzel had noted his own progress towards abstraction in *Composition in Red I*, which 'yields something completely new, to the extent that in it concrete reality is in large measure suppressed in favour of the basic expression of colour and form. For although landscape elements on the one hand and figural elements on the other are still recognisably suggested, in the final artistic analysis they are no longer relevant.'[174] Yet the retreat from naturalism took place only gradually and haltingly. Even in some of Hölzel's wartime compositions motifs like the Virgin and Child are still discernible. Kandinsky, in his *Almanac* essay 'On the Question of Form', suggested that the artist could combine both representational and abstract elements to convey 'the spirit, the *inner sound* in all things'.[175] It was only during the war, back in Russia, that he finally abandoned representation for 'Expressive non-iconic Abstraction'.[176]

The slow emergence of fully abstract art was partly explained by the artists' hesitancy about what they saw as a step into the unknown. They were therefore alert to other movements and cultural phenomena that seemed germane to their own ideas. It was significant that the decade between the mid-nineties and about 1905, vital formative years for many avant-garde painters, saw the rediscovery of German Romantic art, especially the work of Runge and Friedrich, which was strongly represented in the 1906 Century of German Art (1775-1875) Exhibition. Romantic nature-mysticism, and the belief that nature could provide new symbols to replace the worn-out ones of Christianity, was an obvious influence on Kandinsky's circle. Marc's view of animals as 'uncontaminated' beings closer than man to cosmic rhythms echoed Runge's belief about the quasi-divinity of flowers and children. Further common ground was the idea of creating a synthesis of painting and music, and with its anti-materialism and desire for a more 'spiritual', less object-bound art, the group was naturally drawn to the Romantic notion of a hierarchy of the arts with music at its summit.[177] 'An artist', wrote Kandinsky in his treatise *On the Spiritual in Art*, 'who sees that the imitation of natural appearances, however artistic, is not for him, the kind of creative artist who wants to express his own inner world, sees with envy how naturally and easily such goals can be attained in music, the least material of the arts today.'[178] Going beyond artists like Klinger, Kandinsky looked for actual chromatic equivalents for musical sounds, so that painting could work directly on the psyche without the mediation of forms borrowed from nature. Both this and the similarly Romantic idea of the 'total work of art' underlay his desire to combine music, colours and rhythmic movement into one harmonious whole, his interest in the contemporary dance movement, and the conception of his 'colour opera' *The Yellow Sound*.[179] Finally, as with many mainstream artists, interest in the dance coincided with a fascination with spiritualism and the occult, especially Rudolph Steiner's theosophical ideas, another link with Romanticism.[180] Exactly how far occult theories influenced early abstract painting is uncertain; Klee, for example, dismissed theosophy as mumbo-jumbo.[181] But for a time Kandinsky and his partner Gabriele Münter were fascinated by Steiner and other occult writers, and some of Kandinsky's pictures, like the enigmatic *Woman in Moscow* of 1912, with its blob-like threatening 'death force', seem explicable only in terms of their beliefs.[182]

In abandoning the object, avant-garde artists forfeited the status conferred by mastery of difficult academic skills, and risked being dismissed as incompetents, tricksters or lunatics, epithets which came easily to their detractors.[183] So it was all the more necessary to invoke the artist's role as prophet and visionary. Thoma, Böcklin and Klinger, with Dürer in the background, were already accepted as such, but it was a conception linked especially to the Romantics, who had consistently ranked inspiration above formal qualities. If Cornelius had rejected prettiness and the mere reproduction of nature as ends in themselves, even regarding colour as a distraction from art's spiritual mission, Kandinsky and his friends worked to eliminate the object as a kind of impurity in the stream of eternal truth. And, like Cornelius, they regarded art not as a frill or luxury but as a deadly serious pursuit, and insisted on the primacy of the creative impulse (indeed, compulsion: 'True art', wrote Klee, 'is not "being able" but "not being able to do otherwise"')[184] over all external rules.

They reacted in the same spirit against the contemporary applied arts movement. Kandinsky saw the artist, like the Saint George figures he painted in the decade before

1914, as a warrior against material culture, not as a kind of decorator employed in its service. There had been significant contacts between Kandinsky and the pioneers of abstract ornament in Munich, Hermann Obrist and August Endell,[185] and the latter probably helped – though in a sense under false pretences – to prepare the public for abstract art. But the painters ultimately rejected ornament for its own sake as a dead end: the kind of work 'that would signify little more than a tie or a carpet'.[186] (One critic remarked in 1910 on Kandinsky's *Composition 2* that it would be less objectionable if captioned 'colour sketch for a modern carpet'.)[187] '*Never*', declared Marc in 1911, 'will I paint a bush blue simply for the sake of decorative effect, but only in order to intensify the horse that stands out against it in the totality of its being.'[188] One reason why the development of abstract art took so long was precisely that it was a matter of creating, not agreeable patterns, but a new symbolic language. Paradoxically, this re-assertion of the separateness of fine and applied art happened just when the institutional barriers between them were coming down. However, what the avant-gardes offered was not decoration but visions, and sometimes, in works as diverse as Meidner's images of Armageddon, Beckmann's *Sinking of the Titanic* and Marc's *Tyrol*, apocalyptic ones.

# 3
# Centres and colonies

The German art world, in contrast to those of France or Britain, was and is markedly polycentric and fragmented. Indeed, in the nineteenth century especially, given the significance of local groups, teachers and traditions, some of the strongest unifying influences came from abroad: Italy in the early decades of the century and later, ever more insistently, Paris, where an increasing number of German painters trained or spent important periods of their careers. In 1906 Hugo von Tschudi and Alfred Lichtwark acknowledged the diverse character of art production in German-speaking Europe by organising the Century of German Art (1775-1875) Exhibition, a landmark of its kind, on a mainly regional basis, around developments in Vienna, Dresden, Munich, Berlin, Hamburg, western and central Germany. The rationale for this arrangement was not only art-historical and practical but political. An important reason for the project's long gestation period – it had been conceived in 1897, and scheduled originally for 1900 – was opposition from a number of German states.[1] One of the most vociferous was Bavaria, which had remained opposed to any initiative liable to promote cultural centralisation in Berlin. In fact, Unification had tended if anything to accentuate diversity, since the minor dynasties and their governments regarded their capitals' cultural reputations as a counterpoise to Prussia's political, military and economic hegemony; and in August 1874 Johann von Lutz, then Bavarian Education Minister, had emphasised that '*a large part of the future role of the individual states* [of the new Empire] *would lie in the cultivation of art and science*'.[2] Here, as in other fields, Bismarck's constitution reflected non-Prussian susceptibilities, and gave the Reich minimal cultural functions except in the areas of press and copyright legislation. Later, even in the desperate conditions after the First World War, countervailing tendencies were consistently blocked. Significantly, both Bavaria and Saxony spent part of their share of the French war indemnity on art-related projects: the former, as we have seen, on a new Munich Academy, the latter on a lavish acquisition programme for the Dresden Royal Gallery. Artists too, particularly in Munich, seem to have become less preoccupied with the creation of national cultural institutions and more identified with their own centres. Diversity was also strengthened, for economic and prestige reasons, by competition between cities, in the visual arts most conspicuously in the field of museum creation. By 1914, despite increasing integration of the market, the German art scene was more varied than ever before.

Yet if by this time city-states like Hamburg and Bremen and cities such as Leipzig, Cologne, Mannheim, Hanover, Elberfeld and many others had fine galleries created by private or public initiative, and in some cases impressive exhibition facilities as well, none of these places was a major centre of art *production*. For this, it was necessary to have a sizeable community of artists, training institutions, certain traditions of patronage, and an infrastructure of models, dealers and other auxiliaries. Mid-nineteenth-century Germany had four cities which met these criteria in full measure: three royal capitals, Dresden, Munich and Berlin; and Düsseldorf, once the capital of the dukes of Jülich, Cleve and Berg and the Electors Palatine, but from 1815 a Prussian city. All still belonged to the major league on the eve of the First World War, although their importance relative to each other had somewhat altered. There was also a handful of secondary centres which, like Königsberg, Karlsruhe and Frankfurt-on-Main, had reputable training establishments and some resident artists. In other places, such as Stuttgart, Weimar and Darmstadt after the turn of the century, bids for cultural 'promotion' were being made, in particular by exploiting developments in the applied arts. Since before 1850, finally, Germany was acquiring a sprinkling of rural painting colonies, although most of them developed within the orbit of the major centres, and even the most remote were firmly linked to the market.

## THE 'BIG FOUR'

Dresden, where the first German academy salon was held in 1764, is magnificently situated astride a curve of the upper Elbe and dominated by the (now rebuilt) dome of the Frauenkirche and the Baroque palaces of the Wettin electors of Saxony.[3] In the eighteenth century Augustus I and Augustus II founded the famous porcelain works downriver at Meissen, created the great Royal Library in the so-called Japanese Palace, and assembled one of Europe's richest art collections; treasures which earned Dresden the title, coined by Johann Gottfried von Herder, of the 'German Florence'. The city suffered badly during the Seven Years War and again during the final struggles against Napoleon, when for a time it was at the centre of vast military campaigns sweeping across central Germany. (In wartime the royal collections and archives were evacuated to the fortress of Königstein perched on a rocky outcrop 22 miles upstream.) Nevertheless, the early nineteenth century was a glorious period for painting, linked with names like Friedrich, Carus, Kersting and Dahl, and with Ludwig Richter, whose career as Germany's best-loved painter–illustrator began there in the 1830s, much assisted by the recently founded Saxon Art Union. After mid-century the visual arts stagnated, as the Academy and art establishment remained dominated by neo-Nazarene idealists. But the situation changed again under the influence of *plein-airistes* around Carl Bantzer and especially Gotthard Kuehl, who joined the Academy in 1894 and did much, in collaboration with Lord Mayor – from 1895 to 1915 – Otto Beutler, to launch a series of major exhibitions to replace its by now defunct salons. The first Dresden International Exhibition, held in 1897 – twenty-eight years after the first Munich one – included not only paintings but modern, mainly French and Belgian, applied art, including the first work by Henry van de Velde to be shown in Germany. This and the creation of the Dresden Workshops in 1898 established the city as a leading centre of modern design, a reputation strengthened by the 1906 National Exhibition of Applied Art. After 1900 work by Van Gogh, Munch and the Neo-Impressionists was shown both by the Art Union and by the dealers Ludwig Gutbier and Emil Richter, and these firms eventually also hosted exhibitions by the *Brücke* painters.[4]

In the second half of the nineteenth century Dresden industrialised rapidly, eventually becoming home to one of Germany's largest banks and producing manufactured goods ranging from photographic materials to Karl Lingner's world-famous Odol mouthwash.[5] Between 1850 and 1914 its population increased from under 100,000 to well over half a million. All this had inevitable negative consequences. Because of brown-coal air pollution the Royal Gallery was the first in Germany systematically to glass in its pictures.[6] The Large (Ostra-)Enclosure, which Friedrich had shown deserted and semi-waterlogged in a sombre late landscape, was banked up and developed into a vast slaughterhouse complex.[7] The *Brücke* group depicted a wilderness of gasometers, factories and shunting-yards.[8] But other aspects of development had obvious benefits for artists. In 1839, when Johann Dahl painted a famous moonlit view of the city, Saxon railway-building began, and in September of that year Carus and his family were able to visit an exhibition in Leipzig, eat, promenade, and return to the capital the same evening: an excursion that would previously have taken some five days.[9] Less than two decades later Prague, Vienna and the Dutch coast could all be reached by train. Dresden's collections, its first-rate orchestra and Gottfried Semper's magnificent opera-house, as well as the charm of Meissen and the fantastic rock-formations and views of 'Saxon Switzerland', drew floods of tourists who added to the wealth created by industry. When Karl Woermann arrived in 1882 the old city was still a majestic sight, topped by its multitude of towers and by the copper-green roofs of the royal palaces, and the Elbe Valley in spring was a sea of cherry-blossom, much as Goethe had described it a century earlier.[10] By 1900 these delights were attracting many affluent new residents, who built picturesque homes in nearby Loschwitz, Blasewitz and Weisser Hirsch, and further away in Hellerau, Germany's first garden suburb. 'With their gables and turrets, airy balconies and high tiled roofs,' remarked a contemporary on these fanciful creations, 'they create an impression of German geniality, and replace the charms lost to the landscape with artistic ones.'[11] Some still survive as monuments to the wealthy and culture-conscious elite that, with tourists, sustained pre-1914 Dresden's approximately 500-strong art community.[12]

In 1815 there was little indication that within a couple of decades Düsseldorf would become Germany's leading painting centre and for many foreigners, especially

Americans, virtually synonymous with German art.[13] Activity at its Academy had practically ceased during the French occupation between 1806 and 1813. Earlier, for reasons of both inheritance and security, the electoral art collection, including forty-five works by Rubens, twenty-five Van Dycks and several major Rembrandts, had been removed to Bavaria, a loss which finally became permanent in 1870.[14] A new era was signalled by the Prussian regime's refounding of the Academy in March 1819 and its shrewd appointment of the locally born Peter Cornelius as its first director. But although the tradition of large-scale history-painting he founded there persisted, with official support, for the rest of the century, Cornelius was only active in Düsseldorf from 1821 until 1825, when he left for Munich, and his influence in the Rhineland was otherwise limited. The choice of Wilhelm Schadow as his successor was much more important. In the first place, he brought with him young talent from Berlin (Lessing, Hildebrandt, Karl Sohn, eventually Eduard Bendemann) as 'yeast' for a Düsseldorf revival.[15] But his prominent role in the foundation of the Rhenish–Westphalian Art Union in 1829, appointment of Schirmer as a landscape teacher the following year, and emphasis on the study of nature, matched contemporary market trends more closely than Cornelius's efforts. Because of his teaching ability and charismatic personality his first decade and a half in office were halcyon years: the art community expanded, and classic Düsseldorf pictures like Jordan's *Marriage Proposal* and Hildebrandt's and Lessing's historical dramas won international acclaim. Outside the Academy there were close links between painters and writers and a lively cultural atmosphere, especially in the mid-1830s with Felix Mendelssohn as Municipal Music Director and Karl Immermann at the Düsseldorf Theatre. The valley of the central Rhine and the landscapes of the Eifel and the Bergische Land were easily accessible, and there were artistic contacts with Antwerp and Paris. Economic conditions were also favourable, with patronage from Crown Prince Friedrich Wilhelm, in residence at Düsseldorf's idyllic *Jägerhof*, sales to steamer-borne tourists and nearby industrialists, and further afield via the Berlin Academy's biennial salons (to which Düsseldorf artists had privileged access) and the art union network. Summarising the painters' situation in 1843, the Swiss writer Wilhelm Füssli wrote: 'Their pictures get good, and a large proportion of them very good, prices. The better artists probably without exception enjoy a completely secure existence.'[16]

But these golden years were followed by a longer period of crisis. Schadow's increasing Catholic and idealist dogmatism had already provoked conflict with the growing band of 'independents' outside the Academy, the most prominent of whom were Schadow's fellow–'easterner' Lessing and the Rhinelander Peter Hasenclever (1810-53), whose 1836 *Studio Scene* lampooned the Academy's ethos and practices.[17] The economic malaise of the mid-1840s depressed the art market and led the State to postpone further expansion of student numbers.[18] Staple products like 'poetic' genre were under increasing critical attack, new developments in historical colourism and naturalistic landscape and genre were happening elsewhere, particularly in Munich and Berlin, and leading figures like Schirmer, Leutze and eventually Lessing left for other places. Meanwhile, Düsseldorf was developing into a major industrial and administrative centre, its population quadrupling to 100,000 between the 1830s and 1882.[19] (By 1910 it had reached 360,000.) Social and economic discontent had erupted in 1848, vividly evoked by Hasenclever's *Workers Before the City Council*,[20] and persisted thereafter, eventually with the additional tensions of the *Kulturkampf*. More serious for artists were a prolonged crisis at the Academy and further economic problems in the late 1870s. 'Sales are effected with difficulty, and at very much reduced prices', reported the American consul in 1878: 'Not a few of the leading artists have been in great pecuniary straits from the lack of commissions, and men who, for years past, have always received fancy prices for their work, have latterly been hardly able to sell a picture at any price.'[21]

Conditions subsequently improved, and late-nineteenth-century Düsseldorf harboured a large art community headed by rich celebrities like Benjamin Vautier and the Achenbach brothers. The Paint-Box, founded originally as an oppositional group, had become, with its bowling-alley, park and opulent wine-cellar, one of Germany's most hospitable artist' clubs.[22] But the city remained overshadowed by Munich, and in 1895 Lichtwark deplored its general air of artistic mediocrity.[23] New initiatives were often frustrated by local conservatism. In 1902 Peter Behrens became director of the stagnant Design School and thoroughly reorganised it, but the impetus was lost when he left for Berlin.[24] In 1909 the Special League (*Sonderbund*) of Western German Art-Lovers and Artists was founded, and the following summer it held a large exhibition including both modern applied art and paintings by Kandinsky, Jawlensky, German Expressionists and French Fauves.[25] But this and another show in 1911 aroused such antagonism that the group's 1912 exhibition – with 577 works by almost every avant-garde group the most comprehensive of its kind yet seen in Germany – had to be held (also controversially) in Cologne. Still, although the Düsseldorf market remained dominated by conventional work, radical younger artists such as Max Clarenbach, Walther Ophey and August Deusser also found outlets, ranging from the long-established Schulte Gallery to the new Tietz department store that, with Clarenbach advising it, promoted work by modern French and Belgian artists and members of the *Sonderbund* and the *Brücke*.[26] At Christmas 1913 Alfred Flechtheim opened a gallery which offered a commercially shrewd mix of salon fare, French Impressionism and Post-Impressionism, and avant-garde work from Munch to Picasso.[27] Like the *Sonderbund*'s exhibitions, this event confirmed the Rhineland's growing importance as a bridge between modern French and German art.

In the second half of the nineteenth century not only Germany's but Central Europe's most important art-production centre was Munich.[28] Situated on a plateau 1,700 feet above sea level, it is separated from the Bavarian Alps in the south by a moraine landscape of forests, lakes and hills, much of it in 1850 still wild and thinly populated, and from the Danube in the north by a broad and fertile arable region. The proximity of this rural hinterland accounted for the semi-rustic aspects of the city's life well into the twentieth century, and the combination of urban and peasant culture, monumental architecture and unspoiled landscape captivated both artists and visitors. 'In conversation today with a Munich painter,' wrote the English art student Anna Howitt in 1851,

> I chanced to observe what a great charm for me the character of Munich had, – not alone its churches, its pictures, its galleries, its beautiful and old-fashioned houses, but its whole poetical, dreamy character; I loved the wild oxen yoked in the heavy wagons, the peasants, the villages, the [River] Isar, the desolate plain, and the glorious chain of Alps, with a peculiar and indefinable love.[29]

Munich's heart at this time was the old city huddled around the twin-towered medieval Frauenkirche and flanked by the vast palace of the Wittelsbachs. To the north and west was a grid of new suburbs along two monumental thoroughfares created by Ludwig I: the broad and treeless Ludwigstrasse running from the Odeonsplatz to the Victory Gate (1850), with the village of Schwabing beyond, and, westwards towards Nymphenburg, the Briennerstrasse terminated by the Königsplatz and another monumental gateway, the neo-classical Propyläen. Central to Ludwig's plan to make his capital one of the obligatory sights of post-Napoleonic '*Teutschland*' were his new museums: Leo von Klenze's Glyptothek on the Königsplatz, containing the Aegina marbles and Cornelius's interior frescoes and, not far away, the two great picture galleries, Klenze's Alte Pinakothek and the Neue Pinakothek designed by Friedrich von Gaertner. After Ludwig's abdication his son Maximilian II began a third great thoroughfare, the Maximilianstrasse, running from the royal palace eastwards across the Isar, flanked by new Government and commercial buildings – including the city's first luxury hotel, the *Vier Jahreszeiten* – and completed in the 1870s.

Thus far, Munich's development had been mainly governed by the dynasty, and at Ludwig II's accession in 1864 this trend seemed set to continue, since Ludwig envisaged yet another major artery, from the Ludwigstrasse to a new opera-house to be built by Semper on the right bank of the Isar. This scheme came to nothing, partly because of local opposition, and the king became increasingly absorbed in projects outside the capital; 1868 saw the first plans for the pastiche-medieval castle of Neuschwanstein in the distant Schwangau.[30] During the rest of Ludwig II's reign and the Regency period, which began just before his dramatic death in June 1886, Munich was further transformed by the creation of new streets, squares and suburbs, and by the demolition of much of the old city. However, although the tradition of regulated development continued – Munich had been the first nineteenth-century European city to be extended according to a systematic plan[31] – the initiative now came much less from the Wittelsbachs than from the State, the municipality and private entrepreneurs. An approximately fivefold population increase, to nearly half a million inhabitants, between 1850 and 1900 made modernisation essential. Howitt's 'beautiful and old-fashioned houses' were verminous and insanitary, with a characteristic stench of sewage and ancient sauerkraut,[32] and in 1873-74 a cholera epidemic killed Academy Director Wilhelm von Kaulbach and hundreds of other people. Eventually a new drainage and water-supply system was constructed, its completion marked by Adolf von Hildebrand's imposing Wittelsbach Fountain, inaugurated in 1895. Appropriately, this was sited in one of the new city's most elegant spaces, later named the Lenbachplatz, after Munich's famous portraitist. Bounded by the new Deutsche Bank, the Bernheimer luxury department store, fashionable art galleries and the Artists' House (*Künstlerhaus*), it symbolised the alliance of art and commerce on which Regency prosperity depended.

One reason for the vitality of Munich art was the coexistence and, to an extent, cross-fertilisation of the historical–monumental mode of painting associated with the dynasty, the State and the Academy with the popular–naturalistic one rooted in the Art Union and the bourgeois market. This owed much to Ludwig I, patron of Cornelius, Kaulbach and Piloty, but also a long-standing Art Union member who added important genre and landscape paintings to the royal collections. His art adviser and gallery director Georg von Dillis (1759-1841) was one of the founders of Bavarian naturalistic landscape.[33] Another was Dillis's near-contemporary Wilhelm Kobell (1766-1855), who created elaborate battle-paintings for King Max Joseph I and Crown Prince Ludwig, but whose crisply executed, topographically and ethnographically precise images of southern Bavaria and its inhabitants identified him with Munich Biedermeier.[34] After 1850 there were important links between the Academy and the main body of Munich artists and their public. Piloty's brand of history-painting was, as we have seen, far more popular than Cornelius's or Kaulbach's, and remained so after the painter's own gradual eclipse in the 1870s and 1880s. And although Piloty's students had to turn out arcane 'historical disasters' at the Academy, his colouristic technique was readily adaptable to the genre painting associated with Defregger, Grützner, Max and other pupils of Piloty, while Defregger was himself an Academy teacher for more than thirty years. Wilhelm Diez, another of the teachers who sustained the Academy's reputation during Piloty's declining years and after his death, was also a prolific illustrator, contributor to the satirical *Fliegenden Blätter*, and painter of brilliantly crafted anecdotal scenes.

Munich's increasing pre-eminence in the 1850s was linked not only to Piloty's role at the Academy but also to the fame of the city's exhibitions, above all the epoch-making national-historical show of 1858. This was followed by an international exhibition in 1863, notable mainly as the first salon organised by the Munich Artists' Guild instead of the Academy, and by the much more important international exhibition of 1869.[35] This comprised some 2,400 paintings, drawings and watercolours (plus sculpture and architectural designs), and included 500 Munich items ranging from Kaulbach's vast *Battle of Salamis* and Piloty's *Mary Queen of Scots* to portraits by Lenbach, scores of landscapes and Leibl's *Mina Gedon*. Particularly significant in retrospect was the work of French artists, including Corot, Millet, Daubigny, Manet and especially Courbet, who had a room to himself with *The Stone-Breakers* and six other large canvases. (Napoleon III's Government gave important practical assistance, doubtless hoping to extend its influence in southern Germany as Prussian power increased.) Corot and Courbet were both decorated by Ludwig II, and the high point of the season was Courbet's arrival in October to receive his medal in person.[36] He was no longer quite the wild man of twenty years previously, and his pictures may have influenced Munich's budding Realists less than Manet's. But his heroic reputation, fabulous drinking capacity and ability to dash off landscapes out of doors in freezing conditions made his visit a sensation, and his encounter with the young Leibl was a crucial event in the latter's career.

The 1869 exhibition attracted tens of thousands of visitors and achieved more than 90,000 *Gulden* (154,260 marks) worth of sales.[37] The resulting publicity for Munich both as a training centre and a gateway to the international art market swelled the influx of artists from other parts of Germany and abroad, including the United States.[38] Quantitatively and qualitatively the show was dominated by naturalistic, non-monumental work, and the French pictures in particular excited younger artists. The Hungarian student Pál Szinyei-Merse, powerfully impressed by Courbet's paintings, wrote home: 'I have decided to leave the school of Piloty and to follow from now on only one teacher who will be my best guide. This master is nature.'[39] Eugène Müntz described the exhibition in the *Gazette des Beaux-Arts* as the start of a new era, and Munich itself as 'a true temple of art', prepared to make impressive sacrifices for its artists.[40] But they were doing well in any case. 'The painters appear to be prosperous,' wrote Beavington Atkinson of the *Art Journal*; 'their studios are spacious, situated among pleasant, picturesque gardens; and the paintings on the easels seem to meet with ready purchasers.'[41] Despite cholera and the 1874 financial crash this prosperity continued through the seventies, strengthened by American buying and the *altdeutsch* boom associated with the 1876 exhibition. However, Courbet's 1869 prediction of a new Realist epoch had been over-optimistic, and over the next decade neither Leibl, Duveneck nor their friends got enough encouragement to keep them in the city. Instead, the 1870s and 1880s were the heyday of Munich School salon genre and landscape.

At the same time the art community grew both in numbers – there were 796 painters (excluding students) and 148 sculptors resident in the year of Ludwig II's and Piloty's deaths, 1886[42] – and in status: partly for the general reasons discussed earlier, but also because of its much-vaunted contribution to the city's economy, and perhaps because its pageants and the glamour surrounding figures like Lenbach and Defregger compensated for the king's virtual abandonment of his capital. The Allotria Club, founded in 1873, began, like the Düsseldorf Paint-Box, as an anti-establishment group, but soon became the most prestigious of the art community's countless societies, dominated in the late nineteenth century by Lenbach (chairman from 1879 until his death in 1904), the architect Gabriel von Seidl and the sculptor Ferdinand von Miller.[43] It entertained Bismarck and other visiting celebrities, not to mention artists' allies in business, the press and politics, organised spectacular festivals, led the campaign for a Munich *Künstlerhaus*, and did much to shape artists' collective image.

But although by 1886 Munich artists had enjoyed more than a quarter of a century of international acclaim and export-led prosperity, there were clouds on the horizon. The trebling of the American art-import duty in 1883 had created serious doubts about the future of the transatlantic market.[44] There was also a growing challenge from Berlin, symbolised by the 1886 exhibition marking the centenary of its first Academy salon.[45] Held in the new National Exhibition Palace by the Lehrter Bahnhof, it was an elaborate affair, subsidised from public funds, attended by well over a million people and achieving a million marks' worth of sales, five times more than the previous salon in 1884. Although Bavarian-based painters were strongly represented and won many prizes, many people felt that the writing was on the wall for Munich's pre-eminence. Its response was twofold: an even vaster Glaspalast exhibition in 1888, and the inauguration in 1889 of international salons to be held annually instead of every four or five years as hitherto.[46] This strategy, designed both to upstage Berlin and revitalise Munich, was backed by a group of forward-looking painters and publicists including Georg Hirth, who was abandoning *altdeutsch* historicism and now saw *plein-airisme* and other international styles as the key to the future.[47] But the three largely successful international salons held between 1889 and 1891 provoked a revolt by the conservative majority of the Artists' Guild, which resented outside competition and 'unfair' inducements offered to foreign exhibitors. The eventual result was the formation in April 1892 of a breakaway Association of Munich Artists – or Secession – by the pro-international minority. Efforts by the city, the Government and Prince Regent Luitpold to avert a final split failed, and the organisation of two separate salons in the summer of 1893, one in the Glaspalast and the other in a rapidly constructed temporary building in the Prinzregentenstrasse, sealed the community's division.

The Secession's foundation, in the words of its second president, Ludwig Dill, followed 'years of bitter, exhausting conflict accompanied by intrigues of the worst kind, hatred and treachery'.[48] The issues were also extremely complicated. Personal animosity, especially towards Lenbach and other leaders of the Guild and the Allotria, was important. But Dill's description of the Secession's objectives indicates long-standing problems of the salon system, and similarities with independent groups elsewhere in Europe: 'Exhibitions of carefully-chosen art, artistically and elegantly presented, no commercial stuff, inclusion of foreign works.'[49] In fact the differences between the two rival 1893 shows were not vast, either in scope or quality. Though their disparity in size was considerable – 2,500 against fewer than 900 items – the latter was still dauntingly large. There was foreign art in both camps, and Böcklin was not the only artist to be represented in both shows.[50] The French pictures at the Secession were neither Post-Impressionist nor Impressionist, but much older Barbizon work. But, once established, the new group maintained its elite principle, spreading its exhibits over two or three select shows each year. It also became broadly identified with the lighter, looser style of international *plein-airisme*, and gave space to modern applied art, prints and photography. And its appearance was symptomatic of increasing centrifugal tendencies in the art world generally, as more and more artists competed in the market. 1894 brought the first secession – the Free Association (*Freie Vereinigung*) around Corinth, Trübner, Slevogt and Behrens – from the Secession, and after 1900 the proliferation of new groups accelerated. This process was encouraged, paradoxically, by the Secession's rapid reabsorption into the establishment and increasing conservatism. From the outset it was accepted that both Guild and Secession would combine to organise the international super-salons held every four years, including 1892; and, as passions cooled, collaboration extended into many other areas. The Secession soon staked an equal claim to official honours, Academy appointments (Stuck became a professor as early as 1895; by 1914, eleven faculty members were Secessionists) and State purchasing funds, and from 1898 it obtained long-term use of Georg Ziebland's handsome classical exhibition building on the Königsplatz. During the rest of the Regency and pre-war period it clearly built up an affluent clientele for work which was pleasing and bankable. In 1906, although the Secession showed Paul Klee's early etching series *Inventions*, it rejected all nine pictures submitted by Kandinsky.[51] In 1914, three years after many of its members had backed Vinnen's *Protest*, it frankly described itself as 'a bulwark against ultra-radical endeavours'.[52]

In the mean time, anxieties about Munich's future continued. Indeed, they were intensified by the appearance in 1898 of the Berlin Secession which, to bolster its position in a much more hostile environment, energetically recruited talent from other places, including Bavaria.[53] Friction between the two groups increased in the spring of 1901, when Hans Rosenhagen, then a leading ally of the Berlin Secession, published two articles on 'Munich's Decline as an Art Centre', for which he blamed both failures in official policy and the complacency of artists, including the Secessionists.[54] Replies to a subsequent questionnaire on the subject were mixed, but Liebermann's was the most acute: the question itself, he wrote, implied the answer: five or ten years earlier, who would have thought of asking it?[55] (In 1899 he had commented privately on Munich art: 'The last twenty years, as with the claret, were bad.')[56] Also worrying was a drain of talent: Corinth, for example, whom the Secession never forgave for his infidelity in 1894, and who, like Slevogt, was attracted by career opportunities in Berlin. Given the increasing importance of modern applied art and design, the loss of major figures in this field seemed particularly serious: Otto Eckmann in 1897, followed by Peter Behrens (1900), Bernhard Pankok (1902) and Bruno Paul (1907). Several of these emigrants shook Munich's dust from their feet with bitterness and scorn: Trübner, for example, who had left in 1896, told a colleague, 'One must avoid a city like Munich, where only kitsch painting gets recognition, as energetically as possible if one doesn't want to do oneself serious harm.'[57]

Other problems stemmed from the role of culture in Munich's economy. There were of course important local industries: not only brewing but engineering, lens and instrument manufacture, furniture-making, publishing and reprography. But planners were determined to curb large-scale industrialisation in order to preserve the city's character as a royal capital and art and luxury consumption centre. The vigorous marketing of culture, from exhibitions and opera festivals to modern design, was central to this strategy, as were clean-air policies and the general improvement of amenities.[58] By the 1880s tourism was becoming vital both for the economy as a whole and for artists, who did much to shape Regency Munich's fun-plus-culture image. This development inevitably had its negative side. In 1901 an anonymous writer claimed that production of tawdry souvenirs and stereotyped 'pix' (*Büldln*) for tourists had become the art community's prime activity.[59] Artists' social and material circumstances were also changing. Before the Regency, material expectations had been modest and prices low: in 1880, for example, Klinger had found rent and food much cheaper than in Berlin or even Karlsruhe.[60] But thirty years later conditions were very different, owing to large-scale redevelopment, the creation of new tourist cafés, wine restaurants and 'American' bars, and inflation. Indeed, in 1911 a British observer commented that, largely through tourism, Munich had 'gained the unenviable reputation of being one of the most expensive centres to live in in the German Empire'.[61] There was also a widening gulf between the elite of very rich and successful artists, with their mansions, limousines, liveried servants and lavish dinner-parties, and ordinary members of the community. By the turn of the century tickets for the great costume festivals had become unaffordable for many artists, as were the facilities offered by the new Artists' House, built at a cost of over a million marks and finally inaugurated in March 1900 with a sumptuous banquet.[62] (Ownership squabbles between the Guild and the Secession also made the new building a symbol of discord rather than harmony.)

Yet there was cause for optimism as well as gloom. Munich's art schools, both public and private, maintained their appeal and attracted a new generation of outsiders, including Jawlensky, Kandinsky, Marianne von Werefkin, Klee and de Chirico. (In 1897 Picasso remarked that if he had a son he would send him to Munich rather than Paris.)[63] Munich had one of German-speaking Europe's most popular traditional satirical papers, the *Fliegenden Blätter*, and its two most brilliant modern ones, *Jugend* and *Simplicissimus*, sustained by an abundance of youthful talent.[64] The city's craftsmen had been stimulated by two national applied-art exhibitions, in 1876 and 1888, and, to a degree, by Ludwig II's building projects. The impact in the late 1890s of modern design led to the creation of the United Workshops for Arts and Crafts, which remained important despite a turnover of talent. Other new ventures included the German (Science) Museum, whose foundation stone was laid in 1906,[65] and the experimental Artists' Theatre, opened in 1908, where Kandinsky and others endeavoured to realise their ideas of a non-naturalistic 'total work of art'.[66] A new festival opera-house, the Prince Regent Theatre, recalled the Semper–Ludwig II project of the 1860s, and there were plans, albeit frustrated by the outbreak of war, to replace the ageing Glaspalast with a complex of modern exhibition buildings.[67] At the same time Munich not only remained Germany's leading art-export centre but, like Dresden, attracted new permanent residents to its modern suburbs and 'villa colonies' whose spending-power probably helped to correct the long-standing imbalance between local and outside support for art.

From the late nineteenth century onwards the importance of Berlin as an art-production centre – and indeed the quality of its culture generally[68] – was constantly debated, until in the 1920s, except for culture-critics of the extreme Right, the question finally ceased to be interesting. Both before and after 1914, however, Berlin struck many people as a forbidding place. The Goncourt brothers in 1860, though charmed by Berlin women and impressed by the lavish entertainment facilities of the new Kroll Opera, likened the city as a whole to 'a barracks built in America'.[69] (Later they ridiculed Munich as 'an ale-house in a *papier-mâché* Parthenon'.)[70] In the Wilhelmine period Karl Scheffler could still describe Berlin as a Spartan 'colonial' capital, overshadowed by Prussia's military past,[71] while August Macke was appalled at the thousands of its artists who went to the wall in the pounding struggle for existence.[72]

The artistic atmosphere had been less hectic before the foundation of the Empire. In the Biedermeier period there were some 470 resident painters and the Academy had a good reputation under the sculptor Gottfried – father of Wilhelm – von Schadow.[73] But, Menzel's achievements apart, the middle decades of the century were a time of stagnation, and with low Academy enrolments and few major dealers or modern collectors Berlin ranked well below Düsseldorf and Munich. However, this situation changed after 1871, as new money was lavished on villas, apartments and works of art to put in them. The Academy's art school was reorganised and in 1875 placed under the vigorous leadership of Anton von Werner, who broadened the curriculum, enlarged the faculty and eventually more than doubled student numbers.[74] In the 1870s and early 1880s the salons were undistinguished, not least because of the absence, for political reasons, of French art, and it was left to dealers like Fritz Gurlitt and private collectors to introduce modern French painting to the public.[75] But the 1886 Centenary Exhibition was widely perceived as the start of a new era. The 'Pergamon' artists' festival which followed its opening symbolised both the vitality of the Berlin art community and Prussia's broader cultural aspirations. Notable too, and a spur to other governments, were the 160,000 marks' worth of official purchases for the National Gallery.[76] Four years later the art historian Wilhelm Lübke enthused over Berlin's rich musical life, well-organised museums, modern electrically-lit theatres and atmosphere of restless enterprise. He also highlighted the State's readiness to spend unstintingly and, compared with the 'nativism' he detected elsewhere in Germany, to recruit talent wherever it could be found, as key factors in the city's cultural development.[77]

There was also the lure of the Wilhelmine capital's ever more colossal private wealth. By 1904, without counting its affluent outlying suburbs, the city yielded one-eighth of Prussia's entire taxable income.[78] Indeed, so rich were its richest citizens that a mere Reich Chancellor, if he had no private fortune, had to vote with his servants in the lowest class of Prussia's wealth-based suffrage system.[79] For artists, despite the high casualty rate, the metropolis offered rewards undreamed of elsewhere. 'A city like Berlin,' wrote the novelist Robert Walser,

> is like an ill-mannered, insolent, intelligent urchin, affirming what it happens to fancy, throwing away what has become boring . . . An artist who has made it lives in the big city as if in an enchanting oriental dream. He swans from one rich and elegant house to the next, sits down without too much ado at the lavish dining-tables and makes conversation chewing and slurping. He lives as if in a state of intoxication.[80]

This might well have been a reference to Corinth, who, even before settling permanently in the capital in 1901, had described himself as 'swimming like a pike' through Berlin society.[81] Julius Meier-Graefe created an even more vivid image of the paunchy east Prussian on the make: 'Like a polar bear with little red eyes he moved through the ballrooms of Berlin. He looked greedily at many a banker and many a banker's wife as she danced in his arms: a pig ripe for the slaughter! . . . At dinner he always had two jugs of wine by his plate.'[82]

By the early nineties there were growing divisions among Berlin artists, although it was not until May 1898 that the Secession was founded.[83] While its origins differed from those of its Munich precursor – partly a response, as we have seen, to the 'threat from Berlin' – there were parallels. Both groups rejected the vast size and poor hanging conditions of the official salons: the exhibition marking the fiftieth anniversary of the Berlin Artists' Association (*Verein Berliner Künstler* (VBK)) in 1891 included no fewer than 4,702 works.[84] Interest in modern foreign art, from countries like Norway and Scotland as well as France, was growing.[85] There was also the contentious role, comparable to Lenbach's, of Werner: as VBK chairman, Academy director and, effectively, Wilhelm II's court painter, tremendously influential; yet facing significant opposition. (In January 1892 the VBK re-elected him by only one vote.)[86] The Secession's artistic roots went back to Liebermann's Realist beginnings in the 1870s, and its more immediate prehistory to the emergence of younger *plein-airistes* and Naturalists like Skarbina and Ury in the late 1880s. In 1889 they and Liebermann (like Menzel) defied the semi-official ban on participation in the Paris World Exhibition. Three years later Liebermann and the young landscapist Walter Leistikow (1865-1908) founded an independent group, the Eleven (*XI*), whose other members included Skarbina and, from 1894, Klinger (Baluschek later became a guest exhibitor), and showed regularly at Schulte's Berlin gallery until 1899. Though attacked by the critical establishment, it was supported by Rosenhagen's paper *Der Atelier* and, from 1895, the prestigious new journal *Pan*. The Munch exhibition in November 1892, which included early versions of works like *The Kiss*, *Absinthe* and *The Sick Child*, provoked predictable outrage and comments such as 'Naturalist excesses never yet exhibited in Berlin . . . formlessness, painterly brutality, coarseness and vileness of sensibility.'[87] But the decision of Werner and a majority of the VBK to close it immediately – the pictures were removed so speedily that some were damaged – caused such anger that an oppositional sub-group, almost a proto-Secession, was formed in protest. The tension was increased by Wilhelm II's aggressive anti-modernism and by right-wing demands, also backed by the emperor, for stricter laws against obscenity and subversion.[88]

Given the importance of official honours, jobs and patronage on the one hand, and the radicals' easy access to commercial gallery-space on the other, the incentive to avoid an open breach with the establishment was strong. Liebermann was no longer an *enfant terrible*, and could probably have negotiated a compromise over exhibiting arrangements for himself and his friends. In 1897, his fiftieth year, he had a retrospective show of thirty-one pictures at the Berlin salon, won a gold medal and subsequently became an honorary professor and an academician. What apparently precipitated the final break was personal antagonism between Leistikow – an Academy expellee – and Werner and the rejection of the former's large *Grunewaldsee* by the 1898 salon jury. (Two other Leistikow pictures, however, were accepted, and *Grunewaldsee* was bought by the department-store owner Richard Israels and presented to the National Gallery.)[89] The Secession was founded on 2 May. Liebermann looked forward to its inaugural exhibition, scheduled for May 1899, with some trepidation: if they failed to attract enough money, or enough good pictures, he told Hugo von Tschudi, they would have to leave Berlin ignominiously, doubtless to Werner's delight.[90] In the event his fears proved groundless, thanks to donations from wealthy sympathisers and participation by many outside artists, including fifty-seven from Munich alone. The exhibition's tone was conciliatory, with no French work included, pictures by Leibl and Böcklin in positions of honour, and a bust of the emperor at the entrance. The cream of Berlin society, including Chancellor Hohenlohe, put in an appearance and a quarter of the exhibits were sold, yielding a substantial profit.

In the longer term, Liebermann's misgivings were more justified. Commercially the Secession was a success, since figures like Liebermann and Leistikow were already well established, and because of the effective marketing strategy of Paul and Bruno Cassirer.[91] But in other respects conditions remained difficult. Some members, including Skarbina, soon returned to the VBK, while royal and official hostility made itself felt in a ban on Secessionist acquisitions by the National Gallery.[92] Relations with the Munich Secession, as already noted, deteriorated after the turn of the century, hindering the creation of a united front at national level.[93] By August 1903 Liebermann was sufficiently weary and depressed to consider dissolving the Secession, but was dissuaded by Tschudi.[94] There was also chronic internal strife, and from about 1906 onwards increasing tension between the Secession's successful, rich and middle-aged leadership and hungrier, more radical new recruits. In 1910 a breakaway New Secession was formed by Emil Nolde, Max Pechstein and other dissidents.[95] More important in making the 'old' Secession seem *passé*, despite the wide range of its exhibitions, was the appearance in March 1910 of Herwarth

Walden's aggressively anti-establishment journal *Der Sturm* which, as Walden's interest in the visual arts grew, became a forum for Expressionist anti-naturalism.[96] The *Sturm* Gallery's exhibitions, beginning with a Blue Rider show in the spring of 1912 and Walden's First German Autumn Salon the following year, embraced practically every major contemporary art movement and – though hardly competing with the Secession's sales – strengthened Berlin's position as a showcase for the international avant-garde.

## MINOR CENTRES

Far removed, even in 1914, from the 'world city' atmosphere of Berlin were Germany's smaller art centres. The capital of the Empire's fourth kingdom, Württemberg, was Stuttgart, a pleasantly situated city of, in 1905, some 250,000 inhabitants.[97] In the reign of King Wilhelm I (1816-64), despite limited resources, State and private initiative had created an art gallery and training institutions, although their prime purpose had been to educate craftsmen and improve the quality of the kingdom's manufactures in the face of French and British competition.[98] In fine art terms Stuttgart remained a backwater until the turn of the century, when it became a battleground between progressive and conservative painters. After the prominent *plein-airiste* Leopold von Kalckreuth (1855-1928) left in 1905, the Academy was dominated by a conventional military specialist, Robert Haug. Efforts to attract Munich Secession President Hugo von Habermann failed (he used the Stuttgart offer to secure a more prestigious post in Munich), but Adolf Hölzel was appointed in November 1905, probably on the strength of his earlier, rather Leibl-esque pictures of Bavarian peasants.[99] In fact Hölzel's development towards abstract art continued fruitfully in Stuttgart, and he attracted pupils such as Ida Kerkovius, Oskar Schlemmer, Johannes Itten and Willi Baumeister, who became important in the Weimar Republic. But he was harried constantly by colleagues in an atmosphere of prudishness, parsimony and the kind of 'nativism' stigmatised by Lübke in his 1890 essay on Berlin. On the eve of Stuttgart's first international exhibition in May 1913, murals by another pupil of Hölzel, Alfred Pellegrini, in the new exhibition building were covered up on Haug's instructions, and were later destroyed;[100] and an earlier bid to strengthen the modernisers against the 'reactionaries' by enlisting Franz Marc to teach a life class had come to nothing.[101] Looking back later, Hölzel described his Stuttgart years without nostalgia: 'Everyone against me. Every dog incited to piss on me. Everyone at pains to drain me of my heart's blood.'[102] Happier were efforts to promote modern applied art, and above all the enlistment of Bernhard Pankok (1872-1943) to head new teaching and experimental workshops.[103] He eventually became director of the reorganised Design School, strengthened links with local industry and narrowed the gap between applied and fine art teaching.

Karlsruhe, capital of the Grand Duchy of Baden, was, with only 111,700 inhabitants at the turn of the century, a typical minor *Residenz*. The Academy acquired a reputation for landscape training during Schirmer's directorship between 1854 and 1863, but then stagnated – in the mid-1870s it had only twenty-five students[104] – under teachers like Ferdinand Keller, creator of vast historical allegories. In 1894 the painter Robert Poetzelberger described Karlsruhe to a Munich colleague as 'a god-forsaken place where artistic stimulus is practically unknown, that is outwardly and inwardly dull and talentless . . . artistically completely outside the world. You would have to live here for a year', he continued, 'to experience this and see what ignorance of outside conditions prevails, and what narrow horizons rule – and are favoured.'[105] The letter also underlined the importance of the Munich Secession, of which Poetzelberger was an external member, in encouraging change far beyond Bavaria, and its influence in Karlsruhe was soon strengthened by the arrival of the Munich animal-painter Heinrich Zügel (1850-1941), who taught at the Academy in 1894/95.[106] Zügel's stay, and the choice of Kalckreuth as his successor (though he left for Stuttgart in 1900), accelerated the creation, in 1896, of Karlsruhe's own Secession, the Artists' League (*Künstlerbund*). Formed just as art lithography in Germany was beginning to revive, it eventually became famous for its attractive and affordable prints.[107] But this development was somewhat overshadowed by the 1899 appointment, as Kunsthalle Director and Academy professor, of Hans Thoma, guru of neo-Romantic visionary art and, after Böcklin's death in 1901, Wilhelmine Germany's most revered image-maker.

Weimar, capital of the Grand Duchy of Saxe-Weimar-Eisenach, had a mere 30,000 inhabitants in 1900, and an atmosphere even sleepier than Karlsruhe's. But its name was forever linked with Goethe, Schiller, Herder and the other literary giants who had lived there in the reign of Grand Duke Karl August (1758-1828), and it had subsequently enjoyed a 'silver age' under his grandson Karl Alexander (1858-1901), founder of an art school and a museum. Nevertheless, prospects at the accession of the young Wilhelm Ernst in 1901 were unpromising. As Lichtwark noted two years later, there was no local art market, and efforts to open up the industrial towns of neighbouring Thuringia had yet to be made.[108] The court and most resident artists, apart from the former Berlin Secessionist Ludwig von Hofmann, were deeply conservative and suspicious of outside influences. Wilhelm Ernst himself seems to have been the worst kind of philistine princeling, a Potsdam-bred military man with little interest in the arts.[109] These conditions hampered the ambitious schemes of Count Harry Kessler, a millionaire banker's son, aesthete and connoisseur, who became Director of the Weimar Museums in the autumn of 1902.[110] He was prominent in launching the secessions' national umbrella organisation, the German Artists' League (*Deutscher Künstlerbund*), in Weimar at the end of 1903, and as Museums Director initiated a programme of modern art exhibitions, as well as theatrical, literary and other projects. But he inevitably became the target of insidious ('Serbian' in his phrase)[111] intrigues, and a scandal over some erotic Rodin drawings was used to discredit him with the Grand Duke; he finally resigned in the summer of 1906. More successful was Kessler's Belgian friend Henry van de Velde (1863-1957), who had been appointed to lead an

'Arts and Crafts Seminar' in 1901, with a general brief, like Pankok's in Stuttgart, to revitalise the applied arts. He survived to become Director of the new State Design School[112] and, though forced to leave Germany when war broke out, was eventually succeeded by a long-time collaborator, the architect Walter Gropius (1883-1969), who headed the school when it was reconstituted in 1919 as the Weimar Bauhaus.

Darmstadt, finally, *Residenz* of the Grand Dukes of Hesse–Darmstadt, was the scene of a particularly interesting artistic experiment: the culmination of a tradition of collaboration between monarchs, artists and citizens which went back to the first Grand Duke, Ludewig I, in the early nineteenth century.[113] Ernst Ludwig, who inherited the title in 1892 at the age of 23, was a grandson of Queen Victoria and an anglophile liberal. Known as the 'Red Grand Duke', he regarded most of his fellow-princes as reactionary, backed important constitutional reforms, and was the only German ex-monarch to remain in his palace after 1918. (The contrast between him and Victoria's other German grandson, Emperor Wilhelm II, was thus extreme.) He had wide-ranging musical and theatrical interests and, in keeping with his commitment to public service, was keen to promote projects beneficial to the local economy: hence, especially, his identification with the famous Mathildenhöhe Artists' Colony. The idea for this project originated with two private citizens, the wallpaper-manufacturer and publisher Alexander Koch and the writer and (later) theatre reformer Georg Fuchs. Both men rejected historicism in architecture, decoration and design, hoped to promote a truly contemporary style, and saw the modern applied art movement as a major opportunity for Darmstadt, which in the nineteenth century had lost its most promising artists to larger centres. Koch, a kind of Darmstadt counterpart of Georg Hirth, was a dynamic character, influential in the Art Union and editor of two important journals, *Die Innen-Dekoration* and *Deutsche Kunst und Dekoration*.[114] In 1898 he organised a design exhibition which included modern work by Otto Eckmann (carpets and tapestries), Margarete von Brauchitsch (embroideries), Karl Köpping and Hans Christiansen (ornamental glasswork), and complete *Jugendstil* interiors. Koch also presented Ernst Ludwig with a memorandum that became the blueprint for the Mathildenhöhe scheme: a new kind of venture, not tied to any existing institution, in which a few outstanding artists, subsidised by royal and public funds but free to work as they pleased, would stimulate local industry and act as a magnet for new talent.

The first seven 'colonists' comprised Christiansen (1866-1945), the architect–designers Josef Maria Olbrich (1867-1908) of Vienna Secession fame, Peter Behrens (1868-1940), and four other extraordinarily versatile figures, Ludwig Habich, Rudolf Bosselt, Patriz Huber and Paul Bürck. Their first joint task was to design the interior of the German Pavilion at the 1900 Paris World Exhibition. But their début in Darmstadt was the remarkable 'Document of German Art' Exhibition held at Mathildenhöhe between May and October 1901. Although it also featured experimental drama and cabaret productions in a temporary theatre, its permanent centrepiece was a studio building and a group of attractive artists' houses, all except Behrens's designed by Olbrich, and 'ready appointed from cellar to attic with every fitting;

everything modern, not a square centimetre unused, down to the smallest thing, to chairs and dining-room crockery; everything artistically thought out and executed in contemporary manner'.[115] However, although the show attracted great interest, poor management made it a financial disaster. Other problems included tensions within the colony – exacerbated by Olbrich's dictatorial style – which led to several departures, and the difficulty, experienced by most artist–designers since William Morris, in creating affordable products. Practically all the items in the exhibition carried luxury price-tags, and Behrens's house and fittings cost 200,000 marks. (By comparison, the cost without fittings of the magnificent, much larger Villa Kustermann in Munich-Bogenhausen, completed in 1902, was 188,000 marks.)[116] In a detailed and candid review, Koch and his associates acknowledged that their aims, especially the launch of a 'refined bourgeois art', had not been realised.[117] One direct consequence was a steep fall in municipal and parliamentary funding, so that Ernst Ludwig had to bear most of the colony's continuing costs, and those of other, ultimately abortive craft projects. The public purse-strings were loosened again by the success of the 1908 Hessian National Exhibition of Fine and Applied Art, but a promising sequel in the summer of 1914 was cut short by the war. In much more difficult conditions after 1918 it proved impossible to regain the earlier momentum.

Although the pre-war modern applied art movement remained dominated by large centres, especially Dresden and Munich, it certainly created openings for cities like Darmstadt and Stuttgart which could not compete across the whole artistic spectrum. Major exhibitions, such as the Dresden one of 1906, enabled the smaller centres both to demonstrate their capabilities and to enlist new talent: in 1906, for example, both the architect Albin Müller and the book-designer Friedrich Kleukens were recruited for Darmstadt. Some of the more extravagant celebrations of the Mathildenhöhe colony, and of Darmstadt as an 'art centre of the future', were really thinly veiled attacks on Munich, and were palpably over-optimistic.[118] As far as architecture was concerned, the colonists were opposed by a conservative establishment at the Polytechnic and won few local commissions outside the circle of those – like the furniture-manufacturer Julius Glückert – already closely associated with Mathildenhöhe.[119] In general, historicism and newer vernacular ('homeland') styles continued to dominate the scene. But in essence the colony scheme was refreshingly original, especially in its refusal to impose routine obligations on the artists and its aim to create links with local manufacturers and consumers. Some firms, especially furniture-makers, clearly stood to gain, and an embryonic local market existed. Darmstadt's population grew from about 72,000 at the turn of the century to 87,000 in 1914, and of 22,000 dwellings extant in that year, 7,000 had been built since 1900, including 845 villas;[120] a trend that offered clear opportunities for applied art. Other aspects of the Darmstadt venture seem distinctively modern. Koch understood the importance of media support for cultural projects, not only making propagandistic use of his own publications but wooing his fellow-journalists, who 'like no other power represent the justified demands of the time, progress and the advancement of humanity'.[121] For his part, Ernst

Ludwig understood the need for a genuine partnership between the Crown, citizen–activists like Koch, and the taxpayer. If grand-ducal money kept Mathildenhöhe afloat through the lean years 1901-08, public funds were essential to create the 1908 exhibition building and additional infrastructure. Aptly enough, the 1914 show contrasted the 'prince-cult' of the *ancien régime* with 'the tasks of the democratic present . . . in which the monarch functions merely as the first and noblest patron of his artists and the appointed propagator both of his own land's culture and that of his larger fatherland, Germany'.[122]

## ELEMENTS OF AN ART CENTRE: TRAINING

Although, like Menzel in Berlin and Spitzweg in Munich, some famous painters succeeded with little or no formal training, and strong currents of anti-academicism persisted throughout the nineteenth century, the reputation of academies and art schools was probably the single most important element in the prestige-ranking of German art centres. Academies were dynastic creations, founded in the late seventeenth and eighteenth centuries to provide rulers with the painters, sculptors and architects they needed to demonstrate their power; and, in the mercantilist era, to stimulate taste and manufactures.[123] As collegiate bodies they also offered honorary membership to outstanding artists. By the early nineteenth century they had become State-funded institutions closely identified with the concerns of governments, for which (although neo-mercantilist ideas persisted in some quarters) art was a means of legitimating the political and social order, integrating new territories and, in the words of one Prussian minister, linking 'exalted spiritual tendencies with the ordinary pleasures of life, and [ennobling] the latter by giving them form and thus raising them to a higher sphere'.[124] Later, as the numbers of artists swelled and parliaments were called upon to vote large sums for salaries and buildings, the purpose of academies was increasingly debated. In particular, the development of the private art market, and growing concern about a struggling 'artistic proletariat', prompted demands for training in genre, landscape and other popular specialisms alongside propagandistic historical art. Viewed from another perspective, however, the scope of academy training became increasingly narrow during the nineteenth century, with applied art confined to design schools (*Kunstgewerbeschulen*), architecture often transferred to polytechnics, and the teaching of sculpture and engraving overshadowed by mass production of easel-painters.

The importance attached to academies by the last decades of the century was symbolised by the construction of elaborate neo-Renaissance buildings in Düsseldorf, Dresden and Munich, where the new Academy (1874-84) built by Gottfried Neureuther and partly funded from the French war indemnity, was described by Friedrich Pecht as the city's 'real victory monument'.[125] (Ironically, both it and the imposing new academies opened in Düsseldorf in 1879 and Dresden in 1893 were highly unsatisfactory in use.)[126] However, while their architecture might impress casual visitors, academies' standing in the art world depended on the quality of teaching they offered. This varied considerably. For years before Werner's arrival in 1875, the Berlin Academy's art school was in a notoriously low state, with a doggedly conservative faculty and only about seventy-five students, most of them confined to the cast-room.[127] The Düsseldorf Academy's decline preceded Schadow's long-overdue resignation in 1859 and continued for years thereafter, with strife within the faculty, student unrest, and the destruction of the building itself by fire in 1872.[128] Although normal conditions were eventually restored, the institution never regained its former pre-eminence, and August Macke recalled his time there between 1904 and 1906 as dreary in the extreme.[129] The Dresden Academy's glory days lay still further in the past, even if the appointment of Kuehl and Bantzer in the mid-1890s and of Robert Sterl in 1904 had a generally rejuvenating effect. In the late 1860s and early 1870s, notwithstanding Piloty's fame, the Munich Academy left much to be desired: with inadequate teaching space, a tiny library and wretched provision for life classes, it was described by a former student in 1880 as 'one of the worst-endowed art-training institutions in the world'.[130] Later, with Wilhelm Diez, Ludwig Löfftz, Wilhelm Lindenschmit and Franz Stuck in the faculty, conditions improved, and – in keeping with its close links with the Secession – it followed the trend towards more life classes and open-air work. Ministers and the regent were jealous of its reputation and ready to respond discreetly to pressure for improvement, although they disliked public debate: in 1887, for example, with competition from Berlin increasing, Lindenschmit was sharply rebuked for actually publishing a programme of reform.[131] Other indicators of academies' perceived importance included the appointment of remarkably young men as directors: Schadow at 37, Werner at 32, and Fritz Kaulbach at 36 when he succeeded Piloty in 1886; and the salary increments and lucrative commissions (for example Piloty's vast *Thusnelda in the Triumph of Germanicus* of 1869-73)[132] which were offered to keep star teachers in place. Smaller centres inevitably had to bid over the odds for first-class talent: in 1905, for instance, Habermann was offered the very handsome salary of 8,000 marks, plus 'incredibly generous' leave allowances, to teach in Stuttgart, but still preferred 4,560 marks and much heavier teaching obligations in Munich.[133]

In quantitative terms, thanks to its teachers' reputations, and to lenient scholastic entry requirements, modest fees and the availability of bursaries and travel scholarships, the Munich Academy was the most successful in central Europe between the 1860s and 1914. In the winter semester of 1878/79 it had 387 students, compared with 195 in Berlin, 145 in Düsseldorf and 121 in Dresden.[134] Enrolments reached 552 by the completion of the new building in 1884, but were subsequently reduced and held to about 400 until the turn of the century. Numbers then rose again and by the winter of 1908/09 had reached 518: more than the complements of the Berlin (218) and Vienna (272) academies combined.[135] As significant as total numbers was the mix of nationalities, and of the 432 Munich students enrolled in the winter of 1881/82, 144 were Bavarians and 100 from other German states, while 188 came from abroad. Of the foreigners, 85 were from the Habsburg Empire, 34 from North America, 16 from Switzerland, 8 each from Scandinavia and Britain, 9 from the Russian Empire (including Russian Poland), 2 from Italy and 1 each from other European countries, Latin America and India.[136] By 1908/09, although Bavarians were still almost a third of the total (157 out of 518) and the proportion of other Germans had risen from nearly a quarter to nearly a third (170), foreigners (191) still made up almost 40 per cent. But the composition of this group had shifted, with only 9 Americans but 28 Swiss and 24 subjects of the Tsar.[137]

Although academy curricula became concerned almost exclusively with fine art during the nineteenth century, there were pressures from at least the 1840s onwards for a broader, more flexible approach to training.[138] One response was the reorganisation of state design schools and the creation of new ones – by 1910 there were about sixty throughout Germany – especially as successive international exhibitions revealed the superior quality of foreign manufactured goods. By the 1860s and 1870s leading institutions were emphasising originality, colour experiments, and workshop training in individual specialisms, instead of mere pattern-copying and perspective exercises. But there were also radical demands for design-school and academy training to be combined, so that students could change direction (or be redirected) after the completion of common basic courses. This, it was hoped, would channel more talent into industry and address the problem, often debated between the 1840s and 1914, of a mass of 'fine' artists who, after years of specialised training, survived with difficulty or sank without trace. One prominent advocate of reform was Franz Kugler. What benefit, he asked in 1845, came from any but the most inspired gallery pictures? Artists would do better 'to impart that nobility of form to the objects that surround our everyday life which, unconsciously but continuously, exalts our senses and our feelings'; yet 'not loudly from above' like paintings, but 'quietly and from below'.[139] In the 1870s, as we have seen, Dürer became a symbol for the synthesis of art and craft,[140] and by the nineties both American influences – mediated by, among others, Wilhelm von Bode[141] – and British ones were working in the same direction.

But resistance to change remained strong. In 1864 Wilhelm von Kaulbach had vigorously defended the Munich Academy's exclusive dedication to 'the cultivation of art for its own sake, for the sake of beauty'.[142] In 1902 Behrens's proposal for an applied art class at the Academy was rejected by both it and the Design School.[143] In Berlin both Werner and his successor Kampf resisted integration for decades. Eventually the 'second division' of State institutions took the lead. The Breslau Art School, for example, where the architect Hans Poelzig (1869-1936) became Director in 1903, evolved a mixed curriculum ranging from painting and sculpture to stained-glass design, weaving and embroidery, and in 1911 was renamed the Royal [Prussian] Academy of Fine and Applied Art.[144] After 1918, with a faculty which included August Endell, Oskar Moll, Otto Müller and Oskar Schlemmer, the breadth and originality of its training rivalled that of the Bauhaus. But the First World War also accelerated more general change. The Düsseldorf Academy, which had already reintroduced architecture in

1909, eventually absorbed some classes from the disbanded Design School.[145] In 1924 the Berlin Academy's art school became the United State Schools for Free and Applied Art. The principal exception remained the Munich Academy, whose faculty continued to block all proposals for amalgamation with the Design School, or even for equality of status between the two institutions.[146]

Although many people, like the young Klee in 1898,[147] regarded academic training as an advantage in the 'struggle for existence', it was not the only way to acquire technical skills, and the 1914 Munich Address Book listed nearly sixty private schools.[148] Private teaching was variable in quality and generally much costlier than at State institutions with their bursaries and subsidised fees: around 1900 the basic charge for Germans at the Munich Academy was 32 marks per semester (foreigners paid 62), whereas Klee regarded 26 marks a month in the private sector as cheap.[149] Artists took up teaching mostly for financial reasons, though sometimes, as in the case of Kandinsky's Phalanx School,[150] out of enthusiasm and missionary zeal as well. An early and important Munich example was the landscape school headed by Adolf Lier between 1869 and 1873, which spread the influence of Barbizon to a large number of painters and temporarily compensated for the lack of landscape training at the Academy. Two notable establishments at the turn of the century were run by Anton Azbé and Heinrich Knirr. The Slovene Azbé was a charismatic, bohemian figure who encouraged his pupils to create boldly expressive compositions with primary colours laid on with a palette-knife, and to paint out of doors; bicycles were essential equipment. His most famous pupils were Kandinsky and Jawlensky, who arrived in 1896 and spent several stimulating years with him.[151] Knirr emphasised life drawing, and Klee found both his teaching and Knirr himself highly congenial.[152] Both schools gave officially recommended preparatory training for the Academy, but also attracted many students whose gender or age disqualified them from entry: two of Klee's fellow-students were retired colonels in their mid-eighties.[153] Also outstanding were the Teaching and Experimental Studios for Applied and Fine Arts, founded in 1902 by Hermann Obrist and Wilhelm von Debschitz, which in less than four years had expanded from 6 to 185 students.[154] Closely identified with the modern applied arts movement, the school offered preparatory classes in which students had to analyse the structure of natural objects like leaves and shells, and workshop training in specialisms ranging from ceramics and printmaking to woodwork, weaving and photography.

It was also strongly committed to gender equality, and in 1904 Obrist welcomed 'the spontaneous creative talent for invention, emerging as it were overnight in the supposedly uncreative female sex', as 'a valuable new revelation of the gifts slumbering in our nation'.[155] In fact women had been admitted to State design schools since 1869 (1872 in Munich) and access widened more rapidly after the turn of the century.[156] But conditions were much less favourable in fine art, even though the proportion of full-time female artists in Germany rose from 10.9 per cent in 1895 to 16.9 per cent in 1907.[157] Only the Cassel Academy and the Städel Institute in Frankfurt were open to women in the nineteenth century, though limited access in Weimar, Königsberg, Stuttgart and

Karlsruhe was available by 1914.[158] But the 'big four' academies in Dresden, Düsseldorf, Munich and Berlin remained firmly closed; indeed, they were inhospitable places for women in any capacity: Neureuther's new Munich building, for example, did not even provide separate lavatories for the many female models and cleaners employed there.[159] For women with the necessary means the best alternative was to go to Paris, the artistic equivalent of Switzerland (until the 1900s) for aspiring doctors. In the French capital, as Paula (later Modersohn-) Becker found in 1900, one could get good-quality teaching, and work from the nude model, at the private schools of Julian or Cola Rossi, join free anatomy classes at the *École des Beaux-Arts*, and lead something like a 'real' artist's life.[160]

In Germany the restrictions imposed on women created considerable financial (and sexual/marital) opportunities for male artists with teaching inclinations. In 1880 Karl Gussow resigned from the Berlin Academy when he found he could earn five times as much from his private female pupils.[161] Corinth cushioned his move to Berlin by opening a school which mainly attracted women, including his future wife Charlotte Berend. Hugo von Habermann's papers contain letters from female pupils over many years, revealing attitudes to the master ranging from adoration to grovelling self-abasement. ('May God be gracious to us *Münchnerinnen*,' wrote one, 'and grant much, much health and strength to the great artists who still live amongst us, so that the little female artists can blossom and flourish in their shadow.')[162] Cheaper and more varied training for women was offered by the 'ladies' academies' created by female artists' associations in Berlin in 1867, Munich in 1884 and Karlsruhe in 1885.[163] The Munich one, attended by women from all over Germany, including Käthe Kollwitz and Gabriele Münter, and from abroad, expanded rapidly and in 1908/09 reached a peak of 270 students.[164] It offered courses by leading Munich artists and by the art historian Karl Voll at its studios near the Carolinenplatz, and ran a summer school by the Chiemsee. It was also graciously commended by the regent, received a modest State grant and, thanks to a favourable report by the educationalist Georg Kerschensteiner in January 1907,[165] support from the city as well. However, patronising or flatly negative responses to its petitions for large-scale funding, or equality of status with the Academy, revealed predictable prejudices. Even liberals like Kerschensteiner referred disdainfully to 'painting females' (*Malweiber*),[166] while Academy Director von Miller, echoing a widely accepted view, told Parliament in 1912 that 80 per cent of female artists saw art as a stop-gap until marriage, and that any increase in training facilities would simply 'breed a mass of unhappy creatures'.[167]

There was, finally, the vexed question of female access to life classes. *Ad hoc* solutions included the formation of private study-groups and even occasionally, as at the Städel Institute in the early 1870s, the discreet connivance of a sympathetic teacher.[168] However, the 'problem' of nudity was endlessly cited as an insuperable obstacle to free and equal admission of women to State academies. There were also larger political factors in play which probably carried more weight in parts of Germany than in countries like Britain or France. In Bavaria especially, the growing power of the Catholic Centre Party and, as we shall see, ministers' more and more beleaguered position, particularly on cultural issues, during the Regency, would have made it practically impossible to open Academy life classes to women. Moreover, this was one issue on which the prejudices of Catholic politicians coincided with those of Munich's large, overwhelmingly male-dominated and increasingly protectionist art community.

## COSMOPOLITANISM

The prevalence of foreign students at academies and private art schools is a reminder of the marked cosmopolitanism of German art centres before 1914. Looking back on Düsseldorf in the 1850s, the American Worthington Whittredge wrote: 'I found the professors of the Academy in Düsseldorf among the most liberal-minded artists I have ever met, extolling English, French, Belgian, Norwegian and Russian art. The Düsseldorf school, when I reached there, was made up from students of all countries . . . '.[169] There were numerous Norwegians around Dahl in early-nineteenth-century Dresden, and in Düsseldorf with Schadow; Munch's career began to take off in the lively Berlin Scandinavian colony of the early 1890s;[170] and in Munich Olaf Gulbransson became one of *Simplicissimus*' best cartoonists. The Poles Wojciech Kossak and Julian Fallat achieved fame in Wilhelmine Berlin,[171] while Munich in the 1870s was the cradle of Polish Realism, which developed in noisy opposition to the historicism of Jan Matejko – a kind of Polish Piloty – at home.[172] Hungary's most celebrated nineteenth-century artist, Mihaly Munkácsy, trained mainly in Düsseldorf, and Munich's Hungarians included the historical painter Gyula Benczur, Pál Szinyei-Merse and Simon Hollósy, who was to found the Hungarian nationalist artists' colony at Nagybanya.[173] Jawlensky, Kandinsky, Marianne von Werefkin and the Burliuk brothers were the latest of a long line of artists from the Russian Empire, some of whom stayed permanently.

At different periods there were also important groups of Americans in both Düsseldorf and Munich. Between the 1840s and the 1860s Düsseldorf had a large colony of Americans, of whom the most prominent was Emanuel Leutze, one of the founders of the Paint-Box in 1848 and, with Schadow the following year, of the Düsseldorf Gallery in New York. Other colony members included Albert Bierstadt (who later named his studio–mansion overlooking the Hudson River 'The Malkasten' after the club),[174] Eastman Johnson and John Caton Woodville. Americans' increasing preference for Munich over Düsseldorf in the 1860s reflected the two centres' shifting relative importance, and between 1870 and 1885 at least 275 Americans studied painting in the Bavarian capital.[175] They included the Realists Duveneck and William Merritt Chase, who arrived in 1871 and left finally, with most of their followers, at the end of the decade. Frank Currier stayed much longer, achieving fame as a cyclist and mountaineer but little commercial success with his landscapes done in 'thundering colour'.[176] By the time he returned to Boston in 1898 the American colony had dwindled considerably, but David Neal, Toby Rosenthal and Carl Marr settled in Bavaria, Marr becoming director of the Academy in 1919.

Foreigners came to study and work in Germany for various reasons that were strongest between the 1840s and about 1880, but less compelling thereafter. Probably most important was the lack of training facilities at home, since many countries, including Norway, Hungary, Greece, German-speaking Switzerland and the United States, were slow to acquire institutions comparable to those in Germany. Many Düsseldorf and Munich Americans had German connections: Leutze, for example, was born in Württemberg, and about two-fifths of the American students at the Munich Academy between 1870 and 1885 had Germanic names; Duveneck still wrote home in German.[177] Political motives doubtless encouraged Hungarians to make for Munich rather than Vienna, and impelled many of the Tsar's subjects to go abroad. There was no painting academy in Warsaw until 1903, and in the nineteenth century the Prussian, Russian and Austrian rulers of Poland limited the development of art training: further (negative) proof of the political significance attached to painting by governments. Especially in Bavaria where, in addition to the American Marr, the Hungarians Benczur and Wagner and the Greek Gysis all obtained Academy posts, career opportunities were equal for natives and foreigners. Stronger still was the lure of the market, since for most of the nineteenth century, in much of Scandinavia, eastern and south-eastern Europe, art-buying publics were small or non-existent, and there was little to compare with Germany's dealers, salons, art-union networks and art-hungry tourists. In 1869, for instance, the young Szinyei-Merse made his first American sale, then attracted the interest of leading Munich dealers, and won a bronze medal at the 1873 Vienna Exhibition.[178] At the same show another pupil of Piloty, the 23-year-old Aleksander Gierymski, made his début with a scene from *The Merchant of Venice* which had already been bought by the London dealer Wallis.[179]

But well before 1900, Germany's appeal for foreigners was waning. One reason, already noted, was the ever-growing magnetism of France; and, ironically, the strong representation of French artists, from the Barbizon painters to Bastien-Lepage, at Munich's international salons tended to make the Bavarian capital into a stepping-stone to Paris. French art's growing popularity in the United States also encouraged American painters to absorb Parisian influence, with a success amply demonstrated at the 1889 World Exhibition.[180] France's attraction for Scandinavian artists was strengthened by political resentments after the Prusso–Danish War of 1864, and by residual German influences at the conservative training and exhibiting institutions against which young painters increasingly rebelled.[181] But by the nineties German art centres were faced simultaneously by the ascendancy of French *plein-airisme* and by the growth of foreign cultural nationalism. The latter led increasingly to the creation of new art schools, colonies like Skagen and Nagybanya, dedicated to the celebration – or invention – of national landscapes, and styles that drew self-consciously on folk traditions and mythology. (In Hungary, *plein-airisme* itself became semi-naturalised as a 'national' style, with Szinyei's 1873 *Picnic*, actually painted in winter in a Munich studio, fêted after years of obscurity as its first masterpiece.)[182] Finally, market conditions in *fin-de-siècle* Europe were also changing, and the purchasing power of successful businessmen like Ernst Thiel in Stockholm, Wilhelm Hansen and Heinrich Hirschsprung in Copenhagen[183] and the developing bourgeois elite in Budapest[184] reduced artists' need to seek purchasers abroad.

## GALLERIES

As we have seen, art museums proliferated all over Germany in the nineteenth and early twentieth centuries, most of them in places without academies or art communities. But for an art-production centre, a *Kunststadt*, an accessible major art collection was almost indispensable. Certainly the removal of Düsseldorf's pictures, leaving little but a Rubens *Assumption of the Virgin,* too huge to carry away, was keenly felt there throughout the nineteenth century. Germany's dynastic galleries, some of them assembled over hundreds of years, varied greatly in size and importance, from the narrowly provincial one in Karlsruhe to the vast and magnificent collections in Dresden and Munich. The eighteenth-century rulers of Saxony acquired large numbers of superb Dutch, Flemish and Italian paintings, including Raphael's *Sistine Madonna* bought by Augustus III in 1745.[185] Goethe was deeply moved when he was allowed to view the pictures in 1768,[186] and in 1817 the Swedish poet Per Atterbom felt faint before 'splendour seething over like the waves of the sea'.[187] Placed under State administration in 1828 and later declared inalienable, the nucleus of the collection was eventually housed in Semper's new Royal Gallery, opened in 1855. Much larger, and still expanding in the early nineteenth century, were the Munich collections accumulated since the early sixteenth century, by fair means and foul, by the Wittelsbach dukes, electors and kings.[188] The dynasty's already huge Bavarian holdings had been swelled in the 1790s and 1800s by inheritance, which added the galleries of Zweibrücken, Mannheim and Düsseldorf, and by the secularisation of Church property, which brought in a further 1,500 items. After 1815 Crown Prince, afterwards King Ludwig I and his adviser Dillis acquired not only the Boisserée collection of north German and Flemish pictures, but many more French, German and Italian old masters.[189] In 1836 some 1,300 paintings – out of total holdings of more than 8,000 – including Altdorfer's *Battle on the Issus* and *Saint George*, Dürer's self-portrait of 1500, the cream of the world's largest Rubens collection (among them *The Fall of the Damned*, a great cascade of flesh that overwhelmed the Goncourt brothers on their visit in 1860),[190] dozens of Dutch landscapes and genre pieces, and Boucher's *La belle O'Murphy*, were hung in the Alte Pinakothek; many other works were displayed in Elector Max Emanuel's palace at Schleißheim. By comparison, although it contained, for example, Watteau's *Gersaint's Shop* and a version of *The Embarcation for Cythera*, the Hohenzollern collection in Berlin was more modest, at least in 1831 when much of it was presented to the State and housed in the Alte

Museum.[191] But royal collecting continued under both Friedrich Wilhelm III and Friedrich Wilhelm IV, and after 1871 a combination of heavy public spending and private generosity raised the Berlin galleries to world-class stature.

Although gallery-going became a major tourist activity in the nineteenth century – by the beginning of the 1880s the Berlin National Gallery was receiving between 250,000 and 300,000 visitors a year[192] – viewing remained for a long time arduous and inconvenient. Primitive or non-existent heating systems made many galleries practically unusable in winter. Opening hours were short and basic information about the exhibits was often lacking. The subdued lighting of Schinkel's Altes Museum, with its temple-like central rotunda, was more conducive to romantic reverie than to study of the pictures.[193] Much superior in this respect was Klenze's Alte Pinakothek, a long rectangular building with high, overhead-lit principal galleries on the main axis of its upper floor, flanked on its north side by a flight of window-illuminated side cabinets.[194] Yet the crowded floor-to-ceiling hanging arrangement inherited from the old dynastic parade-galleries made it hard to view some works even with opera-glasses. Semper in Dresden set out to combine Klenze's long galleries and cabinets with an 'art sanctum' under a central cupola where the visitor would contemplate the *Sistine Madonna* and other masterpieces.[195] But this was too dark for the purpose, and had to be hung with tapestries instead, while the other galleries were crammed with some 2,200 pictures. Space became a more and more acute problem everywhere during the nineteenth century, especially as State acquisition of modern works increased. Although in 1909 and 1910 Tschudi in Munich and Hans Posse in Dresden boldly rehung their collections to create better-spaced, more enjoyable displays, plans for essential new buildings were frustrated by the First World War. Finally, if conditions for visitors were less than ideal, they were no better for the pictures. Old masters that had survived innumerable wars, fires and evacuations up till 1815 now faced the wear and tear associated with masses of visitors, the destructive effects of central heating, and pollution. Worse still were horrendous cleaning and 'restoration' methods, including retouching by unqualified elderly painters. Max Doerner, one of the twentieth-century experts who were to shift the emphasis from restoration to conservation, told the Bavarian Government in 1918 that even Tschudi had permitted risky cleaning procedures, and added that restorers, like artists, knew less about their own craft than any other profession.[196] (Doerner, originally a painter, then a lecturer on painting materials at the Munich Academy, eventually wrote a standard textbook on the subject and founded the Munich Doerner Institute.)

Restoration was one of several contentious issues connected with the management of old master collections. Tschudi's rehanging of the Alte Pinakothek, for example, which involved the transfer of important works from provincial galleries to the capital, initially provoked fierce local protests. But, as the debates about the acquisition of French art have already shown, the shaping of modern galleries could be far more controversial. A particularly vexed question concerned the influence of local artists on purchasing policies, since the direct (cash-in-hand) and indirect (prestige, market status) advantages of getting work into museums were considerable. The Prussian LKK was dominated by artists from the outset, and in 1862 the Catholic parliamentarian August Reichensperger had predicted that democracy of this kind would mainly deliver hand-outs to the mediocre.[197] In the event, until Justi's reforms just before the First World War, self-interest clearly influenced the LKK's decisions, which occasionally even approved commissions and purchases of work by its own current members.[198] In Munich artists' leverage was even stronger, partly because of their close ties with the dynasty and local prestige, but also because of the explicit linkage between increased State spending from the late 1880s and support for the city's exhibitions. Consequently the art budget remained largely shackled to the salons, despite their declining quality, and 'sympathy purchases' and horse-trading between factions were rife. Prince Regent Luitpold, who had many artist friends, was also an obstacle to change; as one lay advocate of reform, the dramatist Wilhelm Weigand, wrote in 1904: 'The gentlemen who stand at the feeding-trough are too powerful, and the Prince Regent clearly desires that State monies should benefit the needy [i.e. often those without talent] as well as the worthy.'[199]

In the same letter, significantly, Weigand named Tschudi as a possible new broom. At all events, by the time he arrived in 1909 the efforts of the outgoing director Franz von Reber, opposition politicians like the Socialist Georg von Vollmar and concerned officials and ministers had failed to loosen artists' grip on the purchasing system and divert funds from local exhibitions. It had therefore been impossible to fill serious gaps in the Neue Pinakothek's collection, which was described by two British writers as a dismal 'picture-shop', overcrowded, poorly hung and dominated by mediocre work.[200] Tschudi's reform efforts aroused furious resistance, and were further hampered both by the impossibility of obtaining extra funds from Parliament and by the fact that the Neue Pinakothek itself was still (until 1915) owned by the Crown. That he did eventually succeed was due, as we have seen, to the support of his wealthy benefactors, some of them in Berlin and Paris; although even here he was obstructed by Luitpold, who opposed not only the acquisition of non-Bavarian works, but even the acceptance of gifts from outside Bavaria.[201] After Tschudi's death another storm was provoked by acting director Heinz Braune's rehanging of the gallery, and the display of at least some of the French and German masterpieces obtained by his late chief.[202] By the outbreak of war, however, it had been accepted in principle that State funds would henceforth be spent primarily on direct purchases from artists, or via the art trade, rather than at the salons.

## FREEDOM

The degree of creative freedom enjoyed by artists varied from one state of the Empire to another. But the situation was complex, and it was not the case that Prussia was in every respect a bastion of authoritarianism compared with the 'libertarian' south and south-west.[203] Of course no artist working in Berlin during Wilhelm II's reign could have ignored his often and loudly proclaimed distaste for modern, especially French-influenced, art. In such matters as the approval of State purchases, the award of prizes and honours and, above all, of commissions for buildings and monuments, his voice could be decisive.[204] Deference, sycophancy and the undeniable populist appeal of Wilhelm's pronouncements also created an oppressive atmosphere, especially in the 1890s. Just after the foundation of the Secession, for example, Walter Leistikow expressed concern about 'the fearfulness with which everyone tries to avoid the merest appearance of opposition to the Government's all-wise dispositions'.[205] The emperor's support for the ADKG's claim to organise Germany's contribution to the 1904 Saint Louis Exhibition in effect prevented the secessions from participating.[206] As late as 1913 he vetoed the award of a gold medal at the Berlin salon to Franz Stuck, one of Bavaria's most famous and highly decorated artists. To those directly affected, such actions did not seem trivial; Stuck, certainly, did not shrug off the royal snub.[207] But the broader picture was less gloomy. Käthe Kollwitz, though also anathema to the emperor and the Berlin establishment, had her prints acquired by the Dresden Graphic Cabinet (from 1898) and other museums and, as we have seen, received a major commission from the Historical Art League. Neither Wilhelm II nor any other German sovereign – for example King Friedrich August III of Saxony, who complained loudly about the nudity on display at the Dresden exhibitions[208] – could simply suppress works of art they disliked. The conservatism of Prussian official patronage was offset, as already suggested, by the purchasing power and generosity of a modern-minded section of the public. Repressive views were also constantly challenged by Berlin's progressive intelligentsia, from the Naturalists of the *Freie Bühne* and Maximilian Harden in *Die Zukunft* to the circles around *Die Aktion* and *Der Sturm*. Important legal safeguards, which were successfully defended in Parliament in the nineties, made it impossible to silence them. The State could not seriously interfere with artists, ban exhibitions or otherwise do much to hinder the workings of the art market. (The closure of Munch's exhibition in November 1892 was, of course, the work of other artists, not the police, and within weeks a larger selection of Munch's pictures was shown in privately rented premises without incident.)[209] By 1914, finally, public disquiet over the 1908 *Daily Telegraph* affair, the Tschudi episode and the emperor's cultural interventions had probably undermined Wilhelm's authority, if not his formal powers.

At first glance the situation in Bavaria seems to have been altogether more favourable. Although he had requested (in Ludwig II's absence) the rehanging of Liebermann's *Young Jesus in the Temple* in 1879,[210] Prince Luitpold was generally undogmatic about art and saw freedom as essential to Munich's reputation, a commitment shared by the liberally minded and mainly Protestant officials who governed Bavaria until 1912.[211] Very occasionally, as in the cases of Klinger's *Crucifixion*, Slevogt's *Danaë* and some of Putz's nudes, controversial pictures might be draped or removed from display. But this did not exclude the individuals concerned from subsequent official patronage or honours. (In theory, artists who worked for publication as cartoonists or illustrators faced greater risks from the criminal law, but the fact that in Bavaria and several other states, though not in Prussia or Saxony, serious press offences had to be tried by jury provided an effective safeguard, as *Simplicissimus*' near-immunity for most of the pre-1914 period demonstrates.)[212] In reality the most serious threat to artistic freedom came from below, because of the growing power of political clericalism. Important milestones were the 1906 franchise reform, which chiefly benefitted the Centre Party, and the appointment in February 1912 of a ministry headed by the conservative Centrist Count Georg von Hertling.[213] Although Hertling had little in common with the Centre's rank and file, his cabinet was dominated for the first time by Catholics, several of whom had links with Munich's militantly anti-modernist and anti-libertarian morality campaigners. The consequence was stricter theatre censorship and more aggressive police activity in a number of areas, from control of the Carnival to surveillance of foreigners, and the creation of what intellectuals perceived as an alarmingly repressive atmosphere.

In fact, conflicts between liberals and clericals over artistic issues had flared continually since the 1860s, when Wilhelm von Kaulbach's anti-papal cartoons had outraged Catholics;[214] while in 1914 Centrist deputies attacked 'insane' or 'negroid' avant-garde art in proto-Nazi terms.[215] In the intervening period the Centre had opposed 'excessive' spending on the new Academy and other prestige buildings, cut or rejected the State art budget, demanded stricter obscenity legislation, and denounced 'indecent' or 'blasphemous' pictures by Stuck, Makart, Uhde and other painters shown at exhibitions or bought for museums. In return, the party's supporters were vilified by liberals inside and outside Bavaria as philistines hostile to progress and civilisation; equating such bigots with medieval priests and monks, wrote Lübke in 1890, would be gravely unjust to the latter.[216] The underlying issues, however, were less clearcut. On the surface, liberals were strongly identified with Munich's modern secular culture, while Catholics, though with varying degrees of sophistication, sincerely detested it. But there were also hidden agendas on both sides. The Centre's leaders could be flexible enough when it suited them, and clearly regarded matters like the art budget largely as bargaining counters with which to obtain concessions in other areas. After 1900 the mobilisation of popular indignation against 'decadent' painters and 'subversive' satirists perhaps helped to maintain a veneer of unity, as divisions widened between rural party radicals and the urban conservatives who sought an accommodation with the political establishment. For liberals, rekindling the passions of the *Kulturkampf* was a diversion from their own electoral decline (between 1887 and 1905 their parliamentary representation fell from seventy-one seats to twenty-two)[217] and a pretext for opposing further democratisation. Episodes like the campaign in early 1900 against the so-called Lex Heinze, an anti-obscenity bill in the Reichstag, gave a textbook opportunity for anti-clerical and libertarian rhetoric, and to affirm Munich's vitality after a period of low morale in the art community when, to quote Liebermann, 'everyone complains and is despondent and – would like to head for Berlin'.[218] The possibility that, in the interests of long–term stability, the regent's advisers might ally with conservative clericals at the expense of cultural freedom, was the liberals' worst nightmare, and the theme recurred constantly in Parliament, newspapers such as the *Münchener Neuesten Nachrichten* and satirical journals like *Jugend* and *Simplicissimus*.

Debates about culture also reflected long-standing tensions between a politically and economically disadvantaged (backward, according to liberals) Catholic majority on the one hand and, on the other, an elite dominated by Protestant immigrants from other states or from the 'new' (post-1806) Bavarian provinces north of the Danube. 'Old' Bavarian Catholics identified these interlopers with the kingdom's absorption into the Prussian-dominated German Empire; with the *Kulturkampf*, led energetically in Bavaria by the Franconian lapsed Catholic von Lutz; and with a modern, big-business-orientated economy. Associated with many of these developments was Munich's highly visible and pampered art community, which had close links with the court, the political establishment and leading businessmen.[219] Lenbach, though an 'old' Bavarian and a Catholic, was related both professionally and by marriage to the Prussian heroes of Unification, and image-maker by appointment to Bismarck: the *bête noire*, not least as Lutz's ally, of many Bavarian Catholics. In June 1892 the ex-Chancellor was invited to Munich by Lenbach, presented to cheering students on the balcony of Lenbach's villa, and royally entertained at the Allotria with Lenbach in the chair.[220] Stuck's banquets were attended by ministers and high officials, the painter himself was associated with the Merck–Finck banking house, and his daughter married into the Heilmann construction and property dynasty. Fritz Kaulbach and Ferdinand von Miller were long-standing hunting companions of the regent and on close terms with his politically influential and economically well-connected entourage.

It was therefore hardly surprising that, on issues ranging from the disposition of State purchasing funds and monumental commissions (both in the capital and the provinces) to the land speculation surrounding the new Prince Regent Theatre, opposition politicians, both Centrist and Socialist, should have scented the operations of a clique of 'pals' (*Spezl*) and 'big shots' (*Gewappelten*) working to keep the spoils of patronage, honours and commercial opportunity for themselves. Further grievances sprang from the inflation and social problems associated with Munich's economic commitment to tourism and luxury consumption. For Catholics especially, the living symbol of all these concerns was Lenbach's neighbour in the Luisenstrasse, Georg Hirth, a Thuringian liberal–nationalist immigrant (and 'enemy' veteran of the 1866 war) who had become co-owner of the *Neuesten Nachrichten* and founder of *Jugend*. He was also a leader of the anti-Lex Heinze campaign, a regular defence witness at obscenity and blasphemy trials, the advocate of every conceivable progressive cause and a freethinker and divorcé to boot.[221] His contribution to Munich's cultural and general modernisation – he was even its first telephone subscriber – would be hard to overstate. Hirth and his allies, for their part, were understandably alarmed by Bavarian political developments, and on the eve of Hertling's appointment he penned a melodramatic leader in the *Neuesten Nachrichten* denouncing 'confessional insatiability', and prophesying cultural and economic decline and even revolution as the result.[222] In reality the 'cultural–commercial complex' to which Hirth belonged had little to fear from the new regime, since the Centre's populist radicals had been marginalised well before 1912. Nevertheless, the Government's repressive stance on many issues, in retrospect a foretaste of much fiercer reaction after 1918, threatened to tarnish Munich's image as Berlin's appeal increased.

## ARTISTS IN THE COUNTRY

The vast popularity of landscape and rustic genre until well into the twentieth century meant that art students and painters spent much time away from the town, glad to escape from studio-bound academy curricula and the tedium of working from urban models. Rural conditions were often primitive, and in their quest for subjects artists frequently had to endure bone-shaking transport, man-trap-like privies and awful food; working on *Three Women in Church* in Berbling, for example, Leibl needed supplies from his family in Cologne to provide relief from dreadful village cooking.[223] At idyllic spots like the Chiemsee island of Frauenwörth, deadly diseases like diphtheria could strike without warning. But the advantages were low living expenses, willing peasant models (except for nude studies) and almost other-worldly solitude and freedom. Leibl's friend Anton von Perfall described summers spent by the Ammersee in the mid-seventies:

> A passion for nature had seized us, an imperious urge to mingle with her more and more and strip away everything that hindered us – the very clothes on our backs repelled us. We spent hours on the open lake naked on the deck of [Leibl's] cutter, now plunging in, now daydreaming on our backs, or fishing, or shooting at gulls and diving-birds . . . The sun scorched us, the rain washed the colours from our clothes; we had become wild men as far as that was still possible.[224]

From 1873 Leibl increasingly abandoned city life and began to move ever deeper into the country; his last years were spent, with Johann Sperl, in the tiny hamlet of Kutterling in the alpine foothills. Such complete self-exile, however, was exceptional, and most artists kept an urban base while spending the summer months 'on location'.

It would be impossible to describe every place or region, even in Germany – many painters favoured the Danish, Dutch or French coasts, or remained faithful to Italy - that inspired artists between the mid-nineteenth century and 1914. In the 1840s and 1850s Eduard Schleich, Karl Spitzweg and their friends criss-crossed Southern Bavaria and the Tyrol, sleeping in barns and subsisting by working in the fields and painting targets for peasant marksmen.[225] Polling, south of the Starnbergersee, with its abandoned monastery and reedy lake, attracted Munich's American Realists in the 1870s.[226] Later, Putz, Edward Cuccuel and others painted open-air nudes and autumn landscapes in the secluded environs of Schloss Hartmannsberg in the Chiemgau.[227]

Wörth on the Upper Rhine, with its filmy atmosphere, well-drilled peasant boys, and draught animals content to stand until feeding time sounded on the village clock, was ideal for Heinrich Zügel's Academy summer school.[228] Erich Heckel, Max Pechstein and Karl Schmidt-Rottluff worked in idyllic nudity with their (urban) models by the lake-girt castle of Moritzburg near Dresden,[229] and were later drawn repeatedly to the vast skies and picturesque fisherfolk of Dangast in Oldenburg.[230]

Different entirely was the walled Franconian town of Rothenburg on the Tauber. Ludwig Richter's description of it, as early as 1826, contains all the elements of nineteenth-century medievalism and Dürer-worship:

> Evening was already falling as I entered the narrow, uneven streets. The houses with their tall pointed gables, each jutting further out than the one below, archaic name-plates and guild signs, Gothic chapels and churches, but hardly anyone in the streets . . . At the tables [in the inn] sat a few men in clothes which also seemed to date from grandfather's time, drinking their beer from tall pewter tankards familiar to me only from Albrecht Dürer.[231]

Such images appeared in many of Spitzweg's pictures in the 1840s, and Rothenburg's time-warp atmosphere was still intact on the eve of the Franco–Prussian War: 'the whole place', recalled the American painter Toby Rosenthal, 'seemed as if draped in cobwebs.'[232] Later it grew increasingly popular with artists and tourists alike (noticing the connection, the town council sensibly made studios available), and became a kind of surrogate for Nuremberg as the latter developed into an industrial city. Kandinsky painted there in 1901 and 1903, inspired by 'the dream of a medieval totality',[233] and depicting the fortifications like a toy-box castle. Later he worked the memory of the bronze George and dragon statue in the market-place into his celebrated rider motif, symbol of art's challenge to contemporary materialism.

The quasi-'oppositional' function of colonies was demonstrated by the village of Willingshausen in the Hessian Schwalmthal.[234] Still at the turn of the century some way from the nearest railway station, it boasted half-timbered houses, a distinctive costume, and a colourful mix of inhabitants in and around the village that included peasants, rural artisans, minor notables like clergymen, teachers and vets, and Jewish tradespeople and gypsies, while the aristocratic Schwertzell family occupied the nearby castle. Willingshausen had been discovered as early as 1814 by the Baltic painter Gerhard von Reutern, who later shared his enthusiasm with colleagues in Düsseldorf. 1849 saw the arrival of the 19-year-old Ludwig Knaus who, allegedly 'infected by political agitation',[235] had decamped from Schadow's Academy. Finding the peasants sympathetic to artists' needs, he stayed to make copious studies, and returned repeatedly in subsequent years. His Willingshausen (and later also Black Forest) material gave his famous rustic scenes a degree of ethnographic and psychological realism which distinguished them, at least to some extent, from the staginess of Düsseldorf genre. Carl Bantzer made the first of countless working visits in 1887, by which time

Willingshausen, mainly thanks to Knaus, was attracting artists from far and wide. But Bantzer had actually been born in nearby Ziegenhain, and as a vet's son become closely acquainted with the peasants and their dialect. Moreover, in Paris in the early 1880s he had encountered *plein-airisme à la* Bastien-Lepage, later becoming one of Dresden's leading artistic radicals and chairman of the Secessionist group founded there in 1893.[236] One of his contributions to the victory of modern painting in Saxony was to lead painting expeditions both to nearby Goppeln and to Willingshausen, where by 1900 he was a commanding figure, equally welcome at the castle and in the village. The major work of his early Willingshausen period, *Communion in a Hessian Village Church*, was an interesting hybrid product, reminiscent of Leibl in its fine detail and rejection of anecdote, yet in other ways closer to the 'constructed' naturalism of French salon artists like Dagnan-Bouveret. The figures (extensively photographed, as we have seen) were selected from three different congregations and posed in a dummy interior modelled on a fourth church some miles away, while lighted altar candles, rare in this evangelical region, were included for visual effect.[237] After 1900, like many other painters of rural life, Bantzer and his circle increasingly followed the trend towards monumentalised 'homeland art'.

Few artists lived in Willingshausen all the year round, and most colonies functioned as such only in the summer months, with painters working up their material at home in the winter. This was certainly true in relation to Frauenwörth – or Frauenchiemsee – a small island in Germany's biggest lake.[238] (Ludwig II built a palace on the larger Herrenchiemsee close by.) It was romantically discovered by the painter Maximilian Haushofer, who was stranded there in a storm in 1828 and later married the innkeeper's daughter. Its charms, in addition to the large and hospitable inn, included a traditional community still fishing from dug-outs, a convent, stately lime trees and stupendous views of the Alps. Although already popular by the 1840s, its classic period was the era of Karl 'Chiemsee' Raupp (1837-1918), who from 1880 to 1914 ran the beginners' class at the Munich Academy, but had first visited the island in 1869. As well as presiding over the colony's illustrated chronicle, Raupp became identified with a branch of genre painting – above all, dramatic scenes of fishergirls and their infants battling with the Chiemsee's deadly squalls – that became hugely popular with the public; indeed, one of his pupils, Joseph Wopfner, repeated a painting of nuns in a boat intoning the *Ave Maria* some twenty-five times. Raupp's own methods exemplified the functional separation between summer and winter, colony and town. While on Frauenwörth practised local assistants helped him to make countless studies, sometimes perched on a platform above the water for off-shore views of the island, his Munich studio incorporated a Chiemsee 'set' complete with costumes, paddles, an authentic fisherman's boat and a dramatically wheeling (stuffed) seagull which featured in his most famous paintings.[239]

More permanent, with about thirty resident artists by 1914, was the colony at the market town of Dachau eleven miles north-west of Munich.[240] As yet untainted by political events, it was an agreeable place, with wide streets, comfortable hostelries, a castle and a park. Another attraction was the traditionally costumed rural population, both retired farmers (*Austrägler*) living in the town and peasants from round about who came in to trade or litigate. (Ludwig Thoma, Bavaria's celebrated author of peasant novels, practised law there in the mid-nineties and, after moving to the capital to edit *Simplicissimus*, returned often for 'a mouthful of milieu'.)[241] But there were also the peculiarities of the nearby Dachauer *Moos*, until the First World War a largely uncultivated and semi-waterlogged stretch of moorland, featureless except for birch-clumps and the occasional peat-cutter's cabin, yet bewitched by light and atmosphere. 'Once one was on the deserted *Moos*, harsh contrasts disappeared', noted a visitor in 1913:

> The moist atmosphere enveloped trees, moor and distant village-topped hills with soft, silvery vapour. Gravel pits with yellowish, grey-blue, greenish stones; dark brown peat-cuttings; light sun-faded walls; plants with delicate white flowers; groups of dark green trees, and motionless waters that reflected the shimmering air back on to the peat banks.[242]

First frequented by Dillis in the 1830s, Dachau drew Munich's Barbizon-influenced 'atmospheric landscapists' in the 1850s and 1860s, and *plein-airistes*, including Uhde, Zügel and occasionally Bantzer, in the 1880s. But it became best known for the so-called 'New Dachau School' of the 1890s: a group of artists who responded to the moorland's atmospheric conditions by suppressing naturalistic detail in favour of increasingly simplified, ornamental compositions. Its leaders were Ludwig Dill (Plate 22), Arthur Langhammer and, as principal theorist, Adolf Hölzel, who between 1890 and 1905, when he left for Stuttgart, moved from the late Realism of subjects like *Old Peasant Woman at Prayer* to the proto-abstraction of *Composition in Red I*.

Also associated with the development of modern painting was Murnau, 46 miles south-west of Munich and commanding a dramatic view, southwards down a tongue of moorland, of the distant Wetterstein range.[243] Anna Howitt, *en route* to Oberammergau in 1850, was thrilled by one of its spectacular sunsets: 'What wonderful gradations of colour! What sharp, bold, stern lines of composition! . . . Even Turner's wonderful tints and magical power over atmosphere seemed cold and feeble in recollection as we gazed at this lovely picture painted for us by God's own hand!'[244] By 1900 Murnau was already popular with Munich artists; the iron-founder Ferdinand von Miller (father of the sculptor) owned an island estate in the nearby Staffelsee, and the architect Emanuel von Seidl had a summer residence in the town. Kandinsky and Gabriele Münter, accompanied by Jawlensky and Werefkin, worked in and around Murnau in the early autumn of 1908 (Plate 23). 'There,' recalled Münter, 'after a brief period of torment, I made a great leap – from reproducing nature – more or less impressionistically – to sensing content – to abstraction – to rendering an extract. It was a beautiful, interesting, joyful working time . . . '.[245] Then and later she painted pictures which, while radically simplified, captured the feel of particular times and places: twilight on the moor with its looming hay-barns; the intense blues

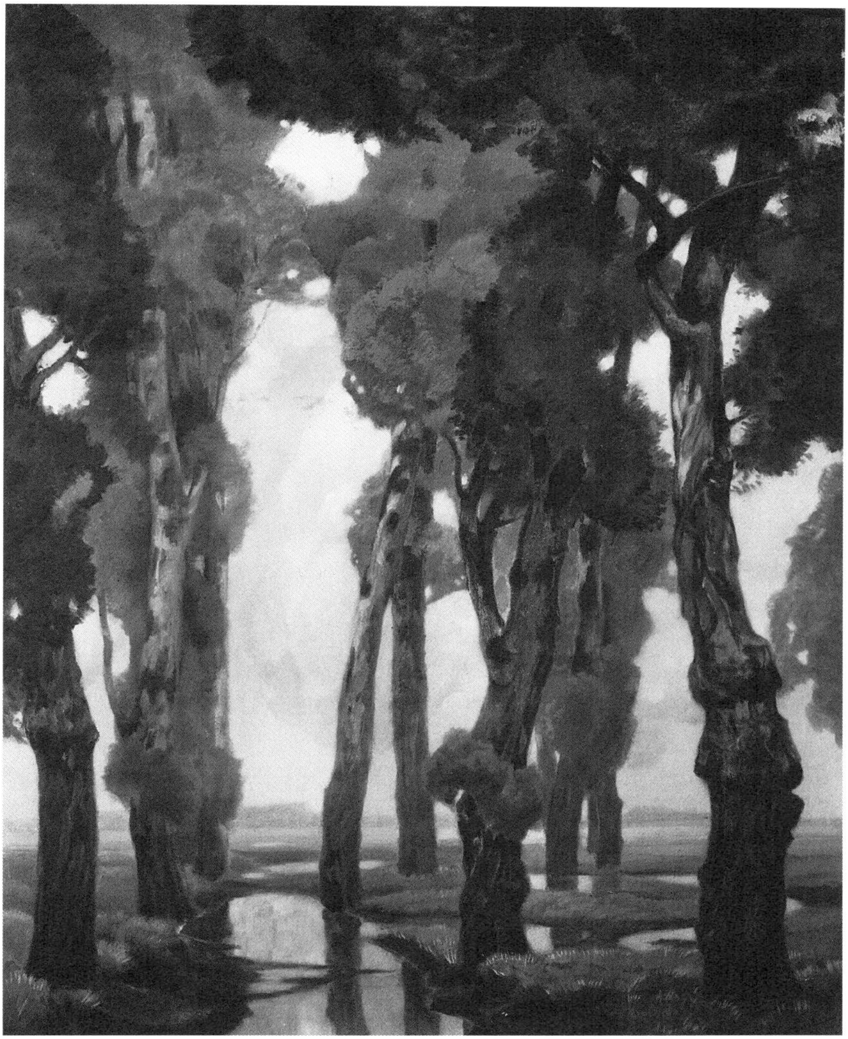

PLATE 22 Ludwig Dill, *Poplars in the Amper Meadows of the Dachau Moos*, 1901, oil on board, 93 x 73 cm. A good example of the rather flat, ornamental compositions inspired by the filmy atmosphere of the semi-waterlogged area along the River Amper. Although Dill had taken up a post in Karlsruhe in 1899, he continued to spend his summers in Dachau.

and greens of afternoons on the high pastures. In the five pre-war years after 1909, when she and Kandinsky acquired the property – dubbed 'the Russians' house' by the locals – which was to remain her home until her death in 1962, undertones of melancholy and isolation crept into her work, perhaps foreshadowing the break-up of their relationship. But it was the end, or nearly so, of a fruitful period in their lives. In Murnau, within cycling distance of Marc in Sindelsdorf, all three artists created their first back-glass paintings and, in 1911-12, worked on the *Blue Rider Almanac*. Kandinsky for his part seems to have found there another refuge from the materialism of the modern world, and transformed the church and castle visible from the *Russenhaus* into images of a hilltop 'spiritual city'.[246] Influenced by the vivid colours and 'sharp, bold, stern lines' of the landscape, he also made his own almost complete transition to abstraction.

Imperial Germany's most celebrated artists' colony and, like Frauenchiemsee, well established in the guide-books by 1914, was the village of Worpswede in the Teufelsmoor north of Bremen.[247] It was founded in 1889 by two disaffected Düsseldorf students, Fritz Mackensen (1866-1953) and Otto Modersohn (1865-1943), who were joined later by Heinrich Vogeler (1872-1942), Carl Vinnen and a Munich friend, Hans am Ende. The art for which, with varying emphases, they eventually became famous, was a blend of *plein-airiste* naturalism, neo-Romantic pathos and, especially in Vogeler's case, elements of Symbolism and *Jugendstil*. Worpswede's own appeal lay in its remoteness, the huge skies and dramatic cloud formations above the flat landscape and, particularly, its distinctive light and atmosphere. 'A journey to Worpswede', wrote Richard Muther in a memorable essay, 'is a cataract operation, as if a grey veil spread between objects and ourselves had suddenly disappeared . . . Have these peasants a colour-demon within them? Or is it only the air, the soft, moisture-saturated air which makes everything so colourful, so resonant and radiant?'[248] In 1895 the group achieved overnight fame at the Munich Glaspalast exhibition, at which Mackensen won the top prize with a picture of peasants listening to an open-air sermon. This success, however, sowed the seeds of future problems, especially jealousies between the painters and an influx of tourists and would-be students. But one of the latter was Paula Becker from Bremen, who worked with Mackensen in the summer of 1897 and returned to stay a year later.[249] Though captivated by the landscape, she soon became aware of the inhabitants' wretched living conditions and drew many of her models from the social rejects in the local poor-house: orphans, battered children and senile old women. Ironically, considering the haze of ruralist nostalgia that came to surround Worpswede, her dark-toned and unidealised early studies of these people, and of 'Old Bredow', the decayed aristocrat, resemble nothing so much as Kollwitz's stark images of the Berlin proletariat.

After 1900 the disintegration of the original colony continued. Overbeck and Vinnen left and Mackensen, who became Director of the Weimar Art School in 1908, ceased to live there permanently. The most prominent figure was now Vogeler, a hugely versatile artist who transformed a dilapidated farmhouse into an exquisite architectural *Gesamtkunstwerk*, the Barkenhoff, and whose fame as a designer attracted numerous craftsmen to the village. Yet Worpswede's ultimately most celebrated painter was Becker, who married the landscapist Modersohn in 1901, but whose own naive–expressionist – in her words, 'runic' – figure painting developed quite differently from his and all the other artists' work (Plate 24). Like other radically unconventional artists, however, she needed far more stimulus than a place like Worpswede could offer. By 1905

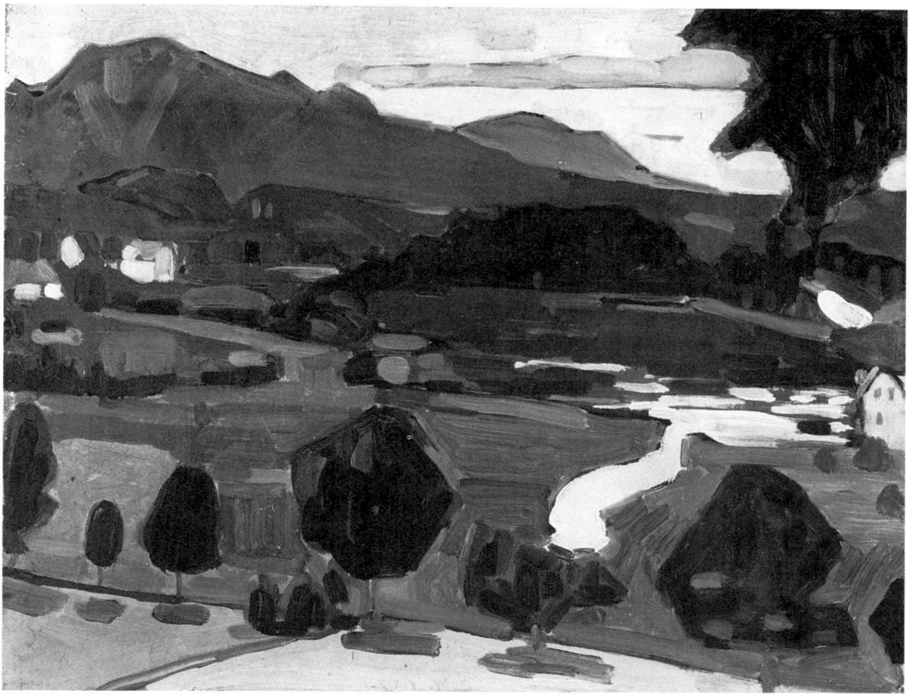

PLATE 23 Vassily Kandinsky, *View of the Staffelsee*, 1908, oil on board, 32.7 x 40.5 cm. © ADAGP, Paris and DACS, London 1997. One of the important series of Fauve-like, more or less proto-abstract landscapes painted in and around Murnau in the late summer of 1908 and the following year.

Modersohn-Becker was disillusioned with her marriage, depressed by the departure (and marriage to the poet Rilke) of her closest friend, the sculptor Clara Westhoff, and stifled by the community's claustrophobic atmosphere. (As early as in February 1899 she had written: 'I believe I will develop away from here. The number of people I can bear to talk to about anything close to my heart and nerves will become ever smaller.')[250] Further progress was possible only through extended visits to Paris. But she died, back in Worpswede, in November 1907 at the age of 31. The colony remained in being during the First World War and, under the leadership of the sculptor Bernhard Hoetger, through the 1920s. In the Third Reich, although Modersohn-Becker's work was rejected as 'degenerate', Worpswede was officially vaunted as a cradle of 'Nordic' art. Since 1945, with its galleries, craft shops and floods of visitors, it has become a textbook example of the modern symbiosis between culture and leisure.

But this was developing even before the turn of the century. 'Art tourism', including visits to the studios of celebrities like Makart, had been growing since the 1870s as journalistic coverage of artists' activities increased, and their rural retreats became

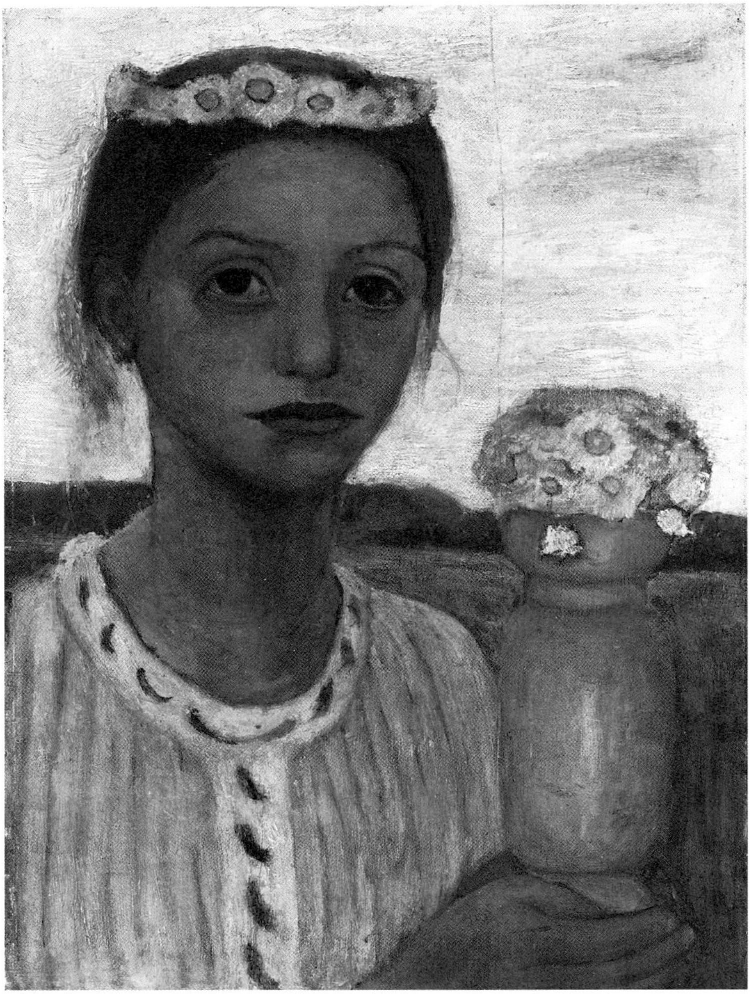

PLATE 24 Paula Modersohn-Becker, *Girl with Flowers*, 1902/3, oil on panel, 48 x 33.5 cm. One of several pictures of fragile and pensive adolescent girls painted between the artist's marriage to Otto Modersohn in May 1901 and the start of her second visit to Paris in February 1903. Her earlier, rather sombre Naturalism has given way to a lighter, more stylised approach, probably influenced by the Worpswede painters Heinrich Vogeler and Ottilie Reyländer.

equally popular. By 1914 railway branch-lines, lakesteamers, motorbuses and cars made even the most remote spots accessible, and commercialisation and overcrowding was spoiling the most popular colonies, attracting Montmartre-style hacks and driving serious artists elsewhere. (In France places like Barbizon, Pont-Aven and Grez-sur-Loing had already gone the same way.) Also disruptive was the boom in summer painting schools. Around Dachau in the 1900s students were scattered over the moor at 50-metre intervals and had to queue for the most popular motifs, while farmers sued over meadows contaminated with palette-scrapings.[251] If teaching fees were an economic necessity, however, so were sales, and even hermit-like ruralists such as Leibl and Sperl maintained their links with patrons and the market. Like the Newlyn painters, whose pictures travelled annually to the Royal Academy by chartered freight van, German artists, wherever they lived, were subject to commercial mechanisms: acceptance by art unions and salon juries and, increasingly, adoption and management by dealers. Within a year of their Munich breakthrough, for example, the Worpswede painters were on show at Schulte's gallery in Cologne.[252] The letters between Marc and Kandinsky in Bavaria and Walden in Berlin reveal how modern communications enabled artists to live and work far from the main centres, while receiving almost daily reports about exhibitions, tours and sales. (By June 1914 Marc even had a telephone in the village of Ried.)[253] They also kept in touch with the aesthetic currents of a vastly extended art world, to which figures like Leibl, Marc and certainly Modersohn-Becker owed at least as much as to their immediate rustic surroundings. Kandinsky, even in *Lederhosen*, was the embodiment of a sophisticated cosmopolitanism nurtured not only by travel but by a constant – indeed often burdensome and disruptive – stream of letters, journals and visitors reaching the alpine foothills from all over Germany, and from as far afield as Amsterdam, Paris, Moscow and Chicago.

# 4
# The market

The basic character of the German art market in this period was of diversity within a framework of increasing integration. The principal integrating mechanism was the development of private picture-buying, as the numbers of artists increased and the relative importance of patronage by dynasties and – despite the post-Unification boom in propagandistic history-painting – governments declined. Even an artist like Franz Defregger, who repeatedly sold outsize historical paintings to museums for five-figure sums, earned most of his considerable income from small– and medium-format works which were snapped up eagerly by private buyers from Königsberg to San Francisco. As the overwhelming majority of painters, regardless of what they had learned as students, also earned their livings from such products, an efficient means of bringing artist and buyer together was essential.

## ART UNIONS

Celebrities like Defregger sold a proportion of their work, some of it even before completion, directly to visiting clients. Lesser-known figures employed cab-drivers and hotel porters to steer tourists towards their studios. [1] But private sales, though evidently widespread, were time-wasting and disruptive for artists, and most pictures probably reached their public via intermediate outlets of one kind or another. Quantitatively the most important of these was the art union network, whose development and broader significance, in relation to both monumental and small-scale art and to museum creation, have already been discussed.[2]

As a market institution, the art unions' distinctive distribution mechanism was a lottery system by which an acquisition committee would spend a statutory proportion of each society's income on works of art which would then be raffled to members, who could increase their chances of winning by buying a number of 'shares'. The development of multi-branch art unions like the Saxon and Rhenish–Westphalian ones, and of regional leagues, allowed the creation of lottery 'pools', thus giving small-town members the opportunity to win works created in the major centres. But the lottery system also enabled committees - which were usually dominated by laymen rather than artists – to guide taste and act as surrogate patrons for young or neglected painters. (The annual presentation of an engraved reproduction to members also steered substantial funds to engravers.) Friedrich's *Large Enclosure Near Dresden*, for example, was bought by the Saxon Art Union at a time when his fortunes were at a low ebb,[3] while in the 1830s Ludwig Richter and his friend Ernst Oehme waited anxiously each spring for the committee's decision, resentful of such dependence, and at seeing their work bestowed by chance, yet aware that few other sales opportunities existed.[4] In Munich Heinrich Bürkel and Philipp Röth had respectively forty and forty-seven works bought by the Art Union in the course of their careers.[5] Although they and other artists – including Franz Marc's father Wilhelm – patronised by the society year after year were respectably talented, such support of so-called 'pensioners' was increasingly attacked, and after the turn of the century lottery winners simply received coupons worth between 100 and 1,500 marks to exchange for works of their own choice. But the lottery system was designed from the outset primarily as a stimulant to ordinary exhibition purchases, which became increasingly important. In 1878, for example, the Munich Art Union's expenditure of 70,725 marks on lottery acquisitions was matched by about 40,000 marks worth of sales,[6] a pattern repeated in proportion by large and small societies across the Empire.

By this time, as we have seen, the art unions were facing increasing criticism, and having to compete with dealers and artists' salons for quality work. Yet the advantages they offered to artists, especially beginners and those at the lower end of the profession, remained considerable: lenient hanging criteria, low commission rates or none at all, and extensive exposure via the touring network. Moreover, the movement as a whole both promoted art as an essential element of national and bourgeois culture and passed enormous amounts of money to artists. In the first half-century of its existence, for example, the Saxon Art Union disbursed 1,101,400 marks on lottery purchases and commissioned engravings.[7] The Munich *Kunstverein* spent some four and three-quarter million marks on lottery items, engravings and acquisitions for its own collection between 1824 and 1904; but with exhibition sales as well the total earned by artists via the society was put at between seven and eight million.[8] Statistics published by the unions' national umbrella organisation in 1911 indicated that in the previous decade the network as a whole had passed an annual average of 1.25 million marks to artists: about as much as the sales yield of all the main artists' salons, and twice the expenditure on art of all German governments and major cities combined.[9]

## SALONS

More prestigious and earlier in origin than the *Kunstverein* exhibitions were the salons organised by the German academies, beginning in Dresden in 1764, Berlin in 1786 and Munich in 1788. Although disrupted during the Napoleonic Wars they were revived after 1815 and were subsequently held at intervals of between one and three years.

(Düsseldorf artists, as already noted, had no formal salon of their own, but enjoyed equal exhibiting rights in Berlin.) They attracted increasing critical attention and grew steadily in size and popularity: according to Kugler, for example, 432 items were shown in Berlin in 1816, 1,065 in 1826 and 1,683 in 1836, this last show attracting almost 112,000 visitors.[10]

Important new developments took place from the 1840s onwards as the numbers of artists grew, and in Düsseldorf tensions between Schadow's Academy and the wider art community increased. The foundation of the Berlin Artists' Association (VBK) in 1841, the Düsseldorf Paint-Box in 1848 and the General German Artists' Guild (ADKG) in 1856 reflected artists' developing sense of professional identity and desire for independence from both academies and art unions. The transfer of responsibility for Munich's salons from the Academy to the Artists' Guild in 1863 was one consequence of this, and opened the way, as we have seen, to more ambitious exhibitions. (The existence of August Voit's Glaspalast, the largest such building in central Europe, was also a vital precondition.) In Berlin the Academy's control continued much longer. But the success, in 1891, of an independent exhibition organised by the VBK to mark its fiftieth anniversary hastened progress towards a system of joint management which increased artists' influence.[11] In Dresden, change was precipitated by the construction of the new Academy between 1885 and 1894, which resulted first in the suspension of the salons and then, because of the inadequacy of the new building, their abandonment. The series of successful fine– and applied-art exhibitions which replaced them, held in the recently completed Municipal Exhibition Hall, were organised by artists themselves in collaboration with the city and the State.[12]

After the hiatus caused by the Franco–Prussian War and the Munich cholera outbreak of 1874, the scale and frequency of exhibitions increased.[13] In Munich, after the 1876 National Applied Art Exhibition, a third international fine art salon was mounted in 1879, and a fourth in 1883. There were also annual, eventually permanent exhibitions of local work organised by the Artists' Guild. The pace quickened further after the Berlin Academy's Centenary Salon in 1886, with Munich's huge – with some 3,500 items – fifth International Exhibition in 1888 (accompanied by a second National Applied Art Exhibition), and in 1889 the first of the annual international salons which were to lead to the formation of the Secession.

Mounting a major exhibition required an enormous organisational effort and cost a fortune – according to Paul Drey, about 125,000 marks for an ordinary Glaspalast show, twice as much for an international one[14] – with governments, municipalities and private subscribers contributing tens of thousands of marks in subsidies and guarantee-funds. International salons were advertised in advance via the diplomatic network, ceremoniously opened by royalty and accompanied by banquets, pageantry and general flag-waving.[15] Serialised reviews in the art journals continued for months, while newspapers printed sales bulletins in the manner of modern sports reports. Profits and the number of visitors were viewed as indicators of an art centre's vitality and of the effectiveness of its training institutions and cultural policies. For individual artists, medals and commendations were important prestige factors, stimulating interest from dealers and justifying higher prices. Financially, salons were important not only for exhibitors but also for artists' organisations hoping to enlarge their funds. Gross sales figures at the Munich international exhibitions rose from 457,786 marks in 1879 to 677,860 marks in 1883 and 1,070,500 marks in 1888 (about the same as the Berlin salon of 1886), and all the national and international Glaspalast shows held between 1879 and 1908 together raised nearly eleven million marks.[16] Exhibitions held independently by the Munich Secession between 1893 and 1908 added another 1,864,139 marks.[17] These figures, of course, must be viewed in the context of expanding art communities and picture-output and, after 1900, inflation. Nevertheless, the big salons made a major contribution to the economics of art production both directly and indirectly – for example through increased dealer– and studio-sales during the exhibition season, and reproduction royalties – and their severe curtailment after the First World War was a serious blow for artists.

The entertainment function of exhibitions was important, and the lush colours and illusionistic detail of *grandes machines* by Piloty, Makart, Defregger and Werner had an appeal equalled only by the panorama and the most elaborate magic-lantern shows. Eye-catching subject-matter was frequently more important than artistic quality. *The Suicide Pact*, a life-size painting of two lovers leaping into a raging torrent, by Emil Neide (remembered today only as a teacher of Käthe Kollwitz), was one of the sensations of the 1886 Berlin salon.[18] In 1892 Georges Rochegrosse's proto-cinematic *Fall of Babylon*, showing Persian warriors about to hurl themselves on revellers prostrated by gluttony and sex, was the talk of central Europe. (The painter's production costs, for models, props and a perspective consultant, were put at 40,000 francs.)[19] In his memoirs the historian Karl Alexander von Müller recalled his boyhood impressions in Munich around 1900:

> Our grandchildren today cannot be more excited before a decisive match than we were then, when, on the first afternoon after the ceremonial opening of a great international exhibition, we entered the broad entrance-hall of the Glaspalast, newly decorated every year according to the plans of Lenbach or Franz Seitz with cool fountains, darkly gleaming laurels and mighty sculptures, while from the nearest rooms to right and left the colours of the well-known masters called.[20]

Still, as a contemporary put it, some people would have been just as happy at the zoo;[21] and by the 1880s 'the state of the salons' had become as vexed a question in German art centres as in Paris or London. (The *Art Journal*'s critic estimated that eight miles of pictures were hung in the 1886 Paris Salon.)[22] Buildings like the Munich Glaspalast accommodated thousands of items hung row on row almost to the ceilings, and huge canvases capable of making an impact in such surroundings were practically unsaleable except to governments, while smaller works were overwhelmed. Year after year painters felt obliged to show predictable 'salon specials' at the expense of their development; works which, in Lichtwark's opinion, were produced simply because the exhibitions existed.[23] Even commercially, despite their impressive-looking sales figures, the salons were inefficient. Between 1890 and 1894, for example, the proportion of works sold to those exhibited for sale in the Glaspalast ranged from approximately 12 to 24 per cent,[24] while for the more prosperous years from 1900 to 1908 Drey cited an annual average of 20.3 per cent.[25]

The vast size and uneven quality of the major salons was, as we have seen, one of the main issues dividing conservative and progressive artists in the late 1880s and 1890s, leading the secessions to mount much more selective, better spaced shows with a minimum of decorative clutter. This trend was further encouraged by the continuing fragmentation of the German art communities. As early as 1893 Ludwig Dill told the Munich City Council on the Secession's behalf that it was 'completely unthinkable to reunite the heterogeneous elements [of the art community] in one society'.[26] New small societies, ranging from the Munich Free Association of 1894 to the Phalanx, the New Artists' Association (*Neue Künstlervereinigung* (NKV)) and the New Secession after the turn of the century, aimed to exhibit the work of members or invited outsiders in hired premises or dealers' galleries. By 1900 even the Munich Artists' Guild had accepted the small group principle to the extent of allowing certain societies to organise separately juried sub-shows in the Glaspalast. In both Munich and Berlin, however, the distinction between the secessions and the older organisations remained, with the latter continuing to show bazaar-like assortments of pictures – a 'mass levy of regulars and territorials', as one guide-book put it[27] – varying enormously in quality, size and subject-matter.

One issue on which the secessions and the older organisations remained united was that of selection by jury, essentially a system by which established artists controlled access to an important market outlet. The problem was, of course, to prevent the main exhibitions from becoming ever more bloated as art production increased; in 1908, for example, a total of 4,445 paintings were shown in the Munich Glaspalast and the three exhibitions put on by the Secession, which rejected nearly 58 per cent of the works submitted (the previous year it had been two-thirds.)[28] Between 1898 and 1908 the Munich Art Union had rejected only some 15 per cent of the 90,684 items submitted to it, but undoubtedly at the cost of its exhibitions' quality. (Only 6.8 per cent of the 77,000 works shown found buyers.)[29] Although alternative arrangements such as quota systems were feasible for small groups, they were hardly practicable for the secessions, let alone for the mass organisations. As the numbers of artists rose the question became increasingly controversial, and formed the background to the foundation in Munich in 1909 of the German Artists' Confederation (*Deutscher Künstlerverband*), which aimed to mount un-juried exhibitions for its members.[30] Though strongly opposed by both Guild and Secession, it was supported by the city government, which made the municipal market-hall available for its exhibitions, the first of which, with 960 items, was held in 1910. The society attracted members from all over Germany, including Emil Nolde and Karl Schmidt-Rottluff, and a sizeable proportion of women, and remained active well into the First World War.

## DEALERS AND AUCTIONEERS

The intimate, harmonious quality of the secessions' exhibitions reflected the influence of the modern commercial galleries – Gurlitt and Schulte in Berlin, for example – which had hosted their precursors' shows, and with which the secessions themselves remained closely linked. In fact the art trade in its modern form was a more recent development in Germany than in countries like Britain, France or Holland. Although before 1800 there had been important private art collections in cities like Hamburg, Leipzig and Cologne,[31] and considerable demand for engravings, in the early nineteenth century there were only a few major German dealers: Boerner and Weigel in Leipzig, Prestel in Frankfurt-on-Main, Arnold in Dresden and Harzen and Commeter in Hamburg. The term 'art dealer' was often applied to people who sold paintings as a sideline alongside books, prints, artists' materials or other goods; in Munich in 1817, for example, Zeller's newly opened 'Establishment for Art and Industry' stocked pipes, boots, optical instruments and toys as well as pictures.[32] While the emerging middle-class picture market was dominated by the art unions until at least the middle of the century, princely patrons such as Ludwig I of Bavaria and Friedrich Wilhelm IV of Prussia used special agents to gather intelligence and negotiate purchases.[33] But economic expansion and improved communications from the 1850s onwards changed this situation. New names appeared such as Boehler and Heinemann in Munich, Lepke, Sachse and Amsler & Ruthardt in Berlin; established firms opened branches in promising new markets, for example Neumann of Vienna in Munich, Schulte of Cologne and Düsseldorf in Berlin; and book- and printsellers expanded into painting. (In minor centres this process took longer; Darmstadt in 1900, for example, still had no specialised dealers, though it had seven by 1910.)[34] A typical modern firm was E. A. Fleischmann in Munich.[35] Founded in 1806 to sell books, it entered the art trade on a modest scale in the 1860s, then opened a gallery and achieved a mass of sales throughout Germany and abroad. Royal patronage, and the parent company's publications, which included prestige works like Nagler's *Artists' Lexicon*, added to its fame. By 1896 it had sold 10,000 paintings – or 15,000 counting auctions – including many by such leading Munich School figures as Max (221), Grützner (*c.* 181), Defregger (154) and Diez (54), as well as celebrities outside Munich like Knaus, Vautier and the Achenbach brothers, and foreigners such as Corot, Bonheur, Israels and Rochegrosse. Similar was the gallery founded by the former painter David Heinemann and taken over by his sons Hermann and Theobald. They too specialised in German and particularly Munich conventional painting. But in 1907 they showed a group of Manets and Monets formerly owned by the Parisian collector Jean-Baptiste Faure, in 1911 sold two Van Goghs to a Berlin businessman and, as occasion arose, also dealt in work ranging from eighteenth-century British paintings to Japanese prints.[36] However, there was a significant distinction between dealers like the Heinemanns, who generally followed current demand, and those who, at least in some of their operations, aimed to promote unknown or controversial artists. A prime example of the latter in Berlin was Fritz Gurlitt, whose gallery was described by an acute French observer as the capital's 'only artistic business',[37] and who not only organised Germany's first Impressionist exhibition in 1883 but represented Klinger and Böcklin long before they became widely accepted.

By 1914 the German art trade was both large – the Munich address-book for that year included no fewer than 171 relevant entries – and extremely varied. At the top end of the market were long-established firms such as Ackermann, Heinemann, Drey, Boehler and Fleischmann, and newer ones like Thannhauser, Goltz and Brakl, whose elegant city-centre premises, accessible only to paying visitors, cultivated a highly exclusive atmosphere. In Berlin the Cassirer Gallery, opened in 1898, had an interior designed by van de Velde. Schulte, at Unter den Linden 1, was noted among other things for its official portraits and prevalence of uniforms, doubtless on its clients as well as on the walls.[38] (Association with controversial groups like the *XI* or *enfants terribles* like Munch – whose first Berlin dealer was Ugo Barroccio at Unter den Linden 16[39] – did not necessarily imply back-street status.) One of Berlin's most ambitious enterprises was Keller & Reiner, which opened at Potsdamerstrasse 122 in 1897 and was extended already the following year.[40] Although it incorporated a conventional picture-gallery, it also set out to show works of art in 'real' surroundings, in rooms decorated and furnished in the latest style by designers like van de Velde and Riemerschmid, and to supply customers with everything from carpets and vases to books in luxury bindings. Ultra-exclusive literary readings, one of which was described by the young Paula Becker in January 1901,[41] further raised the establishment's tone, and there was even a library with the latest art literature. In much of this, especially the presentation of ready-designed interiors, Keller & Reiner mirrored the modern applied-art exhibitions being held in cities like Dresden and Munich, and also set an example to department stores, some of which eventually opened art galleries of their own.

Lower down the scale the picture was more colourful. At the bottom were junk-dealers and flea-market stallholders – such as those in the Munich Au – where the alert buyer could find collectable drawings and studies, and perhaps the occasional Holbein, amid stacks of chromolithographs and discarded art union engravings. Like 'Old' Tanguy in Paris, framers and colourmen handled commission sales on the side, while some collectors occasionally doubled as dealers. As in seventeenth-century Delft or twentieth-century St Ives, so did some artists, like the Munich animal-painters Braith and Mali, who opened a gallery in the resort of Bozen in the South Tyrol.[42] There were also dealers, finally, who resisted the trend towards specialisation. Hermann Pächter, for example, a former Berlin brewer who became Menzel's principal dealer, handled paintings by Liebermann (with whom he had a contract for a time) and the French Impressionists, Japanese prints, and also weapons, Persian carpets, jewels, patent certificates and other rare and curious items.[43]

If dealers' backgrounds and interests varied greatly, so did their honesty. So-called 'flying' operators, some of them linked to shady picture-factories turning out stereotyped kitsch – the equivalent of today's Far Eastern imports – worked resorts and spas using various tricks to gull the public.[44] A series of sensational forgery trials in Munich in the mid-1890s revealed an underworld of junk-merchants, antique dealers, 'restorers' and failed painters working up stolen or discarded Lenbach studies into finished, signed and expensive paintings.[45] More worrying, as the defendants included respected names such as Heinemann and Ackermann (although they were ultimately acquitted), was the unclear boundary between criminals and mainstream dealers, and the multitude of accepted but often dubious and misleading trade practices that the trials exposed. In another Munich case in 1908 a large courtroom was piled high with fakes attributed to well-known artists.[46] One of the culprits, a barely literate former gravedigger, seems at first sight to have fitted the stereotype of the semi-criminal fringe dealer. Yet in addition to shipping bulk consignments of nudes to the King of Siam he handled mainstream products, and after leaving prison was back in business in high-class city-centre premises.[47] Whether honest or not, however, dealers in Germany clearly had an image problem for much of the period. Probably for many people the very notion of trading in something so 'ideal' as art was repugnant, and making any money was equivalent to profiteering. 'I would so like to convince you', wrote Paul Boerner to his friend Eduard Cichorius in 1866, 'that the interests of my collectors are more important to me than profit':[48] a pathetic statement in view of Boerner's years of dedication to Cichorius's collection. Anti-trade paranoia was rife: dealers, alleged one writer, cared as much about artists as coffee-merchants about plantation workers.[49] Anti-Semitism also played a role, given that many dealers were Jews, and it was perhaps significant that a 1913 advertisement for gallery staff stipulated Protestantism as well as commercial and linguistic skills.[50] But by the turn of the century dealers' regulatory role in the market-place, like that of literary and theatrical agents, seems to have been widely recognised. And sources like the Heinemann business archive, containing masses of data about clients, artists and prices, confirm the view of art-trade apologists like the dealer's son Drey that experienced dealers were commercially far more efficient than artists and their organisations and deserved their profits.[51] The increasing willingness of governments to buy from the trade also enhanced the latter's respectability. By 1914 not only the Heinemann brothers' elegant salon but also their close links with the Bavarian State Galleries and other museums, the bursaries they endowed at the Munich Academy, and the honours they received in return, proclaimed their membership of Imperial Germany's business elite.

Dealer–artist relationships varied considerably. Probably most common were commission-selling agreements and informal understandings of one kind or another which limited the dealer's risk but offered continuity to both parties. One example, perhaps, was the arrangement between the Heinemann Gallery and regular 'suppliers' like the flower-painter Marie Nyl, who sold 106 pictures through the firm between 1900 and 1914.[52] Another was that between Fleischmann on the one hand and Defregger and Grützner on the other, which began when the painters were still students in the late 1860s and lasted, as we have seen, for decades. By the turn of the century, if not earlier, more exclusive contracts were also being made. In September 1899, for instance, the Cassirers undertook to handle all of Max Slevogt's work except portraits (but they also offered to arrange portrait commissions), in return for a minimum annual income of 4,000 marks for three to four years,[53] and similar arrangements seem to have been made with Corinth, Barlach and Kokoschka later on. In April 1905 Wilhelm Suhr, proprietor of the Hamburg firm of Commeter, contracted to pay Munch 3,000 marks a year against sales of his paintings and drawings.[54] The dealer was assigned 25 per cent commission on sales he achieved in Germany, apart from Hamburg, and Austria; 15 per cent on Hamburg sales; and 15 per cent on transactions negotiated by Munch himself. But although Suhr arranged two large shows in Hamburg and sent consignments of pictures on tour every month, the contract was terminated prematurely after only two years. One reason for this was that Munch was a notoriously difficult character, although a bad experience with Bruno Cassirer over the sale of his prints encouraged him to distrust dealers.[55] But the ever-increasing complexity of the market, and artists' need to find as many outlets as possible, was doubtless also a factor. This certainly showed in the contract Kandinsky drafted in September 1912 between himself and the Munich dealer Hans Goltz.[56] Under its terms the painter was to have a one-man show two months later, and the right to two square metres of wall space in Goltz's gallery whenever he needed it for a period of five years. While Goltz was recognised as the artist's principal representative, with 25 per cent commission on Munich sales, the draft also attempted, as far as touring proceeds were concerned, to make complicated commission-sharing arrangements between him and Kandinsky's other dealer, Herwarth Walden in Berlin. Not surprisingly, the agreement soon broke down with recriminations on all sides, and the Munich exhibition, hosted by yet another gallery, was delayed until January 1914.

Another facet of the art trade's development was the increase of auctions.[57] Pre-1871 Germany's two leading auction houses, Boerner–Weigel in Leipzig, and Commeter, both specialised in prints, but newer firms responded to growing demand for precious objects of all kinds. In Munich Fleischmann moved into auctioneering, establishing itself with the 350,000 marks sale of the Salm-Reifferscheid collection of nineteenth-century paintings in 1888, and other six-figure yields in subsequent years.[58] Its rival Hugo Helbing, founded in 1885, eventually became one of south Germany's most important firms.[59] Gutekunst in Stuttgart for a time dominated the print market, its leisurely sales providing Lichtwark and other connoisseurs with happy days of bidding and gossip in the relaxed atmosphere of the Württemberg capital.[60] But Germany's most important firm, and the first to establish an international reputation, was that of Rudolph Lepke in Berlin, founded in 1853.[61] By the mid-1890s it was issuing an average of fifty catalogues a year, covering not only pictures but books, coins, furniture, porcelain and antiques of all kinds. Between 1909 and 1911 it auctioned the fabulous Lanna collection of applied art (the prints were sold by Gutekunst), that fetched record prices amid fiercely competitive bidding. In February 1912 the firm inaugurated its palatial new premises in the Potsdamerstrasse by selling the old masters of the Hamburg patrician Eduard Weber, an event which confirmed Berlin's position as a world-class auction centre. Like the trappings of successful ordinary dealers, Lepke's new building and lavish scholarly catalogues, whose excellence was praised by mandarins like Bode, symbolised the art trade's commercial and cultural respectability.

Although it is convenient to examine the different types of market outlet separately, there were actually many overlaps between them. Art unions often made lottery purchases at academy salons as well as at their own exhibitions; Friedrich's *Evening on the Baltic*, bought in Dresden by the Saxon Art Union in 1831, was an early example.[62] In 1836 the touring exhibitions of the art union circuits west and east of the Elbe included Düsseldorf works from that year's Berlin Academy salon, and in the late 1840s the Academy and the art unions shared the cost of sending pictures to Danzig and Königsberg.[63] Co-operation between art unions and dealers also became commonplace, with the latter regarding the former as useful talent pools. (Franz Marc's belief, expressed in June 1913, that 'if we [i. e. the Blue Rider group] can win over the *art unions* the benefit will be incalculable, especially the effect on the art dealers'[64] suggests that this still held good in the pre-war period.) Leipzig's second Art Union, founded in 1848, made all its lottery purchases from the del Vecchio Gallery, and by 1878 had spent nearly 220,000 marks there.[65] For a dealer trying to open up a new market the local art union was an obvious point of entry. In 1897, for example, the Gurlitt Gallery mounted a show of fifty-six Realist and other modern paintings at the Darmstadt *Kunstverein*.[66] In 1908 a large Van Gogh touring exhibition assembled by Paul Cassirer ended at the Frankfurt *Kunstverein*, and five years later the dealer not only opened a branch of his firm in Cologne but also became artistic director of the art union there, which was housed in the same building.[67] But in general successful dealers were on the look-out for novelty wherever it appeared. Schulte showed Munch's pictures in Düsseldorf and Cologne immediately after the 1892 scandal – whose main effect, Munch reported to his family, was to advertise his work[68] – and, as we have seen, snapped up the Worpswede painters after their 1895 triumph in Munich. The Gurlitt Gallery hosted Corinth and other renegades from the Munich Secession in 1894,[69] and the New Dachau School apparently had its first group show with Keller & Reiner in 1898.[70] Cassirer's intimate relationship with the Berlin Secession, of which he actually became president in 1912, was one of the most fruitful associations of the entire period, giving the artists the benefit of Cassirer's formidable business skills, and letting the dealer share the society's aura of heroic altruism.[71]

## BUYERS

It is generally much easier to find detailed information about market institutions than about the people who acquired pictures; although the Heinemann archive, covering the period from about 1900 to the 1930s, lists thousands of German and foreign clients – from small-scale occasional buyers to industrialists who spent fortunes on whole galleries of pictures – together with the works they bought and the prices they paid. Contemporary commentators were agreed that large holdings of modern (post-1800) and contemporary German art were rare before the turn of the century, and handbooks showed that collections of Oriental art, weapons, coins and old master, especially Dutch, paintings were much more common.[72] (In 1912 Lichtwark deplored pre-1900 Germany's lack of a non-dynastic collecting culture, and especially the neglect of early-nineteenth-century painters.)[73] The modern private galleries that did exist are mostly well documented, often in lavish catalogues produced by their owners or by auction houses. But a broader picture of art ownership in Germany can only be constructed from a jumble of disparate sources: artists' letters, sale reports, lists of museum donors and the catalogues of exhibitions like the Menzel memorial show of 1905 and the Century of German Art (1775-1875) Exhibition of 1906.

A high proportion of the pictures painted by German-based artists between the 1850s and 1914 were acquired, as almost obligatory status-symbols, by small-scale buyers and art union lottery-winners. The art union movement's journal, the *Deutsche Kunstblatt*, exhorted in 1855: 'Just as the well-appointed house should have its musical gathering-point, the piano, and the glass-fronted bookcase should harbour its favourite poets, so its walls must show that the visual arts are alive and at home with us.'[74] Probably tens of thousands of middle-class Germans acknowledged this imperative by paying out the quite small sums necessary, at art-union prices, to buy at least one or two original canvases. A more affluent and committed stratum of buyers would have included those who acquired Karl Spitzweg's pictures before the price-rise following the painter's death in 1885,[75] Heinemann's humbler clients, and the pathetic band of officials, retired officers and others who paid substantial sums for fake Lenbachs, Defreggers and Böcklins.[76] No doubt many collections too small to appear in the handbooks, like that of the Leipzig physician A. Ulrich, who bought three major Corinth paintings in 1898-99,[77] contained items of significant quality. Some collectors belonged to the art and literary communities: in Munich, for example, in addition to numerous painters, the writer Paul Heyse, the stained-glass designer Carl de Bouché and the sculptor Wilhelm von Rümann; and the dramatist Weigand, who owned important German Realist paintings and prints by Klinger and Greiner.[78] During the Wilhelmine period medium-sized private collections clearly began to multiply. In 1907, for example, the Saxon Art Union in Dresden organised an exhibition of 400 modern works, most of them bought in the previous twenty years, lent by some sixty local owners, and could easily have assembled twice the number.[79]

One of the few major collectors of modern art in Germany before the 1860s was Joachim Wagener, whose pictures, as we have seen, eventually became the nucleus of the National Gallery. Wagener's fellow-Berliner, the iron-merchant Louis Ravené, assembled a modern gallery in the 1850s which, expanded by his heirs, was still one of the sights of the city in the 1900s.[80] A third important but isolated mid-nineteenth-century figure was the Mecklenburg nobleman, poet and Orientalist Count Adolf Friedrich von Schack. After settling in Munich in 1857 he created a collection that was eventually dominated by works – both bought and commissioned – by Schwind, Lenbach, Böcklin, Hans von Marées and Anselm Feuerbach, most of whom were still unrecognised.[81] The gallery contained no French work, which the Count considered greatly overrated, and no original old masters (though a number of specially commissioned copies). Although Schack was a dedicated collector, artists often found his difficult, demanding and tight-fisted behaviour tolerable only because, in the 1850s and 1860s, no alternatives were available. 'He paid miserable prices,' recalled Lenbach later,

> but he was the only one who paid anything at all; and although every artist who had dealings with him at one time or another had reason to be resentful towards him, one should never forget that he and he alone opened his wallet at a time when all other rich men kept theirs closed, and would have calmly looked on while people like Arnold Böcklin, Anselm Feuerbach and others dedicated themselves to stone-breaking or some similarly healthy but not very lucrative occupation.[82]

The collection became accessible to the public in 1865, was practically complete a decade later, and on Schack's death in 1894 was bequeathed to Emperor Wilhelm II. With uncharacteristic sensitivity, and to the disgust of the Prussian National Art Commission, Wilhelm allowed it to stay in Munich, where it remained a popular tourist attraction. Its quaintness as a showcase of 'poetic' narrative painting, detached from the mainstream of increasingly French-influenced naturalism, was conveyed with Gallic scorn by the journalist Jules Huret, who described it in 1911 as ' . . . nothing but an old romantic attic in which mediocre German painters rub shoulders with each other amid discarded Italian bric-à-brac'.[83]

The upswing of the central European economy in the 1860s and 1870s rapidly stimulated luxury spending. Contemporary painters were not the only beneficiaries of this, since art from many periods and cultures found its way into the lavish new residences of Berlin and other cities. Buyers' motives undoubtedly varied. The Lenbach portraits of Bismarck and Wilhelm I commissioned by Gerson Bleichroeder for his marble-clad mansion in the capital,[84] the trainloads of pictures needed to fill Silesian coal-millionaires' castles[85] and the uninspiring old master gallery in the Krupps's Villa Hügel near Essen[86] arguably reflected representational needs rather than a passion for beauty. Aesthetically more engaged, perhaps, was the railway magnate Bethel Henry Strousberg, owner of Liebermann's *Goose-Pluckers*, although this and his other pictures soon came under the hammer after his bankruptcy in 1875.[87] The Berlin stockbroker Adolf von Liebermann assembled two successive collections and for a time owned Menzel's *Rolling-Mill*.[88] An exceptionally fine gallery, to which Lichtwark paid enthusiastic tribute on its owner's death in 1902, was that of the Hamburg banker Eduard Behrens,[89] containing prime examples of German salon work, seven Menzels, including the intricately detailed *Paris Street Scene* of 1869 and, virtually obligatory for a 'blue chip' collection of the time, pictures by Corot, Daubigny and other masters of the Barbizon School.

Three other, less orthodox galleries reflected personal relationships between collectors and artists. The earliest belonged to the Worms industrialist Maximilian von Heyl, who in 1890 moved to Darmstadt to occupy an elegant neo-Renaissance mansion, the Heylshof, built for him by the Munich architect Gabriel von Seidl.[90] The von Heyl gallery was large, rich and eclectic, including works of many periods acquired during its owner's travels throughout Europe. The modern part of the collection – which, like Schack's, contained no French works – was shaped by von Heyl's friendship with three pillars of the 1870s Munich art scene, Lenbach, Fritz Kaulbach and the architect Lorenz (husband of Mina) Gedon. The two painters not only contributed a number of portraits, including one of Lenbach's best portraits of Bismarck, but probably also introduced von Heyl to Böcklin, who was eventually represented in the Heylshof by fifteen paintings, including the powerful *Prometheus Landscape* and numerous drawings. A second notable collection was that of the Berlin dealer–*amateur* Ernst Seeger, who became Leibl's friend and patron in the five years before his death in 1900.[91] Buying just before the artist's prices began to soar, Seeger came to own twenty-five major works which, after his own death in 1911, were acquired, by purchase or donation, by the Wallraff–Richartz Museum. Much larger and more varied were the holdings of the Munich publisher Thomas Knorr, who shared his business partner and neighbour Georg Hirth's enthusiasm for the unconventional and provocative.[92] He bought Slevogt's controversial *Danaë*-as-prostitute, but also works by Makart, the Realists, the Munich Secession, the Glasgow Boys, fashionable French contemporaries like Jacques Emile Blanche, and Toulouse-Lautrec.

Finally, in a class by itself, was the collection of Prince Luitpold of Bavaria, who spent almost 900,000 marks of his private fortune on it between the early 1850s and his death in 1912.[93] Although Luitpold was never a patron on the scale of his father Ludwig I, pictures, like hunting, were among his greatest passions, and he was clearly as keen to see a Monet show at the Phalanx Society as he was to inspect the annual parade in the Glaspalast.[94] He bought from the Munich Art Union throughout his adult life and in cash terms was Munich's most important collector. Between 1890 and 1894 alone, for example, he spent 92,050 marks at the Glaspalast, equivalent to almost 4 per cent of the total turnover of the exhibitions.[95] His taste was eclectic, extending even to Japanese art, although his local purchasing decisions were often influenced by friendship. An inventory compiled after his death listed 529 items, mostly by Munich artists, including 108 animal or hunting pictures, 185 landscapes, architectural pieces and interiors, 122 genre scenes, 7 religious works, 42 still lifes, 9 battle paintings and 56 portraits. The painters ranged from the genre specialist Wilhelm Marc to Max Slevogt, son of one of Luitpold's old army comrades, with a broad selection of major and minor figures from both the Artists' Guild and the Secession.

## INTEGRATION

It is clear that by the middle of the nineteenth century, at the latest, it would have been impossible for the expanding art communities of cities like Dresden, Düsseldorf and Munich to have sustained themselves by local sales alone. (Berlin, increasingly, was in a class by itself.) The Munich population's platonic attitude to art was almost proverbial, and of almost three million marks spent at major Glaspalast shows between 1889 and 1894 less than one-tenth came from private local residents.[96] After 1900, as already suggested, an influx of well-off new residents probably helped to redress the balance, and the Heinemann archive recorded many actual and potential local clients. But it remained true that national and international integration of the market, allowing maximum mobility for products and buyers alike, was vitally important, even for star portraitists like Lenbach, Kaulbach and Stuck, many of whose clients came from other parts of Germany and abroad.

The foundations of an integrated market had been laid by the art unions. The Hamburg society's very first show in April–May 1826, comprising ninety works, included not only pictures by Friedrich and Dahl in Dresden – doubtless sent by boat down the Elbe – but a fresco cartoon by the Nazarene Johann Friedrich Overbeck in Rome.[97] In the late 1830s the associated art unions of Halberstadt, Magdeburg, Hanover, Brunswick and Halle were showing pictures from all the major German centres, and from the Low Countries, Switzerland and France.[98] Of the 194 artists who exhibited at the Hamburg *Kunstverein*'s spring show in 1846, 33 were from Düsseldorf, 32 from Munich, 23 from Berlin, 9 from Dresden and 4 from Frankfurt, with others from Vienna, Geneva, Paris, Brussels and towns in Holland.[99] The far-flung membership of the larger societies was giving wide exposure to German art by this time: in 1835, for instance, Friedrich's *Memories of the Riesengebirge* was raffled from Dresden to P. Durnovo in St Petersburg;[100] one of the winners of the 1849 Munich lottery was Tsar Nicholas I;[101] and the same year twelve of the fifty-one winning members of the Rhenish–Westphalian Art Union lived in the United States.[102] Later, artists' salons also became increasingly international in scope. The 1869 Munich International Exhibition included works from America as well as France, and the 'universal expositions' in Paris (1867, 1878, 1889 and 1900), Philadelphia (1876), Sydney (1879), Chicago (1893), St Louis (1904) and San Francisco (1915) all had German participants, as did major shows in Italy, Spain and Latin America and, by the turn of the century, regular international salons like the Venice Biennale (from 1895) and the exhibitions at the Carnegie Institute in Pittsburgh.[103] Dealers both exploited and extended this network. David Heinemann, for example, ran a '*palais des beaux-arts*' in Nice and mounted exhibitions in other German cities, Switzerland and London (at the Grafton Gallery) in addition to his main operation in Munich,[104] and by 1914 his firm had huge numbers of clients and dealer-associates in Europe, the Middle East and the United States. In its first twenty-five years of dealing Fleischmann sold at least a quarter of its pictures abroad.[105] Finally, as we shall see, collaboration between German and French dealers helped to bring Impressionism to Germany, and foreigners contributed substantially to the fortunes of the avant-garde.

By the middle of the nineteenth century the economics of art in Germany was being significantly influenced by tourism.[106] Its earliest effects were probably felt in Düsseldorf and the Rhineland, where from the 1820s onwards steamer travel, guidebooks and eventually package tours created one of Europe's classic tourist clichés. Dresden and the Elbe Valley, as already noted, drew increasing numbers of visitors as communications improved. Munich became important in the last third of the nineteenth century, thanks to local health and sanitary improvements and to the completion of the long-distance European rail network, which placed it at the intersection of two great transport axes, from Paris to the Near East and from north-central Europe and Scandinavia to Italy.[107] (North-south travel had been revolutionised by the completion of the Brenner line over the Alps in 1867.) Other Bavarian attractions included mountaineering and eventually winter sports, the decennial Passion Play at Oberammergau, which received its first Cook's tour in 1880, and Ludwig II's castles, opened to visitors soon after his death in 1886. By the eve of the First World War, when Munich itself was receiving over half a million staying visitors a year,[108] a network of local rail and bus routes had turned southern Bavaria into a travel 'package' which could be sold by Cook, Lunn and their competitors in conjunction with tours in eastern Switzerland and the Tyrol.[109] This was the background for Regency Munich's visitor-orientated development plans and for the major cultural projects of the period, from the annual international salons launched in 1889 to the Mozart and Wagner festivals at the Prince Regent Theatre. These were aimed unequivocally – tickets for the *Ring* cost over 100 marks in 1913[110] – at the same international clientele which travelled on the Orient or the Egypt Express, alighted at the *Vier Jahreszeiten* and patronised the city's most exclusive shops and galleries.

Exhibition sales figures and museum statistics illuminate only one aspect of the complex relationship between art and tourism. Both before and after 1850, some of the earliest visitors to the new 'landscapes of leisure' of Germany, Austria and Switzerland were artists, who sometimes risked life and limb to capture images of dramatic weather and scenery that in turn undoubtedly stimulated travel. Especially important in the late nineteenth century, at least for German tourists, were family journals like *Die Gartenlaube*, whose middle-class readers were increasingly in a position to take holidays away from home.[111] By the mid-eighties, when its circulation was nearing 250,000, the *Gartenlaube* alone was publishing hundreds of tourism-related items every year: reproductions of paintings by Defregger, Raupp and other genre specialists, articles and novels by the young Ludwig Ganghofer and travel pieces by popular topographers like Max Haushofer. A classic of its kind was an 1885 feature on the Paznaun Valley in the Northern Tyrol with illustrations by a longstanding *Gartenlaube* contributor and native of the region, Matthias Schmid.[112] On the eve of its penetration by the new Arlberg railway, the area was described in brochure-like terms as an idyllic spot with stunning views, poor but industrious inhabitants, picturesque skirmishes between gendarmes and smugglers, and a liberal innkeeper/postmaster defying clerical harassment. Prospective bourgeois visitors were also reassured about the absence of beggars and 'the feeling for order and cleanliness that is noticeable everywhere'. Other passages about the clear air, peaceful atmosphere and nocturnal stillness broken only by bird-cries and the sound of the River Trisanna, now read like a subliminal indictment of tourists' urban habitat. Similar material, published in huge quantities in books and periodicals, continued to feed the tourist industry for decades, and by the 1900s artists were also illustrating guide-books and, like the Anglo–Bavarian alpine landscapist Edward Compton, contributing to the publicity campaigns mounted by local authorities, private pressure groups and State railways.[113]

Many visitors to the beauty-spots of Bavaria and Saxony came from other parts of Germany, especially Berlin and the industrial cities of the north-west. Descriptions of resorts like Partenkirchen as 'Kurfürstendamm in costume'[114] and the emergence of the brash Berliner in department-store *Lederhosen* as a stock figure of fun reflected both ritual anti-Prussianism and economic reality: some 9.2 per cent of overnight visitors to Munich between 1 April 1913 and 31 March 1914 came from in and around Berlin.[115] (Another 35 per cent came from elsewhere in Germany, excluding Bavaria.) Tourism statistics, which only began to be gathered systematically just before the war, do not coincide with detailed figures available for exhibition sales, but some congruence can be assumed. At any rate, about one-third of the money spent at the Glaspalast between 1889 and 1894 was spent by Germans living outside the Bavarian capital.[116] Another important group (11.6 per cent) of visitors to Munich in 1913-14 came, not surprisingly, from Austria–Hungary. Their compatriots had spent 8.3 per cent of the Glaspalast purchase-money in 1889-94 and, according to Drey, the Habsburg Empire absorbed easily the largest share (21.2 per cent by value) of all German art exports between 1900 and 1908.[117]

The British were probably the first sizeable group of foreign visitors after the end of the Napoleonic Wars, and continued to come, thanks partly to entrepreneurs like Cook, in significant numbers until 1914. Anna Howitt's pilgrimage to Munich in 1850 to experience the 'unbounded imagination, philosophic thought and studious research' of Wilhelm von Kaulbach's art was probably a late consequence of Nazarene influence in England.[118] But although by the 1860s the term *Engländer* was apparently synonymous with 'wealthy art-lover',[119] hard evidence of British buying is patchy. While working in the Rhineland in the 1870s and 1880s, for example, the Scottish railway entrepreneur James Staats Forbes added German pictures to his large collection of European art,[120] and in the same period London's fashionable French Gallery was clearly an important showcase for contemporary Munich painting.[121] In the 1880s Hans Thoma found more buyers in Liverpool and Manchester than in Germany.[122] Sale-room evidence, however, suggests that British collectors generally favoured French salon painters and Hague School artists like Israels and Mauve much more than their German counterparts.[123]

Of greater concern than exports to Britain by the turn of the century were those to the United States. This was because the American presence on the German market had earlier been very large, but had subsequently declined with painful consequences for artists. Although the Munich landscape and genre specialist Heinrich Bürkel had made the first of many transatlantic sales as early as 1839,[124] it seems to have been about another decade before American buying began to have a major impact. By 1853 the *Deutsche Kunstblatt* was complaining that American (and British) 'speculators' were buying up too many 'pearls of German artistic genius . . . as though [the pictures] were weary of Europe and homeless on German soil'.[125] In the background was the sizeable American membership of organisations like the Rhenish–Westphalian Art Union and the existence of a lively export trade from Düsseldorf to New York. The latter owed its success partly to the contacts created by Leutze and other 'Düsseldorf Americans', but mainly to the efforts of the German-American wine merchant John Godfrey (Johann Gottfried) Boker, who had emigrated from Remscheid before 1825, later served as American Consul in Düsseldorf, and in 1849 opened a gallery of Düsseldorf paintings on New York's Broadway.[126] In 1850 he also tried to launch a German–American Art Union which would distribute selected German pictures by lottery to American subscribers.[127] Although this project came to nothing, the Düsseldorf Gallery prospered and continued to import new works: in 1851, for example, Lessing's huge *Martyrdom of Hus*, for which Boker paid 10,000 thalers ($7,500).[128] Financial difficulties in the late 1850s, however, Boker's death in 1860, and then the Civil War eventually ended its operations.

The huge post-Civil War upswing of the American economy stimulated both travel to Europe and demand for works of art. Americans were much in evidence both at the Paris Exhibition of 1867 and the Munich one of 1869: as the *Art Journal* noted, 'the Americans especially think that a Munich picture is a fine sort of thing to carry home, and they are quite right'.[129] Munich dealers opened branches in the United States, especially New York, and Wimmer–Humpelmayr fixed English-language labels to pictures as a matter of course.[130] Transatlantic buyers accounted for 19 per cent of the money spent at the 1879 International Exhibition and an astonishing 31 per cent in 1883.[131]

But that year brought what was widely perceived as a body-blow for German artists: the raising of the US art-import tariff from 10 to 30 per cent. Protests were fruitless and, apart from a tariff-free interlude in 1894-97, the duty remained – at least for recent work – at between 15 and 30 per cent until a campaign led by the New York collector John Quinn finally led to its abolition in the autumn of 1913.[132] Another long-term problem was the continuing shift of American interest to Paris. In the 1880s the Barbizon craze, especially in the New York–Boston–Philadelphia 'triangle', continued to generate record prices, Durand-Ruel sent his first Impressionist paintings to America, and millionaires vied for works by Meissonnier, Bonheur and Breton.[133] The Columbian World's Exposition in Chicago in 1893 demonstrated France's strong influence on American taste. Nevertheless, American spending on German art remained significant throughout the Belle Époque. Between 1889 and 1894, for example,

Americans still accounted for an average of over 15 per cent of expenditure at the Munich Glaspalast, although this figure conceals a variation between 30 per cent (143,810 marks) in 1889 and a mere 1.7 per cent (6,600 marks) in 1893, when both the Chicago Exposition and a financial crash kept many Americans at home.[134] But the uncertain future of the American market clearly unsettled the German art world and especially Munich where, together with the challenge from Berlin, it was one of the key themes of the Secession's manifesto of June 1892.

By 1900 'recapturing the American market' had become a prominent issue in German cultural politics. But it was also complicated by disputes between the secessions and the ADKG, aggravated by the interventions of Wilhelm II. One consequence was the furore over German participation in the Saint Louis International Exposition of 1904, when the decision of the emperor, egged on by Werner, to overrule his officials and reaffirm the ADKG's sole right to organise exhibitions abroad provoked a virtual boycott by the secessions, the creation of the rival (Secessionist) German Artists' League and an outcry in the Reichstag.[135] The experience – like the Lex Heinze episode a few years previously – was so bruising for the State bureaucracy that for the next decade it remained reluctant to become directly involved in the promotion of German art abroad. This stance was illustrated by the exhibition of some 150 items of painting and sculpture held at the Metropolitan Museum in New York, the Art Institute of Chicago and in Boston in 1909.[136] The project in fact involved the collaboration of Bode and other German officials on both sides of the Atlantic and even the loan of works owned by Wilhelm II. But its organisation and funding (costs eventually reached 150,000 marks) were the responsibility of the German-American businessman Hugo Reisinger, who was rewarded in due course with both Prussian and Bavarian decorations. The tour's unofficial status made it possible to include work from both sides of the art-political divide, to keep the ADKG at arm's length, and thus to avoid another fiasco *à la* Saint Louis. (German participation in the Rome International Exhibition of 1911 also seems to have bypassed the ADKG.)[137]

In the background was what the German Trade Attaché in New York had described in a memorandum of July 1907 (the latest of several since 1900)[138] as the 'highly unsatisfactory' level of German art exports to the United States, the overwhelming preponderance of French art – in 1906, 57.2 per cent of US imports, compared with 5.1 per cent from Germany – and the perception that most Americans regarded 'us Germans as art barbarians'.[139] In fact officials were pessimistic about the chances of improving sales, and regarded art mainly as a vehicle for general cultural propaganda. But artists and their organisations remained fixated on America as, in the words of a parliamentarian in 1904, 'the main art market of the future'.[140] This was understandable. Indeed, although by 1913 ultra-sophisticated Americans were fascinated by the Armory Show, and the rich and fashionable had long been buying Impressionism, first-generation provincial art-lovers – successors of the 'Giottos of Griggsville [Illinois]' who had fêted Oscar Wilde on his 1882 lecture tour[141] – and inhabitants of the new cities of the Mid– and far west probably constituted a vast potential market for conventional art: if not exactly the salon fare of the 1880s, then certainly the kind of *juste milieu* Secessionism in evidence in Reisinger's 1909 touring show and at venues like the Carnegie Institute salons.

After 1900 Munich continued to have easily the largest share of Germany's transatlantic art exports, in 1907, for example, 76.1 per cent by value.[142] Between that year and 1913, according to official statistics, 7,752,331 marks' ($1,824,078) worth of oil paintings were cleared through the city's United States consulate.[143] Not all exported works, of course, were by living or local artists, and the abolition in 1909 of duty on pictures over twenty years old boosted sales of older work at the expense of the new.[144] Nevertheless, painters probably continued to enjoy substantial dollar earnings until exports finally dried up in about 1915. In the winter of 1905/06 Kaulbach painted three members of the Rockefeller family, supposedly for the fabulous sum of 150,000 marks,[145] and Stuck, now approaching middle age, found American commissions helpful in maintaining his opulent lifestyle. Dealers also did well. The Heinemann Gallery, for example, which had clients and contacts in more than forty American towns and cities by 1914, earned handsomely from transatlantic sales. A random selection from its archive includes dealings with Emil Blatz of Milwaukee (41,950 marks for 16 items in 1903); the film magnate Carl Laemmle (600 marks for 2 pictures, 1908-09) and another Chicago collector, C. M. Hewitt (142,608 marks for 20 pictures, 1902-12); Seymour H. Knox in Buffalo (23,375 marks for 2 paintings in 1907); and two New Yorkers, Hugo Reisinger (39,000 marks for a Manet and 8 other pictures between 1900 and 1909) and Henry Goldman (67,000 marks for Lenbach portraits of Bismarck and Mommsen in 1913).[146]

Despite the tiny contribution made by paintings to Germany's total export earnings – in 1907, for example, a mere 0.15 per cent[147] – the international traffic in art aroused strong passions. On the one hand, great efforts were made before 1914 to increase foreign sales and open up new markets, both for profit and to enhance Germany's cultural influence. The Society for German Art Abroad (*Gesellschaft für deutsche Kunst im Auslande*), for example, founded at the end of 1908, took on both tasks.[148] By 1911 it had nearly 600 members – including 15 art unions and the ADKG – about half of whom were artists, and its committee, though chaired by a painter, included Bode and assorted notables like the President of the Prussian Central Land Bank, the Chairman of the German South American Society and Field Marshal Colmar von der Goltz. Through exhibitions, lectures and publications it boosted German picture sales and secured monument commissions in a number of South American countries. It also received State subsidies, and indeed was just the kind of establishment-dominated but private body whose activities officials liked to support. On the other hand, however, strong reservations were expressed about artistic commerce with other nations. The issue of imports, especially from France, was, as we have seen, controversial long before Vinnen's *Protest*: in 1892, for instance, Friedrich Pecht had crabbily declined to support the VI. Munich International Exhibition's guarantee fund and thus 'to inflict yet more foreign competitors on our art comrades here'.[149] But concern also about 'excessive' art exports went back at least to the 1850s and the campaign to create the Historical Art League. Half a century later the idea that cultural production was a kind of vital substance which should not be dispersed abroad was still potent, and in 1909 Lichtwark not only attacked the Society for German Art Abroad but declared that exporting Germany's best work would be tantamount to treason.[150] Fortunately, he added, only second-rate pictures had crossed the Atlantic in the previous century, for 'where would we be if we had lost the best Menzels, Böcklins, Leibls, Thomas, Schwinds, Feuerbachs to the Americans?' Three years later he pronounced again: 'The great deeds of visual artists . . . have the same transforming effect as Goethe's *Faust* or Mozart's *Figaro*. Thus for a people to retain possession of the works of its great painters and sculptors is a matter of national existence.'[151]

## PRICES AND PATRONAGE

Another important characteristic of the period from 1850 to 1914 was rising prices. 'One fact is indisputable,' wrote Julius Meier-Graefe in the first of three articles on the art trade published in 1913, 'inflation in the art market. Values are going up like balloons. And values in every area: pictures, sculptures, carpets, tapestries, furniture, ornaments; Europe, China, Japan.'[152] Two years earlier Tschudi had commented that would-be collectors of old masters, even American multi-millionaires, needed to 'reach to the ceiling'.[153] Whereas in 1865, for example, the Dresden Royal Gallery had acquired Dürer's *Christ on the Cross* for the equivalent of 6,000 marks,[154] on the eve of the war Meier-Graefe could cite numerous instances of six-figure sums for individual pictures. Rembrandt's prices had soared – in 1905 the Städel Institute had paid 336,000 marks for his *Blinding of Samson*[155] – and by 1914 good-quality Dutch landscapes and genre scenes were affordable only by the very rich.[156] Artists whose work had long been neglected, like Goya, or practically forgotten, like El Greco, were now being lucratively promoted by dealers like Durand-Ruel.

For modern work the picture was more varied and more difficult, now, to reconstruct. Lists of prices realised at auctions, published in *Die Kunstchronik* from the 1860s onwards and later, voluminously, in specialist journals like *Der Kunstmarkt* (1903) and *Der Cicerone* (1909), are an important source. They certainly helped dealers to navigate the market, and for artists like Defregger, Knaus or Grützner, whose subjects, popularity and creative powers remained consistent over decades, they probably corresponded quite closely to 'studio-door' prices for current work. But for many other artists this was not the case, and one must guess, and guess cautiously, about remuneration. 'The number of artists of whom one knows that they actually get the prices they ask', commented Lichtwark in 1909, 'is astonishingly small in Germany.'[157] The papers of well-informed figures like Munich Secession President Hugo von Habermann indicate that a combination of economic need, tight-fisted buyers and turnover-conscious salon managers often forced even established artists to accept knock-down prices.[158]

Three of German-speaking Europe's most highly valued painters, who died within a few years of each other near the turn of the century, were Böcklin, Menzel and Leibl. Between 1893 and his death in 1901 Böcklin earned 256,000 marks from sales, at an average price per canvas of 16,000 marks: four times as much as in the decade 1874-85 preceding his breakthrough.[159] (Around 1900, by way of comparison, it cost from 30,000 to 60,000 marks to build a one-family villa in Blankenese or Gross-Flottbek near Hamburg.)[160] In 1901 his *Sea Idyll* (1887) went to the New Gallery in Vienna for the enormous sum of 100,000 marks and his prices, despite the attacks of writers like Meier-Graefe, remained very high for the rest of the pre-war period. In 1911 the Berlin National Gallery paid at least 180,000 marks for one of his watery fantasies, *Triton and Sea-Nymph*, which the LKK had refused to buy for 16,000 marks in 1876.[161] Menzel when he died in 1905 was also at the very top of the scale, his prices further inflated by the special purchasing fund for his work created by Wilhelm II and the Prussian State. Thus in 1906 and 1907 Tschudi could pay 160,000 marks for *Supper at the Ball* and, respectively, 165,000 marks and 95,000 marks for two much earlier pictures, *Garden of the Prince-Albrecht-Palais* (1846-76), and *Théâtre du Gymnase* (1856).[162] In 1883 Leibl had sold *Three Women in Church* to a private collector in Worms for 40,000 marks:[163] much less than he had expected for his years of labour, but still remarkable for a non-academic painting of that time, and far more than Leibl received for other pictures in his lifetime. (Knaus's conventional *Hessian Funeral* of 1871 had originally fetched 60,000 marks.)[164] But growing appreciation of Realism by the time of his death in 1900 meant that museums or their benefactors soon had to pay huge prices for his best works: for example, 112,000 marks for *Three Women* by the Hamburg Kunsthalle in 1906, and 180,000 marks for *Frau Gedon* for the Neue Pinakothek in 1911.[165] That year the Wallraff–Richartz Museum paid over a million marks for a dozen or so of the Leibl paintings formerly owned by Ernst Seeger (others were presented by private donors).[166]

Other Realists lived to enjoy their rise in status. In 1910, for example, the Berlin National Gallery paid 25,000 marks for Trübner's *Portrait of Mayor Hofmeister* (1872) and by this time, according to Meier-Graefe, his other works of the 1870s were fetching comparable five-figure sums. More important for the artist, since there was no *droit de suite* in Germany, was the success of his current work, and the Bremen Kunsthalle paid 20,000 marks for a 1910 landscape.[167] Liebermann was probably Wilhelmine Germany's top-earning artist, although partly through print sales. The Hamburg Kunsthalle paid 60,000 marks for the notorious *Young Jesus in the Temple* (1879) in 1911, while Cassirer was asking from 15,000 to 25,000 marks apiece for new paintings.[168] Such rewards, however, were far above the norm. In 1910 Drey cited between 200 and 1,000 marks as the going rate for 'good' pictures, and 1,000 to 10,000 marks for 'very good' ones.[169] Munch was undoubtedly getting four-figure prices by the time he was honoured with a room to himself at the 1912 *Sonderbund* show. But between 1903 and 1906 he had sold two paintings to Gustav Schiefler for 750 marks, done a head-and-shoulders portrait of Count Kessler for 400 marks, and painted the physicist Felix Auerbach in Weimar for 500 marks.[170] Even for an eminent mainstream figure like Habermann, obtaining 5,000 marks – minus commission – for a picture was a notable achievement, although a couple of such sales a year would have meant a comfortable income. (In 1912 a white-collar Siemens employee earned 2,620 marks a year;[171] the janitor of the Munich Glaspalast, after ten years' service, 1,800 marks, and the rector of a Bavarian humanistic *Gymnasium* with equal seniority, 8,700 marks.)[172] The many painters whose outlets were art unions or back-street dealers would have reckoned their prices in tens or hundreds of marks rather than thousands.

The reasons for the rising cost (much faster than general inflation) of 'classic' art, both pre-1800 and modern, are clear enough: economic expansion and the growth of affluence; increased public awareness of art as museums became more accessible, journals proliferated and reproduction methods improved; and more opportunities to acquire it as the art trade developed and great aristocratic collections came on the market. Another conspicuous inflationary influence by the turn of the century was the activity of American buyers, animated by dealers like Knoedler and Duveen. *Kunst und Künstler*'s very first article was a complaint by the otherwise rather pro-American Wilhelm von Bode about the apparent distortion of the market by a new generation of super-collectors like J. P. Morgan.[173] Seven years later, after the abolition of US import duty on older art, Bode cited a string of old master prices in excess of one million marks and reiterated his argument that European galleries were quite unable to compete except in fields still unexplored or unfashionable across the Atlantic, at least from their regular funds.[174]

An area in which Americans had a big influence on prices was modern French art and particularly, from the late 1880s onwards, Impressionism.[175] The pre-war climax of this development came at the Rouart sale in Paris in December 1912, when Degas's *Dancers Practising at the Bar*, for which the artist had originally received less than 500 francs, was sold to Durand-Ruel, for Harry and Louisine Havemeyer, for $95,700 (401,940 marks).[176] But from the late 1890s German museums and private collectors had also been reinforcing this trend. At least ten works by Manet and Monet from the Faure collection, for example, found their way to Hamburg and Berlin.[177] Lichtwark, in Paris with a crowd of his compatriots for the Rouart sale, wrote: 'The prices of French pictures are today mainly pushed upwards by German [museum] directors and dealers.'[178] (Afterwards, Lichtwark was glad to secure Renoir's large and rather grimy *Riders in the Bois de Boulogne*, which had hung on Henri Rouart's staircase, for the Kunsthalle for 90,000 marks.)[179] In March 1911, vainly attempting to get special funds from the Bavarian State for a 'shopping list' of French art since David, Tschudi had compiled a 'tariff' for prime works by painters including Monet (60,000 marks), Renoir (100,000 marks), Degas (100,000 marks) and Cézanne (50,000 marks).[180] He put Manet at 280,000 marks, only 40,000 marks more than the price of *Breakfast in the Studio*, which was presented to the Neue Pinakothek later that year.[181]

Museums' regular acquisition funds were wholly inadequate in this situation. In Bavaria the annual recurrent grant of 30,000 marks for old masters and 90,000 marks for modern painting and sculpture remained static from the turn of the century until 1914.[182] In Saxony the financial buoyancy of the 1870s and 1880s gave way to stringency later on, and in 1910 the Dresden Royal Gallery could afford only one painting out of its recurrent budget.[183] The pinch was felt even in Prussia, where in 1913 over a fifth of ordinary State spending on art and science was devoted to the Berlin museums.[184] Although the total regular funds spent on them had risen nearly threefold since 1876 their personnel costs had grown almost fivefold, and their acquisition funds, on average, by only about half. The National Gallery's purchasing budget rose by somewhat less than a third, and it also received a smaller share than other institutions of the substantial extraordinary funds – more than thirty million marks, for all purposes – granted for museums between 1876 and 1913. The clear implication, and not only in Berlin, was that future growth required the large-scale mobilisation of private wealth.

In France and Britain support organisations like the *Amis du Louvre* (1897) and the National Art Collections Fund (1903) were being created for exactly this purpose. (In a different patronage environment, the Friends' Association of the Metropolitan Museum in New York had been founded already in 1870.)[185] In Germany the idea went back, in essence, to the early nineteenth century since, as we have seen, many art unions sooner or later founded galleries, and in many cases maintained close links with them. Other associations were formed specially to create museums, in Düsseldorf in 1846, for example, although its aim was not achieved until 1913.[186] Similar groups appeared after 1871 in industrial cities such as Krefeld (1883), Elberfeld (1892), Essen (1901) and Halle (1912). A third kind of organisation developed to fund acquisitions for existing institutions, like the elite association created in 1896 by Bode to support the Kaiser-Friedrich-Museum. With a minimum annual subscription of 500 marks, it was spending on average more than 50,000 marks a year by 1906, and eventually built up funds of 250,000 marks.[187] But more broadly based societies had already been founded for the Wallraff–Richartz–Museum in 1856 and the Hamburg Kunsthalle in 1870. The Städel Institute's *Museumsverein*, formed in 1899, helped it, in conjunction with other donors, to acquire a succession of major works including Leibl's *Ill-Matched Couple*, Rembrandt's *Blinding of Samson*, and Cranach's *Torgau Altar*.[188] Associations in Stuttgart (1906)[189] and Dresden (1911)[190] funded significant acquisitions for the royal galleries, and the latter also campaigned for a new museum of modern art. Such bodies greatly increased the weight of German museums in the market and, in Lichtwark's view, fuelled the 'feverish competition' for works of art.[191]

Other funds came from individuals. Bode was outstandingly successful over many years in inducing Berlin's wealthy businessmen – figures like the textile magnate James Simon, for example[192] – to donate works of art, cash or entire collections to the capital's museums. In 1913 the Prussian Parliament learned that he and his colleagues had obtained gifts worth 4,680,000 marks in the previous four years alone.[193] At the National Gallery, Tschudi's circle of donors included not only Simon but also Prince Guido Henckell von Donnersmarck, the coal millionaire Eduard Arnhold and the bankers Julius Stern, Karl Hagen and Ernst and Robert von Mendelssohn. All the Manets, Monets and Renoirs acquired in the Tschudi era, plus Courbet's *Wave*, Daumier's *Don Quixote* and many other works, were given or bequeathed by them or other private individuals.[194] As already mentioned, Tschudi used the same strategy in Munich between 1909 and 1911, and contributors to the Tschudi Donation included, in addition to several members of the Berlin circle, Count Harry Kessler, the Munich writer and connoisseur Alfred Walter Heymel, the Starnberg businessman Georg Schmidt-Reissig, who presented Manet's *Breakfast in the Studio*, and dealers such as Durand-Ruel, Vollard, Böhler and Thannhauser.[195] No doubt simple altruism played some part in this generosity. For the dealers, however, getting 'their' artists into museums offered obvious commercial advantages, and for many of the others desire for honours was important: in Bavaria applications by Tschudi for the award of titles and decorations in return for gifts were a routine aspect of fund-raising.[196]

By 1914 the large-scale mobilisation of private wealth by museums was becoming widespread. It enabled the Mannheim Gallery, for example, to buy Manet's *Execution of Maximilian* in 1910. But the outstanding example was Lichtwark's programme in Hamburg. Like Tschudi, he regarded private art collecting as an important – and in nineteenth-century Germany underdeveloped – cultural activity offering long-term benefits for individual collectors, artists and ultimately the whole community.[197] Both men sought to promote a symbiotic relationship between museums and private collections, with the former encouraging active appreciation of art, and thus also art-buying, and the latter, created without bureaucratic (or democratic) constraints, serving as reservoirs for the museums of the future. The result, Lichtwark believed, would be a life-enhancing process of visual education in a society in which experience of art was over-mediated by the written word. (In 1897 Liebermann argued that 'We must learn once again to see with our eyes. The Lübkes bear much of the blame for the fact that in Germany the sense for visual art is less developed than in other countries'.)[198] Other aspects of this project were the encouragement, as we have seen, of art education in schools and the promotion of a wide range of activities by amateurs, from photography and printmaking to garden design.

In seeking support for his aims Lichtwark had to contend both with opposition from conservative local artists and the Art Union and with Hamburg's workaholic commercial culture, with its disdain for leisure and retirement and suspicion of aesthetic pursuits.[199] (Significantly, and in rather American fashion, Lichtwark strove to enlist wealthy women as taste-makers and participants in his schemes.) However, he generally worked well with the Kunsthalle's governing Art Commission and gained increasing freedom of action as his stature in the museum world increased. He also dedicated himself heroically to tapping Hamburg's enormous wealth; as a colleague later recalled, no dinner was too boring for him if it produced funds for the Kunsthalle.[200] Names like Amsinck, Beit, Behrens, Diederichsen and Warburg gradually enabled Lichtwark to emulate the old princely patrons whom he admired. The fruits of their generosity included major Romantic paintings – still absurdly undervalued at the turn of the century – such as Friedrich's *Polar Sea*, Runge's *Morning* and *Flight into Egypt*, and works by Kersting, Dahl and Carus; Menzel's unfinished *March [1848] Casualties Lying in State*; Leibl's *Three Women* and *Countess Treuberg*; and the largest Liebermann collection anywhere.[201] But Lichtwark's style as director–patron was most in evidence in his creation of a gallery of commissioned Hamburg views and portraits; a means to use his public's involvement with familiar subjects to deepen its interest in art. In 1910, for example, he simply informed the Art Commission that he wanted a Corinth portrait of the historian Eduard Meyer, and that funds were available; and induced the artist to place his subject off-centre and against the light in a daringly unorthodox composition.[202] Corinth's painting, the following year, of Carl Hagenbeck and Pallas the walrus in Hamburg's famous zoo[203] and the pictures created by Vuillard and Bonnard in 1913 were also paid for by Lichtwark's private benefactors.

## DIVERSIFICATION

By the end of the nineteenth century the formerly overwhelming market dominance of the highly finished oil painting was being undermined. Diversification away from fully worked-up exhibition canvases – 'rounded-off, real pictures', in Werner's phrase[204] – was encouraged by the Century of German Art (1775-1875) Exhibition, with its contingent of newly discovered 'private' paintings, and by the previous year's Menzel show, which included nearly 80 sketchbooks and over 4,000 individual sketches and studies in various media.[205] Many choice items in both exhibitions were already owned by museums, and both the Hamburg Kunsthalle and the Berlin National Gallery had begun to acquire Menzel studies well before the painter's death. In January 1908 even the conservative General Council of the Bavarian State Galleries accepted unanimously that 'good studies, which are often much more valuable than completed "gallery pictures", should definitely be added to the Neue Pinakothek'.[206] By 1914 the tyranny of 'finish' was largely a thing of the past.

Related to this development was increasing demand for watercolours, pastels and drawings. These had been popular in the 1800s and remained so, clearly, at the art unions. But during the great expansion of the market between the 1830s and the 1880s only 'minor' media works by well-known oil painters could command serious prices. Thus, for example, although Menzel's watercolour *In the Second-Class Railway Compartment* fetched 2,450 marks in 1882,[207] the Munich Americans Frank Currier and Sion Longley Wenban, whose pastels and watercolours were later much sought after, led marginal existences, ignored by both dealers and buyers.[208] Watercolours were certainly less durable than oils, and unable to match the intricate detail and saturated colours of post-Biedermeier salon painting. According to the critic Max Schasler, who in 1866 advocated international watercolour salons to stimulate German artists, they were also negatively identified with amateurs, especially women, whose numbers increased as easy-to-use manufactured materials became available.[209] By the mid-1880s, however, attitudes were changing, watercolour societies began to proliferate, and in 1887 a series of international 'minor' media exhibitions commenced in Dresden. Most of the items in these shows were by established male professionals, who in 1892 included Andreas Achenbach, Leibl, Liebermann, Leistikow and Kuehl. They were also more than solidly priced; indeed in 1892 large-format seascapes by Hans von Bartels were set at the amazingly high level of five and ten thousand marks.[210] The simultaneous pastel revival seems to have been encouraged – as was the case with watercolours – by technical improvements. With drawings, increasing use of charcoal matched the vogue for *plein-airiste* spontaneity, while Max Klinger's treatise *Painting and Drawing*, first published in 1891, argued that whereas painting was best suited to naturalism, '*Griffelkunst*' (both drawings and black-and-white prints) was the ideal medium for fantastic and visionary images. By 1919 the book had gone through six editions, and probably influenced many artists, from Germany's modern cartoonists to Klee and Kubin. In general, even if most artists' prices did not rise dramatically until the inflationary conditions of the First World War, demand for 'minor media' clearly expanded during the Wilhelmine period, encouraged both by the secessions, which organised regular specialised shows, and by dealers like Gurlitt in Berlin and Brakl in Munich, who promoted them as valid alternatives to oils for the less affluent buyer.[211]

Although prints had been avidly collected in cities like Leipzig and Hamburg in the early decades of the century, Germany later fell behind other countries: not only France and Britain, where a print renaissance began soon after mid-century, but also Austria, where central Europe's most important print society, the Vienna Association for Reproductive Art, was founded in 1871. As printmakers, Menzel in the 1840s and 1850s and Leibl in the 1860s and 1870s remained isolated figures; the Düsseldorf Society for Original Etching formed in 1879 soon petered out for lack of support,[212] and in 1892 it was claimed that there were only two or three artists in Germany who specialised in the medium.[213] The post-1830s colour craze seems to have been partly responsible for this situation, together with widespread ignorance about non-oil media and, in particular, haziness about the concept of an original print: 'A generation ago,' wrote the graphic expert Hans Wolfgang Singer in 1914, 'one could still meet good connoisseurs of painting and collectors who thought an etching and a pen-drawing were one and the same thing.'[214] Also important was the largely auxiliary role of graphic techniques for much of the nineteenth century. Lithography, for example, although a German invention with huge creative potential, had soon become a commercial medium; and, well into the 1870s, woodcutting, wood engraving and, to a lesser extent, etching were used mainly for reproduction and illustration.

Change was facilitated by the development of new mass reproduction methods, many of them pioneered in Germany. (By 1900 technically and commercially innovative firms like Bruckmann and Hanfstaengl in Munich, Seemann in Leipzig and the Photographic Union in Berlin had become major employers and export earners.)[215] Partly because art unions and governments for a time continued to commission them,[216] quality engraved or etched reproductions were not eliminated overnight. Nevertheless, the revolution in methods of reproduction decimated the old reprographic industry's army of craftsmen and artist–engravers – accustomed to spend two or three years on the reproduction of a single large painting – who ultimately shared the fate of portraitists made redundant by photography. Those graphic artists who survived, however, most of whom were also painters, were able to exploit the emerging market for original prints.

A parallel development was the quickening interest in old master prints from the 1870s, especially as American museums and private collectors entered the field.[217] But contemporary work was also increasingly reproduced and discussed in new specialist journals, particularly the Viennese *Graphische Künste* (from 1879), and later the short-lived but influential *Pan* (1895-1900) in Berlin and *Ver Sacrum* (1898-1903) in Vienna.[218] By the 1900s also older periodicals like the *Zeitschrift für bildende Kunst* were not only giving space to modern prints but offering their readers tipped-in etchings by artists as unorthodox as Heinrich Zille.[219] There was, also, the contribution of Klinger, both as an influence on other graphic artists such as Karl Stauffer, Otto Greiner and later Munch and Kollwitz, and in generating wider interest in prints. Klinger had taken up etching initially, at his dealer's suggestion, as a means of reproducing his drawings.[220] But he had soon found it ideal for his special brand of music-inspired fantasy and eroticism and by the mid-nineties had completed twelve of his fourteen graphic cycles (totalling 243 images). Collected first by a small band of devotees such as Dr H. H. Meier in Bremen and Weigand in Munich, they eventually attracted increasing attention from both buyers and gallery-goers: in 1896, for example, a tally of request slips at the Dresden Gallery's Graphic Cabinet showed that Klinger's prints were not only five times more popular than those of Rembrandt, Menzel and Böcklin but, remarkably, three times more so than Dürer's.[221]

Museums, in fact, were prominently involved in all these developments. In Vienna the work of experts like Josef Meder at the Albertina helped to prepare the ground for the drawing revival associated with Klimt and the Secession. It was probably no accident that the Dresden 'minor' media salons began only a few years after the arrival in 1883 of Max Lehrs at the Graphic Cabinet.[222] During his long career, Lehrs – who became director in 1896 – and his colleague H. W. Singer not only vastly increased the Cabinet's holdings of nineteenth-century and, up to a point, contemporary watercolours and drawings, but also made them more accessible to the public through exhibitions and publications. In 1881, meanwhile, the Berlin National Gallery, which had already bought drawings by Klinger, had mounted a large loan exhibition of modern French and British etchings,[223] and six years later paid 2,500 marks for two etched portraits of Gustav Freytag by Stauffer.[224] In the 1890s, assisted by a large increase in funds, the Dresden Graphic Cabinet acquired a huge range of nineteenth-century

German and European prints, and Lehrs and Singer continued their publishing activity with monographs on contemporary artists, *œuvre* catalogues for Stauffer (Lehrs) and Klinger (Singer), and technical treatises. The scope of the collections also widened, incorporating playing-cards from 1885, posters (1895), artists' postcards (1898), modern photographs (1899), and daguerrotypes (1915).[225] In 1896 the Cabinet also began to acquire Japanese prints, and the following year Woldemar von Seidlitz, an art historian in the Saxon Gallery Administration, published a classic study of the subject.[226] In Hamburg Lichtwark was not only enlarging the Kunsthalle's already considerable graphic collection, but also playing an active role in what he regarded as another key area of contemporary taste formation. In the nineties he provided a press for Hamburg's amateur print-makers, and in the winter of 1903/04 sponsored an ambitious international graphic exhibition.[227] It was organised by the Hamburg collector Gustav Schiefler, who assembled some 1,750 works by Klinger, Liebermann, Kollwitz, Munch, Toulouse-Lautrec, Zorn and a variety of British and Belgian artists. The show resulted in 22,000 marks' worth of sales, many of them to buyers in and around Hamburg.[228] (In fact, a substantial number of Germany's pre-war print-collectors seem to have lived in this area.)[229]

After the turn of the century, also encouraged by the secessions, the volume and range of print production grew rapidly. Two thousand items were submitted for a salon organised by the German Artists' League in Hamburg in 1910, and 4,500 for another in 1913.[230] One of the most popular techniques was etching, practised by leading Berlin Secessionists like Liebermann, Corinth and Slevogt, several Worpswede artists, and Kollwitz. From 1911, however, Kollwitz turned increasingly to lithography, which had revived strongly in the previous decade and a half. (Lehrs, in an 1896 *Pan* article commemorating the centenary of Alois Senefelder's invention, had commented that the term usually conjured up memories of dusty pictures in provincial hotels, with titles like *His First Pair of Trousers*, or *Granny's Darling*, and labelled 'The . . . Art Union's Subscription Print for 1864'.)[231] Although German artists' efforts lagged behind the brilliant developments in colour lithography taking place in 1890s Paris, lithographs were eventually more successful than other types of original print in reaching a broad market. The contribution of the Karlsruhe Artists' League (i.e. Secession) under Kalckreuth to this has already been mentioned. The firm of R. Voigtländer in Leipzig published lithographs by artists like Thoma and Bantzer at prices, according to format, of between 2.50 and 6 marks. Its 1912 catalogue was dominated by religious and patriotic subjects and views of lakes, mountains and picturesque old towns like Rothenburg, and its publicity articulated fashionable ideas about beautifying homes and schools and bringing culture to the masses.[232] Interestingly, despite their plainly bourgeois subject-matter, these prints were enthusiastically endorsed by the Education Committee of the Social Democratic Party.[233]

The exact size and value of the contemporary print market is hard to determine. Only a small minority of works in the 1903/04 Hamburg exhibition were priced at over 100 marks,[234] and it was not apparently until 1917 that the Berlin Secession's winter graphic shows (including watercolours and drawings as well as prints) actually showed a profit.[235] But old master prices were soaring long before this, and Rembrandt etchings reached levels of over 14,000 marks apiece at the Lanna sale in Stuttgart in 1909, the beginning of a decade-long print boom.[236] Of work by living artists, Klinger's 1884 cycle *A Life*, which had sold originally for 450 marks, was fetching over 6,700 marks by 1908, and individual prints for which Singer had paid 6 marks in the nineties were approaching 4,500 marks by 1907.[237] Also according to Singer, a single etching by the Norwegian Anders Zorn, one of the most sought-after graphic artists of the pre-1914 period on both sides of the Atlantic, fetched 10,000 marks shortly before the war.[238] This was clearly exceptional, and much work by Zorn himself and other modern masters – Whistler, Munch, Toulouse-Lautrec – could be picked up far more cheaply at pre-war sales.[239] But the nature of the graphic medium meant that a few modestly priced editions could bring a useful return for the artist. Vogeler in Worpswede, who liked to keep his paintings, seems to have lived mainly from print-making.[240] Liebermann, Singer calculated, could in theory have earned as much as 80,000 marks from prints in 1912 alone.[241]

In the international survey of modern graphic art he published in 1914, Singer made the interesting remark that, qualitatively, the German print revival was already petering out by about 1905.[242] This judgement, of course, was possible only because he ignored Germany's enormously vigorous and prolific avant-garde print-makers: Kirchner, Heckel, Schmidt-Rottluff, Pechstein, Nolde and the rest. Ten years earlier the mandarins of the Graphic Cabinet had overlooked the *Brücke* artists on their doorstep; just as, in the nineties, they had apparently paid no attention to Munch, whom Singer described in his book as 'the father and direct instigator of everything in the very latest graphic art which is beyond the pale'.[243] This was disappointing in view of Singer's and Lehrs's strong support for Böcklin and Klinger in the 1880s, and for Kollwitz from the turn of the century, although it was perhaps inevitable that Expressionist primitivism and eroticism were too much for them in middle age. (Predictably, Lehrs in 1913, by now Director of the Berlin Graphic Cabinet, was disorientated and repelled by his first experience of the cinema.)[244] Even Munch, however, described the first Schmidt-Rottluff lithograph he saw as 'insane'.[245]

The non-oil work of the Expressionists continued a European tradition going back to Carstens and Blake, of rebellious artists turning to new or neglected media.[246] In 1906 Klee declared graphic art to be his 'true domain',[247] and by 1914 he was on the way to recognition without having exhibited a single notable oil painting. Other avant-garde artists in various parts of Germany produced, in addition to their oils, a large volume of work in other media: small– and large-format watercolours, drawings and prints of all kinds; Kirchner alone in the course of his career made almost 1,000 woodcuts, more than 650 etchings and drypoints and over 450 lithographs.[248] He and Heckel were among the first twentieth-century German artists to print their own lithographs, and devised a method of 'turpentine etching' which radically distinguished their prints from the more conventional ones of the secessions.[249]

Nevertheless, the avant-garde owed a great deal to technical developments, changes of sensibility and improvements in sales opportunities that were already taking place by 1900. As early as 1888 a critic at the Dresden 'minor' media salon had praised watercolours by the Flemish artist Gustave den Duyts in which drawing had given way to spontaneous flourishes of liquid colour.[250] By 1914, although oil paintings still dominated the major salons, the range of exhibitable media available to artists was vastly greater than it had been, for example, for Leibl and his friends in the 1870s. This not only created greater scope for artistic expression, but was important economically, since a proportion of avant-garde collectors were probably youngish people with limited budgets. Prints by the Finn Axel Gallen-Kallela found ready buyers at the Munich Phalanx show in June 1902 (and were soon taken on by Schulte),[251] and although the more radical *Brücke* work seems to have attracted little interest until 1914[252] even a trickle of sales at two- or three-figure prices – Schmidt-Rottluff was asking on average 200 marks for drawings in 1907[253] – helped the artists to survive until their oils began to sell. Munch, already much more widely exposed, earned an estimated 4,000-5,000 marks a year from prints in 1902-04 and about 11,000 in 1908–09, and stepped up production to a total pre-1914 level of approximately 10,000 individual items.[254]

## IMPRESSIONISM

By 1914 Imperial Germany had become the most important foreign market for French Impressionism after the United States; indeed, it was perhaps more important than France itself. That this was possible despite the political climate of the Wilhelmine period owed much to the general market developments already described. In the first place, although the Impressionists and their friends had been appearing at German salons well before 1900,[255] and special shows of their work were put on by artists' societies and art unions thereafter, Impressionism's penetration of the German market was due primarily to dealers, whose increasing status helped them to establish alternative canons of aesthetic value alongside conventional–academic ones. Secondly, the growing internationalisation of the market facilitated both regular collaboration between dealers like Durand-Ruel in Paris and Cassirer in Berlin and operations like the Faure (1906) and Pellerin (1909) sales, for which they and Bernheim Jeune formed a consortium.[256] Thirdly, receptiveness to Impressionism was encouraged by the declining importance of 'finish'. Finally, the steep price increase of work by modern French artists since Manet undoubtedly made them increasingly attractive as objects of investment and speculation.

By the pre-war period probably most of Germany's principal modern dealers were handling Impressionist and Post-Impressionist work, including Keller & Reiner, from whom Tschudi bought a Signac in 1898,[257] Gutbier–Arnold in Dresden, who held a large Manet-to-Lautrec show the same year,[258] Schulte in Berlin and the Rhineland,

and Heinemann and Thannhauser in Munich. But the main players were Durand-Ruel and Cassirer. The former, of course, had offset his financial problems in the early 1880s by moving into the American market which, since his first New York show in 1886, had become increasingly profitable.[259] But 1883, when he had exhibited Impressionist paintings in Boston (and made his first American visit), saw the introduction of the 30 per cent US import tariff, which had presented him with a significant hurdle. Perhaps this influenced Durand-Ruel's decision to send work to Gurlitt's Impressionist show in Berlin that same autumn. But by this time in any case Germany (like Britain) must have looked from Paris like another potentially lucrative, but tariff-free, foreign market. Between 1892 and 1895 he arranged small exhibitions at the Berlin Kaiserhof Hotel, attracting buyers who subsequently became major collectors.[260] Later, as demand built up, he developed close relationships with the Cassirers and other German dealers, and with museums. He supplied the National Gallery with many of its modern French works (in 1897 he more than halved the price of Millet's *November Evening* for Tschudi's donors),[261] and contributed, as we have seen, to the Tschudi Donation to the Neue Pinakothek in 1911.

For their part, the Cassirer cousins played an enormously important part in selling Impressionism, as well as the work of Liebermann and other Secessionists, to museums and wealthy private collectors. (The association with Liebermann, highly advantageous to the painter, was crucial for the gallery, given the former's friendships and contacts throughout the German and French art worlds, and his dual status by 1898 as both 'leader of the opposition' and academician.) The nucleus of this operation, which financially ballasted the firm well into the First World War, was the dissemination of Impressionism/Secessionism through a network of the cousins' and Liebermann's friends, relations and business associates, who in turn acted as 'multipliers' among other buyers in Berlin and elsewhere.[262] Like Durand-Ruel, the Cassirers worked closely with museums, not only selling to Tschudi in both Berlin and Munich but also, for example, supplying most of the Bremen Kunsthalle's pre-war Impressionist acquisitions and Manet's *Execution of Maximilian* for the Mannheim Gallery.[263] After the dealing partnership between the cousins ended in 1901, Bruno's publishing activities remained a key commercial asset (Paul too was active as a publisher from 1908). Most important was the lavishly illustrated journal *Kunst und Künstler*, launched in 1903. Cheaper and with a much larger circulation than its luxurious but unviable precursor *Pan*, it published not only translations of classic pro-Impressionist texts by writers like Duret, Laforgue and Zola, but also heavyweight pieces by contemporaries such as Liebermann, Lichtwark, Meier-Graefe, Scheffler and Tschudi. Also notable was its series of articles on outstanding private galleries, a feature calculated to promote competitive buying on Cassirer-approved lines. A similar if more diffuse effect was doubtless achieved by the firm's books, ranging from polemics like Meier-Graefe's *Böcklin Affair* to scholarly monographs and *livres de peintres* illustrated by Corinth, Slevogt, Barlach and other Cassirer artists.

The principal entry-point for modern French art in Germany was Berlin. Its pioneering collector was the jurist Carl Bernstein, who was introduced to it in Paris in 1882 by his cousin Charles Ephrussi, the editor of the *Gazette des Beaux-Arts*, and returned home with a selection of works by Manet and the Impressionists.[264] The collection remained unique for a number of years and was much ridiculed, both by the public at large when it was exhibited by Gurlitt in 1883, and by Bernstein's friends and acquaintances; Menzel, for example, expressed amazement that he should have spent money on such 'daubs'.[265] Others who were more enthusiastic, however, included Klinger, Liebermann and eventually Tschudi. In 1892 Liebermann received a Manet flower-painting from Bernstein in exchange for a portrait, and by 1914 had acquired another sixteen Manets, including *The Bundle of Asparagus*, and works by Monet, Pissarro, Degas and – probably the limit of his taste – Cézanne.[266] Also outstanding were the holdings of Eduard Arnhold, described by Tschudi in 1909 as 'probably the most artistically valuable modern collection' in Germany.[267] Arnhold's taste, doubtless like that of other major collectors, was eclectic, and his three residences in Berlin and the Mark contained old masters, nineteenth-century salon works and pictures by his friend Böcklin. But for Tschudi the heart of the collection comprised German Realist works by Leibl (the so-called *Village Politicians*) and Liebermann, paintings by Monet, Renoir and Degas, which he had begun to buy at the Kaiserhof in the early nineties, and several important Manets, including *Le Bon Bock*. A third, less outstanding collection belonged to the banker Julius Stern.[268] In addition to works by Stern's friend Liebermann and other Secessionists it included a Manet and a sizeable group of Impressionists, and works by Bonnard, Vuillard and Denis, but also Munch and Nolde etchings and a Picasso painting, *Woman in Crinoline*.

Paul Cassirer's decision to open a branch in Cologne in 1913 indicates that Berlin was not the only lucrative market in Germany. Several years earlier, indeed, the French writer Octave Mirbeau, on a motoring tour of the Rhineland, had dined with a Mainz industrialist whose house contained paintings by Monet, Cézanne, Renoir, Vuillard, Bonnard, Roussel, Van Gogh, Vallotton, a 'whole suite of Lautrec pastels, some of them very free', and 'bronzes by Rodin and delightful wood-carvings by Maillol'.[269] Important modern collectors in other places included Count Kessler in Weimar,[270] Karl Ernst Osthaus, founder of the Folkwang Museum, in Hagen,[271] Theodor Behrens in Hamburg, owner of Manet's *Nana*,[272] and bank director Alfred Wolff, whose house on the Munich Carolinenplatz contained paintings by Cross, Signac, Luce and Rysselberghe.[273] Also notable were two closely (and literally) related collections in Dresden–Blasewitz. One belonged to Oscar Schmitz, who had bought heavily from Durand–Ruel in Paris in the 1890s, but continued to collect after moving to Saxony in 1903.[274] He owned French paintings from Delacroix to Gauguin, works by Liebermann and other Secessionists, and sculpture by Rodin and Maillol. Schmitz's brother-in-law Rothermundt owned a similarly rich collection, though it was weighted more heavily towards German art, and its seventeen Liebermanns formed the largest collection of the artist's work outside the Hamburg Kunsthalle. (Paul Fechter's *Kunst und Künstler* article on Rothermundt's gallery, incidentally, was typical of many such pieces in that it contained practically no information about the collector himself, in fact not even his first name.)[275] Finally, the Lübeck eye specialist Max Linde owned, in addition to a bizarre Böcklin, Whistler's *American Girl*, paintings by Leibl, Liebermann and Manet, a range of Impressionists, Vuillard and Bonnard, Japanese prints and the finest collection of Rodin sculptures after Rodin's own.[276] He was also, of course, one of Munch's most important patrons, and in 1902 wrote a book about him – rejected, significantly, by Bruno Cassirer – which predicted the supercession of Impressionist naturalism by the 'art of the future'.[277] No doubt the combination of Munch and Rodin, two of the most controversial foreign artists of the day, explains the hostility with which Linde and his treasures were regarded locally. (Worse still, he opposed the erection of a 'William the Great' monument in Lübeck.)

The Linde collection was remarkable not only for its range and quality but also for its setting, a century-old mansion in the Danish 'Empire' style, restored to its original purity after 'historicisation' in the 1860s. Its high, airy rooms, with large windows and light-coloured décor, were the perfect environment for Linde's modern paintings, prints and watercolours; Whistler's full-length *American Girl*, for example, was the centrepiece of the spacious classical dining-room with its 'Lübeck Chippendale' furniture and Art Nouveau light fittings.[278] (The Rodin sculptures were distributed among the oval music-room, the conservatory and the garden.) Among the factors tending to increase demand for modern art in Wilhelmine Germany, the transformation of interior design during this period (promoted, as we have seen, by modern galleries like Keller & Reiner) was clearly of particular importance. An approximate starting-point was the Biedermeier revival of the mid-nineties. But over the next two decades, influenced by a succession of exhibitions, by new journals such as Alexander Koch's *Deutsche Kunst und Dekoration*, and by the work of outstanding German and foreign architects and architect–designers, it continued to develop in several directions: *Jugendstil* (Olbrich, van de Velde), neoclassicism (Troost, Schultze-Naumburg), and an increasingly Spartan modernism (Behrens, Loos, Gropius). Broadly characteristic of all these styles, and underpinned by progressive notions about comfort and hygiene, was their emphasis on light and space and rejection of historicist murk and clutter. If, as already noted, pundits like Jakob von Falke had prescribed old masters and sombre salon paintings for the *Dürerzeit* interior, Impressionism and international *plein-airisme*, both in oils and more intimate 'minor' media, were ideal for the 'house beautiful' of the *fin-de-siècle*. The extent of modern housebuilding after 1890, especially in Germany's rapidly expanding green-belt suburbs, gives an approximate measure of the opportunities emerging not only for architects and designers but also for painters and art dealers.

Jewish dealers, collectors and critics have also been given much of the credit for the breakthrough of modern art; or, of course, blamed for it.[279] After the 1892 scandal, Munch received a number of invitations from wealthy Berliners and noted 'practically all of them from Jews'.[280] Bernstein was Jewish, as were Liebermann, Meier-Graefe, and the Cassirers and many of their inner circle of clients and associates, and the papers of Secessionists like Corinth indicate the importance of a substantial body of rich and modern-minded Jewish patrons. But the argument can be sustained only up to a point. Fritz Gurlitt, collectors like Arnhold, Kessler, Osthaus and Linde were not Jews; some Jewish collectors – James Simon, for example – had other interests; and, undoubtedly, many Jews and non-Jews were either indifferent to art or patronised the conventional salons. (It was also difficult for Jews to become directors of State galleries, as it was for them to obtain other top official posts; Max Friedländer, for example, seems to have been rejected as Tschudi's successor in Munich on overtly anti-Semitic grounds.)[281] In general, as far as Imperial Germany is concerned, individual nuances and complexities of taste of the kind revealed by Raymonde Moulin's interviews with post-1945 French collectors can now only be guessed at.[282] (Was the appeal of Munch and the Expressionists, for example, influenced mainly by *Angst* about materialism and possible armageddon? Or was it part of a process of 'self-fashioning' through possessions characteristic of an expanding consumer society?[283] There can be no definite answers.) More specifically, lack of evidence and insoluble problems of identity-definition make it impossible, now, to determine how far the position, real and perceived, of Jews in Wilhelmine Germany influenced artistic preferences, or whether affluent Jews and gentiles alike may have been motivated to much the same extent by considerations of fashion, status, financial gain or, perhaps especially in Berlin, by an urge to bait the establishment and assert their autonomy in an authoritarian society.

One might speculate, however, that the vogue for Impressionism/Secessionism, like the contemporary migration to the suburbs, was linked to the strains of urbanisation. As far as Impressionism was concerned, German collectors, like American ones, evidently preferred flowerpieces and landscapes to subjects suggestive of industrialism or social tension. The painted countryside, moreover, was not that of Courbet, Millet or even Bastien-Lepage, with their dominant foreground figures of toiling peasants, but a 'leisure zone' in which nature combined with modern amenities to create settings for boat-trips, beach promenades or *parties de campagne*.[284] Such images by Monet, Renoir, Sisley and their colleagues no doubt appealed to modern Germany's second-generation bourgeois elite much as the Arcadian scenes of Watteau, Boucher and Fragonard had pleased the eighteenth-century aristocracy. On the other hand, the role of Realism (Leibl, early Liebermann) in many modern collections also suggests an opposite mechanism: acknowledgment of work, inequality and poverty, but their 'safe' confinement within the pictureframe.[285] And a number of writers, from Scheffler to the historian Karl Lamprecht and the sociologist Georg Simmel, predictably linked the apparently haphazard, snapshot-like quality of modern art to the 'impressionist' flux of the metropolis. Describing a Slevogt portrait-in-motion of the Berlin cultural historian Eduard Fuchs, owner of sketches and studies by Slevogt, Daumier and Liebermann, the critic Robert Breuer wrote: ' . . . one detects the tempo in which Berlin has to live, senses this compulsion of the moment, the sporting, surgical element, the training to seize character in the whirling kaleidoscope'.[286] Finally, attaining a kind of critical mass by about 1905, was the sheer respectability and bankability of the new art, both French and German. This owed much to the Cassirers' marketing strategy. But other (related) developments combined, despite protests about 'the degradation of German art by the supporters of Impressionism',[287] to give it an ever brighter aura of aesthetic correctness: the appearance of pro-modernist art-historical surveys, from Muther (1893/94) to Meier-Graefe (1904), the conquest of the museums and, again, modern art's apparently unstoppable rise in value.

## SELLING THE BLUE RIDER

A particularly interesting and well documented market case-study is that of the artists around Kandinsky and the *Blue Rider Almanac* by 1914. In the first decade of the century, as is well known, Kandinsky moved gradually from a representational style influenced by Symbolism and Munich *Jugendstil* towards abstraction.[288] The first society he founded, the Phalanx (1901-04), was eclectic, exhibiting works by artists ranging from Monet and the Neo-Impressionists Seurat, Signac and Luce to Kallen-Gallela, members of the Darmstadt Colony, and artists associated with the Munich satirical cabarets. In 1909 Kandinsky and Münter, with Jawlensky, formed the NKV, which was much more closely identified with the international painting avant-garde. But in December 1911 controversy over Kandinsky's increasingly abstract tendencies led to his and Münter's withdrawal, together with Marc who had joined the NKV earlier in the year. In the rural seclusion of Sindelsdorf and Murnau they had already begun work on the *Almanac*, which was published in May 1912 by Reinhard Piper. The book gave its name to a group whose other principal members included Jawlensky, Werefkin, Kubin and, for a time, Macke. Also associated with it, and a participant in its second show, was Klee who, like the Russians, had trained and worked in Munich, with interludes abroad, since the late 1890s.

All three NKV exhibitions and the first Blue Rider one (December 1911–January 1912) were hosted by one of Munich's most successful modern dealers, Heinrich Thannhauser, and the second Blue Rider show by his rival Hans Goltz. Given the importance of the art trade by this time, as well as the conservatism of the Secession, dealers were the obvious port of call for hopeful new groups, and in the pre-war period the proliferation of firms and intense competition between them created plenty of openings for work with a suitable aura of novelty.[289]

One of Munich's longest-established progressive firms was that of J. Littauer on the Odeonsplatz, which in 1896 had shown Hermann Obrist's daring semi-abstract textile designs, and in the 1900s was selling prints by Munch.[290] But the first of a new generation of Regency dealers was the former singer and theatre-manager Franz Josef Brakl, who in 1906 opened a luxurious salon in the Goethestrasse which, partly in association with Cassirer, offered a range of Impressionist, Secessionist and related wares.[291] But Brakl's mainstay was the work of Leo Putz and the Munich *Scholle* group, whose constant exposure in *Jugend*, colourful decorative style – Putz did murals for the Brakl

Gallery – and attractive, unproblematical subject-matter made them an eminently bankable proposition. By the end of 1909, however, increasing competition, especially from his former partner Thannhauser, forced Brakl to look further afield. Attempting to find work that was unfamiliar but not too difficult or startling, he began to stock animal lithographs by Marc – who had contacts in the *Scholle* – and gave him a one-man show in February 1910. (Six months later the dealer was practically begging for the privilege of showing Macke's pictures as well.)[292] The association had far-reaching consequences for Marc, since it brought him in touch not only with Piper but with Helmuth and August Macke and, through them, with the Berlin collector Bernhard Koehler.

Thannhauser, meanwhile, not only took over some of Brakl's artists but also his safety-plus-novelty business concept and, evidently, his links with Cassirer, which soon enabled him to become Munich's leading Impressionist gallery.[293] He also handled a wide range of other French work from Corot onwards, and choice examples of German Realism and Secessionism. But the need for a distinctive profile also led him to the NKV and the Blue Rider, to Amiet and Giacometti, and to Klee and Picasso, who in 1911 and 1912 respectively held their first German one-man exhibitions in his gallery. A third key figure was Hans Goltz, a bookseller who had moved into modern art-dealing via exhibitions of fine illustrated books and prints.[294] He too was forced by competitive pressure to offer constant variety; hence, probably, his decision to put on the Blue Rider's second Munich show in the spring of 1912. But although his dealings with some of the artists lasted until the summer of 1913, they clearly brought him more trouble than profit. Marc in particular complained constantly about his alleged shortcomings, described him as a 'wolf' and a 'megalomaniac'[295] and, in Paris with him in the autumn of 1912, as embarrassingly ignorant by comparison with his French colleagues.[296] The following year he was delighted when the dealer was assaulted by a dissatisfied American customer.[297] Still, Goltz persevered through the war with artists like Klee and Schiele and eventually became a figure of some substance. Max Dietzel, initially in partnership with the pro-Expressionist writer Paul Ferdinand Schmidt, also cultivated the international avant-garde and in 1913 dealt with both Münter and Marc; who, however, described his elegant salon as a 'cheese shop' whose motto should be 'rest in peace'.[298]

By the end of 1911 Kandinsky, Marc and their friends had some cause for satisfaction and optimism. The riposte to Vinnen had revealed the strength of the modernist camp and located them alongside Liebermann, Cassirer and other pillars of the progressive establishment. At the same time the break with the NKV, the acceptance of the rapidly assembled Blue Rider collection by a leading dealer, and the prospective appearance of the *Almanac* marked important steps in their move away from naturalism. They also had the support of a major patron, Koehler. Already in late September Kandinsky had told Marc of his strong sense of anticipation, 'As with an approaching, vastly interesting mountain trip, but one on which one must crawl through chimneys and ride along ridges. Is it possible that, after many years of expectation, of disappointments and bitter hours, finally and so suddenly etc. [*sic*]?'[299]

Even mundanely defined (i.e. leaving aside the turbulence of Kandinsky's inner development at this time), however, the 'chimneys' and 'ridges' were still daunting. In the first place, the artists well understood the importance of Berlin in their efforts to achieve greater exposure and sales, and in the summer of 1910 Marc had clearly regarded Brakl and Thannhauser as stepping-stones to Cassirer.[300] Yet his attempt, during a visit to the capital in January 1912, to interest the 'dictator'[301] in the Blue Rider had achieved no definite result.[302] Secondly, the group needed a publicity machine. The relationship with Piper, although it produced the *Almanac*, was far from ideal. Marc and Kandinsky evidently disliked him from an early stage (Marc described him as a 'typesetter's apprentice'),[303] while the publisher had some reason to resent their lofty disdain for the details of book production.[304] (Much later, Piper glossed over these tensions, but also confessed his lack of enthusiasm for the new art.)[305] This, broadly, was the situation when, at the beginning of March 1912, a telegram arrived from Herwarth Walden offering to show the Blue Rider in what was to become the *Sturm* Gallery in a rented villa in the Berlin Tiergarten.[306] The exhibition, which opened on 12 March and lasted until early April, marked the beginning both of Walden's career as a dealer in avant-garde painting and of an association which gave the artists many advantages unavailable to them in Munich.

For the first time they had a dealer who really understood and admired their work. 'You are a quite extraordinary artist', Walden told Kandinsky just before the show he organised for him in October 1912. 'I am very proud of the exhibition. The strongest thing that Europe has to offer . . . What a genius! What a life! Strength and art!'[307] Moreover Walden made available not only a journal but also polemical and propagandistic talents already honed to razor-sharpness by a two-year period of warfare – much of it in partnership with the Viennese satirist Karl Kraus – with the Berlin cultural establishment and 'quality' press.[308] This gave the Blue Rider a publicity apparatus comparable to that wielded by the Cassirers for Impressionism/Secessionism and by Apollinaire in Paris for Cubism. From 1912 Marc and Kandinsky had free access to *Der Sturm*, while Walden organised two major manifestations on behalf of Kandinsky: a series of endorsements by leading figures in the art world published in the journal in March and April 1913, and the illustrated monograph *Kandinsky 1901-1913*. Finally, Walden was vastly more energetic than the Munich dealers in handling practical matters. The increasing complexity of the market was making the business side of artists' careers ever more burdensome, and the conscientious Kandinsky was often overwhelmed. 'I'm doing a great deal of work', he told Walden in March 1914. 'And people and more people constantly keep coming. The talk is about all kinds of important matters. And letters, letters. Often bundles of them come 3-4 times a day one after the other. Among them always urgent things.'[309] In such circumstances dealers were bound to assume an increasingly managerial role. (In 1920 Goltz was to describe the modern dealer as a 'path-breaker, intermediary, secretary, stockist, shipping agent, book-keeper and banker' for his artists.)[310] Yet Walden's capacity for work was phenomenal: for organising exhibitions with all the details of publicity, insurance and catalogue production; keeping track of works on tour, rescuing lost or damaged pictures, or retrieving ones which the artists suddenly needed from remote places; negotiating with other dealers; nursing potential buyers, haggling over prices and extracting payment. He also found himself mediating in disputes with Piper and handling the artists' proliferating lawsuits: 'Naturally Walden can do all that', noted Marc in June 1913 about yet another one.[311] In fact, a decision by the artists to do anything, Kandinsky admitted six months later, meant 'dear Herr Walden, take the dirty business on yourself again!!'[312] And all these services seem to have been provided for a flat 15 per cent commission on sales, compared with 25 to 33 per cent for allegedly sluggish efforts by Goltz.[313]

The artists warmly appreciated Walden's efforts. 'I really want to thank you for the beauty and creative strength of your activity', wrote Kandinsky in February 1914. 'It's always a great pleasure to watch you at work.'[314] A year earlier there had been talk of luring Walden to Munich to head a new kind of art union – with no artist–members! – to support the avant-garde, a move which Marc believed (briefly) would tilt the whole balance of art politics back against Berlin.[315] However, the alliance with Walden also had major drawbacks. In the first place it clearly scotched the chance of an arrangement with Cassirer, one of the leaders of the Berlin 'culture industry' that Walden loved to hate, and relations with him continued to deteriorate. A second problem was Walden's chronic lack of funds, especially after his break with the wealthy Kraus in the summer of 1912.[316] *Der Sturm* was anything but profitable, and Walden's iconoclastic image isolated him from the kind of support readily available to Cassirer; in September 1912 he frankly admitted to Kandinsky, in asking for a 500-mark loan, that he was so detested in Berlin that no-one there would help him.[317] (Walden's initial approach to the Blue Rider had possibly been influenced by its known links with the wealthy Koehler.) Walden's perpetual cash-flow problems, ever-unsuccessful capital-raising schemes, frantic appeals for loans and delays in remitting purchase-money not only increasingly irritated the artists but further soured their already tense relationships with the Munich dealers.[318]

Kandinsky's apparent failure to sell anything at his *Sturm* Gallery retrospective in October 1912[319] and the financial disaster of the First Autumn Salon a year later suggest that, apart from Koehler, there was as yet little interest in Berlin in 'the art of the future'. One reason, perhaps, was that the progressive 'slot' of the market was already effectively occupied by the art promoted by Cassirer, but in Germany generally there was a growing, though scattered and heterogeneous band of avant-garde buyers. One of the earliest and most important was Karl Ernst Osthaus, who had bought Renoir's *Lise* in 1901, but then moved on to become the first private German collector of Van Gogh, then Gauguin, and eventually also the patron of the *Brücke* artists Heckel and Kirchner, Rohlfs, Kokoschka and other avant-garde figures.[320] In December 1911 he had bought Marc's large *Red Horses* for the Folkwang Museum for 750 marks,[321] one of the artist's earliest major sales. Another important west German collector was the banker Baron August von der Heydt in Elberfeld. His generosity, both directly and via the local Museum Association, made the Elberfeld Museum one of the most interesting modern galleries in Europe with, by 1914, works by Vlaminck, Friesz, Picasso, Jawlensky, Erbslöh and Van Dongen.[322] By the end of the war the baron himself owned sculpture by Bernhard Hoetger – of whom he was a major patron – and paintings by Braque, Derain, Bechtejeff, and practically every important member of the German avant-gardes, including Modersohn-Becker (with twenty-eight items).[323]

At the other end of the scale, doubtless encouraged by the modest prices of most avant-garde work, were comparatively small-scale collectors, such as the Berlin doctor, Schultz, to whom Klee apparently made his first sale in April 1906,[324] and the Oldenburg lawyer Ernst Beyersdorfer, a lay member of the *Brücke* and friend of Heckel and Schmidt-Rottluff.[325] Some minor buyers looked at first like major ones; Madame Dorian from Paris, for example, described by Marc as a 'courageous monied lady' who expressed tremendous enthusiasm, bought a few prints, and then vanished into the blue.[326] An intriguing case was that of the young recluse Franz Kluxen from the North Sea island of Föhr. At the *Sonderbund* exhibition in Cologne in the summer of 1912 he showed strong interest in works by Kandinsky and Picasso and bought a picture by Macke (who reported to Marc that he hoped to create a 'Blue Rider villa' on Föhr),[327] and by the autumn was even negotiating for Kandinsky's large *Composition 6,* priced at 20,000 marks. Walden was ecstatic, telling Kandinsky at the end of October, 'He will later buy very, very much from you. Also be advised in his collecting only by me. I believe that in a few years' time he will also help the *Sturm* very much.'[328] Four days later he wrote to Münter: 'Kluxen will buy more from K[andinsky] (and soon also from you), and for tens of thousands! If I'm sure, then it's true!'[329] However, although Kluxen eventually seems to have acquired works by Kandinsky, Marc and Münter, hopes that he might become a kind of latter-day Ludwig II for the Blue Rider faded as it emerged that he was neither willing nor able to pay serious prices, and early in 1913 he admitted that 'I am . . . not a rich collector, but an enthusiast occasionally indulged with money by my father'.[330]

Both wealthy and committed, by contrast, was Bernhard Koehler, a middle-aged manufacturer whose collecting interests were initially quite conventional.[331] But his link by marriage with Macke brought him in contact with the avant-garde and, in January 1910, with the almost penniless Marc, to whom he eventually paid an allowance of 200 marks a month in return for collecting advice and (the crux of the arrangement was unclear and later led to dispute)[332] a certain number of pictures. By 1914 he had acquired numerous works by Marc and the Blue Rider, as well as other items – for example El Greco's *John the Baptist* – with which the artists felt a strong affinity. His collection, which was accessible to interested outsiders, became an important showcase in the otherwise unsympathetic environment of Berlin. In fact Koehler, like Osthaus, was much more than a mere buyer, clearly enjoying the company of artists and even helping them to hang their shows. As well as subsidising Marc, he settled all or most of the debts incurred by the *Almanac*, covered the Autumn Salon's 20,000-mark deficit[333] and paid for Macke's fruitful visit to North Africa with Klee in the spring of 1914. This princely generosity undoubtedly outweighed Koehler's at times difficult personality – Marc wrote of a 'caustic, pessimistic armour'[334] surrounding him – his insistence on substantial price reductions and his dislike of dealers, especially Walden. (With Koehler, as with other major buyers, both dealer and artists worried constantly that competing 'influences' might divert his interest elsewhere.)

The fact that, apart from Koehler, sales prospects in both Berlin and Munich remained limited made it essential to exploit the wider market for all it was worth. Between the spring of 1912 and the outbreak of war the Blue Rider artists, either individually or collectively, showed at art unions, dealers' salons and other venues in an extraordinary number of places in Germany and abroad: in Kandinsky's case, for example, (in chronological order) Paris, Cologne, London, Hagen, Zürich, Rotterdam, Budapest, Düsseldorf, Vienna, Saint Petersburg, Amsterdam, Dresden, Helsingfors [Helsinki], Trondheim, Göteborg, Tokyo, Amsterdam and Malmö.[335] Macke in the same period had one-man exhibitions in Cologne (Feldmann), Bonn (Friedrich Cohen), Jena (Art Union, twice), Barmen (Hall of Fame), Dresden (Arnold), Hamburg (Louis Bock) and Stuttgart (Art Union), but also had work shown in many other places including Moscow, Budapest and several Scandinavian cities.[336]

Walden and Kandinsky pursued such a strategy not only as committed internationalists but also because sales abroad were an essential supplement to those in Germany. In fact, although Walden developed extraordinary virtuosity in shuttling pictures around the international circuit, the financial yield was often meagre: 'The exhibition in Copenhagen', Walden told Münter in June 1913, 'was held at the *Sturm*'s expense and of course as usual showed a big deficit . . . '.[337] But at least some of the sales and self-confidence generated in the pre-war period were due to the dealer's ability to cast the net so wide. Foreign visitors to Germany also played an important role, both financially and psychologically. In May 1913 Marc excitedly told Walden, 'A prince from Siam has bought up half the Munich art trade, also a few little things by Kandinsky and me; the whole lot is heading for the Siamese royal palace!'[338] A couple of months later Willem Beffie from Amsterdam called unexpectedly on Marc and spent '2,600 Mk!!!'[339] By the autumn he owned at least three Kandinskys – including the important *Small Pleasures* – and was still interested the following year. (However, as Marc told Kubin in 1914, Beffie 'like all of them, including Koehler', wanted to pay as little as possible.)[340]

Potentially much more important were American buyers. Already in July 1912 Walden was hoping to send the Blue Rider across the Atlantic, but circumstances, including shortage of funds, thwarted the scheme.[341] The decisive breakthrough was brought about by the New York Armory Show of February–March 1913, Kandinsky's contribution to which, *Improvisation 27*, was bought by Alfred Stieglitz for 1,260 marks.[342] The picture clearly also impressed the Chicago collector Arthur J. Eddy, who visited Murnau in the summer and by the end of the year had bought more than twenty Kandinskys of various periods,[343] as well as Münter's *Still Life with Queen*[344] and Marc's *Red Deer* and *Enchanted Mill*.[345] Eddy, who subsequently wrote a book on Cubism, was a flamboyant figure who enjoyed shocking friends and clients with his modern pictures – which he compared to 'an explosion of fireworks'[346] – and whose style, in contrast to hesitant and penny-pinching Europeans, plainly appealed to Kandinsky. Eddy also lent three of his Kandinskys to the Allied Artists' exhibition in London in 1913, where they were enthusiastically reviewed by Roger Fry, and encouraged the New York motor manufacturer Edwin R. Campbell to give the painter a 2,000 mark commission for four wall panels of the seasons for his Park Avenue apartment.[347] The coming of war thus destroyed a link that might otherwise have become as important as American support for the Impressionists in the late nineteenth century.

In his already frequently cited study of the contemporary market, published in 1910, Paul Drey asserted that 'The genius who shows new ways to a new goal is denied economic success; he to whom art gives its greatest delights is denied his daily bread.'[348] It is interesting to see how far these romantically-tinged remarks applied to the Blue Rider group by 1914. In fact the evidence suggests a more complex picture. It is certainly true that the artists spent most of the period between early 1912 and mid-1914 in a state of chronic insolvency, although they probably exaggerated their difficulties to Walden in order to extract payments and deflect the dealer's own appeals for cash. Marc wrote on 13 February 1913: 'I'm under such ridiculous pressure that I'm practically paralysed. I get whole bills in Leporello format, three- and four-figure [sums]. I've put off so many payments, for years, always in the hope of better times! But they don't come, on the contrary.'[349] Kandinsky and Münter, despite their comfortable backgrounds, also had financial problems by this time, aggravated by tax demands and a hernia operation for Kandinsky. (He acknowledged, however, that they also had a 'rather opulent' lifestyle, which included extensive travel and residences in both Murnau and Munich.)[350] Jawlensky's position, complicated by his stormy relationship with the wealthy Marianne von Werefkin, was apparently far worse, and in June 1914 he was practically desperate for funds.[351]

In market terms, secondly, none of the painters could match prosperous Berliners like Liebermann, Corinth and Slevogt, fashionable Munich painters like Putz, who could ask up to 8,000 marks for a picture by 1912,[352] or the leader of the Munich New Secession, Albert Weisgerber, whose annual pre-war income was approximately 25,000 marks.[353] However, Marc seems to have been hanging on commercially, while by 1914 Kandinsky was beginning to do much better. Marc's financial mainstay, like that of other avant-garde artists, was probably income from 'minor' media: according to Goltz's accounts in the summer of 1912 he was selling lithographs and woodcuts at between 25 and 40 marks (gross), and watercolours at between 40 and 150 marks.[354] These were useful, if not princely sums, and windfalls like the Beffie purchase in July 1913, including one painting for 1,500 marks, encouraged Marc to hold firm with the prices of his oils, some of which he listed prior to an exhibition in Amsterdam that autumn.[355] They included *Cows* (1911, 83.3 x 137.2 cm), 600 marks; *Foxes* (1913, 88 x 66 cm), 900 marks; *Shepherds* (1912, 100 x 135 cm), *Horses and Eagles* (1912, 101 x 135 cm) and *Deer in the Forest [1]* (1913, 100.9 x 104.7 cm), each at 1,000 marks; and *Waterfall* (1912, 165 x 158 cm), 1,600 marks. For *Horses and Eagles* and the two 1913 paintings Marc stipulated that 'under no circumstances' would he go lower.[356] Early the next year, discussing yet another vacillating buyer, he told Walden that, although completely broke, he would insist on 800 marks for a pair of nudes which the previous summer could have been had for 400: 'the nudes', he wrote, 'have simply got more expensive, like all my pictures; if he goes on waiting I hope they will become dearer still'. (He also reported that a lady from Krefeld had paid Thannhauser 700 marks for his *Donkey Frieze*, which had earlier been priced at 300.)[357] Despite this brave stance, however, Marc's finances remained precarious[358] and, ironically, it was not until his apotheosis as a 'fallen hero', and in the inflationary conditions of the mid-wartime market, that sales of his work took off.

Kandinsky's performance matched his higher profile in the art world, even though his latest work was certainly less accessible than Marc's. (By the autumn of 1913 the Russian painter had few of his older pictures left.)[359] In November 1913 he instructed Walden to make a series of large price increases, for example raising *Composition 1* from 1,800 marks to 5,000, and *Composition 2* from 15,000 marks to 20,000, ambitious levels even by mainstream standards.[360] It hardly needs to be reiterated that such 'list' prices bore no necessary relation to actual receipts, and Kandinsky usually gave sizeable discounts to important patrons like Koehler and Eddy, and when he urgently needed money. However, his bullish attitude at this time was based on some real successes, in particular 11,000 marks' worth of sales – probably mostly to Eddy – in 1913 alone.[361] Klee, by contrast, although getting increasing exposure by 1914 and blossoming as a watercolourist since his North African trip, did not become commercially established until the latter part of the war. And Münter, of all the Bavarian-based artists, seems to have found it consistently most difficult to sell her work.

By criteria other than sales, the Blue Rider group occupied a position in the German art world by 1914 that was by no means obscure or marginal, even if their theoretical aims were probably not widely understood. Marc must have been one of the very few artists of the Wilhelmine period to reject an exhibition offer from Cassirer, which he did, with relish, in August 1912.[362] Also, Kandinsky, Marc and Jawlensky had all crossed the museum 'threshold' well before the war. Although Tschudi's death put paid to any chance of entering the Bavarian State Galleries, other doors were opening, including, in addition to the Elberfeld and Folkwang Museums, the Barmen Hall of Fame (Marc, Kandinsky, Werefkin),[363] and the Reiff Museum in Aachen, which bought Kandinsky's *Improvisation 24* and *Blue Mountain* in January 1914.[364] There can be no doubt, either, about the artists' fame – or notoriety – thanks both to Walden's efforts and to Kandinsky's and Marc's own considerable talents for self-advertisement. By June 1913 the *Almanac* had sold 807 copies (some of which found their way into such staid institutions as the Strasbourg City Library)[365] and eventually went into a second edition, while Kandinsky's writings were being translated into several languages. In November Kandinsky complained that Thannhauser 'hasn't a clue what position my pictures now have, how much is written about them everywhere'.[366] A few weeks later, describing a well-attended private view at the Cologne 'Art Circle', he told Walden that although a reading from his poem cycle *Sounds* had been laughed at, 'the pictures were taken seriously: on that score the time for laughing is already past'.[367]

Most significant, perhaps, was the positive notice being taken outside the modernist camp. In fact an acute appreciation of the Blue Rider was published by the Austrian art historian (and Dürer expert) Hans Tietze in the popular *Kunst für Alle* as early as September 1912. In a piece in which sympathy and scepticism were finely balanced (Kandinsky was praised more as a theorist than as an artist, and described as overdue for an academy chair), Tietze acknowledged the group's radicalism but doubted whether it would succeed in creating a wholly new and autonomous artistic language; art was too closely entwined with the culture of particular societies. It was also unlikely that the artists' ideas would ever become common property: '[The new art] will not be able to become the general mode of expression because it will be unable to tear down the mighty wall of centuries-old tradition . . . unless there is a colossal, catastrophic shock to our entire culture'.[368] Yet the writer believed that it would be profoundly influential, in Germany and beyond, as a salutary reminder, after decades of Impressionism, that art's purpose was not the reproduction of external reality, and that 'the glorious privilege claimed for the artist by Albrecht Dürer' was the power to create a world from within himself.

# Epilogue: war and its aftermath

'Dear Herr Walden, so now we have it!' wrote Kandinsky on 2 August 1914, the day after Germany's declaration of war on Russia.[1] 'Isn't it fearful? I feel as if torn from a dream. Within myself I was living in a time when such things would be impossible. My illusion was taken from me. Mountains of corpses, all kinds of dreadful torments, spiritual culture wound back for an indefinite time.' In the margin he added: 'Of the sixteen years I have been living in Germany I have given up not a few completely to German artistic life. How am I suddenly to feel myself an alien here?' These remarks, reflecting both the painter's humanity and his status as a Russian citizen, were prescient. The war's first casualty was the cosmopolitanism of Germany's art centres. Chauvinistic frenzy was erupting everywhere by the time Kandinsky, accompanied by Münter, left for Switzerland on 3 August. Jawlensky and Werefkin, making for the same destination, were spat on as soldiers escorted them to the harbour at Lindau.[2] In Weimar Henry van de Velde took refuge in a psychiatric clinic until the first wave of xenophobia had subsided.[3] Munich's right-wing press exulted at the imminent 'cultural struggle' against French atheism and Russian barbarism, gloated over the expulsion of subversive and promiscuous '*Schlawiner*' from the bohemian enclave of Schwabing, and trumpeted the supremacy of 'German discipline'.[4] Countless artists and intellectuals shared the general euphoria. 'Despite all the miseries that war brings with it,' wrote Adolf von Hildebrand, 'the air has become immensely clean.'[5] Marc, contemplating the 'colossal, catastrophic shock' of which Hans Tietze had written two years earlier, told Kandinsky on 26 September that he was profoundly thankful for the war: 'There was no other way to the era of the spirit. Only so could the Augean stable, the old Europe, be cleansed . . . '.[6] But a month later, though still affirming the conflict's purifying power, he wrote: ' . . . I have the sorrowful feeling that this war will flow between us and divide us like a great torrent; the one can barely see the other on the distant bank. All calling is in vain, writing perhaps also. At such a time everyone, whether he will or no, is snatched back into his [own] nation.'[7]

The war affected artistic life in all kinds of ways. Training of male artists contracted dramatically, and troops were billeted in the Munich Academy. The authorities were besieged by painters, some of them disreputable or deranged, hoping to serve as war artists.[8] After initial confusion arrangements were made, under the aegis of the General Staff, for a limited number of individuals - like Richard Benno Adam, as we have seen - to depict operations under strict supervision and in some cases, as in 1870, to double as correspondents for papers like the *Leipziger Illustrierte Zeitung*.[9] (Not all of them could bear the horrors they encountered: Slevogt, for example, returned after only a fortnight, appalled by the vision of 'a world desecrated by blind destruction'.)[10] In Dachau, where the outbreak of war had been announced by a town crier, enemy prisoners arrived to cultivate the *Moos*, beginning the destruction of its unique atmosphere. Another nearby beauty spot, the Würmwald, became the site of an ammunition factory, whose fenced-off rows of wooden barracks would later become the Third Reich's first regular concentration camp.[11] Germany's outstanding commercial artists, men like Lucien Bernhard and Ludwig Hohlwein, switched their talents from car and travel advertisements to posters for war loans and disability funds.[12] The main artists' societies organised travelling exhibitions designed to promote the Empire's image in neutral countries or, in occupied territory, to 'instruct, edify and amuse' the troops.[13]

Chance, physical fitness and the vagaries of official policy governed the fate of artists eligible for active service. Macke, Weisgerber and Marc were all dead by the spring of 1916. Of those who were psychologically traumatised, Kirchner, Beckmann and Grosz were only the best known. The Munich etcher Willi Geiger, serving as a balloon observer, was transferred in January 1917 from the comparative quiet of Macedonia to the terrors of the Western Front. Attacked by fighters in the air, strafed and bombarded on the ground, he was soon in a state of nervous collapse, and embarked on a lengthy process of lobbying, petitions and medical investigations that eventually removed him from the fighting.[14] Klee was called up on 11 March 1916, but probably saved from the trenches by top-level concern about the casualty rate among Bavaria's artists.[15] (By February 1916 the Berlin authorities had resolved to withdraw a certain number of outstanding individuals from combat, but the decision was implemented too late to prevent Marc being killed, near Verdun, on 4 March.)[16] Told at the last minute that he had volunteered for a flying unit, Klee was transferred to an aircraft repair and construction depot near Schleissheim, and in the winter of 1916/17 spent weeks escorting dismantled aeroplanes on vast and leisurely train journeys to their operational bases. The sights he recorded in his letters, windswept coastal aerodromes, mud-covered infantrymen looking more like slaves than soldiers, and nocturnal Cologne with criss-crossing searchlight beams and a zeppelin floating above the cathedral, were transmuted in due course into haunting, spidery images. Moved once again to a flying school near Augsburg, he obtained a desk job which enabled him to work more productively than ever before, all the while maintaining a strict detachment from the activities around him. 'In the evenings', he told his wife in February 1918, 'I am completely in charge in the office and can spread myself out comfortably, my surroundings recede, and good works create themselves before me . . . My hand is entirely the instrument of a distant sphere.'[17] Ten months later, following an 'inner command' - and the example of tens of thousands of other servicemen - he decided to demobilise himself: 'I shall take my leave gracefully, send back written greetings, and quote a passage from *Götz* [*von Berlichingen*].'[18]

The breakdown of peace in Europe had begun to send tremors through the economy as a whole and the art market even before 1914. The outbreak of the first Balkan War in October 1912 had caused panic selling on the exchanges, and in November Walden had ridiculed the refusal of Goltz, anxious about possible German involvement, to take on a successful Futurist exhibition: 'He's obviously afraid that the Bulgarians or Montenegrans will come to Munich and steal his pictures so that he has to pay compensation to the *Sturm Verlag*.'[19] Not surprisingly, therefore, the onset of the First World War had an initially paralysing impact: 'Naturally all exhibitions are completely dead', Walden told Münter in late September 1914.[20] But this situation (like the dramatic rise in unemployment that followed the start of hostilities) was short-lived. In April 1915 Corinth, on the eve of a new show, reported that conditions in Berlin were 'pretty lively',[21] and by 1916 the whole market was booming, with steeply rising prices not only for paintings and prints but for valuables of all kinds - except, apparently, weapons[22] - and dealers scurrying to find new kinds of object to sell. In October 1916, after the Schmeil collection of some 150 modern paintings had raised almost 1,200,000 marks (including 60,000 for Liebermann's 1872 *Women Making Jam*) at auction, *Der Kunstmarkt* commented that works of art were being traded like stocks and shares.[23] The five-figure sums paid for Julius Stern's Impressionist and Post-Impressionist pictures earlier that year demonstrated that, war or no war, demand for modern French art was as strong as ever.[24] In the autumn of 1917, after a succession of record-breaking old master sales, Bode blamed the buying public's 'lack of taste, ignorance of artistic and market value and, above all, brash ostentation' for what he regarded as an alarming trend.[25]

Another 1917 article, by Emil Waldmann, attempted a deeper analysis. Not only demand for works of art, but increasing numbers of museum visits, argued Waldmann, indicated that art had become a significant distraction from the tribulations of war. But the art market was also attracting money that in peacetime would have been spent on other luxuries, such as travel. 'Because', he wrote, 'people who earlier never looked at a picture but went to Ceylon, or gambled away their money in Cairo, are now buying pictures whether they like it or not, unless they want to put all their earnings in their bottom draw, the circle of art consumers has become much larger. For the number of former Ceylon-travellers is not small.'[26] In addition there was the mark's exchange weakness that, for example, had encouraged the Stockholm Museum to pay 27,000 marks - but 'really' only 20,000 – for a Degas ballerina picture at the Stern sale. Still more fundamental and, as Waldmann acknowledged, also apparent in neighbouring countries, was the depreciation of money and the transfer of assets into other stores of value. (In 1915 alone prices in Germany had risen more than in the previous forty-five years together; by the end of 1918 the pre-war mark had lost about three-quarters of its 1913 value.)[27] In this situation the condition and subject-matter of pictures became less and less important, so that even dark and difficult old Italian paintings found ready buyers.

The war's effect on artists trying to earn a living with current work was uneven. On the positive side, most of the main salons not only continued, albeit in streamlined form, but achieved impressive sales.[28] At the same time, however, the disappearance of American buyers and restrictions on trade with Austria from 1916 onwards created a huge financial shortfall, especially in export centres like Munich, which can hardly have been filled by domestic sales. Individuals with established reputations, like the veterans of the Berlin Secession, enjoyed ever-rising prices and insatiable demand for their work. Corinth, for example, spent the proceeds of prestigious portrait commissions on black-market luxuries, kept several servants and was ready to oblige farmers with paintings in exchange for meat and poultry.[29] In February 1918 he wrote: 'The art business is going well, there's no reason to complain.'[30] But lower down the scale, as sources like the Habermann papers reveal, hundreds of rank-and-file artists were in desperate straits, dependent on semi-charitable royal purchases and in some cases reduced to virtual beggary; in April 1916, indeed, one painter appealed to the kindly Secession President for his cast-off clothes and shoes.[31]

The fortunes of the avant-garde and its allies were also mixed. While some dealers, such as Flechtheim, eventually had to suspend their operations, others struggled on despite wartime difficulties. Walden not only continued to promote those artists who were still within reach but, subsidised by his wife's lucrative war work, extended his gallery, started an art school and opened a shop for his publications.[32] In general, despite the hopes of reactionaries, the war tended to hasten the acceptance of the new art rather than eliminating it, and in 1917 Klee suggested to Walden that *Der Sturm* was no longer an appropriate title for his journal.[33] Other changes both reflected and accelerated this trend: in November 1917 Wilhelm Hausenstein, an enthusiast for Expressionism and admirer of Klee, replaced the conservative Fritz von Ostini as art critic of the *Münchener Neuesten Nachrichten*,[34] and before the war's end even the *Leipziger Illustrierte Zeitung*, 'the old aunt', was soliciting pictures from Klee for a feature 'under the flag of Expressionism'.[35] Among patrons, Osthaus ran into serious financial difficulty and withdrew increasingly from the scene.[36] But others appeared: the tea- and coffee-importer Markus Kruss, for example, who sold his Impressionist and Secessionist pictures and devoted himself entirely to the work of Nolde, Heckel, Schmidt-Rottluff and Kirchner.[37] Adolf Hölzel, after years of financial dependence on his Stuttgart job, saw his boat come in when he met the Hanover biscuit-maker Hermann Bahlsen in the middle of 1915.[38] Bahlsen commissioned three large stained-glass windows for his factory, bought fifteen of Hölzel's paintings, and in 1918 arranged a major exhibition of his work at the Hanover Kestner Society. A week after it opened another local industrialist, the Pelikan pen-manufacturer Fritz Beindorff, bought up the entire collection of more than fifty works. Klee, finally, was not only able to work comfortably throughout much of his war service, but at last achieved commercial success via exhibitions (for which he was usually granted leave) with

Walden, Goltz and societies like the Munich New Secession.[39] In addition to welcome critical attention, these yielded, in the last two years of the war, 21,040 marks, or 10,829 in 1914 gold–mark terms.[40]

Conditions in the immediate post-war period were in some respects worse than during the war itself. To shortages of food, fuel and housing, the paralysis of transport and the psychological burden of defeat were added political turbulence, to which German society had long been unaccustomed. Max Beckmann's fearful image of personal and domestic violation, *Night* (1918/19) (Plate 25), reflected chaos and insecurity in the cities. But in the spring of 1919 Dachau was occupied for a time by troops of the Munich Soviet,[41] and in Worpswede Vogeler's Barkenhoff became a centre of revolutionary agitation.[42] (Vogeler, whose war experiences had converted him to Communism, eventually emigrated to the Soviet Union.) Between the end of 1918 and the end of 1923 spiralling inflation and the collapse of the exchange rate sucked thousands of works of art out of the country and pushed art prices to truly hypertrophic levels. Already in November 1921, for example, Anselm Feuerbach's *Children on the Shore* was auctioned in Munich for 1,000,010 marks, although the cost to its Swiss purchaser was little more than 15,000 francs.[43] The following March the studies and drawings picked up years before, for a few marks each, by the Munich actor Alois Wohlmuth, fetched five-figure sums.[44] For practising artists the situation became ever more nightmarish, and a survey published by the *Frankfurter Zeitung* in 1922 listed them among the self-employed groups particularly vulnerable to inflation.[45] Some prominent figures, it is true, like Putz and (again) Corinth were able to live comfortably by bartering pictures for what they needed; the latter, indeed, had had a new house built at Urfeld near the Walchensee, and had travelled magnificently back to Bavaria by airship to take possession of it.[46] But the rest found themselves facing the worst-case conditions of a flooded market already anticipated by *Der Kunstmarkt* in the first autumn of the war: 'the total destruction of all previous yardsticks and foundations . . . which must be the inevitable consequence of massive emergency sales'.[47] Crisis measures co-ordinated by the Reich Government in the second half of 1923 to subsidise materials and exhibition costs and to buy pictures not only proved wholly inadequate, but in states like Bavaria - even in the blizzard conditions of hyper-inflation - triggered perennial anxieties about cultural centralisation in Berlin.[48]

Although the stabilisation of the currency by 1924 restored a veneer of normality, several long-term changes continued to blight artists' economic environment for the rest of the Weimar period. In the first place, because of the immense cost of war, defeat and demobilisation, State and municipal funds remained extremely tight, so that museum budgets were pared to the bone and major schemes for new galleries and exhibition facilities had to be abandoned.[49] (Royal patronage had ceased with the fall of the monarchies in November 1918.) Secondly, and noted by experienced market-watchers even during the paper-price frenzy of the inflation,[50] there was a severe price-slump for the conventional landscapes and narrative subjects from which many

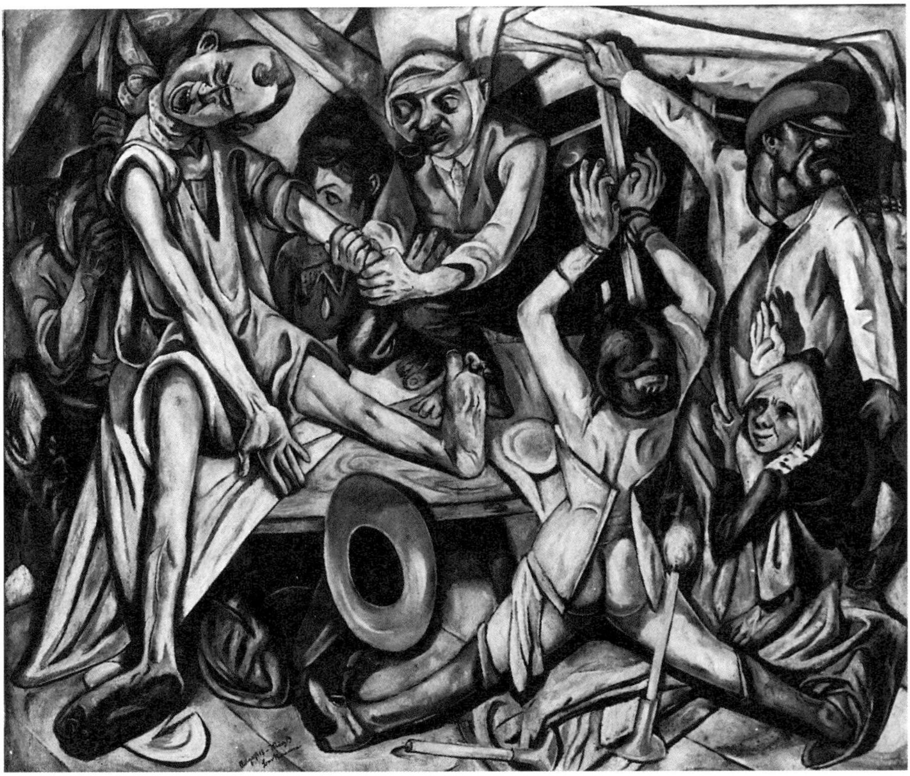

PLATE 25 Max Beckmann, *Night*, 1918/19, oil on canvas, 133 x 154 cm. © DACS 1997. Painted in Frankfurt between August 1918 and March 1919, the picture reworks themes of violence and destruction which had preoccupied the painter for at least a decade, but with special intensity since his wartime experiences as a medical orderly and his mental breakdown in 1915. The scene's inherent nightmarishness is heightened by its disturbing spatial organisation. On the right, young Peter Beckmann is being abducted by one of the intruders, while on the left Beckmann himself is being tortured and strangled: the artist as Christ-like victim and martyr. Although *Night*'s autobiographical and iconographical origins are complex, it clearly relates on one level to the upheavals in post-war Germany. A lithographed version formed part of a series, *Hell*, which included images of Spartacist violence and the murder of Rosa Luxemburg in January 1919.

artists had made a living; Knaus's *Hessian Funeral* of 1871 which, it will be recalled, had originally fetched 60,000 marks, was auctioned in 1931 for 5,000.[51] This trend was international, and was to last until well after the Second World War. Thirdly, notwithstanding an influx of foreign bargain-hunters during the inflation, there was a prolonged depression in the tourist industry, especially in the luxury sector, once so crucial for the art market; indeed, in parts of Switzerland over-capacity in the 1920s actually led to the demolition of hotels.[52] (The great international exhibitions that, for all their shortcomings, had provided useful sales, especially to foreigners, also failed to revive on their pre-war scale.) Fourthly, professional overcrowding among artists remained at least as serious a problem as before the war, especially in centres like Munich, that were now unmistakably overshadowed by Berlin. Inevitably, therefore, long-overdue egalitarian measures such as the admission of women to academies (in Munich, from the winter semester of 1920/21) provoked protests from men fearful, as in other occupations, of female competition.[53] Finally, there was the significant redistribution of wealth and income in Germany caused by the upheavals of 1914-23.[54] *Rentiers* at all levels were, for obvious reasons, hard hit. Within the middle class which, as a whole, was by no means 'annihilated' by the inflation, senior and medium-level civil servants, academics, teachers and some members of the 'free' professions also emerged relatively impoverished. It seems highly probable, as we have seen, that people like this (who had made up 42 per cent of the non-artist membership of the Munich *Kunstverein* in 1905; a further 10 per cent had been royalty, high aristocrats and officers, also 'yesterday's men' in Weimar terms)[55] had formed the backbone of the pre-war art-buying public. Their reduced circumstances, therefore, and the likely preference of those whose position had improved - large and middling businessmen and organised white- and blue-collar workers - for 'cars, radios and amusements'[56] rather than high culture, also help to explain the economic insecurity and low morale widespread among artists after 1923, and underline the importance of August 1914 as a major watershed.

# Notes

## INTRODUCTION

1 Lübke, *Die moderne französische Kunst*, p. 29.
2 J. Osborne, R. Lenman and E. Sagarra, Imperial Germany: towards the commercialisation of culture, in Burns (ed.), *German Cultural Studies*, p. 15.
3 See Niederhauser, Literature and the arts.
4 Berghahn, *Imperial Germany*, p. 43.
5 *Ibid.*, pp. 47, 312 (Table 37); H. Matzerath, Berlin 1890-1940, in A. Sutcliffe (ed.), *Metropolis 1890-1940*, London, Mansell, 1984, pp. 289-304.
6 Bessel, *Germany after the First World War*, p. 223
7 Ribbe, *Geschichte Berlins*, Vol. 2, p. 764.
8 E. Roters, Kunst im Widerspruch, in Boberg *et al.* (eds.), *Industriekultur . . . : Die Metropole*, pp. 57-8.
9 D. Bieber, Peter Janssens Wandgemälde für Erfurt. Monumentalmalerei und ihre politische Bedeutung, in Mai and Waetzoldt (eds.), *Kunstvervaltung, Bau und Denkmalpolitik*.
10 H.-T. Wappenschmidt, Rathäuser im rheinisch-westfälischen Industriegebiet. Die Bildprogramme in Krefeld, Bochum und Elberfeld, in Mai, Pohl and Waetzoldt (eds.), *Das Rathaus im Kaiserreich*.
11 See Reulecke, *Geschichte der Urbanisierung*, pp. 139-46.
12 Berman, *All That is Solid*, p. 16.
13 L. Müller, The beauty of the metropolis: toward an aesthetic urbanism in turn-of-the-century Berlin, in Haxthausen and Suhr (eds.), *Berlin*, p. 40.
14 See Ribbe, *Geschichte Berlins*, Vol. 2, pp. 721-30.
15 K. Strohmeyer, Rhythmus der Großstadt, in Boberg *et al.* (eds.), *Industriekultur . . . : Die Metropole*, pp. 32-51.
16 *Berlin und die Berliner*, p. 273.
17 Strohmeyer, Rhythmus der Großstadt, p. 45; and see also H. Bergius, Berlin als Hure Babylon, in Boberg *et al.* (eds.), *Industriekultur . . . : Die Metropole*, pp. 102–19.

18 Prolog vor dem Kino (1912), in Kaes (ed.), *Kino-Debatte*, p. 43.
19 *Franz Marc 1880-1916*, p. 39: Marc to Klee, 11 December 1912.
20 Goncourt, *Journal*, Vol. 1, p. 794: 6 September 1860.
21 See especially *Stadtbilder*; Roper, *German Encounters*; Haxthausen and Suhr (eds.), *Berlin*.
22 Müller, The beauty of the metropolis, pp. 48-55.
23 See D. Bartmann, Das Großstadtbild Berlins in der Weltsicht der Expressionisten, in *Stadtbilder*, pp. 254-7; and cat. nrs. 157-64.
24 See. H.-U. Thamer, Sammler und Sammlungen in der frühen Neuzeit, in Mai and Paret (eds.), *Sammler, Stifter und Museen*, pp. 44-62.
25 *KVB*, 1918.
26 Pecht, *Geschichte der Münchener Kunst*, p. 270.
27 Osborne, Lenman and Sagarra, Imperial Germany, p. 13.
28 *Ibid.*, p. 23.
29 Freytag, *Soll und Haben. Ein Roman*, Leipzig, Reclam, n. d., Vol. 2, pp. 407-9.
30 Kocka, The European pattern and the German case, in J. Kocka and A. Mitchell (eds.), *Bourgeois Society in Nineteenth-Century Europe*, Oxford and Providence, Berg, 1993, p. 5. For valuable discussions of the German middle class, see also D. Blackbourn, The German bourgeoisie: an introduction, in Blackbourn and Evans (eds.), *The German Bourgeoisie*; Blackbourn, *Populists and Patricians*, chs. 4-5.
31 See *Verzeichnis der Mitglieder des Sächsischen Kunstvereins im Jahre 1842*, Dresden, 1842.
32 *KVB*, 1905. Munich's status as a royal capital probably explains the high percentage of officers (370), *Rentner/Privatier* (500), high aristocrats (30) and royalty (53).
33 Berghahn, *Imperial Germany*, p. 303 (Table 17).
34 *Ibid.*, pp. 8-9.
35 L. Gall, 'Ich wünschte ein Bürger zu sein'. Zum Selbstverständnis des deutschen Bürgertums im 19 Jahrhundert, *Historische Zeitschrift*, 245 (1987), p. 618.
36 See E. Altenloh, *Zur Soziologie des Kinos. Die Kinounternehmung und die sozialen Schichten ihrer Besucher*, Jena, Spamer'sche Buchdruckerei, 1913.
37 Ranke, *Zille*, p. 9.
38 Berghahn, *Imperial Germany*, p. 161.
39 See Abrams, *Workers' Culture*.
40 Berghahn, *Imperial Germany*, p. 64.
41 See *Schilder, Bilder, Moritaten*.
42 Berghahn, *Imperial Germany*, p. 60.
43 J. Wolff, The culture of separate spheres: the role of culture in nineteenth-century public and private life, in Wolff and Seed (eds.), *The Culture of Capital*, p. 125.
44 See Oettermann, *Das Panorama*.

45 *Offizieller Katalog der internationalen Ausstellung von Amateur-Photographien in der Kunsthalle zu Hamburg*, Berlin, Mosse, 1893, advertisement section.
46 R. Vierhaus (ed.), *Das Tagebuch der Baronin Spitzemberg*, Deutsche Geschichtsquellen des 19. und 20. Jahrhunderts, 43, 2nd edn., Göttingen, Vandenhoeck & Ruprecht, 1961, p. 261, 20 June 1889.
47 See *Schilder, Bilder, Moritaten.*
48 Döblin, Das Theater der kleinen Leute, reprinted in Kaes (ed.), *Kino-Debatte*, pp. 37-8; and see also Abrams, *Workers' Culture*, ch. 7.
49 Nochlin, Why have there been no great women artists? (1971), in her *Women, Art and Power*, p. 150.
50 For a good overview, see Frevert, *Women in German History*, especially chs. 7, 10 and 11.
51 Hirth, *Das deutsche Zimmer*, p. 29.
52 Frevert, *Women in German History*, p. 322.
53 See Berghahn, *Imperial Germany*, pp. 65-78; Frevert, *Women in German History*, ch. 10.
54 Frevert, *Women in German History*, p. 122.
55 See Helmut Fritz, *Die erotische Rebellion. Das Leben der Franziska Gräfin zu Reventlow*, Frankfurt-on-Main, Fischer, 1980.
56 Frevert, *Women in German History*, pp. 123-4.
57 Baisch (ed.), *Aus der Töchterschule ins Leben.*
58 See *Adressbuch für München*, 1887, Pt. 2; *Statistik des Deutschen Reichs*, Vol. 209 (1910), pp. 439-63. Further north, another 133 lived in Berlin-Charlottenburg alone (*ibid.*, p. 53).
59 Modersohn-Becker, *Briefe und Tagebuchblätter*, p. 31: letter to her parents, 7 November 1897.
60 See Taylor, *Tini Rupprecht.*
61 See Gillett, *The Victorian Artist's World*, chs. 5 and 6; Garb, Gender and representation, in Blake *et al.*, *Modernity and Modernism.*
62 See *Jubiläums-Ausstellung . . . : Katalog.*
63 See Teufel, *Ateliers.*
64 Warburg Institute, London and Zentralinstitut für Kunstgeschichte, Munich: Berlin and Munich Secessions and *Deutscher Künstlerbund* catalogues.
65 HSA/M, MK 14 163; SAM/M, Polizeidirektion 3428.
66 See for example the papers of Munich Secession President Hugo von Habermann.
67 Anna Bertram, In der Gesellschaft, in Baisch (ed.), *Aus der Töchterschule*, pp. 60–77; and compare Gillett, *The Victorian Artist's World*, p. 165.
68 Singer, *Die Moderne Graphik*, p. 128.
69 Falke, *Die Kunst im Hause*, pp. 448, 449, 450; and compare Garb, Gender and representation, p. 231.
70 Falke, *Die Kunst im Hause*, p. 455.

71 Uhr, *Corinth*, pp. 96-9.
72 Klinger, *Briefe*, pp. 145-7, letter to Alexander Hummel, 12 June 1901.
73 Compare Gillett, *The Victorian Artist's World*, pp. 176-91.
74 See Nagel, *Kollwitz*; Carey and Griffiths, *The Print in Germany*, pp. 21-45.
75 Singer, *Die moderne Graphik*, pp. 128-9.

## CHAPTER I

1 See A. Wolff, Der Kölner Dom, in Trier and Weyres, *Kunst des 19. Jahrhunderts im Rheinland*, Vol. 1; Das Kölner Dombaufest, *KChr* 16/2 (21 October 1880), cols. 17-23; and the essays in *Der Kölner Dom im Jahrhundert seiner Vollendung*, Vol. 2.
2 Das Kölner Dombaufest; Hartmann, *Der Historische Festzug*, pp. 37-41; Hartmann, 'Historische Wahrheit - Künstlerische Weihe'.
3 C. v. L[ützow], Die Vollendung des Kölner Doms, *ZfbK*, 15 (1880), p. 365.
4 See especially Nipperdey, Nationalidee und Nationaldenkmal; also L. Tittel, Monumentaldenkmäler von 1871 bis 1918 in Deutschland. Ein Beitrag zum Thema Denkmal und Landschaft, in Mai, *et al.*, *Kunstverwaltung, Bau- und Denkmalpolitik*; Hardtwig, *Geschichtskultur*, ch. 8; H.-E. Mittig, Das Denkmal, in Busch, *Funkkolleg Kunst*, Vol. 2.
5 Nipperdey, Nationalidee und Nationaldenkmal, p. 559.
6 Tittel, Monumentaldenkmäler, p. 238.
7 Arndt, Das Kyffhäuser-Denkmal; Hardtwig, *Geschichtskultur*, pp. 245-51.
8 Woermann, *Lebenserinnerungen*, Vol. 1, pp. 362-3; and see A.-M. Hürlimann, Die Eiche, heiliger Baum deutscher Nation, in *Waldungen*; Schama, *Landscapes of Memory*, pp. 81-112; C. Tacke, Die 1900-Jahrfeier der Schlacht im Teutoburger Wald 1909: von der 'klassenlosen Bürgergesellschaft' zur 'klassenlosen Volksgemeinschaft'?, in Hettling and Nolte, *Bürgerliche Feste*.
9 R. Dieckhoff, Vom Geist geistloser Zustände. Aspekte eines deutschen Jahrhunderts, in *Der Kölner Dom*, Vol. 2, pp. 64-5.
10 *Ibid.*, p. 79.
11 Goethe, Von deutscher Baukunst; and see J. Leighton, The *Winter Landscape*, in *Friedrich: Winter Landscape*, pp. 47-8.
12 Lützow, Die Vollendung des Kölner Doms, p. 369.
13 Hürlimann, Die Eiche, p. 67.
14 D. Kimpel and R. Suckale, Die gotische Kathedrale: Gestalt und Funktion, in Busch (ed.), *Funkkolleg Kunst*, Vol. 1, p. 32.
15 Grote, *Die romantische Entdeckung Nürnbergs*, p. 18.
16 Hartmann, *Der Historische Festzug*, p. 40.
17 For the background, see Vierhaus, Preussen und die Rheinlande.
18 Rave, Anfänge preussischer Kunstpflege am Rhein, p. 201.

19 See C. Weinstock, Die Restaurierung des Aachener Rathauses und seines plastischen Bildschmucks im 19. Jahrhundert, in Mai, Pohl and Waetzoldt (eds.), *Das Rathaus im Kaiserreich*; and F. Büttner, Geschichte für die Gegenwart? Der Streit um die Karlsfresken Alfred Rethels, in Althoff (ed.), *Die Deutschen und ihr Mittelalter*.
20 Nipperdey, Kirche und Nationaldenkmal, pp. 187-8.
21 Carr, *History of Germany*, pp. 24-5.
22 Das Kölner Dombaufest, cols. 19-20.
23 See Blackbourn, Progress and piety, in his *Populists and Patricians*; Nipperdey, *Deutsche Geschichte*, pp. 403-6.
24 Bussmann, *Zwischen Preussen und Deutschland*, p. 172.
25 See Bayerle, *Johann Huss*; Uechtritz, *Blicke in das Düsseldorfer Kunst- und Künstlerleben*, Vol. 1, pp. 418-52; Füssli, *Zürich und die wichtigsten Städte am Rhein*, Vol. 2, pp. 197-204.
26 Büttner, Geschichte für die Gegenwart?, pp. 114-15.
27 Tacke, 1900-Jahrfeier, p. 200; and see G. Unverfehrt, Arminius als nationale Leitfigur. Anmerkung zu Entstehung und Wandel eines Reichssymbols, in Mai and Waetzoldt (eds.), *Kunstverwaltung, Bau- und Denkmalpolitik*, pp. 315-40.
28 See G. Unverfehrt, Bistum, Stadt und Reich. Das Programm der Fresken Hermann Prells, in Mai, Paul and Waetzoldt (eds.), *Das Rathaus im Kaiserreich*, pp. 231-60; Nipperdey, Religion und Gesellschaft.
29 H. Steuer, Industrialisierung und Domvollendung, in *Der Kölner Dom*, Vol. 2.
30 See U. Krings, Eisenbahn- und Strassenbrücken, in Trier and Weyres (eds.), *Kunst des 19. Jahrhunderts im Rheinland*, Vol. 2; and Hartmann, *Der Historische Festzug*, p. 39.
31 U. Krings, Hochbauten der Eisenbahn, in Trier and Weyres (eds.), *Kunst des 19. Jahrhunderts im Rheinland*, Vol. 2, pp. 78-81.
32 D., Kimpel, and R., Suckale, Wie entsteht eine gotische Kathedrale?, in Busch (ed.), *Funkkolleg Kunst*, Vol. 1.
33 Hartmann, *Der Historische Festzug*, pp. 32-7.
34 By P. Ritter; figures identified for me by Baron Wolfgang von Stromer. For Cologne, see Hartmann, 'Historische Wahrheit - Künstlerische Weihe', pp. 237-8.
35 Mommsen, Stadt und Kultur im deutschen Kaiserreich, p. 82; and see H. v. Dijk, Bürger und Stadt, in Kocka (ed.), *Bürgertum im 19. Jahrhundert*, Vol. 3, pp. 458–65; Sheehan, Liberalism and the city.
36 E. Kleinertz, Grundzüge der Geschichte Kölns im 19. Jahrhundert, in *Der Kölner Dom*, Vol. 2.
37 *Ibid.*, p. 59; and Kleinertz, Einige Aspekte der Geschichte Kölns, in *Der westdeutsche Impuls 1800-1814 (Köln)*.
38 Sheehan, Liberalism and the city, p. 132.

39 O. Most, Deutsches Städtewesen, in *Deutschland als Weltmacht*, pp. 175, 180.

40 See H. Theissing, 'Romantika und Realistika'. Zum Phänomen des Künstlerfestes im 19. Jahrhundert, in Trier (ed.), *Zweihundert Jahre Kunstakademie Düsseldorf*, pp. 185-202.

41 J. Steen, Nationalfeste - Geschichte als reale Utopie (1838-1862), in *Trophäe oder Leichenstein?*

42 *Ibid.*, pp. 171-2.

43 J. Steen, Die preussische Besetzung und die Weltgeschichte, in *Trophäe oder Leichenstein?*, pp. 182-94.

44 See below.

45 See the discussion in M. Hettling and P. Nolte, Bürgerliche Feste als symbolische Politik im 19. Jahrhundert, in *Bürgerliche Feste*, pp. 18-26.

46 See Nipperdey, *Deutsche Geschichte*, pp. 498-519; G. G. Iggers, Geschichtswissenschaft in Deutschland und Frankreich 1830 bis 1918 und die Rolle der Sozialgeschichte, in Kocka (ed.), *Bürgertum im 19. Jahrhundert*, Vol. 3; more generally, Löfgren, The nationalisation of culture.

47 W. Hardtwig, Geschichtsinteresse, Geschichtsbilder und politische Symbole in der Reichsgründungsära und im Kaiserreich, in Mai and Waetzoldt (eds.), *Kunstverwaltung, Bau- und Denkmalpolitik*, p. 49.

48 Thomas Nipperdey, quoted in R. Chickering, *Karl Lamprecht: A German Academic Life (1856-1815)*, Atlantic Highlands, NJ, Humanities Press, 1993, p. 394.

49 Iggers, Geschichtswissenschaft, pp. 175-7.

50 Hardtwig, *Geschichtskultur*, pp. 233-4.

51 P. Johanek, Mittelalterliche Stadt und bürgerliches Geschichtsbild im 19. Jahrhundert, in Althoff (ed.), *Die Deutschen und ihr Mittelalter*, pp. 95-6.

52 See P. M. Lützeler, Bürgerkriegs-Literatur. Der historische Roman im Europa der Restaurationszeit, in Kocka, *Bürgertum im 19. Jahrhundert*.

53 H. Boockmann, Ghibellinen oder Welfen, Italien- oder Ostpolitik. Wünsche des deutschen Mittelalters an das Mittelalter, in Elze and Schiera (eds.), *Das Mittelalter*, pp. 132-3.

54 See Hochreiter, *Vom Musentempel*, pp. 58-125.

55 See v. Einem, Cornelius.

56 I. Jenderko-Sichelschmidt, Profane Historienmalerei: Die grossen Bilderzyklen, in Trier and Weyres (eds.), *Kunst des 19. Jahrhunderts im Rheinland, 3: Malerei*, pp. 145-6.

57 *National-Galerie zu Berlin: Verzeichnis* (1934), pp. vi, 23-5.

58 Haack, *Die Kunst des 19. Jahrhunderts*, p. 104.

59 *Ibid.*, p. 109.

60 *Ibid.*, p. 107.

61 See Büttner, Geschichte für die Gegenwart; Paret, *Art as History*, pp. 86-92; Vaughan, *German Romantic Painting*, pp. 229-31.

62 Rosenblum and Janson, *Art of the Nineteenth Century*, p. 267.
63 See I. Jenderko-Sichelschmidt, Die Düsseldorfer Historienmalerei 1826 bis 1860, in *Die Düsseldorfer Malerschule*.
64 Contemporary review of Lessing's *Hus at the Council of Kostnitz*, quoted in Bayerle, *Johann Huss*, p. 55.
65 Füssli, *Zürich und die wichtigsten Städte am Rhein*, Vol. 2, p. 591.
66 C. Heilmann, Zu Ludwigs Kunstpolitik und zum Kunstverständnis seiner Zeit, in *'Ihm, welcher der Andacht Tempel baut*, p. 19.
67 See R. Schoch, Die belgischen Bilder; C. Heilmann, Zur französisch-belgischen Historienmalerei und ihre Abgrenzung zur Münchener Schule, in *Die Münchener Schule*; Paret, *Art as History*, pp. 91-2; also Wind, The revolution of history painting.
68 *Lebenserinnerungen*, Vol. 2, p. 107.
69 See Nipperdey, Verein als soziale Struktur, pp. 200-201.
70 Reprinted in *Trophäe oder Leichenstein?*, pp. 126-7.
71 Sendschreiben an Herrn Dr Ernst Förster in München über die beiden Bilder von Gallait und de Bièfve, in *Kleine Schriften*, Vol. 3, p. 407.
72 *Allgemeine Zeitung*, 24 February 1863, reprinted in Schnorr, *Künstlerische Wege*, p. 249.
73 Paret, *Art as History*, p. 22.
74 F. v. Schiller, *Geschichte des Dreissigjährigen Krieges*, ed. W. Böhme, Vienna, Freytag, 1917, pp. 289-93. See also M. Bringmann, Tod und Verklärung. Zum Dilemma realistischer Historienmalerei am Beispiel von Pilotys 'Seni vor der Leiche Wallensteins', in Mai (ed.), *Historienmalerei in Europa*; *Neue Pinakothek, München, VI*, pp. 262-5.
75 Munich International Exhibition, p. 315.
76 O. Berggrün, Makarts 'Einzug Karls V in Antwerpen', *KChr*, 13/28 (25 April 1878), cols. 441-6; Franke, Publikum und Malerei, pp. 105-6; *Hamburger Kunsthalle: Meister des 19. Jahrhunderts*, pp. 202-4.
77 With, Menzel, pp. 194-208.
78 See Paret, *Art as History*, ch. 1.
79 *Adolph von Menzels Briefe*, p. 205: Menzel to Dr Puhlmann, 2 August 1866.
80 See Hermand, *Adolph Menzel: Das Flötenkonzert*.
81 See Förster-Hahn, Adolph Menzel's 'daguerrotypical' image of Frederick the Great, p. 255.
82 F. Förster-Hahn, Die 'formende Kraft' historischer Bilder. Adolph Menzels und Anton von Werners Darstellungen deutscher Geschichte, in *Anton von Werner. Geschichte in Bildern*, p. 81; also D. de Chapeaurouge, Menzels Friedrichsbilder im 'historischen Genre', in Mai (ed.), *Historienmalerei in Europa*.
83 With, Menzel, p. 205.
84 W. Schlink, 'Kunst ist dazu da, um geselligen Kreisen das gähnende Ungeheuer,

die Zeit, zu töten . . . '. Bildende Kunst im Lebenshaushalt der Gründerzeit, in Lepsius (ed.), *Bildungsbürgertum*, p. 80.

85 See the painting by F. Kops, *Ein neuer Menzel*, *Jubiläums-Austellung . . . : Katalog* (1886), nr. 635.

86 Scheffler, *Menzel*, p. 61.

87 See Schivelbusch, *Lichtblicke*.

88 Needham, *Nineteenth-Century Realist Art*, p. 177; With, Menzel, pp. 168-78.

89 Förster-Hahn, Die 'formende Kraft', p. 87; and see A. Rosenberg, Ein neues Bild von Adolf Menzel, *KChr*, 14/17 (6 February 1879), cols. 265-70. The picture was copied by Degas.

90 De Chapeaurouge, Menzels Friedrichsbilder, p. 219.

91 Kugler, Über die gegenwärtigen Verhältnisse der Kunst zum Leben, in *Kleine Schriften*, Vol. 3, p. 225.

92 Eberlein, *Geschichte des Kunstvereins*, pp. 40-1, 53-63.

93 See Langenstein, *Der Münchener Kunstverein*, pp. 183-8; *SHKK*, 1880, pp. 246-9.

94 Förster-Hahn, Die 'formende Kraft', p. 85.

95 E. Mai, Nationale Kunst. Historienmalerei vor und nach 1870. Von der Romantik der Geschichte zur geschichtlichen Wirklichkeit, in *Anton von Werner. Geschichte in Bildern*, p. 26.

96 Deiters, *Geschichte*, pp. 5-6; Zur Geschichte der deutschen Kunstgenossenschaft, *KChr*, 3/22 (28 August 1868), cols. 185-6.

97 See Holt (ed.), *The Art of All Nations*, pp. 214-40.

98 Deiters, *Geschichte*, p. 9 (Hermann Becker).

99 *Ibid.*, p. 11 (Feodor Dietz).

100 Pevsner, *Academies of Art*, pp. 232-4; E. Mai, Die Berliner Kunstakademie im 19. Jahrhundert. Kunstpolitik und Kunstpraxis, in Mai and Waetzoldt (eds.), *Kunstverwaltung, Bau- und Denkmalpolitik*, pp. 444-8.

101 Munich International Exhibition, p. 315.

102 With, Menzel, p. 253.

103 Werner, *Erlebnisse*, pp. 57-61; *Anton von Werner. Geschichte in Bildern*, pp. 315-17.

104 *KChr*, 6/24 (6 October 1871), col. 196.

105 E. Mai, Kunstpolitik am Rhein. Zum Verhältnis von Kunst und Staat am Beispiel der Düsseldorfer Kunstakademie, in Trier and Weyres (eds.), *Kunst des 19. Jahrhunderts im Rheinland*, Vol. 3, p. 30.

106 See Bartmann, *Werner*; *Anton von Werner. Geschichte in Bildern*.

107 T. W. Gaehtgens, Anton von Werner und die französische Malerei, in *Anton von Werner. Geschichte in Bildern*, pp. 53-6.

108 R. Heller, Anton von Werner, der Fall Munch und die Moderne im Berlin der 1890er Jahre, in *Anton von Werner. Geschichte in Bildern*, p. 108.

109 Werner, *Erlebnisse*, p. 261.

110 R. Bothe, Stadtbilder zwischen Menzel und Liebermann. Von der Reichsgründungsepoche zur wilhelminischen Großstadt, in *Stadtbilder*, p. 184.

111 See Werner, *Erlebnisse*, ch. 3; Bartmann, *Werner*, pp. 96-102; Paret, *Art as History*, pp. 165-80; *Anton von Werner. Geschichte in Bildern*, pp. 332-69.
112 Werner, *Erlebnisse*, pp. 337-41.
113 Rosenberg, Die Kaiserproklamation in Versailles von Anton von Werner, *KChr*, 12/27 (12 April 1877), cols. 430-2.
114 Modersohn-Becker, *Briefe und Tagebücher*, p. 182, 14 February 1903.
115 Mai, Nationale Kunst, p. 31.
116 Bröhan, *Baluschek*, pp. 19-20.
117 See T. Burollet, Le vertige du mur. Du 'Cycle des Nibelungen' au 'Christ dans l'Olympe', in *Symboles et réalités*; Biehn, *Residenzen der Romantik*.
118 Rall and Petzet, *König Ludwig II*, p. 18; and see *Designs for the Dream King*.
119 Lindsay, *Courbet*, p. 239.
120 Burollet, Le Vertige du mur, p. 56.
121 J. Paul, Das 'Neue Rathaus' - eine Bauaufgabe des 19. Jahrhunderts, in Mai und Waetzoldt (eds.), *Das Rathaus im Kaiserreich*, p. 29.
122 Unverfehrt, Bistum, Stadt und Reich, pp. 245-6.
123 See W. Lübbeke, Das kleine bayerische Rathaus, in Mai, Pohl and Waetzoldt (eds.), *Das Rathaus im Kaiserreich*, pp. 301-58.
124 Paul, Das 'Neue Rathaus', pp. 76-80.
125 See Arndt, Das Kyffhäuser-Denkmal; Boockmann, Ghibellinen oder Welfen.
126 Mende, *Im Namen Dürers*, pp. 136-7, 214-15.
127 Arndt, Das Kyffhäuser-Denkmal.
128 See Schulte-Wülwer, *Das Nibelungenlied*; Lankheit, Nibelungen-Illustrationen der Romantik; R. Mattausch and V. Schmidt-Linsenhoff, Vom Nationalepos zur Weltanschauungsoper: die Rezeption des Nibelungenliedes, in *Trophäe oder Leichenstein?*; W. Frühwald, Wandlungen eines Nationalmythos: der Weg der Nibelungen ins 19. Jahrhundert, in Borchmeyer (ed.), *Wege des Mythos*.
129 Dieckhoff, Vom Geist geistloser Zustände, p. 94.
130 Hartmann, *Der Historische Festzug*, pp. 27-31.
131 See Hettling and Nolte (eds.), *Bürgerliche Feste*; and, for example, Scheffel's letters to Werner: *Briefe von Viktor Joseph von Scheffel*, pp. 185, 189, 194.
132 Hartmann, *Der Historische Festzug*, p. 29.
133 *Der grüne Heinrich*, Berlin, Schreiter, n. d., Part III, ch. 13; Lüdecke and Heiland (eds.), *Dürer und die Nachwelt*, pp. 394-6; Wolf, *Münchener Künstlerfeste*, pp. 35–48. Keller's account is second-hand, as he did not arrive in Munich until May.
134 *Allotria*, pp. 146-53.
135 Werner, *Erlebnisse*, pp. 463-7.
136 Hartmann, *Der Historische Festzug*, p. 35.
137 *Hamburger Kunsthalle: Meister des 19. Jahrhunderts*, pp. 202-4.
138 A. Zweite, Aspekte der Münchener Landschaftsmalerei, in *Münchner Landschaftsmalerei*, p. 22.

139 Ranke, *Lenbach*, p. 174.
140 Lieb, *München*, p. 241.
141 Deiters, *Geschichte*, p. 8.
142 Hartmann, *Der Historische Festzug*, p. 30.
143 See Honour, *Romanticism*, ch. 12.
144 *Ibid.*, p. 246.
145 *Ibid.*, p. 245; printed in full in Busch and Beyrodt (eds.), *Kunsttheorie und Kunstgeschichte*, pp. 13-18.
146 Nipperdey, Religion und Gesellschaft, p. 610.
147 Giorgio Vasari, *Lives of the Artists*, abridged edn., trans. G. Bull, London, Penguin, 1965, p. 284.
148 Grote, *Die romantische Entdeckung*, pp. 20-7.
149 Busch and Beyrodt (eds.), *Kunsttheorie und Kunstgeschichte*, p. 47.
150 See Lüdecke and Heiland, *Dürer und die Nachwelt*; Bialostocki, *Dürer and his Critics*, ch. 5; Hutchison, *Dürer*, ch. 18.
151 For example Pecht, *Geschichte der Münchener Kunst*, pp. 454-5.
152 See Aubert, Der Landschaftsmaler Friedrich, col. 290
153 Hutchison, *Dürer*, pp. 164-5.
154 Wolfmann, *Holbein*, p. 4.
155 Thausing, *Dürer*, Vol. 1, pp. 32-4.
156 Eitelberger, Die deutsche Renaissance, p. 81.
157 Pecht, *Geschichte der Münchener Kunst*, pp. 400-1.
158 Lüdecke and Heiland, *Dürer und die Nachwelt*, pp. 187-210, 384-91.
159 *Ibid.*, p. 191.
160 Bussmann, *Zwischen Preussen und Deutschland*, p. 182; and see also H. Glaser, Souveränität und Integration - Leitschienen bayerischer Politik im Vormärz, in *Biedermeiers Glück und Ende*.
161 Lüdecke and Heiland, *Dürer und die Nachwelt*, p. 198.
162 Jules Michelet, seeing the painting in 1842, commented '[Dürer] was not, as Michelangelo was, a titan of art, but he was a Christ' (Bialostocki, *Dürer and his Critics*, p. 97). See also W. Busch, Die Autonomie der Kunst, in Busch (ed.), *Funkkolleg Kunst*, Vol. 1, pp. 233-8.
163 Mende, *Im Namen Dürers*, p. 92.
164 See Waetzoldt, *Deutsche Kunsthistoriker*, Vol. 2, pp. 214-39.
165 Grimm, *Dürer*, p. 44.
166 Muther, *Geschichte der Malerei*, Vol. 2, p. 145; for the background, see Bialostocki, *Dürer and his Critics*, ch. 8.
167 Kiaulehn, *Berlin*, p. 296.
168 *Deutsche Renaissance. Eine Sammlung von Gegenständen der Architektur, Dekoration und Kunstgewerbe in Original-Aufnahmen, 1: Nürnberg*, ed. A. Ortwein, Leipzig, Seemann, 1871– .
169 See C. Segieth, Zwischen Historismus, 'Secession' und 'Jugend'. Georg Hirth,

ein Kunstagitator der Jahrhundertwende, in Prinz and Krauss (eds.), *München*.

170 Grote, *Die romantische Entdeckung*, p. 13.

171 W. Schwemmer, Kunst und Kunstpolitik in der zweiten Hälfte des 19. Jahrhunderts, in Pfeiffer (ed.), *Nürnberg*, p. 433; *Kunsthandbuch für Deutschland*, pp. 263-5.

172 W. Schultheiss, Im Bismarckreich, in Pfeiffer (ed.), *Nürnberg*, pp. 391-3.

173 M. Th[ausing], Eine unblutige Commune in Deutschland, *ZfbK*, 7 (1872), pp. 69-74.

174 Thausing, *Dürer*, Vol. 1, ch. 2; Woltmann, *Holbein*, pp. 21-4; compare R. Endres, Sozialstruktur Nürnbergs, in Pfeiffer (ed.), *Nürnberg*.

175 See H. Eckert, Nürnbergs Sozialstruktur 1818-1918 und ihre politischen Auswirkungen, in Pfeiffer (ed.), *Nürnberg*.

176 Lübke, Die heutige Kunst, p. 7.

177 *Ibid.*, p. 4.

178 Eitelberger, Die deutsche Renaissance, p. 82.

179 Thausing, Kunstliteratur, *ZfbK*, 6 (1871), col. 313.

180 Muther, *Geschichte der Malerei*, Vol. 3, p. 137.

181 S. Lichtenstein, Die deutsche Kunst- und Kunstindustrieausstellung in München, *ZfbK*, 11 (1876), p. 290.

182 Hirth, *Das deutsche Zimmer*, p. 2.

183 *Ibid.*, p. 63; and see W. Brönner, Schichtenspezifische Wohnkultur: die bürgerliche Wohnung des Historismus, in Mai, Pohl and Waetzoldt (eds.), *Kunstpolitik und Kunstförderung*.

184 Falke, *Die Kunst im Hause*, p. 287.

185 See chapter 2 below.

186 *ZfbK*, 19 (1884), p. 260.

187 E. Kedourie, *Nationalism*, London, Hutchinson, 1960, p. 61.

188 See Weber, *Der Gegensatz*.

189 Lübke, *Die moderne französische Kunst*, p. 1.

190 Miller, Die bayerische Abgeordnetenkammer und der Neubau der Münchener Kunst-Akademie, *KChr*, 9/43 (7 August 1874), col. 691.

191 Schmaedel, Zweck und Ziel der allgemeinen deutschen Kunst- und Kunstindustrieausstellung in München, *KChr*, 11/34 (2 June 1876), pp. 540, 541.

192 *Paris 1889*, p. 33.

193 Uhr, *Corinth*, p. 25.

194 Paul, *Tschudi*, pp. 27, 106-7.

195 On the background, see Hochreiter, *Vom Musentempel*, section A; for statistics, *SHKK* and *KHB*.

196 Hochreiter, *Vom Musentempel*, p. 17.

197 W. Hardtwig, Privatvergnügen oder Staatsaufgabe? Monarchisches Sammeln und Museum 1800-1914, in Mai and Paret (eds.), *Sammler, Stifter und Museen*, p. 87.

198 W. Kemp, Kunst kommt ins Museum, in Busch (ed.), *Funkkolleg Kunst*, Vol. 1, p. 209.
199 Hochreiter, *Vom Musentempel*, pp. 18-19.
200 Kemp, Kunst kommt ins Museum, pp. 216-17.
201 *Ibid.*, pp. 218-19; Nipperdey, Verein als soziale Struktur, pp. 192-3.
202 Dube, *Munich Gallery*, p. 50.
203 Hochreiter, *Vom Musentempel*, pp. 24-5.
204 *Ibid.*, p. 51; and see Cleve, *Geschmack, Kunst und Konsum*, pp. 320-31, for similar developments in Württemberg.
205 See *'Ihm, welcher der Andacht Tempel baut . . .* '; Mittlmeier, *Neue Pinakothek*.
206 Hardtwig, Privatvergnügen, p. 77.
207 See E. Mai, 'Wallraffs Chaos' (Goethe) - Städels Stiftung, in Mai and Paret (eds.), *Sammler, Stifter und Museen*.
208 *Ibid.*; and Verbeek, Das erste Wallraff–Richartz-Museum.
209 For a complete list up to 1904, see *Kunsthandbuch für Deutschland*.
210 Dibbern, *Hamburger Kunsthalle*, pp. 15-19.
211 See Teupser (ed.), *Kunst und ihre Sammlung in Leipzig*.
212 Mende, *Im Namen Dürers*, pp. 38, 41.
213 See Eberlein, Vorgeschichte und Entstehung; Idee und Entstehung; and Rave, *Geschichte der Nationalgalerie*, pp. 4-27.
214 Carr, *History of Germany*, p. 69.
215 H. Börsch-Supan, Zur Deutung der Kunst Caspar David Friedrichs, *Münchener Jahrbuch für bildende Kunst*, 27 (1976), p. 213.
216 Gaehtgens, *Berliner Museumsinsel*, p. 75.
217 W. Feldenkirchen, Staatliche Kunstfinanzierung im 19. Jahrhundert, in Mai, Pohl and Waetzoldt (eds.), *Kunstpolitik und Kunstförderung*, pp. 44-7.
218 *BVKS/D*, 1874/75, pp. 3-11; Richter, *Geschichte der Stadt Dresden*, p. 258, puts the regular annual budget from 1874 at 72,000 marks.
219 Spindler (ed.), *Handbuch*, Vol. 4/1, pp. 337-9.
220 Lenman, *Kunst, Macht und Geld*, pp. 71-3.
221 With, *Landeskunstkommission*; according to Rave, *Geschichte der Nationalgalerie*, p. 13, it was founded in 1859.
222 Bay. Kultusministerium, Bekanntmachung vom 29. April 1907, *Ministerialblatt*, 14 (30 April 1907), pp. 243-8.
223 Woermann, *Lebenserinnerungen*, Vol. 2, pp. 7-28.
224 *Ibid.*, p. 21.
225 *BVKS/D*, 1882/83, p. 12.
226 Paul, *Tschudi*, p. 59.
227 With, *Landeskunstkommission*, pp. 35-9.
228 See especially Paul, *Tschudi*; also With, *Landeskunstkommission*; and Teeuwisse, *Vom Salon zur Secession*, pp. 197-220.
229 Lichtwark, *Kauffmann*, p. 15.

230 *SHKK*, 1880, p. 19.
231 Cecil, *Wilhelm II*, p. 276.
232 Tschudi, Ausstellung deutscher Kunst aus der Zeit von 1775-1875, in *Gesammelte Schriften*, p. 174.
233 *SBPrAH*, 5th session 1898, Vol. 2, p. 1525: v. Heeremann, 16 March 1898.
234 Paul, *Tschudi*, pp. 253-76.
235 La réorganisation des musées bavarois par M. Hugo v. Tschudi, *Journal des débats*, 2 November 1910.
236 With, *Landeskunstkommission*, pp. 129-44.
237 Martin, *Tschudi-Spende*; HSA/M, MK 14 284: Heinrich Braune to Kultusministerium, 30 January 1912.
238 Paul, *Tschudi*, pp. 58, 94.
239 See *Städel'sches Kunstinstitut: Verzeichnis*.
240 Gutbrod, Rezeption, pp. 96-100; Dibbern, *Hamburger Kunsthalle*, pp. 66-7.
241 See *Hamburger Kunsthalle: Katalog*; also Lichtwark, *Briefe*, Vol. 2, pp. 490-2: 17 and 31 January 1913.
242 See Sutton, Bonnard and Vuillard.
243 W. v. Seidlitz, Courbet's *Steinklopfer*, *Dresdner Jahrbuch 1805. Beiträge zur bildenden Kunst*, ed. K. Koetschau and F. v. Schubert-Soldern, Dresden, 1905.
244 Vinnen, *Ein Protest*; see also Paret, *Berlin Secession*, pp. 182-99; Paul, *Tschudi*, pp. 319-27.
245 Gutbrod, Rezeption, pp. 104-5; Ott, Erinnerungen.
246 GNMAbK/Nbg, Marc Papers: FM IIc, Marc to Reinhard Piper (copy), 7 May 1911.
247 Rosenhagen, Die Wilden (January 1911), reprinted in *Der Blaue Reiter: Dokumente*, pp. 27-9.
248 *Im Kampf*, p. 7 (L. Kaemmerer).
249 Rosenberg/Rosenhagen, *Handbuch*, pp. v–vi.
250 Tschudi, Kunst und Publikum, 27 January 1899, in *Gesammelte Schriften*, pp. 56-75.
251 Werner, *Erlebnisse*, p. 413.
252 *Anton von Werner. Geschichte in Bildern*, nr. 420, pp. 310-14.
253 HSA/M, MK 14 283: Dieffenbacher to Kultusministerium, 18 October 1910; Tschudi to Kultusministerium, 29 October 1910.
254 Carey and Griffiths, *The Print in Germany*, p. 67; StG/W, Nachlass Habermann: Vinnen to Habermann, 15 April 1908, on non-historical subjects purchased.
255 Oettermann, *Panorama*, pp. 192-3.
256 Tacke, 1900-Jahrfeier, pp. 212-13.
257 Schweinitz (ed.), *Prolog vor dem Film*, p. 61.
258 See Jensen, *Marketing Modernism*, ch. 5.
259 *Albrecht Adam und seine Familie*, nrs. 246, 383, pp. 272, 355.

## CHAPTER 2

1 Uechtritz, *Blicke*, Vol. 1, p. 3.

2 *Kgl. Akademie der Künste: Katalog der Jubiläums-Ausstellung . . . 1885*, introduction.

3 Drey, Der Kunstmarkt, p. 157.

4 *KVB*, 1908.

5 C. Heilmann, Die Sammlung zeitgenössischer Malerei König Ludwig I in der Neuen Pinakothek, in Mittlmeier, *Neue Pinakothek*, p. 125.

6 *Statistik des Deutschen Reichs*, 209 (1910), pp. 47-67, 439-63; 211 (1913), appendix, p. 59.

7 Mende, *Im Namen Dürers*, pp. 10-12.

8 *SHKK*, 1880, pp. 250-87.

9 *KVB*, 1911, p. vii.

10 Kalkschmidt, *Spitzweg*, pp. 151-61.

11 Ruederer, *München*, p. 58.

12 *150 Jahre Württembergischer Kunstverein*, pp. 37-9.

13 Lankheit, *Marc*, p. 89.

14 *150 Jahre Württembergischer Kunstverein*, p. 17.

15 Hardtwig, Privatvergnügen oder Staatsaufgabe?, in Mai and Paret (eds.), *Sammler, Stifter und Museen*, p. 99.

16 Wichmann, *Realismus und Impressionismus*, p. 21.

17 Holt, *Art of All Nations*, p. 237.

18 Mitchell, *Art and Science*, p. 161.

19 See V. Leuschner, Der Landschafts- und Historienmaler Carl Friedrich Lessing (1808-1880), in *Die Düsseldorfer Malerschule*.

20 See R. Theilmann, Schirmer und die Düsseldorfer Landschaftsmalerei, in *Die Düsseldorfer Malerschule*.

21 See Mai, 'Unsere Düsseldorfer Schule . . . '.

22 Muther, *Geschichte der Malerei*, Vol. 2, pp. 542-3.

23 *Ibid.*, pp. 485, 550-1.

24 U. Ricke-Immel, Die Düsseldorfer Genremalerei, in *Die Düsseldorfer Malerschule*, p. 155.

25 *Ibid.*, nr. 110 (Kunstmuseum Düsseldorf), p. 345.

26 See Pietsch, *Knaus*; Rosenberg, *Vautier*; Defregger, *Defregger*.

27 *Die Gartenlaube*, 1885 (1), p. 17.

28 Pecht, *Geschichte der Münchener Kunst*, pp. 335-6.

29 See F. Sengle, Wunschbild Land und Schreckbild Stadt; E. Sagarra, *Blut und Boden* fiction and the tradition of popular reading culture in Germany, in M. Laffan (ed.), *The Burden of German History, 1939-45*, London, Methuen, 1988, pp. 30-47.

30 Weimar, *Daguerrotypie*, pp. 26-30.

31 Peters, *Stilgeschichte*, pp. 89-92; Scharf, *Art and Photography*, ch. 2.
32 See J. A. Schmoll, gen. Eisenwerth, Lenbach und die Photographie, in *Franz von Lenbach*.
33 Voss, *Stuck*, pp. 255-7.
34 See Zimmermanns, *Kaulbach*.
35 Taylor, *Rupprecht*, p. 21.
36 See Kaufhold, *Bilder des Übergangs*, ch. 2.
37 *Lovis Corinth*, p. 58: Liebermann to Corinth, 12 February 1900.
38 S. Pucks, 'Und die Deutschen begannen, mich kräftig zu unterstützen'. Edvard Munchs Förderer in Deutschland 1902-1912, in *Munch in Deutschland*, p. 96.
39 T. Munro, quoted in Mitchell, *Art and Science*, p. 3.
40 See G. Himmelheber, Kunst des Biedermeier, in *Kunst des Biedermeier*.
41 Peters, Schadow, p. 14.
42 Rosenberg, *Vautier*, pp. 47-8, 56-7.
43 Rosenberg, *Defregger*, p. 42, and illustration, p. 33.
44 Mayr, *Leibl*, p. 220.
45 See *Leibl zum 150. Geburtstag*, pp. 240-2.
46 See Duveneck, *Duveneck*; M. Quick, Munich and American Realism, in *Munich and American Realism*.
47 M. Eberle, Max Liebermann zwischen Tradition und Opposition, in *Liebermann in seiner Zeit*, pp. 16, 26.
48 *Menzel der Beobachter*, pp. 177-82.
49 See Eberle, Liebermann; and C. Lenz, Wilhelm Leibl - der Maler, in *Leibl zum 150. Geburtstag*.
50 *Leibl zum 150. Geburtstag*, nr. 83 (Städel'sches Kunstinstitut, Frankfurt-on-Main), pp. 314-15.
51 Mayr, *Leibl*, p. 218.
52 *Leibl zum 150. Geburtstag*, pp. 343-4.
53 G. Czymmek, Wilhelm Leibls Leben in seinen Briefen und in der Überlieferung seiner Freunde, in *Leibl zum 150. Geburtstag* pp. 24-5.
54 Diem, *Sperl*, p. 26.
55 With, Menzel, pp. 275-6.
56 *Liebermann in seiner Zeit*, pp. 178-9.
57 Mayr, *Leibl*, pp. 145-6.
58 Langer, *Leibl*, p. 41.
59 See Eberle, Liebermann; in 1913 he owned capital of 6.1 million marks.
60 Quick, Munich and American Realism, pp. 25-6.
61 *Triumph of Realism*, no. 15, p. 64.
62 See *Ein Jahrhundert deutscher Kunst*.
63 *KChr*, 8/28 (25 April 1873), cols. 448-9.
64 Pecht, *Geschichte der Münchener Kunst*, p. 345.
65 See chapter 3 below.

66 *Kunstmuseum Düsseldorf. Führer*, nr. 296, pp. 164-5.
67 *Ibid.*, nr. 311, p. 173; Rosenhagen, *Kampf*, pp. 25-6.
68 For classic overviews, see Hamann and Hermand, *Deutsche Kunst und Kultur, 2: Naturalismus*; A. Soergel, *Dichtung und Dichter der Zeit*, Leipzig, Voigtländer, 1911, bk. 1.
69 See Bothe, Stadtbilder zwischen Menzel and Liebermann, in *Stadtbilder*; Bröhan, *Baluschek*; Nagel, *Kollwitz*.
70 See chapter 3 below.
71 See S. Miller, Critique littéraire de la social-démocratie allemande à la fin du siècle dernier, *Le Mouvement Social*, 1967, pp. 50-69.
72 Bröhan, *Baluschek*, pp. 68, 73.
73 Woermann, *Lebenserinnerungen*, Vol. 2, pp. 21-2.
74 Weisberg, *Beyond Impressionism*, p. 188.
75 See L. Merrill, *A Pot of Paint. Aesthetics on Trial in Whistler v. Ruskin*, Washington and London, Smithsonian Institution Press and Freer Gallery of Art, 1992.
76 Woermann, *Von Apelles bis Böcklin*, Vol. 2, p. 230.
77 Wichmann, *Realismus und Impressionismus*, p. 21.
78 See Weisberg, *Beyond Impressionism*, chs. 2 and 3.
79 *Carl Bantzer*, pp. 21-5, 72-93.
80 *Leibl und sein Kreis*, pp. 55-60; *Leibl zum 150. Geburtstag*, pp. 71-2.
81 W. Neite, Die Frühzeit der Photographie in der Rheinprovinz, in Trier and Weyres (eds.), *Kunst des 19. Jahrhunderts im Rheinland*, Vol. 3, p. 360; N. Rosenblum, *A World History of Photography*, New York, Abbeville, 1984, pp. 18, 20.
82 *Das Photoalbum*, p. 82.
83 See Gebhardt, *Königlich Bayrische Photographie* and *Hanfstaengl*; and Ranke, *Albert*.
84 Ranke, *Albert*, pp. 18-33, 52-69.
85 *Kandinsky in Munich*, pp. 34-5.
86 Gebhardt, *Königlich Bayrische Photographie*, p. 93.
87 See Peters, *Stilgeschichte*, chs. 8 and 9; Kaufhold, *Bilder des Übergangs*.
88 *BVKS/D*, 1898/99, p. 57.
89 A. Effner, Frank Eugene Smith: Grenzgänger zwischen Malerei und Photographie, in *Frank Eugene*, p. 258.
90 Lichtwark, Einleitung, *Jahrbuch der Gesellschaft Hamburgischer Kunstfreunde*, 1 (1894), pp. 5-6.
91 See A. Krase, 'daß ich . . . innerlich mit dieser Stellung so verwachsen bin: Frank Eugene Smith an der Leipziger Akademie 1913-1927, in *Frank Eugene*, pp. 201-35.
92 H. and A. Gernsheim, The first photographs taken in Germany, *Image*, 9 (1960), p. 45.

93 See Scharf, *Art and Photography*; *Malerei nach Photographie*.
94 Starzynski, *Gierymski*, figs. 10, 11.
95 Weiss, *Kandinsky in Munich*, p. 32.
96 Klee, *Tagebücher*, p. 187, nr. 639 (1905); *Briefe*, Vol. 1, pp. 263-4, 337: to Lily Klee, 24 August 1902 and 12 July 1903.
97 R. Gollek, Murnau, in Wietek (ed.), *Deutsche Künstlerkolonien*, p. 186.
98 See Schmoll, Lenbach und die Photographie.
99 Compare, for example, T. H. Breen, The meaning of 'likeness': American portrait painting in an eighteenth-century consumer society', *Word and Image*, 6 (1990), pp. 325-67.
100 Zimmermanns, *Kaulbach*, pp. 35-8.
101 See Rosenblum, *A World History of Photography*, ch. 5; and especially Scharf, *Art and Photography*.
102 Schmoll, Lenbach und die Photographie, pp. 73-4.
103 HSA/M, MK 14 225: Kultusminister v. Landmann to v. Wiedenmann, 3 February 1902 (draft).
104 *Hessen in der deutschen Malerei*, pp. 62-4.
105 Imiela, *Slevogt*, p. 351, n. 12.
106 Ranke, *Zille*, p. 19.
107 Schmoll, Lenbach und die Photographie, p. 71.
108 *Ibid.*, p. 67; and see Eggum, *Munch and Photography*.
109 See P.-K. Schuster, 'München leuchtete'. Die Erneuerung christlicher Kunst in München um 1900, in *'München leuchtete'*.
110 Woermann, *Von Apelles bis Böcklin*, Vol. 2, pp. 218-20.
111 *München und seine Kunst- und Kunst-Gewerbe-Ausstellung*, Zurich, 1888, p. 41.
112 M. Bernstein, Von einem Panorama, *KfA*, 2/6 (15 December 1886), pp. 105-10.
113 Franke, Publikum und Malerei, p. 116.
114 P.-K. Schuster, Religiöses bei Hanfstaengl, in *'München leuchtete'*, p. 90.
115 See Pascal, *From Naturalism to Expressionism*, ch. 7.
116 Rosenberg, *Gebhardt*, pp. 12-22; and see D. Bieber and E. Mai, Gebhardt und Janssen - religiöse und Monumentalmalerei im späten 19. Jahrhundert, in *Die Düsseldorfer Malerschule*, pp. 166-76.
117 *'München leuchtete'*, p. 198.
118 Venzmer, *Hölzel*, p. 94.
119 See *'München leuchtete'*; and C. Chassé, *The Nabis and Their Period*, trans. M. Bullock, London, Lund Humphries, 1969, ch. 9.
120 See Gumppenberg, *Lebenserinnerungen*, pp. 108-9, 141-52; Pascal, *From Naturalism to Expressionism*, pp. 174-7.
121 *Neue Pinakothek München, VI*, pp. 129-32; *'München leuchtete'*, pp. 164-5.
122 HSA/M, MK 14 308: Kultusminister v. Lutz to Ludwig II, 2 May 1885; and see *Neue Pinakothek München, VI*, pp. 239-40; *'München leuchtete'*, pp. 162-3.
123 StB. M/Mon, Künstlergenossenschaft Papers: Alfred Seifert.

124 Knackfuss, *Menzel*, p. 42 and ill. 58.
125 Leiss, *Kunst im Konflikt*, pp. 95-101; *Liebermann in seiner Zeit*, p. 31.
126 *Max Klinger, 1857-1920*, p. 268.
127 For example H. Eisentraeger, Die moderne Malerei, in Weber (ed.), *Die Wissenschaften und Künste der Gegenwart*, p. 281.
128 Venzmer, *Hölzel*, pp. 86-94.
129 *Neue Pinakothek München, VI*, pp. 142-4.
130 See Schmoll, Salome 1900; Jones and Kingsley, Salome.
131 M. Hürlimann, Wie schön ist die Prinzessin Salome heut' Nacht, *Du*, 8 (1981), p. 23.
132 In the Museum der bildenden Künste, Leipzig. See Uhr, *Corinth*, pp. 119-20; Dijkstra, *Idols of Perversity*, pp. 381-401.
133 *Neue Pinakothek München, VI*, pp. 331-2; *'München leuchtete'*, pp. 196-7.
134 Imiela, *Slevogt*, pp. 36-8, 50, 355-6.
135 *Ibid.*, p. 362, n. 34; *Neue Pinakothek München, VI*, pp. 315-16.
136 See *Leo Putz 1869-1940*.
137 C. J. Bailey, Caspar David Friedrich: an introduction, in *Friedrich: Winter Landscape*, p. 9; and see in general Rosenblum, *Modern Painting and the Northern Romantic Tradition*.
138 Quoted in Bailey, Friedrich, p. 8.
139 Aubert, Der Landschaftsmaler Friedrich, col. 288.
140 Woermann, *Lebenserinnerungen*, Vol. 2, p. 55.
141 See Angermeyer-Deubler, Thoma.
142 See M. Nissen, *Der Rembrandtdeutsche Julius Langbehn*, Freiburg im Breisgau, Herder, 1926, ch. 11.
143 Haack, *Die Kunst des 19. Jahrhunderts*, p. 403.
144 *SBPrAH*, second session 1900, Vol. 2, 14 March 1900 (Metger), col. 3010.
145 See the essays in *Arnold Böcklin. Die Gemälde*; and J. Wissmann, Zum Nachleben der Malerei Arnold Böcklins, in *Arnold Böcklin 1827-1901*.
146 Wissmann, Zum Nachleben, p. 28.
147 See especially I. Koszinowski, Böcklin und seine Kritiker: zu Ideologie und Kunstbegriff um 1900, in Mai, Wolandt and Waetzoldt (eds.), *Ideengeschichte und Kunstwissenschaft*; and Paul, *Tschudi*, pp. 231-6.
148 Koszinowski, Böcklin und seine Kritiker, p. 281.
149 See W. Ranke, Böcklinmythen, in *Arnold Böcklin. Die Gemälde*.
150 Wissmann, Zum Nachleben, p. 37.
151 Koszinowski, Böcklin und seine Kritiker, p. 286.
152 *Ibid.*, p. 287.
153 M. Dottin, Laforgue, Böcklin, Klinger, in Hiddleston (ed.), *Laforgue aujourd'hui*, p. 192.
154 Böcklin, *German Masters of the Nineteenth Century*, p. 62. Böcklin's original title was *A Silent Place*.

155 Wissmann, Zum Nachleben, p. 28.
156 *Ibid.*, p. 31.
157 See Brandes, *Moderne Geister*, pp. 57-72; and in general *Max Klinger, 1857-1920*.
158 *Briefe von Max Klinger*, pp. 42-3, letter to H. Meier, 11 July 1883.
159 Lehrs, Max Klingers 'Brahms-Phantasie', *ZfbK* NS 6 (1895), p. 118.
160 U. Planner-Steiner, 'Auf der Suche nach dem Reich der Kunst'. Malerei und Gesamtkunstwerk, in *Max Klinger, 1857-1920*, p. 56.
161 In the Museum der bildenden Künste, Leipzig.
162 See M. Lehrs, Alexander Hummel und Max Klinger, *ZfbK* NS 26 (1914), pp. 131-73.
163 See Vaughan, *German Romantic Painting*, ch. 3.
164 See M. Bisanz-Prakken, *Gustav Klimt: Der Beethovenfries. Geschichte, Funktion und Bedeutung*, Munich, dtv, 1980.
165 Lehrs, Alexander Hummel und Max Klinger, p. 170.
166 Dottin, Laforgue, Böcklin, Klinger, p. 194.
167 See in general Gordon, *Expressionism*; *Expressionism: A German Intuition*; Eschenburg, *Landschaft*, pp. 182-93; N. Lynton, The New Age: primal work and mystic nights, in *Towards a New Art*.
168 See *Munch und Deutschland*; D. E. Gordon, Expressionism and its publics, in W. Schadendorf (ed.), *Beiträge zur Rezeption der Kunst*, p. 88.
169 Przybyszewski, *Das Werk von Edvard Munch*, pp. 25, 26,
170 Wissmann, Zum Nachleben, p. 37.
171 *Alexei Jawlensky 1864-1941*, p. 48.
172 Paul, *Tschudi*, pp. 205-15.
173 *Ibid.*, pp. 229-30.
174 W. Venzmer, Dachau bei München, in Wietek (ed.), *Deutsche Künstlerkolonien*, p. 52.
175 *The Blaue Reiter Almanac*, p. 56.
176 H. Osborne (ed.), Abstraction, in *The Oxford Companion to Twentieth-Century Art*, Oxford, University Press, 1981, p. 3.
177 See P. Vergo, Music and abstract painting: Kandinsky, Goethe and Schoenberg, in *Towards a New Art*.
178 *Ibid.*, p. 41.
179 Weiss, *Kandinsky in Munich*, pp. 96-8.
180 See especially S. Ringbom, Kandinsky und das Okkulte, in *Kandinsky und München*; and Weiler, *Jawlensky*, pp. 70-2.
181 *Briefe*, Vol. 2, p. 882: to Lily Klee, 14 October 1917.
182 In the Städtische Galerie im Lenbachhaus, Munich; and see Ringbom, Kandinsky und das Okkulte, pp. 94-5.
183 See Gordon, Expressionism and its publics, p. 88; *Der Blaue Reiter: Dokumente*.
184 *Briefe*, Vol. 1, p. 338: to Lily Stumpf.
185 See Weiss, *Kandinsky in Munich*, ch. 4.

186 P. Vergo, Introduction, in *Abstraction: Towards a New Art*, p. 15.
187 Vergo, Music and abstract painting, p. 52.
188 Lankheit, *Marc*, p. 72: Marc to Maria Marc, 10 February 1911

## CHAPTER 3

1 A. Lichtwark, Die Vorarbeit, in *Ein Jahrhundert deutscher Kunst*, Vol. 1, pp. vii–viii.
2 *KChr*, 9/44 (14 August 1874), p. 707.
3 See Richter, *Geschichte*; Schumann, *Dresden*; and Woermann, *Lebenserinnerungen*.
4 See Gordon, Kirchner in Dresden.
5 Richter, *Geschichte*, p. 219.
6 Woermann, *Lebenserinnerungen*, Vol. 2, p. 15.
7 Richter, *Geschichte*, pp. 163-4.
8 B. Hünlich, Dresdener Motive in Werken der Künstlergemeinschaft 'Brücke', *Jahrbuch der Staatlichen Kunstsammlungen Dresden*, 13 (1981), pp. 67-100.
9 Carus, *Lebenserinnerungen*, Vol. 2, p. 60.
10 Woermann, *Lebenserinnerungen*, Vol. 2, pp. 1-8; Heres, Gloria Dresdensis.
11 Richter, *Geschichte*, p. 209; and see V. Helas, *Villenarchitektur/Villa Architecture in Dresden*, Cologne, Taschen, 1991.
12 *Statistik des Deutschen Reichs*, Vol. 209, p. 581.
13 See Trier (ed.), *Zweihundert Jahre Kunstakademie Düsseldorf*; *Die Düsseldorfer Malerschule*; *Der westdeutsche Impuls (Düsseldorf)*.
14 Dube, *Munich Gallery*, pp. 46-7; Woermann, *Lebenserinnerungen*, pp. 334-5.
15 Peters, Schadow, p. 71.
16 Füssli, *Zürich und die wichtigsten Städte am Rhein*, Vol. 2, p. 551.
17 In the Kunstmuseum Düsseldorf; and see H. Gagel, Die Düsseldorfer Malerschule in der politischen Situation des Vormärz und 1848, in *Die Düsseldorfer Malerschule*, p. 70.
18 R. Andrée, Böcklin in Düsseldorf, in *Arnold Böcklin 1827-1901* (1974), p. 16.
19 Most, Deutsches Städtewesen, in *Deutschland als Weltmacht*, p. 168; and see H. A. Peters, W. Schepers S. v. Wiese, Düsseldorf - eine Großstadt auf den Weg in die Moderne, in *Der westdeutsche Impuls (Düsseldorf)*.
20 In the Kunstmuseum Düsseldorf; and see *Die Düsseldorfer Malerschule*, nr. 97, pp. 329-31.
21 *Commercial Relations of the United States*, 1878, pp. 426-7.
22 See Woermann, *Lebenserinnerungen*, pp. 357-70.
23 *Briefe*, Vol. 1, pp. 196-8: 13 July 1895.
24 G. Moeller, Peter Behrens und die Düsseldorfer Kunstgewerbeschule 1903-7, *Der westdeutsche Impuls (Düsseldorf)*.
25 M. Moeller, Der Sonderbund.
26 J. Hülsewig, Moderne Kunst in Düsseldorfer Galerien.

27 D. Teuber, Die Galerie Alfred Flechtheim, Düsseldorf, in *Der westdeutsche Impuls (Köln)*; and *Alfred Flechtheim.*

28 See in general Lieb, *München*; *Die Münchner Schule*; Ludwig, *Münchner Malerei.*

29 Howitt-Watts, *An Art Student in Munich*, Vol. 1, p. 232.

30 Rall and Petzet, *Ludwig II*, p. v.

31 D. Klein, Bürgerliches Bauen in der Prinzregentenzeit, in Prinz and Krauss (eds.), *München*, p. 90.

32 See Wilberforce, *Social Life in Munich*, ch. 17.

33 See *Johann Georg von Dillis.*

34 G. Himmelheber, Kunst des Biedermeier, in *Kunst des Biedermeier*, pp. 38-9.

35 See *München 1869-1958*; Holt, *Art of All Nations*, pp. 493-532.

36 See E. Ruhmer, Courbet in der Sicht des Leibl-Kreises, in *Courbet und Deutschland*, and pp. 49, 366.

37 Wolf, Sechzig Jahre, p. 295.

38 See Andrée, Böcklin in Düsseldorf; *Munich and American Realism.*

39 Bernáth, *Szinyei-Merse*, p. 9.

40 Cited in Holt, *Art of All Nations*, pp. 521, 529-30.

41 Atkinson, Munich International Exhibition, p. 327.

42 *Adressbuch für München*, 1887, pt. 2, pp. 43-56.

43 See *Allotria.*

44 See chapter 4 below.

45 See *Jübiläums-Ausstellung . . . : Katalog*; *KfA*, 2 (1886), p. 377.

46 See Betz, Kunstausstellung und Tagespresse, pp. 20-8; Makela, *Munich Secession*, ch. 2.

47 See Segieth, Zwischen Historismus, 'Secession' und 'Jugend', in Prinz and Krauss (eds.), *München*, pp. 253-4.

48 GNMAbK/Nbg: Dill Memoirs (typescript), p. 64.

49 *Ibid.*, p. 61.

50 See *Münchener Jahresausstellung* and *Verein bildender Künstler* catalogues, 1893; and Bierbaum, *Aus beiden Lagern.*

51 Klee, *Briefe*, Vol. 1, p. 647: Klee to Lily Stumpf, 12 June 1906; StG/W, Habermann Papers: Kandinsky to Secession Committee, 1 June 1906.

52 HSA/M, MK 14 359: Secession to Education Ministry, 14 June 1914.

53 See Paret, *Berlin Secession*, pp. 95-102; W.-D. Dube, Die Kunstsituation in Berlin und Corinth, in *Lovis Corinth 1858-1925: Gemälde und Druckgraphik.*

54 Rosenhagen, Münchens Niedergang als Kunstzentrum, *Der Tag*, nrs. 143, 145, 13 and 14 April 1901.

55 Engels, *Münchens Niedergang*, p. 12.

56 PStB. H/B, Tschudi Papers: Liebermann to Tschudi, 3 April 1899.

57 StG/W, Breyer Papers: Trübner to Robert Breyer, *c.* 1901.

58 See A. Andersen and R. Falter, Die 'Rauchplage': Grosstechnologie und frühe Großstadtkritik, and H. Karch, Das München-Bild und seine Vermarktung, in

Prinz and Krauss (eds.), *München*; Hardtwig, Soziale Räume und politische Herrschaft.

59 Isarius, Darmstadt - die 'werdende Kunststadt', *Deutsche Kunst und Dekoration*, 9 (1901/02).

60 Klinger, *Briefe*, pp. 32, 34: letters to his parents, June and July 1880.

61 *House of Commons Sessional Papers 1911*, Vol. 93: *Commercial Reports*, no. 4798, Bavarian Commerce 1910/11, p. 17.

62 See StadtAM/M, KA 148 (Künstlerhausverein); G. Hch., Das Münchener Künstlerhaus: zu seiner Einweihung, *KfA*, 15/15 (1 May 1900), pp. 339-50.

63 M. Eksteins, When Death was young . . . : Germany, modernism and the Great War, in R. J. Bullen *et al.* (eds.), *Ideas into Politics. Aspects of European History 1880–1950*, London and Totowa, NJ, Croom Helm, p. 28.

64 See Herrmann, Die 'Jugend' und ihr Künstlerkreis; *Simplicissimus: eine satirische Zeitschrift 1896-1914*, Munich, Haus der Kunst, 1977.

65 See Hochreiter, *Vom Musentempel*, pp. 126-79.

66 See Weiss, *Kandinsky in Munich*, ch. 9.

67 See material in HSA/M, MK 14 359 (Ausstellungsgebäude für Kunst und Kunstgewerbe).

68 See Zammito, Der Streit um die Berliner Kultur.

69 Goncourts, *Journal*, Vol. 1, p. 794: 6 September 1860.

70 *Ibid.*, p. 808: 18 September 1860.

71 Scheffler, *Berlin*, pp. 11-16.

72 Vriesen, *Macke*, p. 22.

73 Himmelheber, Kunst des Biedermeier, p. 37.

74 Bartmann, *Werner*, pp. 168-71; Teeuwisse, *Vom Salon zur Secession*, pp. 29-37.

75 See chapter 4 below.

76 *KChr*, 22/5 (11 November 1886), col. 76.

77 Lübke, Berliner Eindrücke (1890) in his *Altes und Neues*.

78 *Berlin und die Berliner*, p. 145.

79 C. Tower, *Germany of Today*, London, Williams & Norgate, 1914, p. 43.

80 Walser, Berlin und der Künstler, *KuK*, 8 (1910), pp. 195, 196.

81 *Lovis Corinth. Eine Dokumentation*, p. 58: Corinth to Josef Ruederer, 28 December 1899.

82 Uhr, *Corinth*, p. 171.

83 See Doede, *Berliner Secession*; Paret, *Berlin Secession*; Teeuwisse, *Vom Salon zur Secession*.

84 Heller, *Munch*, p. 100.

85 Heller, Anton v. Werner, der Fall Munch und die Moderne, in *Anton von Werner. Geschichte in Bildern*, p. 102.

86 *Ibid.*

87 *KChr*, NS 4/5 (17 November 1892), col. 74.

88 See Lenman, *Kunst, Macht und Geld*, ch. 1.

89 Paul, *Tschudi*, pp. 105-6.
90 PStB. H/B, Tschudi Papers: Liebermann to Tschudi, 3 April 1899.
91 See Tafel, Paul Cassirer als Vermittler; and chapter 4 below.
92 *Liebermann in seiner Zeit*, p. 286.
93 See StG/W, Habermann Papers, for example Paul Cassirer to Habermann, 6 June 1901 and 12 March 1903.
94 PStB. H/B, Tschudi Papers: Liebermann to Tschudi, 20 and 28 August 1903.
95 See Paret, *Berlin Secession*, ch. 6.
96 Godé, *Der Sturm*.
97 See Baum *et al.* (eds.), *Die Stuttgarter Kunst*.
98 Cleve, *Geschmack, Kunst und Konsum*, ch. 5.
99 Venzmer, *Hölzel*, pp. 20-1.
100 *Ibid.*, pp. 27-8.
101 *Franz Marc 1880-1916*, pp. 39-40: Dr Hans Hildebrandt to Marc, 25 April 1913.
102 Venzmer, *Hölzel*, p. 28.
103 *Ibid.*, p. 20; M. Diez, Die kgl. Kunstgewerbeschule und die Lehr- und Versuchswerkstätte, in Baum *et al.* (eds.), *Die Stuttgarter Kunst*.
104 Klinger, *Briefe*, p. 14: Klinger to his father, 6 October 1875.
105 StB. M/Mon, Langhammer Papers: Poetzelberger to Arthur Langhammer, 25 January 1894.
106 HSA/M, MK 18 160: Zügel, curriculum vitae.
107 W. von zur Westen, Moderne Arbeiten der angewandten graphischen Kunst in Deutschland: die Reklame-Kleinkunst, *Zeitschrift für Bücherfreunde*, 5 (1901/02), pp. 389-90; Singer, *Moderne Graphik*, p. 12.
108 *Briefe*, Vol. 2, p. 58: 8 October 1903.
109 Hofmannsthal–Kessler, *Briefwechsel*, pp. 111-12, 114-15: Kessler to Hofmannsthal, 6 December 1905 and 8 March 1906.
110 See Bismarck, Kessler und die französische Kunst.
111 Hofmannsthal–Kessler, *Briefwechsel*, p. 118: Kessler to Hofmannsthal, 24 June 1906.
112 See van de Velde, *Geschichte meines Lebens*, chaps. 8-11.
113 See Franz, Der erste und der letzte Grossherzog von Hessen; and in general *Ein Dokument . . . : Darmstadt 1901-1976*, Vols. 1-5.
114 H. Kleinstück, Der Kunstverein Darmstadt um 1900 als Wegbereiter der Mathildenhöhe, in *Ein Dokument . . . : Darmstadt 1901-1976*, Vol. 3, pp. 9-11.
115 [Deiters], *Bericht*, p. 5.
116 Windsor, *Behrens*, p. 18; *München und seine Bauten*, p. 387.
117 See Koch in *Ein Dokument deutscher Kunst*, p. 10; and other contributions.
118 For example Isarius, Darmstadt.
119 E. Reinhold-Postina, *Jugendstil, Traditionalismus und Heimatliche Bauweise*, Darmstädter Architekturgeschichte, Vol. 3, Darmstadt, Roether, 1991, p. 9.
120 E. G. Franz, Die Stadt der Künstlerkolonie: Darmstadt 1900-1914, in *Ein Dokument . . . : Darmstadt 1901-1976*, pp. 12, 22, 34.

121 Koch, *Darmstadt*, p. ii.
122 P. F. Schmidt, Die Künstlerkolonie zu Darmstadt 1899-1914, in *Festschrift zum 25jährigen Regierungsjubiläum*, p. 83.
123 See E. Mai, Die Berliner Kunstakademie im 19. Jahrhundert: Kunstpolitik und Kunstpraxis, in Mai and Waetzoldt (eds.), *Kunstverwaltung, Bau- und Denkmalpolitik*, pp. 431-4; and in general Pevsner, *Academies of Art*.
124 Mai, Kunstpolitik am Rhein, in Trier and Weyres (eds.), *Kunst des 19. Jahrhunderts im Rheinland*, p. 17.
125 *KfA*, 1 (1885), p. 117.
126 See HSA/M, MK 14 144-5 (Munich Academy 1886-1908); Woermann, Zur Geschichte der Düsseldorfer Kunstakademie, in *Von Apelles bis Böcklin*, Vol. 2, pp. 221-3; Richter, *Geschichte*, pp. 191-3.
127 Bartmann, *Werner*, pp. 168-71.
128 See Woermann, Zur Geschichte der Düsseldorfer Kunstakademie; *Lebenserinnerungen*, Vol. 1, pp. 343-50.
129 *August Macke*, p. 13.
130 J. Krsnjavi, Der Kunstunterricht an der Münchener Akademie, *ZfbK*,15 (1880), pp. 110-16.
131 In *KfA*, 2/9 (1 February 1887), pp. 129-38; and see HSA/M, MK 14 113: Prime Minister Lutz to Prince Regent, 17 April 1887.
132 *Neue Pinakothek München: Erläuterungen*, p. 255.
133 See HSA/M, MK 18 133 (Habermann), especially Habermann to Education Ministry, early November (?) 1905.
134 *SHKK*, 1880, pp. 167-91.
135 HSA/M, MK 14 095: Education Minister Wehner to Prince Regent, 29 April 1909.
136 *KChr*, 17/16 (2 February 1882), col. 256.
137 Figures in HSA/M, 14 155 (Academy enrolments 1889-1921).
138 See Mai, Kunstakademien im Wandel: zur Reform der Künstlerausbildung im 19. Jahrhundert: die Beispiele Berlin und München, in Wingler (ed.), *Kunstschulreform*.
139 Kugler, Über den Pauperismus auch in der Kunst, in *Kleine Schriften*, Vol. 3, p. 556.
140 See chapter 1 above.
141 See Von der Weltaussellung in Chicago (1893), in *Kunst und Kunstgewerbe*, pp. 39-44.
142 Mai, Kunstakademien im Wandel, p. 34.
143 HSA/M, MK 14 095: Academy Directorate to Education Ministry, 27 March 1902.
144 See J. Rickert, Das pädagogische Prinzip der Breslauer Kunstakademie (1900–1932), in Wingler (ed.), *Kunstschulreform*.
145 S. v. Wiese, Die Düsseldorfer Kunstakademie 1900-14 zwischen Restauration und Reform, in *Der westdeutsche Impuls (Düsseldorf)*, p. 103.

146 K. H. Meissner, Die Geschichte der Akademie der bildenden Künste in München, in *Die Zwanziger Jahre in München*.
147 *Briefe*, Vol. 1, pp. 15-16: Klee to Ida Klee, 16 October 1898.
148 *Adressbuch für München und Umgebung*, 1914, pt. 4, pp. 116-17, 121-2.
149 *Satzungen für die Studierenden der Kgl. Bay. Akademie der bildenden Künste in München*, Munich, 1890, § 6; Klee, *Briefe*, Vol. 1, pp. 17-18: Klee to Ida Klee, 19 October 1898.
150 Weiss, *Kandinsky in Munich*, pp. 63-5.
151 *Ibid.*, ch. 1; *Alexei Jawlensky 1864-1941*, pp. 41-3.
152 See Klee, *Briefe*, Vol. 1: letters from late 1898 to late 1899.
153 Klee, *Tagebücher*, nr. 81, p. 45.
154 See W. v. Debschitz, Eine Methode des Kunstunterrichts, and H. Obrist, Die Lehr- und Versuchateliers für angewandte und freie Kunst, *Dekorative Kunst*, 7 (1903/04), pp. 209-27 and 228-32; H. Schmoll gen. Eisenwerth, Die Münchener Debschitz-Schule, in Wingler (ed.), *Kunstschulreform*.
155 Obrist, Die Lehr- und Versuchateliers, p. 231.
156 Berger, *Malerinnen*, pp. 91-3.
157 Drey, *Die wirtschaftlichen Grundlagen*, p. 73.
158 Berger, *Malerinnen*, pp. 92-4.
159 HSA/M, MK 14 146: Academy Directorate to Education Ministry, 26 June 1916.
160 See Modersohn-Becker, *Briefe und Tagebuchblätter*, pp. 87-119.
161 Werner, *Erlebnisse*, p. 275.
162 StG/W, Habermann Papers: Dorothea Dieckhoff to Habermann, 1 November [?].
163 Berger, *Malerinnen*, p. 91.
164 GStA/M, MA 92 294: undated typescript memo. (probably spring 1914); and see material in StadtAM/M, KA 133 (Künstlerinnenverein).
165 StadtAM/M, KA 133: memo. of 12 January 1907.
166 StadtAM/M, KA 189 (Die Juryfreien): memo. of 8 October 1909.
167 StadtAM/M, KA 133: Künstlerinnenverein annual report for 1911/12, pp. 49-50.
168 Berger, *Malerinnen*, p. 140; and compare Gillett, *The Victorian Painter's World*, ch. 6, and Garb, Gender and Representation, in Blake *et al.*, *Modernity and Modernism*.
169 D. F. Hoopes, The Düsseldorf Academy and the Americans, in *The Düsseldorf Academy and the Americans*, p. 26.
170 See U. Schneede, 'Aus der Erinnerung und mit der Phantasie': Skandinavien in Berlin – Munchs 'zweite Heimat', in *Munch und Deutschland*.
171 Brunn and Reulecke (eds.), *Berlin*, p. 187.
172 See A. Morawinska, Zur polnischen Malerei des 19. und beginnenden 20. Jahrhunderts, in *'Ein seltsamer Garten'*; Jensen (ed.), *Polnische Malerei*.
173 See Jacobs, *The Good and Simple Life*, ch. 7.
174 *Albert Bierstadt*, p. 36.
175 Quick, Munich and American Realism, in *Munich and American Realism*, p. 22;

and see E. Ruhmer, München um 1875: Schnittpunkt internationaler Kunstbeziehungen, in *Die Münchner Schule*, pp. 82, 84.

176 White, *Currier*, p. 29 (quoting Marr).

177 Quick, Munich and American Realism, p. 23; and Duveneck, *Duveneck*.

178 Jeszenszky, 'Le déjeuner sur l'herbe' de Szinyei, p. 24.

179 Starzynski, *Gierymski*, p. 9.

180 See H. B. Weinberg, Cosmopolitan attitudes: the coming of age of American art, in *Paris 1889*.

181 Jacobs, *The Good and Simple Life*, pp. 88-9; and see *Dreams of a Summer Night: Scandinavian Painting at the Turn of the Century*, London, Arts Council, 1986.

182 Jeszenszky, 'Le déjeuner sur l'herbe' de Szinyei, pp. 18-25.

183 K. Varnedoe, Nordic art at the turn of the century, in *Northern Light*, pp. 17-19.

184 G. Éri and Z. Jobbágyi (eds.), *A Golden Age: Art and Society in Hungary 1896-1914*, Budapest, London and Miami, 1989, p. 43.

185 See *BVKS/D*, 1870/71, pp. 3-6; *Dresden Royal Gallery: Catalogue*, pp. xi–xx.

186 Heres, Gloria Dresdensis, pp. 11-12.

187 *Aufzeichnungen des . . . Dichters P. D. A. Atterbom*, p. 92.

188 See Dube, *Munich Gallery*.

189 *Ibid.*; and Hardtwig, Privatvergnügen oder Staatsaufgabe? in Mai and Paret (eds.), *Sammler, Stifter und Museen*.

190 Goncourts, *Journal*, Vol. 1, p. 809: 18 September 1860.

191 See Osborn, *Berlin*, ch. 12; Hochreiter, *Vom Musentempel*, pp. 41-4.

192 *SHKK*, 1880, p. 21; 1881, pp. 24-5.

193 Hochreiter, *Vom Musentempel*, pp. 33-40; Rave, Schinkels Museum; H. Menz, Die Dresdener Gemäldegalerie im Semperbau 1855-1960, *Jahrbuch der staatlichen Kunstsammlungen Dresden*, 16 (1984), pp. 83-4.

194 Menz, Dresdener Gemäldegalerie, pp. 85-6.

195 *Ibid.*, pp. 86-90.

196 HSA/M, MK 18 129: Doerner, Über Gemälderestaurierung, November 1918.

197 With, *Landeskunstkommission*, pp. 27-8.

198 For example Karl Steffeck in 1883 and 1886: With, *Landeskunstkommission*, p. 48.

199 MFM/W, Weigand Papers: Weigand to Hermann Eichfeld, 15 October 1904.

200 Ansell and Fraprie, *The Art of the Munich Galleries*, ch. 8.

201 Paul, *Tschudi*, p. 294.

202 Martin, *Tschudi-Spende*, pp. 18-20; Die Änderung in der obersten Leitung der bayrischen Galerien, *KChr*, NS 25/41 (21 August 1914), cols. 601-2.

203 See Lenman, *Kunst, Macht und Geld*, ch. 1.

204 *Ibid.*; and see E. Roters, Kunst im Widerspruch, in Boberg, Fichter and Gillen (eds.), *Industriekultur in Berlin im 19. Jahrhundert: Die Metropole*.

205 Bröhan, *Leistikow*, p. 120: Leistikow to Theodor Wolff, 29 June 1898.

206 See Paret, *Berlin Secession*, ch. 4.

207 *Vossische Zeitung*, 4 December 1913; HSA/M, MK 18 155: Stuck to Education Ministry, 17 December 1913.
208 Woermann, *Lebenserinnerungen*, Vol. 2, p. 86.
209 Schneede, 'Aus der Erinnerung und mit der Phantasie', in *Munch und Deutschland*, pp. 14-16.
210 Leiss, *Kunst im Konflikt*, pp. 95-101.
211 See in general Möckl, *Prinzregentenzeit*; and F. Prinz, Annäherung an München: postmoderne Rückblicke auf die Geburt einer Großstadt, in Prinz and Krauss (eds.), *München*.
212 See Lenman, Politics and culture.
213 Möckl, *Prinzregentenzeit*, pp. 541-7.
214 Rosenberg, *Friedrich August Kaulbach*, p. 3; *Art Journal*, NS 9 (1870), p. 81.
215 For example *SBBayKdA*, 2 May 1914, pp. 720-2 (Siben).
216 Lübke, Berliner Eindrücke, p. 437.
217 Lenman, *Kunst, Macht und Geld*, p. 51.
218 PStB. H/B, Tschudi Papers: Liebermann to Tschudi, 9 September 1898; and see Lenman, *Kunst, Macht und Geld*, pp. 41-52.
219 See Prinz, Annäherung an München, pp. 17-21; and Möckl, Hof und Hofgesellschaft, pp. 211-13.
220 Ranke, *Lenbach*, pp. 291-3.
221 See Segieth, Zwischen Historismus, 'Secession' und 'Jugend'.
222 Nr. 71, 10 February 1912.
223 Mayr, *Leibl*, p. 127.
224 *Ibid.*, p. 100.
225 Wichmann, *Meister, Schüler, Themen*, pp. 35-6.
226 White, *Currier*, pp. 22-3.
227 Stein, *Putz*, pp. 42-52.
228 E. T. Rohnert, *Heinrich von Zügel: Ein Malerleben*, Berlin, 1941, p. 78.
229 Jähner, *Künstlergruppe Brücke*, pp. 46-9.
230 G. Wietek, Dangast am Jadebusen, in Wietek (ed.), *Deutsche Künstlerkolonien*.
231 Johanek, Mittelalterliche Stadt, in Althoff (ed.), *Die Deutschen und ihr Mittelalter*, p. 89.
232 Rosenthal, *Erinnerungen*, p. 45.
233 R. Sheppard, Kandinsky's *œuvre* 1900-14: the avant-garde as rear-guard, *Word and Image*, 6 (1990), p. 45.
234 See Bantzer, *Hessen in der deutschen Malerei*; K. Kaiser, Willingshausen in der hessischen Schwalm, in Wietek (ed.), *Deutsche Künstlerkolonien*.
235 *Die Düsseldorfer Malerschule*, p. 369.
236 See G. Krüger, Goppeln bei Dresden, in Wietek (ed.), *Deutsche Künstlerkolonien*.
237 *Carl Bantzer*, pp. 72-97.
238 See A. Sailer, Frauenchiemsee in Oberbayern, in Wietek (ed.), *Deutsche Künstlerkolonien*; Raupp and Wolter, *Künstlerchronik von Frauenchiemsee*.

239 See Teufel, *Ateliers*: Raupp.
240 See Venzmer, Dachau, in Wietek (ed.), *Deutsche Künstlerkolonien*; Rössler, *Neu-Dachau*.
241 F. Heinle, *Ludwig Thoma*, Reinbek, Rowohlt, 1963, p. 95.
242 H. Hildebrandt, *Adolf Hölzel als Maler*, Stuttgart, 1913, p. 7.
243 See R. Gollek, Murnau, in Wietek (ed.), *Deutsche Künstlerkolonien*.
244 Howitt-Watts, *An Art Student in Munich*, Vol. 1, p. 51.
245 Gollek, Murnau, p. 179.
246 Sheppard, Kandinsky's *œuvre*, p. 46.
247 See Jacobs, *The Good and Simple Life*, ch. 6; K. V. Riedel, Worpswede im Teufelsmoor bei Bremen, in Wietek (ed.), *Deutsche Künstlerkolonien*.
248 Worpswede, in *Aufsätze*, Vol. 3, p. 279.
249 See Perry, *Modersohn-Becker*; Berger, *Malerinnen*, pp. 261-95.
250 Modersohn-Becker, *Briefe und Tagebücher*, p. 74: letter to her family, 12 February 1899.
251 Venzmer, Dachau, p. 54.
252 S. Weltge-Wortmann, *Die ersten Maler in Worpswede*, Worpswede, Worpsweder Verlag, 1979, p. 36.
253 PStB. H/B, *Sturm* Archive: Marc to Walden, 3 (?) June 1914: 'I've now got a *telephone*! (Benediktbeuern 20)'.

## CHAPTER 4

1 Drey, Kunstmarkt, p. 12.
2 See chapters 1 and 2 above.
3 Vaughan, *German Romantic Painting*, p. 21.
4 Richter, *Lebenserinnerungen*, pp. 370-1.
5 Kalkschmidt, *Spitzweg*, p. 43; *KVB*, 1922/23, p. 55.
6 See *KVB*, 1878.
7 *KChr*, 13/28 (25 April 1878), cols. 451-2.
8 *KVB*, 1903.
9 *KVB*, 1911, p. vii.
10 Über die gegenwärtigen Verhältnisse der Kunst zum Leben, in *Kleine Schriften*, Vol. 3, pp. 218-19.
11 Bartmann, *Werner*, pp. 179-87.
12 Schumann, *Dresden*, pp. 253-6.
13 See Betz, Kunstausstellungen und Tagespresse, p. 18; Wolf, Sechzig Jahre.
14 Drey, Kunstmarkt, pp. 61-2.
15 See SAM/M, Polizeidirektion 1025: international exhibitions, 1879-1913.
16 StB. M/Mon: Künstlergenossenschaft annual reports; *KChr*, 22/5 (11 November 1886), col. 76; Drey, Kunstmarkt, p. 170.

17 Drey, Kunstmarkt, p. 171.

18 Franke, Publikum und Malerei, p. 107.

19 See *KChr*, NS 4/6 (24 November 1892), cols. 92-3; *ZfbK*, NS 3 (1891/92), p. 304.

20 Müller, *Aus Gärten der Vergangenheit*, p. 198.

21 Franke, Publikum und Malerei, p. 35, citing H. E. v. Berlepsch.

22 Milner, *Studios of Paris*, p. 48.

23 Franke, Publikum und Malerei, p. 34.

24 StB. M/Mon: Künstlergenossenschaft reports (only those for 1892-94 show how many items were not for sale).

25 Drey, Kunstmarkt, p. 123.

26 StadtAM/M, KA 148 (Künstlerhausverein): Dill to städt. Baucommission, 20 May 1893.

27 *Berlin und die Berliner*, p. 263

28 Drey, Kunstmarkt, pp. 170-1.

29 *Ibid.*, pp. 172-3.

30 See StadtAM/M, KA 189 (Die Juryfreien).

31 See H.-U. Thamer, Sammler und Sammlungen in der frühen Neuzeit, in Mai and Paret (eds.), *Sammler, Stifter und Museen*. On the art trade generally, see Drey, Kunstmarkt, pp. 129-50; Moulin, *Le marché de la peinture en France*; Jensen, *Marketing Modernism*.

32 A. Zweite, Aspekte der Münchener Landschaftsmalerei, in *Münchner Landschaftsmalerei*, p. 23.

33 Hardtwig, Privatvergnügen oder Staatsaufgabe? in Mai and Paret (eds.), *Sammler, Stifter und Museen*, p. 89.

34 *Adressbuch der Haupt- und Residenzstadt Darmstadt*, 1900, pp. 505-6; 1910, p. 563.

35 See *E. A. Fleischmanns Hofkunsthandlung*; *KChr*, 16/43 (15 September 1881), col. 734.

36 GNMAbK/Nbg: Heinemann Archive; also Kahn, *Münchens Grossindustrie*, pp. 291-2.

37 Jules Laforgue, in Teeuwisse, *Vom Salon*, p. 104.

38 *Berlin und die Berliner*, p. 263.

39 *Munch und Deutschland*, p. 249.

40 See Teeuwisse, *Vom Salon*, pp. 235-6.

41 *Briefe und Tagebücher von Paula Modersohn-Becker*, pp. 144-5.

42 Bühler, *Anton Braith, Christian Mali*, p. 37.

43 Teeuwisse, *Vom Salon*, pp. 230-4; Meier-Graefe, Handel und Händler, pp. 32-4.

44 F. Hellwag, Die 'fliegenden' Kunsthändler, *Die Kunst*, 28 (1911), pp. 418-24; Drey, Kunstmarkt, pp. 152-3.

45 See J. Eltz, Der grosse Bilderdiebstahl oder das 'originale' Fälschen, in *Franz von Lenbach 1836-1904*.

46 See *Münchener Neuesten Nachrichten*, nrs. 552-82, 25 November-10 December 1908; *KM*, 6/2 (10 October 1908).
47 *Adressbuch für München und Umgebung*, 1912.
48 *Handzeichnungen . . . aus der Sammlung Cichorius*, p. 12.
49 Kutter, *Das materielle Elend*, p. 11.
50 *KM*, 10/35 (30 May 1913), p. 304.
51 Drey, Kunstmarkt, pp. 49-50, 122-4, 151-2.
52 GNMAbK/Nbg, Heinemann Archive: artist index.
53 Imiela, *Slevogt*, p. 52.
54 S. Pucks, 'Und die Deutschen begannen, mich kräftig zu unterstützen'. Edvard Munchs Förderer in Deutschland 1902-1912, in *Munch und Deutschland*, p. 97.
55 *Ibid.*
56 StGL/M, Gabriele-Münter-Stiftung: Kandinsky to Goltz (pencil draft), 12 September 1912.
57 See in general Mühsam, *Kunstauktion*.
58 *E. A. Fleischmanns Hofkunsthandlung*, p. 6.
59 Mühsam, *Kunstauktion*, pp. 169-73; Kahn, *Münchens Grossindustrie*, pp. 302-3.
60 M. Lehrs, Alfred Lichtwarks Briefe, *ZfbK*, NS 53 (1918), p. 189.
61 Mühsam, *Kunstauktion*, pp. 176-82.
62 Bailey, Friedrich, in *Friedrich: Winter Landscape*, p. 29.
63 Dr Lucanus, Der Kunstverein zu Halberstadt, *DKB*, 1/6 (11 February 1850), pp. 47-8.
64 PStB. H/B, *Sturm* Archive: note on back of letter from Galerie Arnold to Marc, 16 June 1913.
65 *SHKK*, 1880, p. 275.
66 *150 Jahre Kunstverein Darmstadt*, p. 27.
67 Jensen, *Marketing Modernism*, p. 76; E. Mai, 'Was vorher war': Kunstleben und Ausstellungswesen in Köln vom 19. und 20. Jahrhundert, in *Der westdeutsche Impuls (Köln)*, pp. 39-40.
68 *Munch und Deutschland*, p. 255; Heller, Anton von Werner, der Fall Munch und die Moderne, in *Anton von Werner. Geschichte in Bildern*, p. 106.
69 *Lovis Corinth. Eine Dokumentation*, pp. 43-4.
70 Venzmer, *Hölzel*, p. 17.
71 See Jensen, *Marketing Modernism*, pp. 190-4.
72 See *KHB*, 6th edn., 1904; and *Pantheon*, 1914.
73 Lichtwark, Der Sammler, 1, pp. 234-40.
74 Langenstein, *Münchener Kunstverein*, p. 192.
75 See the list of purchasers printed in Roennefahrt, *Spitzweg*.
76 Münchener Neuesten Nachrichten, nr. 522, 25 November 1908.
77 See *Lovis Corinth. Eine Dokumentation*, p. 382, and further correspondence; Uhr, *Corinth*, pp. 113, 115-16.

78 StB. M/Mon, Helbing sale catalogues; *KHB*, 6th edn., 1904, p. 255; Weigand, *Welt und Weg*.

79 Schumann, *Dresden*, p. 39.

80 *KHB*, 6th edn., 1904, p. 81; With, Menzel, pp. 179-81.

81 See A. Pophanken, Graf Adolf Friedrich von Schack und seine Galerie: Anmerkungen zur Münchner Sammlungsgeschichte, in Mai and Paret (eds.), *Sammler, Stifter und Museen*; E. Ruhmer, Adolf Friedrich von Schack und seine Sammlung, in *Arnold Böcklin 1827–1901* (1974); and Schack, *Meine Gemäldesammlung*, pp. 125-46.

82 Lenbach, *Gespräche und Erinnerungen*, p. 48.

83 Huret, *En Allemagne*, pp. 27-8.

84 Stern, *Gold and Iron*, pp. 478, 482.

85 See Grundmann, Schlösser und Villen.

86 See R. Köhne-Lindenlaub, Private Kunstförderung im Kaiserreich am Beispiel Krupp, in Mai, Pohl and Waetzoldt (eds.), *Kunstpolitik und Kunstförderung*.

87 *Aspekte der Gründerzeit*, pp. 62-4.

88 See *Die Gemälde-Galerie des verstorbenen Herrn Adolf von Liebermann in Berlin*, ed. J. M. Heberle, Cologne, Lempertz, 1894.

89 See *Die Sammlung Eduard Behrens zu Hamburg*, ed. E. Heilbut, 1891; Lichtwark, Eduard L. Behrens: Schlussworte bei der Gedächtnisfeier im Kunstverein 1895, in *Aus der Praxis*, pp. 86-92.

90 G. Howaldt, Zur ehemaligen Kunstsammlung Heyl in Darmstadt, in *Arnold Böcklin 1827–1901* (1974).

91 G. Czymmek, Wilhelm Leibls Leben, in *Leibl zum 150. Geburtstag*, pp. 41-2.

92 See *Die Galerie Thomas Knorr*.

93 See Pixis, *Verzeichnis*.

94 Weiss, *Kandinsky in Munich*, p. 68.

95 StB. M/Mon, Künstlergenossenschaft reports, 1890-94.

96 StB. M/Mon, Künstlergenossenschaft reports, 1889-94; Drey, Kunstmarkt, p. 20.

97 Warburg Institute, London, CPE 574: Kunst-Kataloge 1815-46

98 Lucanus, Der Kunstverein zu Halberstadt, pp. 47-8.

99 Warburg Institute, London, CPE 574: Kunst-Kataloge 1815-46.

100 *German and Austrian Painting in the Hermitage*, Leningrad, Aurora, 1986, p. 66.

101 *DKB*, 1/9 (4 March 1850), p. 72.

102 *DKB*, 1/24 (17 June 1850), p. 192.

103 See Victoria & Albert Museum, London, 78.P: Carnegie Institute catalogues (from 1896); Alloway, *The Venice Biennale*.

104 Kahn, *Münchens Grossindustrie*, pp. 291-2.

105 *Fleischmanns Hofkunsthandlung*, p. 4.

106 See Lenman, Art and tourism in southern Germany.

107 M. Krauss, *Die Grundlagen des Fremdenverkehrs in München und im bayerischen Hochland*, Munich, 1917, pp. 43-4.

108 *ZBSL*, 47 (1915), p. 36.
109 See for example Continental Travel Ltd., London (Lunn), *The Travel Handbook and Calendar, Summer 1911*.
110 StadtAM/M, KA 397 (Prinzregententheater): Wagner/Mozart festival programme.
111 See H. Gebhardt, Illustrierte Zeitschriften in Deutschland am Ende des 19. Jahrhunderts, *Börsenblatt für den deutschen Buchhandel* (1983), pp. 41-65.
112 'V. D. N.', Das Paznaunerthal, *Die Gartenlaube*, 33 (1885), nr. 21, pp. 345-8 and nr. 22, pp. 363-7.
113 See for example Bay. Staatsbibliothek, Munich: Bayerischer Fremdenverkehrsrat, Jahresbericht 1910/11.
114 A. Stark, Die Bauern bei Ludwig Thoma mit besonderer Berücksichtigung der Dachauer Bauern, PhD dissertation, Munich, 1937, p. 15.
115 *ZBSL*, 47 (1915), pp. 36-7.
116 StB. M/Mon: Künstlergenossenschaft reports, 1889-94.
117 Drey, Kunstmarkt, p. 168.
118 Howitt-Watts, *An Art Student in Munich*, Vol. 1, p. 21.
119 *Briefe von Josef Viktor von Scheffel*, p. 88: Scheffel to Werner, 24 June 1868.
120 See *Dictionary of National Biography*, 2nd Supplement, 1901-11, Oxford, University Press, 1912, Vol. 2, pp. 37-9.
121 See catalogues in Victoria & Albert Museum, London, 200.B.170-1.
122 Angermeyer-Deubler, Thoma, p. 160.
123 See Graves, *Art Sales*.
124 *The René von Schleinitz Collection*, p. 63.
125 Quoted in Langenstein, *Münchener Kunstverein*, p. 185.
126 See R. L. Stehle, The Düsseldorf Gallery of New York, *New York Historical Society Quarterly*, October 1974, pp. 304-17.
127 H. Weiss, Für deutsche Künstler, *DKB*, 1/22 (3 June 1850), pp. 169-70
128 Stehle, Düsseldorf Gallery, p. 309.
129 Atkinson, Munich International Exhibition, p. 327.
130 Bühler, *Anton Braith, Christian Mali*, p. 57.
131 Makela, *Munich Secession*, p. 17.
132 *KChr*, 20/24 (26 March 1885), cols. 415-16; and see *61st Congress, 2nd Session 1909-10: House Documents Vol. 129: Tariff Acts Passed by the Congress of the United States from 1789 to 1909*, pp. 342, 406, 500, 590, 759; J. Zilczer, *'The Noble Buyer': John Quinn, Patron of the Avant-Garde*, Washington, DC, Smithsonian Institution Press, 1978, pp. 28-31.
133 See H. W. Morgan, *New Muses. Art in American Culture, 1865-1920*, Norman, University of Oklahoma Press, 1978, chs. 2, 4.
134 StB. Mon/M: Künstlergenossenschaft reports, 1889-94. In 1893 some dollars probably went to the Secession.
135 See Paret, *Berlin Secession*, pp. 112-55.

136 See GStA/M, MA 92 358: art sales to America and other foreign countries.
137 GStA/M, MA 92 358: Prime Minister Podewils to Adjutant-General v. Wiedenmann, 1 December 1909.
138 Paret, *Berlin Secession*, pp. 121-3.
139 GStA/M, MA 92 358: memo. of German Trade Attaché Waetzoldt in New York, 24 July 1907.
140 *SBRT*, Vol. 192, 15 February 1904, cols. 1018-19 (E. Müller-Meiningen).
141 *The Letters of Oscar Wilde*, ed. R. Hart-Davis, London, Rupert Hart-Davis, 1962, p. 103: Wilde to Mrs George Lewis, March 1882.
142 Drey, Kunstmarkt, p. 24.
143 See figures in *ZBSL*, 41 (1909) to 46 (1914).
144 *KM*, 9/13 (29 December 1911), p. 124.
145 Zimmermanns, *Kaulbach*, p. 252.
146 GNMAbK/Nbg, Heinemann Archive: client index.
147 Drey, Kunstmarkt, p. 22.
148 See Ludwig, *Kunst, Geld und Politik*, pp. 255-7.
149 StB. M/Mon, Künstlergenossenschaft Collection 182/67: authorisation form annotated by Pecht; and see Drey, Kunstmarkt, pp. 19-23.
150 Der junge Künstler und die Wirklichkeit, *JbGHK*, 15 (1909), pp. 60-1.
151 Lichtwark, Der Sammler, 1, pp. 229-30.
152 Meier-Graefe, Handel und Händler, 1, p. 30; and see also Drey, Kunstmarkt, pp. 24-48.
153 Tschudi, *Gesammelte Schriften*, p. 230.
154 Die Böhm'sche Kunstauction in Wien, *KChr*, 1/1-2 (30 January 1866), pp. 1-2.
155 *Bericht über die Tätigkeit des Städel'schen Kunstinstituts 1894-1907*, pp. 10-11.
156 See Martin, *Alt-Holländische Bilder*, ch. 3.
157 Lichtwark, Der junge Künstler und die Wirklichkeit, p. 56.
158 See for example StG/W, Habermann Papers: Ludwig Dill to Habermann, 29 November 1900.
159 H. Holenweg, Das Schicksal der Gemälde Arnold Böcklins, in *Arnold Böcklin. Die Gemälde*, pp. 99-100.
160 See G. H. Grell and A. Löwengard, Städtische und ländliche Einzelhäuser unter Berücksichtigung der Umgegend Hamburgs, in *Hamburg und seine Bauten*, Hamburg, Architekten- und Ingenieurverein, 1914, Vol. 1.
161 HSA/M, MK 14 284: Tschudi to Bavarian Education Ministry, 1 March 1911; Holenweg, Das Schicksal, p. 100, states 200,000 marks.
162 Meier-Graefe, Handel und Händler, 3, pp. 306-7.
163 *Leibl zum 150. Geburtstag*, p. 344.
164 Bantzer, *Hessen in der deutschen Malerei*, p. 32.
165 Lenman, *Kunst, Macht und Geld*, pp. 78, 79.
166 Meier-Graefe, Handel und Händler, 3, p. 308.
167 *Ibid.*

168 *Ibid.*; but note the much lower 1911 auction prices in *Jahrbuch der Bilder- und Kunstblätterpreise*, pp. 206-8.
169 Drey, Kunstmarkt, p. 44.
170 Pucks, 'Und die Deutschen begannen . . . ', pp. 94-5.
171 Berghahn, *Imperial Germany*, p. 9.
172 *Münchener Handbuch*, 26 (1913), pp. 412-14.
173 Bode, Die amerikanische Konkurrenz.
174 Bode, Die Berliner Museen und die amerikanische Konkurrenz.
175 See Distel, *Impressionism*, chs. 20 and 21; S. Schaeffer, Impressionism and the popular imagination, in *A Day in the Country*, pp. 342-5.
176 Weitzenhoffer, *The Havemeyers*, p. 208; Lichtwark, *Briefe*, Vol. 2, pp. 484-7: 11 December 1912.
177 Tschudi, Die Sammlung Arnhold, 2, *KuK*, 7 (1909), p. 57.
178 Lichtwark, *Briefe*, Vol. 2, p. 476: 7 December 1912.
179 *Ibid.*, p. 486: 11 December 1912.
180 HSA/M, MK 14 284: Tschudi to Education Ministry, 1 March 1911.
181 HSA/M, MK 14 283: Education Minister Wehner to Prince Regent Luitpold, 30 December 1911.
182 HSA/M, MInn 14 163: Education Ministry to Foreign Ministry, 26 January 1900.
183 Woermann, *Lebenserinnerungen*, Vol. 2, pp. 86-8; ZIK/M: Dresdener Museumsverein, Jahresbericht 1911/12.
184 Feldenkirchen, Staatliche Kunstfinanzierung, in Mai, Pohl and Waetzoldt (eds.), *Kunstpolitik und Kunstförderung*, pp. 39-43.
185 Seidlitz, Museumsvereine, p. 36.
186 *KHB*, 6th edn., 1904, pp. 627-8; *Kunstmuseum Düsseldorf: Führer*, p. 5.
187 Seidlitz, Museumsvereine, pp. 39-40.
188 *Ibid.*, p. 40; *Bericht über die Tätigkeit des Städel'schen Kunstinstituts, 1894-1907*, pp. 2-4, 38-42.
189 Bruns, *Württemberg*, p. 636.
190 ZIK/M: Dresdener Museumsverein, Jahresbericht 1911/12.
191 *Briefe*, Vol. 2, p. 458: 24 October 1912.
192 See H.-G. Wormit, James Simon als Mäzen der Berliner Museen, *Jahrbuch der Stiftung Preussischer Kulturbesitz*, 1 (1963); and see also T. Gaehtgens, Wilhelm Bode und seine Sammler, in Mai and Paret (eds.), *Sammler, Stifter und Museen*.
193 *SBPrAH*, 21. Leg.-Periode, 5. Sess., 1912/13, Vol. 10, 12 April 1913, pp. 13987-8; and see Gaehtgens, *Berliner Museumsinsel*.
194 With, *Landeskunstkommission*, pp. 98-9; also *Nationalgalerie Berlin: Verzeichnis*.
195 HSA/M, MK 14 284: Directorate of Bavarian State Galleries (Heinz Braune) to Education Ministry, 30 January 1912; and Paul, *Tschudi*, pp. 314-15.
196 Examples in HSA/M, MK 14 283.
197 Lichtwark, Der Sammler; and Dibbern, Hamburger Kunsthalle, pp. 25-37, 80-99.

198 Schlink, 'Kunst ist dazu da . . . ', in Lepsius (ed.), *Bildungsbürgertum*, p. 78.
199 Lichtwark, Hamburg, *Pan*, 2 (1896), pp. 313-23; and Dibbern, Hamburger Kunsthalle, p. 235, note 47.
200 Lehrs, Lichtwarks Briefe.
201 See *Hamburger Kunsthalle: Katalog*, 1969.
202 Hentzen, Die Entstehung der Bildnisse.
203 *Hamburger Kunsthalle: Katalog*, 1969, nr. 1821.
204 Werner, *Erlebnisse*, p. 63.
205 See *Ausstellung von Werken . . . Menzels*, 1905.
206 HSA/M, MK 14 278: minutes of meeting, 13 January 1908.
207 *KChr*, 17/28 (27 April 1882), col. 452.
208 See White, *Currier*; and Weigmann, *Wenban*.
209 Article reprinted in *Von Wilhelm Leibl bis Lovis Corinth*, pp. 18-19.
210 See *Katalog der III. internationalen Ausstellung . . . zu Dresden*.
211 M. Michel, Ein moderner Kunstsalon in München, *Dekorative Kunst*, 9 (1906), p. 542; and in general sale results published in *KM*, 1903-14.
212 Horn, *Düsseldorfer Graphik*, p. 149.
213 Graul, *Vervielfältigende Kunst*, p. 79.
214 Singer, *Die moderne Graphik*, p. 1.
215 See for example T. Goebel, Die grossen deutschen Verlagsanstalten: die Verlagsanstalt F. Bruckmann A.-G. in München, *Zeitschrift für Bücherfreunde*, 4 (1900).
216 K. Voll, Die Reform der deutschen Kunstvereine, illustriert am Münchener Verein, *KfA*, 14/17 (1 June 1899), p. 259; *BVKS/D*, 1878/79, p. 17.
217 C. Herchenroider, *Meistergraphik, Graphikmarkt: Sammeln, Preise, Geschmack*, Munich, Kunst und Antiquitäten, 1983, p. 13.
218 See C. M. Nebehay, *Ver Sacrum 1898-1903*, Munich, dtv, 1979.
219 For example, G. K., Heinrich Zille, *ZfbK*, NS 15 (1904), p. 224, with his etching *Nacht*.
220 Singer, *Die moderne Graphik*, p. 60.
221 *BVKS/D*, 1896/97, p. 43.
222 See W. v. Seidlitz, Max Lehrs, in *Dresdner Jahrbuch. Beiträge zur bildenden Kunst*, 1905, pp. 113-20.
223 A. Rosenberg, Ausstellung in der Nationalgalerie, *KChr*, 16/34 (2 June 1881), cols. 545-9.
224 *Franz von Lenbach 1836-1904*, p. 95, n. 25.
225 Lehrs, Daguerreotypen, *ZfbK*, NS 28 (1917), pp. 181-96.
226 Seidlitz, *Geschichte des japanischen Farbenholzschnitts*, Dresden, 1897, 1910.
227 Warburg Institute, London, CPE 574: *Gesellschaft Hamburgischer Kunstfreunde* [GHK]: *Katalog*.
228 G. Schiefler, Die graphische Ausstellung der GHK im Jahre 1903, *JbGHK*, 10 (1904), pp. 102-4.

229 Carey and Griffiths, *The Print in Germany*, p. 18.
230 Singer, *Die moderne Graphik*, p. 4.
231 Die Kunst des Steindrucks, *Pan*, 2/3 (1896), p. 233; and see A. Griffiths, Starting again from scratch: lithography in Germany from the 1890s to the 1920s, in Gilmour (ed.), *Lasting Impressions*.
232 *Die farbige Künstlerlithographie und ihre Bedeutung für die künstlerische Kultur*, Leipzig, Voigtländer 1912. (copy held in the library of the Victoria & Albert Museum, London).
233 Victoria & Albert Museum, London: *Künstlerischer Wandschmuck. Eine Anregung und ein Verzeichnis. Herausg. vom Bildungsausschuss der Sozialdemokratischen Partei Deutschlands*, Berlin, 1909, p. 5.
234 *GHK Katalog*, 1903/04.
235 *Lovis Corinth. Eine Dokumentation*, p. 223: Corinth to H. Struck, 29 June 1917.
236 Herchenroider, *Meistergraphik*, pp. 73-4.
237 Singer, *Die moderne Graphik*, p. 70.
238 *Ibid.*, p. 2.
239 See *KM*, 10/23 and 10/36 (7 March and 6 June 1913), pp. 202, 308-10; and *Jahrbuch der Bilder- und Kunstblätterpreise*, 1912.
240 Lichtwark, *Briefe*, Vol. 2, p. 141: 10 June 1905.
241 Singer, *Die moderne Graphik*, p. 1.
242 *Ibid.*, p. 2.
243 *Ibid.*, p. 429.
244 Lehrs, Kunst und Kino, in *Gesammeltes*, pp. 205-10.
245 Griffiths, Starting again, p. 193.
246 Rosenblum and Janson, *Art of the Nineteenth Century*, p. 60.
247 Klee, *Briefe*, Vol 1, p. 650: to Lily Stumpf, 24 June 1906.
248 Carey and Griffiths, *The Print in Germany*, p. 107.
249 Griffiths, Starting again, pp. 193-8.
250 H. A. Lier, Die Aquarellistenausstellung in Dresden, *ZfbK*, 23 (1888), pp. 66-7.
251 P. Weiss, Kandinsky und München: Begegnungen und Wandlungen, in *Kandinsky und München*, p. 49.
252 Griffiths, Starting again, p. 198.
253 Hesse-Frielinghaus, *Osthaus*, p. 195.
254 G. Woll, Munchs Graphik in Deutschland: vom Zustandsdruck zur Massenauflage; and Pucks, 'Und die deutschen begannen . . . ', in *Munch und Deutschland*, pp. 46, 50, 97.
255 Gutbrod, Rezeption, pp. 122-5.
256 *Ibid.*, pp. 64-5; Jensen, *Marketing Modernism*, p. 79.
257 Paul, *Tschudi*, p. 202; and in general especially Jensen, *Marketing Modernism*, ch. 2.
258 Gutbrod, Rezeption, p. 105.
259 See Distel, *Impressionism*, pp. 233-5; Weitzenhoffer, *The Havemeyers*, ch. 8.
260 Gutbrod, Rezeption, p. 59.

261 Paul, *Tschudi*, p. 91.
262 See especially Tafel, Paul Cassirer als Vermittler; also Teeuwisse, *Vom Salon*, pp. 236-41; Gutbrod, Rezeption, pp. 61-71.
263 Gutbrod, Rezeption, pp. 100-1, 104-5.
264 See Tschudi, Die Sammlung Bernstein, *Gesammelte Schriften*, pp. 232-7; Teeuwisse, *Vom Salon*, pp. 98-104; B. Paul, Drei Sammlungen, pp. 11-15.
265 Teeuwisse, *Vom Salon*, p. 103.
266 P. Krieger, Max Liebermanns Impressionisten-Sammlung und ihre Bedeutung für sein Werk, in *Liebermann in seiner Zeit*; Paul, Drei Sammlungen, pp. 15-19.
267 Tschudi, Die Sammlung Arnhold, 1, *KuK*, 7 (1909), p. 4; Paul, Drei Sammlungen, pp. 19-25.
268 E. Hancke, Die Sammlung Stern, *KuK*, 8 (1910), pp. 536-48; Warburg Institute, London: Helbing–Cassirer sale catalogue, May 1916.
269 *Bonnard: Sketches of a Journey. Travels in an early motorcar. From Octave Mirbeau's journal 'La 628-E8'. With illustrations by Pierre Bonnard*, London, Philip Wilson, 1989, p. 168.
270 See Bismarck, Graf Harry Kessler und die französische Kunst.
271 See Hesse-Frielinghaus, *Osthaus*.
272 Gutbrod, Rezeption, pp. 64-5.
273 Uhde-Bernays, *Im Lichte der Freiheit*, p. 312.
274 P. Fechter, Die Sammlung Schmitz, *KuK*, 8 (1910), pp. 15-25.
275 P. Fechter, Die Sammlung Rothermundt, *KuK*, 8 (1910), pp. 346-55.
276 E. Heilbut, Die Sammlung Linde in Lübeck, *KuK*, 2 (1903/04), pp. 6-20, 303-25.
277 Pucks, 'Und die Deutschen begannen', pp. 93, 97.
278 Heilbut, Die Sammlung Linde, 1, p. 20.
279 See P. Paret, Bemerkungen zu dem Thema: jüdische Kunstsammler, Stifter und Kunstsammler, in Mai and Paret (eds.), *Sammler, Stifter und Museen*.
280 Heller, Werner, der Fall Munch und die Moderne, in *Anton von Werner. Geschichte in Bildern*, p. 106.
281 GStA/M, MA 92 302: Education Minister Wehner to Prime Minister Podewils, 2 December 1911.
282 Moulin, *Le Marché de la peinture en France*, ch. 5; and compare Vollard, *Souvenirs*, ch. 4.
283 Compare T. H. Breen, The meanings of things: interpreting the consumer economy in the eighteenth century, in Brewer and Porter (eds.), *Consumption and the World of Goods*, pp. 249-60; and on the question of evidence, S. Schama, Perishable commodities: Dutch still-life paintings and the 'empire of things', especially pp. 483-4.
284 See Schaeffer, Impressionism and the popular imagination; Herbert, *Impressionism*, pp. 303-6.

285 Compare Halle, *Inside Culture*, ch. 5, on 'primitive' art in modern American homes.
286 Breuer, Die Sammlung Eduard Fuchs, *KuK*, 10 (1912), p. 460.
287 Alt, *Die Herabwertung der deutschen Kunst*.
288 See Weiss, *Kandinsky in Munich*.
289 See StadtAM/M, KA 189 (Die Juryfreien): Georg Fuchs to Verwaltungsrat des städt. Ausstellungs-Areales, 21 July 1909.
290 Makela, *Munich Secession*, p. 135; Woll, Munchs Graphik, p. 54.
291 See Michel, Ein moderner Kunstsalon in München; *Leo Putz 1869-1940*, pp. 51, 54.
292 Macke–Marc, *Briefwechsel*, pp. 19-20: Marc to Macke, 30 August 1910.
293 See *Moderne Galerie Heinrich Thannhauser München: Eröffnungs-Austellung November 1909*; G. Biermann, Die Kunst auf dem internationalen Markt, 1: Gemälde aus dem Besitz der Modernen Galerie Thannhauser, München, *Der Cicerone*, 5 (1913), pp. 309-26.
294 See K. Lochmaier, Die Galerie 'Neue Kunst Hans Goltz' in München, in Junge (ed.), *Avant-Garde und Publikum*.
295 PStB. H/B, *Sturm* Archive: Marc to Walden, 31 August 1912.
296 Kandinsky–Marc, *Briefwechsel*, p. 191: Marc to Kandinsky, 1 October 1912.
297 PStB. H/B, *Sturm* Archive: Marc to Walden, [1913].
298 *Ibid.*: Marc to Walden, 22 February and 15 June 1913; and see *Münter*, ed. Mochon, p. 40.
299 Kandinsky–Marc, *Briefwechsel*, p. 61: Kandinsky to Marc, 21 September 1911.
300 Macke–Marc, *Briefwechsel*, pp. 19-20, Marc to Macke, 30 August 1910.
301 Kandinsky–Marc, *Briefwechsel*, p. 203: Marc to Münter, 10 December 1912.
302 *Ibid.*, pp. 109-26: Marc to Kandinsky, 10, 14, 18/19, 23 January 1912.
303 *Ibid.*, p. 38: Marc to Kandinsky, [1 March] 1912.
304 See Marc–Piper letters in GNMAbK/Nbg, Marc Papers, FM IIc.
305 Piper, *Mein Leben*, pp. 296-9.
306 Kandinsky–Marc, *Briefwechsel*, p. 138: Marc to Kandinsky, [1 March] 1912; and see Strauss, Kandinsky and 'Der Sturm'; Godé, *Der Sturm*, pp. 93-6.
307 StGL/M, Gabriele-Münter-Stiftung: Walden to Kandinsky, 2 October 1912.
308 Godé, *Der Sturm*, ch. 1 and pp. 31-41.
309 PStB. H/B, *Sturm* Archive: Kandinsky to Walden, 11 March 1914.
310 Lochmaier, Die Galerie 'Neue Kunst Hans Goltz', p. 108.
311 Kandinsky–Marc, *Briefwechsel*, p. 228: Marc to Kandinsky, 16 June 1913.
312 PStB. H/B, *Sturm* Archive: Kandinsky to Walden, 6 January 1914.
313 StGL/M, Gabriele-Münter-Stiftung: Walden to Kandinsky, 22 August 1912; Kandinsky to Goltz (draft), 12 September 1912; Walden to Münter, 18 January 1913; GNMAbK/NbG: Marc Papers, FM Ib/6a, Goltz account, *c.* August 1912.
314 PStB. H/B, *Sturm* Archive: Kandinsky to Walden, 25 February 1914.

315 *Ibid.*: Marc to Walden, 22 February 1913.
316 Godé, *Der Sturm*, p. 91.
317 StGL/M, Gabriele-Münter-Stiftung: Walden to Kandinsky, 28 September 1912.
318 Many of the letters deal with these issues.
319 StGL/M, Gabriele-Münter-Stiftung: *Der Sturm* to Goltz, 16 December 1912; Walden to Kandinsky, 18 December 1912.
320 Hesse-Frielinghaus, *Osthaus*, pp. 137-55, 195-200.
321 *Franz Marc 1880-1916*, p. 36.
322 *Der westdeutsche Impuls (Wuppertal)*, pp. 100-1.
323 *Ibid.*, pp. 90-98; *Die Sammlung . . . von der Heydt*.
324 Klee, *Tagebücher*, p. 212: nr. 765, 13 April 1906.
325 Wietek, Dangast, in Wietek (ed.), *Deutsche Künstlerkolonien*, p. 176.
326 PStB. H/B, *Sturm* Archive: Marc to Walden, 27 and 29 August 1912.
327 Macke–Marc, *Briefwechsel*, p. 135: Macke to Marc, 1 July 1912.
328 StGL/M, Gabriele-Münter-Stiftung: Walden to Kandinsky, 31 October 1913.
329 *Ibid.*: Walden to Münter, 3 (5?) November 1913.
330 GNMAbK/Nbg, Marc Papers, FM IIIc: Kluxen to Walden (copy), 30 January 1913.
331 See Schmidt, Koehler.
332 GNMAbK/Nbg, Marc Papers, FM Ic: Koehler to Marc, 18 and 23 July 1910; *Franz Marc 1880-1916*, pp. 26-7.
333 Schmidt, Koehler, p. 84.
334 PStB. H/B, *Sturm* Archive: Marc to Walden, 11 (?) August (?) 1913.
335 Gordon, *Modern Art Exhibitions*, Vol. 1, p. 339.
336 *August Macke*, p. 515; Macke was distancing himself from the Blue Rider by the autumn of 1913, although he had a one-man show with Walden the following January.
337 StGL/M, Gabriele-Münter-Stiftung: Walden to Münter, 11 June 1913.
338 PStB. H/B, *Sturm* Archive: Marc to Walden, 10 May 1913.
339 *Ibid.*: Marc to Walden, 23 July 1913; Kandinsky–Marc, *Briefwechsel*, pp. 233-7: Marc to Münter, 23 and 27 July, 7 August 1913; *Franz Marc 1880-1916*, p. 40: Marc to Klee, August 1913.
340 *Franz Marc 1880–1916*, p. 125.
341 Kandinsky–Marc, *Briefwechsel*, pp. 184, 186: Marc to Münter, 19 and 21 July 1912.
342 *Ibid.*, p. 212: Kandinsky to Marc, 8 March 1913. Other, overlapping links were via the 1912 Sonderbund exhibition and Stieglitz's friend Marsden Hartley.
343 PStB. H/B, *Sturm* Archive: Kandinsky to Walden, 18 November 1913 (Kandinsky referred to 'a collector in Chicago'). See Röthel and Benjamin, *Kandinsky. Catalogue Raisonné*, nos. 437, 441, 452, 455, 460, 468, 477.
344 *Münter*, ed. Mochon, p. 51, nr. 47.
345 Kandinsky–Marc, *Briefwechsel*, p. 244: Marc to Kandinsky, *c.* mid-November 1913.

346 Lindsay, Kandinsky in 1914 New York, p. 33.
347 *Ibid.*; they reached New York, after being exhibited in Stockholm, in the summer of 1916.
348 Drey, *Die wirtschaftlichen Grundlagen*, pp. 64–5.
349 PStB. H/B, *Sturm* Archive: Marc to Walden, 13 February 1913.
350 *Ibid.*: Kandinsky to Walden, 29 September 1912.
351 *Ibid.*: Jawlensky to Walden, 30 June 1914.
352 Stein, *Putz*, p. 46.
353 BKrA/M, OP 69691: Reserve-Jäger-Regt. 16 to 12 Bav. Reserve Infantry Brigade, 18 March 1915.
354 GNMAbK/Nbg, Marc Papers, FM Ib/6a: Goltz accounts, summer 1912.
355 PStB. H/B, *Sturm* Archive: Marc to Walden, 23 July and [after 24] September 1913. The present location of the pictures is, respectively: private collection; Kunstmuseum Düsseldorf; Staatsgalerie Moderner Kunst, Munich (loan); Städt. Galerie Hanover; Phillips Collection, Washington, DC; Robert Gore Rifkind Collection, Los Angeles.
356 *Ibid.*: Marc to Walden, [after 24] September 1913.
357 *Ibid.*: Marc to Walden, [after 25] February 1914.
358 *Ibid.*: Marc to Walden, 10 June 1914. Still, the sale of Marc's parents' home had enabled him to acquire a substantial house in Ried near Benediktbeuren in April 1914.
359 *Ibid.*: Kandinsky to Walden (card), 27 September 1913.
360 *Ibid.*: Kandinsky to Walden, 12 November 1913.
361 *Ibid.*: Kandinsky to Walden, 18 November 1913.
362 *Ibid.*: Marc to Walden, 31 August 1912.
363 *Der westdeutsche Impuls (Wuppertal)*, p. 142.
364 PStB. H/B, *Sturm* Archive: Kandinsky to Walden, 2 January 1914.
365 GNMAbK/Nbg, Marc Papers, FM Ic: Koehler to Marc, 14 January 1915; PStB. H/B, *Sturm* Archive: Kandinsky to Walden, 7 February 1914.
366 PStB. H/B, *Sturm* Archive: Kandinsky to Walden, 18 November 1913.
367 *Ibid.*: Kandinsky to Walden, 7 February 1914.
368 Tietze, Der Blaue Reiter, p. 549; and see Lankheit, A history of the Almanac, in *The Blaue Reiter Almanac*, p. 44.

## EPILOGUE

1 PStB. H/B, *Sturm* Archive.
2 Weiler, *Jawlensky*, p. 89.
3 Hesse-Frielinghaus, *Osthaus*, pp. 84–5.
4 See F. Abel, Mars regiert die Stunde, and F. Rainer, Schwabings Untergang, *Allgemeine Rundschau*, 8 August and 14 November 1914.

5 *Adolf von Hildebrand und seine Welt*, p. 625: Hildebrand to Prince Rupprecht, 18 September 1914.
6 *Franz Marc 1880-1916*, p. 44.
7 *Ibid.*, Marc to Kandinsky, 24 October 1914.
8 See BKrA/M, MKr 1710: war artists and reporters, 1906-18.
9 BKrA/M, MKr 1710: Hans von Hayek to Bavarian War Ministry, 9. September 1914.
10 E. Mai, 'Ja, das ist der Krieg!' Zur Militär- und Schlachtenmalerei im Kaiserreich, in *Die letzten Tage der Menschheit*, p. 257.
11 Thiemann, *Erinnerungen*, pp. 36-8.
12 See D. Vorsteher, Bilder für den Sieg: das Plakat im Ersten Weltkrieg, in *Die letzten Tage der Menschheit.*
13 StG/W, Habermann Papers: Richard Winternitz to Habermann, 1 October 1917.
14 See BKrA/M, OP 19 650: Willi Geiger.
15 Werckmeister, *The Making of Paul Klee's Career*, p. 81.
16 *Franz Marc 1880-1916*, p. 47; on Marc's war service and death, see BKrA/M, OP 1602.
17 Klee, *Briefe*, Vol. 2, p. 908: letter of 28 (?) February 1918.
18 *Ibid.*, p. 946: Klee to Lily Klee, 16 December 1918.
19 StGL/M, Gabriele-Münter-Stiftung: Walden to Münter, 9 November 1912.
20 StGL/M, Gabriele-Münter-Stiftung: Walden to Münter, 24 September 1914.
21 *Lovis Corinth. Eine Dokumentation*, p. 194: Corinth to Otto H. Claass, 2 April 1915.
22 Waldmann, Der Krieg und die Bilderpreise, p. 378.
23 *Der Kunstmarkt*, 14/5 (27 October 1903), p. 31.
24 *KM*, 13/36 (2 June 1916), pp. 167-70; and Warburg Institute, London, Helbing–Cassirer sale catalogue, May 1916.
25 Donath, *Der Kunstsammler*, p. 151.
26 Waldmann, Der Krieg und die Bilderpreise, p. 380.
27 Bessel, *Germany after the First World War*, p. 31.
28 *KM*, 14/1 (5 October 1917), pp. 5-6.
29 *Lovis Corinth. Eine Dokumentation*, p. 229: Corinth to Schwarz, 30 September 1917.
30 *Ibid.*, p. 231: Corinth to H. Struck, 10 February 1918.
31 StG/W, Habermann Papers: Fritz Schreiber to Habermann, 4 April 1916.
32 Godé, *Der Sturm*, pp. 153-6.
33 Werckmeister, *The Making of Paul Klee's Career*, p. 96.
34 Klee, *Tagebücher*, p. 389: nr. 1092, 15 November 1917.
35 *Ibid.*, p. 408: nr. 1126a, 24 August 1918.
36 Hesse-Frielinghaus, *Osthaus*, pp. 137-55.
37 See B. Söntgen, Markus Kruss - ein Sammler von 'Brücke'-Künstlern, *Zeitschrift des deutschen Vereins für Kunstwissenschaft*, 40 (1988).

38 Venzmer, *Hölzel*, pp. 28–33.
39 See Klee, *Briefe*; and Werckmeister, *The Making of Paul Klee's Career*, esp. chs. 3–5.
40 Werckmeister, *The Making of Paul Klee's Career,* pp. 137–9.
41 Thiemann, *Erinnerungen*, p. 42.
42 See Riedel, Worpswede, in Wietek (ed.), *Deutsche Künstlerkolonien.*
43 Donath, *Der Kunstsammler*, p. 138.
44 StB. M/Mon: annotated Helbing sale catalogue, 14–16 March 1916.
45 Holtfrerich, *The German Inflation*, pp. 241–2.
46 *Lovis Corinth. Eine Dokumentation*, pp. 256, 261, 263.
47 *Der Kunstmarkt,* 12/9 (30 November 1914), p. 29.
48 See HSA/M, MK 14 237: Notgemeinschaft der deutschen Kunst, I, 1923–30.
49 V. L. Lidtke, Museen und die zeitgenössische Kunst in der Weimarer Republik, in Mai and Paret (eds.), *Sammler, Stifter und Museen*, pp. 220–2; also HSA/M, MK 14 359: Ausstellungsgebäude für Kunst und Kunstgewerbe.
50 For example A. Donath, Der Kunstmarkt 1922, *Jahrbuch für Kunstsammler*, 3 (1923).
51 Bantzer, *Hessen in der deutschen Malerei*, p. 32.
52 Lenman, Art and tourism in southern Germany, p. 176.
53 See for example HSA/M, MK 14 102: protest declaration of 13 February 1919; and Bessel, *Germany after the First World War*, p. 119.
54 See Holtfrerich, *The German Inflation*, pp. 266–78.
55 *KVB*, 1905.
56 StB. M/Mon: R. Hendschel, Einige Erlebnisse und Erfahrungen im Kunstreferat aus den Jahren 1915–1933 (typescript), p. 5.

# Bibliography

## UNPUBLISHED SOURCES

The available unpublished material relating to art and artists in the period covered by this book is very extensive, and likely to become much more so as more collections of private papers reach the archives. The documentary sources used here are located as follows:

### *Baldham*

Private collection: the Franz von Stuck Papers (correspondence, photographs, press material).

### *Berlin*

Preussische Staatsbibliothek, Handschriftenabteilung: the *Sturm-Archive Herwarth Walden* (letters from the Blue Rider artists, buyers, dealers and art arganisations); the *Hugo von Tschudi Papers* (letters from Max Liebermann and other artists).

### *London*

Public Record Office (Kew): FO 9 and FO 149 (Munich Consulate: diplomatic and economic reports and general correspondence).

### *Munich*

Private collection: Franz von Defregger Papers (diaries, some correspondence).

The Bavarian State Archives contain a mass of material relating to art in this period. The largest holdings are those of the Ministry of Church and School Affairs (MK) in the Bay. Hauptstaatsarchiv (Allgemeine Abteilung), dealing with museums, exhibition buildings, the Academy, honours, artists' models and many other matters. The Bavarian Foreign Ministry (MA) files in the Geheime Staatsarchiv cover international exhibitions, cultural relations with other German and foreign states, and proposed Reich legislation (for example on copyright, and sections of the Criminal Code pertaining to freedom of expression). The Geheime Hausarchiv contains papers relating to the patronage activities of Kings Ludwig II and III and Prince Regent Luitpold. The Bayerische Kriegsarchiv (MKr) holds dossiers on artists who served in the Bavarian army and material on war artists.

The Kulturamt (KA) files in the Münchener Stadtarchiv contain important material on aspects of the city's artistic life, especially the activities of the Secession and other societies, the Künstlerhaus, exhibitions and major cultural projects like the construction and running of the Prinzregententheater.

The Münchener Stadtbibliothek, Monacensia-Abteilung contains, in addition to a huge range of printed sources (newspapers, Art Guild and Art Union reports, address books and so on), useful collections of papers relating to the Art Guild and individual artists.

### *Nuremberg*

Germanisches Nationalmuseum, Archiv für bildende Kunst: *Franz Marc Papers* (correspondence with artists, Reinhard Piper, Bernhard Koehler and others); *Ludwig Dill Papers*: (typescript memoirs); *Heinemann Archive* (very extensive card indexes of buyers, artists and other dealers).

### *Würzburg*

Main–Fränkisches Museum: *Wilhelm Weigand Papers* (private and literary correspondence: letters from artists whose work Weigand collected, and relating to Weigand's activity as an adviser to the Bavarian State Galleries).

Städtische Galerie: *Hugo von Habermann Papers* (very large collection of letters and other material pertaining to many aspects of artistic life, especially the Munich Secession and its relations with other groups, from the late nineteenth century until Habermann's death in 1929); *Robert Breyer Papers* (letters from Trübner, Slevogt and others).

## HANDBOOKS AND OFFICIAL PUBLICATIONS

*Allgemeines Lexikon der bildenden Künste von der Antike bis zur Gegenwart, begr. von U. Thieme und F. Becker*, ed. H. Vollmer, Leipzig, Seemann, 1931.

*Berichte über die Verwaltung der königlichen Sammlungen für Kunst und Wissenschaft zu Dresden*, Dresden, various years.

*Jahrbuch der Bilder- und Kunstblätterpreise. Verzeichnisse der wichtigsten Versteigerungsergebnisse des deutschen Kunstmarktes*, ed. E. Mennbier, Vol. 2, Vienna, 1912.

*Kunsthandbuch für Deutschland. Verzeichnis der Behörden, Sammlungen, Lehranstalten*

*und Vereine für Kunst, Kunstgewerbe und Altertumskunde*, 6th edn., ed. M. Creutz, Berlin, Reimer, 1904.
*Münchener Handbuch. Kalender für Bureau, Comptoir und Haus*, Munich, various years.
*Pantheon . . . ein Handbuch für das Sammelwesen der ganzen Welt*, ed. J. Zenker, Esslingen, Neff, 1914.
*Statistik des Deutschen Reichs*, Berlin, various years.
*Statistisches Handbuch für Kunst und Kunstgewerbe im Deutschen Reich*, Berlin, 1880 and 1881.
*Stenographische Berichte über die Verhandlungen der Bayerischen Kammer der Abgeordneten,* Munich, various years.
*Stenographische Berichte über die Verhandlungen des Preussischen Abgeordnetenhauses,* Berlin, various years.
*Stenographische Berichte über die Verhandlungen des Reichstags*, Berlin, various years.

## PUBLISHED LETTERS, DIARIES AND MEMOIRS

*Aufzeichnungen des schwedischen Dichters P. D. A. Atterbom über berühmte deutsche Männer und Frauen nebst Reise-Erinnerungen aus Deutschland und Italien aus den Jahren 1817-19*, trans. F. Maurer, Berlin, 1867.
*Der Blaue Reiter: Dokumente einer geistigen Bewegung*, ed. A. Hüneke, Leipzig, Reclam, 1991.
Bode, W. v., *Mein Leben*, 2 vols., Berlin, Reckendorf, 1930.
Carrière, M., *Dreissig Jahre an der Akademie der Künste in München*, Brunswick, Westermann, 1888.
Carus, C. G., *Lebenserinnerungen und Denkwürdigkeiten*, ed. E. Jansen, 2 vols., Weimar, Kiepenheuer, 1966.
*Lovis Corinth. Eine Dokumentation*, ed. T. Corinth, Tübingen, Wasmuth, 1979.
Falke, J. v., *Lebenserinnerungen*, Leipzig, Meyer, 1897.
Goering, B. T., *Dreissig Jahre München: kultur- und kunstgeschichtliche Betrachtungen*, Munich, Beck, 1904.
Goncourt, E. and J. de, *Journal. Mémoires de la vie littéraire*, 4 vols., Paris, Fasquelle & Flammarion, 1956.
Gumppenberg, H. v., *Lebenserinnerungen. Aus dem Nachlass des Dichters*, Berlin and Zurich, Eigenbrödler-Verlag, 1930.
*Adolf von Hildebrand und seine Welt: Briefe*, ed. B. Sattler, Munich, Callwey, 1962.
Hugo von Hofmannsthal–Harry Graf Kessler, *Briefwechsel 1898-1929*, ed. H. Burger, Frankfurt-on-Main, Insel, 1968.
Wassily Kandinsky-Franz Marc, *Briefwechsel. Mit Briefen von und an Gabriele Münter und Maria Marc*, ed. K. Lankheit, Munich and Zurich, Piper, 1983.
Klee, P., *Briefe an die Familie 1893-1940*, ed. F. Klee, 2 vols., Cologne, DuMont, 1976.
Klee, P., *Tagebücher 1898-1918*, ed. F. Klee, Cologne, DuMont, 1957.

*Briefe von Max Klinger aus den Jahren 1874 bis 1919*, ed. H. W. Singer, Leipzig, Seemann, 1924.

Lenbach, F. v., *Gespräche und Erinnerungen. Mitgeteilt von W. Wyl*, Stuttgart and Leipzig, Deutsche Verlags-Anstalt, 1904.

Lichtwark, A., *Briefe an die Kommission für die Verwaltung der Kunsthalle*, ed. G. Pauli, 2 vols., Hamburg, Westermann, 1924.

August Macke–Franz Marc, *Briefwechsel*, ed. W. Macke, Cologne, DuMont, 1974.

*Adolph von Menzels Briefe. Mit Unterstützung der Erben des Meisters gesichtet und herausgegeben von Hans Wolff*, Berlin, Bard, 1914.

*Briefe und Tagebuchblätter von Paula Modersohn-Becker*, ed. S. D. Gallwitz, Munich, Wolff, 1922.

Müller, K. A. v., *Aus Gärten der Vergangenheit. Erinnerungen 1882-1914*, Stuttgart, Kilpper, 1951.

Pecht, F., *Aus meiner Zeit. Lebenserinnerungen*, 2 vols., Munich, Verlagsanstalt für Kunst und Wissenschaft, 1894.

Piper, R., *Mein Leben als Verleger: Vormittag, Nachmittag*, Munich, Piper, 1947, 1964.

Richter, L., *Lebenserinnerungen eines deutschen Malers*, ed. M. Fleischhack, Berlin, Evangelische Verlagsanstalt, [n. d.].

Rosenthal, T., *Erinnerungen eines Malers*, Munich, Pflaum, 1927.

Schack, A. F. Graf v., *Meine Gemäldesammlung*, 6th edn., Stuttgart, Cotta, 1891.

*Briefe von Josef Viktor von Scheffel an Anton von Werner 1863-1886*, ed. A. v. Werner, Stuttgart, Bonz, 1915.

Schlittgen, H., *Erinnerungen*, Munich, Langen, 1926.

Schnorr v. Carolsfeld, J., *Künstlerische Wege und Ziele. Schriftstücke aus der Feder des Malers*, ed. F. Schnorr v. Carolsfeld, Leipzig, 1909.

Thiemann, C., *Erinnerungen eines Dachauer Malers. Beiträge zur Geschichte Dachaus als Künstlerort*, Dachau, 1966.

Uhde-Bernays, H., *Im Lichte der Freiheit. Erinnerungen aus den Jahren 1880 bis 1914*, Frankfurt-on-Main, Insel, 1947.

Velde, H. van de, *Geschichte meines Lebens*, Munich, Piper, 1962.

Vollard, A., *Souvenirs d'un marchand de tableaux*, Paris, Albin Michel, 1948.

Weigand, W., *Welt und Weg. Aus meinem Leben*, Bonn, 1940.

Werner, A. v., *Erlebnisse und Eindrücke, 1870-1890*, Berlin, Mittler & Sohn, 1913.

Woermann, K., *Kunst- und Naturskizzen aus Nord- und Sud-Europa. Ein Reise-Tagebuch*, 2 vols., Düsseldorf, Voss, 1880.

Woermann, K., *Lebenserinnerungen eines Achtzigjährigen*, 2 vols., Leipzig, Bibliographisches Institut, 1924.

## CATALOGUES

*Abstraction: Towards a New Art. Painting 1910-20*, London, Tate Gallery, 1980.

*Albrecht Adam und seine Familie. Zur Geschichte einer Münchner Künstlerdynastie im 19. und 20. Jahrhundert*, ed. U. v. Hase-Schmundt, Munich, Wolf & Sohn, 1981.

*American Expatriate Painters of the Late Nineteenth Century*, ed. M. Quick, Dayton, Ohio, Dayton Art Institute, 1976.

*Aspekte der Gründerzeit*, Berlin, Mann, 1974.

*Ausstellung von Werken Adolph von Menzels, 1905*, Berlin, National-Galerie, 1905.

*Biedermeiers Glück und Ende . . . die gestörte Idylle 1815-1848*, ed. H. Ottomeyer and U. Laufer, Munich, Stadtmuseum, 1987.

*Albert Bierstadt, Art and Enterprise*, ed. N. K. Anderson and L. S. Ferber, New York, Hudson Hills Press, 1990.

Kgl. Ältere Pinakothek in München, *Katalog der Gemälde-Sammlung*, Munich, Bruckmann, 1904.

*Carl Bantzer 1857-1941. Foto, Zeichnung, Gemälde: Synthetischer Realismus*, Marburg, Kunstgeschichtliches Seminar, 1977.

*Arnold Böcklin 1827-1901*, Düsseldorf, Kunstmuseum, 1974.

*Arnold Böcklin 1827-1901. Gemälde, Zeichnungen, Plastiken. Ausstellung zum 150. Geburtstag*, Basel and Stuttgart, Schwabe, 1977.

*Arnold Böcklin. Die Gemälde*, ed. R. Andrée, Basle and Munich, Reinhardt/Prestel, 1977.

*Lovis Corinth 1858-1925*, ed. Z. Felix, Cologne, DuMont, 1986.

*Lovis Corinth 1858-1925: Gemälde und Druckgraphik*, Munich, Prestel, 1975.

*Courbet und Deutschland*, ed. W. Hofmann, Cologne, DuMont, 1978.

*A Day in the Country. Impressionism and the French Landscape*, by R. R. Bretell, S. Schaefer, S. Gache-Patin and F. Heilbrunn, Los Angeles and New York, Los Angeles County Museum/Abrams, 1984.

*Designs for the Dream King. The Castles and Palaces of Ludwig II of Bavaria*, London, Debrett's, 1978.

*Johann Georg von Dillis 1759-1841. Landschaft und Menschenbild*, ed. C. Heilmann, Munich, Prestel, 1991.

*Ein Dokument deutscher Kunst: Darmstadt 1901-1976*, 6 vols., Darmstadt, Roether, 1976-77.

Dresden Royal Gallery, *Catalogue of the Pictures*, 8th edn., Berlin, Bard, 1912.

Dresdner Galerie, *Neue Meister*, ed. H. Zimmermann, Leipzig, Seemann, 1965.

*Dritte internationalen Ausstellung von Aquarellen, Pastellen, Handzeichnungen und Radirungen zu Dresden, 10 August–25 September 1892: Katalog*, Dresden, Kunstgenossenschaft, 1892.

*De Dürer à Friedrich. Dessins allemands du Wallraff–Richartz Museum de Cologne*, Rennes, Musée des Beaux-Arts, 1994.

*The Düsseldorf Academy and the Americans*, Atlanta, High Museum of Art, 1973.

*Die Düsseldorfer Malerschule*, Mainz, Philipp von Zabern, 1979.

*Frank Eugene. The Dream of Beauty*, ed. U. Pohlmann, Munich, Stadtmuseum and Nazraeli Press, 1995.

*Expressionism: A German Intuition 1905-1920*, New York and San Francisco, Guggenheim Museum/Museum of Modern Art, 1980.

*Alfred Flechtheim: Sammler, Kunsthändler, Verleger*, Düsseldorf, Kunstmuseum, 1987.

*Caspar David Friedrich, 1774-1840*, ed. W. Hofmann, Munich, Prestel, 1974.

*Caspar David Friedrich: Winter Landscape*, ed. J. Leighton and C. J. Bailey, London, National Gallery, 1990.

*Caspar David Friedrich to Ferdinand Hodler: A Romantic Tradition. Nineteenth-Century Paintings and Drawings from the Oskar Reinhart Foundation, Winterthur*, ed. P. Wegmann, Frankfurt-on-Main and Leipzig, Insel, 1993.

*Die Galerie Thomas Knorr in München*, ed. F. v. Ostini, Munich, Knorr & Hirth, 1906.

*Gesellschaft Hamburgischer Kunstfreunde: Katalog der graphischen Ausstellung 1903-4*, Hamburg, 1903.

Hamburger Kunsthalle, *Katalog der Meister des 19. Jahrhunderts*, ed. E. M. Krafft and C.-W. Schumann, Hamburg, 1969.

Hamburger Kunsthalle, *Katalog der neueren Meister*, Hamburg, 1910.

Hamburger Kunsthalle, *Katalog der neueren Meister*, 2nd edn., Hamburg, 1926.

*Handzeichnungen deutscher Künstler des 19. Jahrhunderts aus der Sammlung Cichorius im königl. Kupferstichkabinett zu Dresden*, ed. J. L. Sponsel, Dresden, 1911.

*'Ihm, welcher der Andacht Tempel baut . . . '. Ludwig I und die Alte Pinakothek. Festschrift zum Jubiläumsjahr 1986*, Munich, Bay. Staatsgemäldesammlungen, 1986.

*Ein Jahrhundert deutscher Kunst. Ausstellung deutscher Kunst aus der Zeit von 1775-1875*, intr. by H. v. Tschudi, 2 vols., Munich, Bruckmann, 1906.

*Alexei Jawlensky 1864-1941*, ed. A. Zweite, Munich, 1983.

*Jubiläums-Ausstellung der kgl. Akademie der Kunst im Landesausstellungsgebäude zu Berlin, von Mai bis Oktober 1886: Katalog*, Berlin, 1886.

*Kandinsky und München. Begegnungen und Wandlungen, 1896-1914*, ed. A. Zweite, Munich, Prestel, 1982.

*Paul Klee. Das Frühwerk*, Munich, Prestel, 1979.

*Max Klinger 1857-1920. Wege zum Gesamtkunstwerk*, Mainz, Philipp von Zabern, 1984.

*Der Kölner Dom im Jahrhundert seiner Vollendung*, ed. H. Borger, 3 vols., Cologne, Historische Museen, 1980.

*König Ludwig II und die Kunst*, ed. M. Petzet, Munich, Prestel, 1968.

*Kunst des Biedermeier, 1815-1835. Architektur, Malerei, Plastik, Kunstgewerbe, Dichtung, Musik und Mode*, ed. G. Himmelheber, Munich, Prestel, 1988.

Kunstmuseum Düsseldorf, *Führer durch die Sammlungen, 1: Alte Kunst, 19. Jahrhundert*, Düsseldorf, Kunstmuseum, 1985.

Kunstmuseum Düsseldorf, *Malerei, 1: Die Gemälde des 19. Jahrhunderts, mit Ausnahme der Düsseldorfer Schule*, ed. R. Andrée, Mainz, Philipp von Zabern, 1981.

*Landschaft im Licht. Impressionistische Malerei in Europa und Nordamerika 1860-1919*, ed. G. Czymmek, Cologne, Wallraff–Richartz Museum, and Zurich, Kunsthaus, 1990.

*Leben und Arbeiten im Industriezeitalter. Eine Ausstellung zur Wirtschafts- und Sozialgeschichte Bayerns seit 1850*, Stuttgart, Theiss, 1985.

*Von Wilhelm Leibl bis Lovis Corinth: Pastelle, Aquarelle und Zeichnungen (1865-1925) aus der Sammlung Georg Schäfer in Schweinfurt*, ed. J. C. Jensen, Schweinfurt, Sammlung Schäfer, 1984.

*Wilhelm Leibl und sein Kreis*, ed. M. Petzet, Munich, Prestel, 1974.

*Wilhelm Leibl zum 150. Geburtstag*, ed. G. Czymmek and C. Lenz, Heidelberg, Braus, 1994.

*Franz von Lenbach 1836-1904*, ed. R. Gollek and W. Ranke, Munich, Prestel, 1987.

*Die Letzten Tage der Menschheit. Bilder des Ersten Weltkrieges*, ed. R. Rother, Berlin, Ars Nicolai and Deutsches Historisches Museum, 1994.

*Max Liebermann in seiner Zeit*, Munich, Prestel, 1979.

*August Macke: Gemälde, Aquarelle, Zeichnungen*, ed. E.-G. Güse, Munich, Bruckmann, 1986.

*Malerei 1800 bis um 1900, im Hessischen Landesmuseum Darmstadt*, Teil 1, ed. G. Howaldt, Kataloge des Hessischen Landesmuseums, Vol. 7, Hanau, Peters, 1979.

*Malerei nach Photographie. Von der camera obscura bis zur Pop Art, eine Dokumentation*, Munich, Stadtmuseum, 1970.

*Franz Marc 1880-1916*, Munich, Prestel, 1980.

*Menzel der Beobachter*, ed. W. Hofmann, Munich, Prestel, 1982.

*Munch und Deutschland*, Hamburg, Kunsthalle, 1994.

*München 1869-1958. Aufbruch zur modernen Kunst*, Munich, Prestel, 1958.

*'München leuchtete': Karl Caspar und die Erneuerung der christlichen Kunst in München um 1900*, ed. P.-K. Schuster, Munich, Prestel, 1984.

*Münchener Jahresausstellung von Kunstwerken aller Nationen im kgl. Glaspalaste: Illustrierter Katalog*, Munich, Hanfstaengl, 1893.

*Die Münchener Secession und ihre Galerie*, Munich, Stadtmuseum, 1975.

*Münchner Landschaftsmalerei 1800-1850*, Munich, Städt. Galerie, 1979.

*Die Münchner Schule, 1850-1914*, Munich, Bay. Staatsgemäldesammlungen & Haus der Kunst, 1979.

*Munich and American Realism in the Nineteenth Century*, Sacramento, Crocker Art Gallery, 1978.

*Gabriele Münter 1877-1962*, ed. R. Gollek, Munich, Stadtgalerie, 1977.

*Gabriele Münter: Between Munich and Murnau*, ed. A. Mochon, Boston, Busch–Reisinger Museum, 1980.

Nationalgalerie Berlin, *Verzeichnis der Gemälde und Skulpturen des 19. Jahrhunderts*, ed. B. Dieterich, P. Krieger, E. Krimmel-Decker, Berlin, Staatliche Museen Preussischer Kulturbesitz, 1976.

National-Galerie zu Berlin, *Verzeichnis der Gemälde und Bildwerke*, Berlin, 1934.

Kgl. Neue Pinakothek, München, *Katalog der Gemälde-Sammlung*, Munich, Bruckmann, 1908.

*Neue Pinakothek München, VI: Malerei der Gründerzeit*, ed. H. Ludwig, Munich, Die

Bayerischen Staatsgemäldesammlungen, Gemäldekataloge, Wolf & Sohn, 1977.
Neue Pinakothek München, *Erläuterungen zu den ausgestellten Werken*, Munich, Bayerische Staatsgemäldesammlungen, 1981.
*Northern Light. Nordic Art at the Turn of the Century*, ed. K. Varnedoe, New Haven and London, Yale University Press, 1988.
*Paris 1889. American Artists at the Universal Exposition*, ed. A. Blaugrund, New York, Abrams, 1889.
*Das Photoalbum 1858-1918. Eine Dokumentation zur Kultur- und Sozialgeschichte*, Munich, Stadtmuseum, 1975.
*Die Prinzregentenzeit*, ed. N. Götz and C. Schack-Simitzis, Munich, Beck, 1988.
*Leo Putz 1869-1940*, Bozen, Athesia, 1980.
*Die Sammlung des Freiherrn August von der Heydt: Ausgewählte Werke der Kunst der Gegenwart*, ed. C. G. Heise, Leipzig, Wolff, 1918.
*Die Sammlung Julius Stern + Berlin. Versteigerung, 22 Mai 1916*, Berlin, Cassirer–Helbing, 1916.
*Schack-Galerie, München*, ed. E. Ruhmer *et al.*, Die Bayerischen Staatsgemäldesammlungen, Gemäldekataloge, Munich, Wolf & Sohn, 1969.
*Schilder, Bilder, Moritaten*, [East] Berlin, Museum für Volkskunde, 1987.
*The René von Schleinitz Collection of the Milwaukee Art Center. Major Schools of Nineteenth-Century Popular Painting*, ed. R. M. Bisanz, Madison, Wisconsin University Press, 1980.
*The Second Empire. Art in France under Napoleon III*, Philadelphia, Museum of Art, 1978.
*'Ein seltsamer Garten': polnische Malerei des 19. Jahrhunderts: Romantik, Realismus und Symbolismus*, Lucerne, Kunstmuseum, 1980.
*Carl Spitzweg und sein Freundeskreis*, Munich, Haus der Kunst, 1967.
Städel'sches Kunstinstitut, *Kurzes Verzeichnis der Gemäldesammlung*, Frankfurt-on-Main, 1907.
Städel'sches Kunstinstitut, *Verzeichnis der Gemälde aus dem Besitz des Städel'schen Kunstinstituts und der Stadt Frankfurt*, Frankfurt-on-Main, 1966.
*Stadtbilder. Berlin in der Malerei vom 17. Jahrhundert bis zur Gegenwart*, Berlin, Arenhövel and Nicolaische Buchhandlung, 1987.
*Franz von Stuck, 1863-1928. Maler, Graphiker, Bildhauer, Architekt*, Munich, Villa Stuck, 1982.
*Symboles et réalités. La peinture allemande 1848-1905*, Paris, Musée du Petit Palais, 1984.
*The Triumph of Realism. An Exhibition of European and American Realist Paintings, 1850-1910*, New York, Brooklyn Museum, 1967.
*Verein bildender Künstler Münchens (a. V.) 'Secession,: Offizieller Katalog der internationalen Kunstausstellung*, Munich, Bruckmann, 1893.
*Waldungen. Die Deutschen und ihr Wald*, ed. B. Weyergraf, Akademie-Katalog 149, Berlin, Nicolaische Buchhandlung, 1987.

Wallraff–Richartz Museum der Stadt Köln, *Verzeichnis der Gemälde*, Cologne, 1965.

*Anton von Werner. Geschichte in Bildern*, ed. D. Bartmann, Munich, Hirmer, 1993.

*Der westdeutsche Impuls, 1900-1914: Kunst- und Umweltgestaltung im Industriegebiet*, 6 vols., Cologne, Essen, Düsseldorf, Hagen, Krefeld, Wuppertal, 1984.

*Heinrich von Zügel 1850-1941. Gemälde und Zeichnungen*, Stuttgart, Stadtgalerie, 1981.

*Die Zwanziger Jahre in München*, Schriften des Münchner Stadtmuseums, Vol. 8, Munich, 1979.

## BOOKS AND ARTICLES

Abrams, L., *Workers' Culture in Imperial Germany. Leisure and Recreation in the Rhineland and Westphalia*, London and New York, Routledge, 1992.

Allotria, *Ein halbes Jahrhundert Münchener Kulturgeschichte, erlebt mit der Künstlergesellschaft Allotria*, Munich, Thiemig, 1959.

Alloway, L., *The Venice Biennale 1895-1969. From Salon to Goldfish Bowl*, London, Faber, 1968.

Alt, T., *Die Herabwertung der deutschen Kunst durch die Parteigänger des Impressionismus*, Mannheim, Nemnich, 1911.

Althoff, G. (ed.), *Die Deutschen und ihr Mittelalter*, Darmstadt, Wissenschaftliche Buchgesellschaft, 1992.

Angermeyer-Deubler, M., Hans Thoma - ein 'Kämpfer für deutsche Kunst'? Ein Beitrag zur Wirkungsgeschichte Hans Thomas, *Jahrbuch der staatlichen Kunstsammlungen in Baden–Württemberg*, 25 (1988), pp. 160-87.

Ansell, F. J., and Fraprie, F. R., *The Art of the Munich Galleries*, London, Bell, 1911.

Arndt, M., Das Kyffhäuser-Denkmal. Ein Beitrag zur politischen Ikonographie des Zweiten Kaiserreiches, *Wallraff–Richartz-Jahrbuch*, 40 (1978), pp. 75-127.

*Ateliers Münchner Künstler. Photographien von Carl Teufel*, 3 vols., Munich, 1889-90.

Atkinson, J. Beavington, Munich International Exhibition. With notes on German art, *Art Journal*, N S 8 (1869), pp. 314-15, 327-8.

Aubert, A., Der Landschaftsmaler Friedrich, *Die Kunstchronik*, NS 7/18 (5 March 1896), pp. 281–93.

Baisch, A. (ed.), *Aus der Töchterschule ins Leben. Ein allseitiger Berater für Deutschlands Jungfrauen*, Stuttgart, Leipzig, Berlin, Vienna, Deutsche Verlags-Anstalt, 1895.

Bantzer, C., *Hessen in der deutschen Malerei, 1: Die Maler der Schwalm*, 3rd edn., Marburg, Elwert, 1950.

Bartmann, D., *Anton von Werner. Zur Kunst und Kunstpolitik im deutschen Kaiserreich*, Berlin, Deutscher Verlag für Kunstwissenschaft, 1986.

Baum, J., *et al.* (eds.), *Die Stuttgarter Kunst der Gegenwart*, Stuttgart, Deutsche Verlags-Anstalt, 1913.

Baumann, B., *Der Münchner Maler Wilhelm Marc 1839-1907. Monographie und Werkverzeichnis*, Miscellanea Bavarica Monacensia, Vol. 139, Munich, 1986.

Bayerle, G., *Johann Huss und das Concilium zu Kostnitz, veranlasst durch Lessings Bild auf der diesjährigen Kunstausstellung, in zwei Abtheilungen*, Düsseldorf, Roschütz, 1842.

Berger, R., *Malerinnen auf dem Weg ins 20. Jahrhundert. Kunstgeschichte als Sozialgeschichte*, Cologne, DuMont, 1982.

Berghahn, V. R., *Imperial Germany 1871-1914. Economy, Society, Culture and Politics*, Providence and Oxford, Berghahn Books, 1994.

*Berlin und die Berliner. Leute. Dinge. Sitten. Winke*, Karlsruhe, 1905.

Berman, M., *All That Is Solid Melts Into Air. The Experience of Modernity*, London and New York, Verso, 1983.

Bernáth, M., *Pál Szinyei-Merse*, Budapest, Corvina, 1981.

Bessel, R., *Germany after the First World War*, Oxford, Clarendon Press, 1992.

Betz, E., Kunstausstellungen und Tagespresse in München an der Wende des 19. Jahrhunderts. Ein Beitrag zum Kunst- und Kulturleben der bayerischen Hauptstadt, PhD dissertation, Munich, 1953.

Beyrodt, W., and Busch, W. (eds.), *Kunsttheorie und Kunstgeschichte des 19. Jahrhunderts in Deutschland, 1: Kunsttheorie und Malerei; Kunstwissenschaft. Texte und Dokumente*, Stuttgart, Reclam, 1982.

Bialostocki, J., *Dürer and his Critics, 1500-1971. Chapters in the History of Ideas, Including a Collection of Texts*, Saecula Spiritualia, Vol. 7, Baden-Baden, Koerner, 1986.

Biehn, H., *Residenzen der Romantik*, Munich, Prestel, 1970.

Bierbaum, O. J., *Aus beiden Lagern. Betrachtungen, Karakteristiken und Stimmungen aus dem ersten Doppel-Ausstellungsjahre in München*, Munich, Schüler, 1893.

Bierbaum, O. J., *Stuck*, Bielefeld and Leipzig, Velhagen & Klasing, 1899.

Bismarck, B. v., Harry Graf Kessler und die französische Kunst um die Jahrhundertwende, *Zeitschrift des deutschen Vereins für Kunstwissenschaft*, 42 (1988), pp. 47-62.

Blackbourn, D., *Populists and Politicians. Essays in Modern German History*, London, Allen & Unwin, 1987.

Blackbourn, D. and Eley, G., *The Peculiarities of German History. Bourgeois Society and Politics in 19th-Century Germany*, Oxford, Oxford University Press, 1984.

Blackbourn, D. and Evans, R. J. (eds.), *The German Bourgeoisie*, London and New York, Routledge, 1991.

Blake, N., Fer, B., Frascina, F., Garb, T. and Harrison, C., *Modernity and Modernism: French Painting in the Nineteenth Century*, New Haven and London, Yale University Press, 1993.

*The Blaue Reiter Almanac, edited by Wassily Kandinsky and Franz Marc*, ed. K. Lankheit, trans. H. Falkenstein, London, Thames & Hudson, 1974.

Boberg, J., Fichter, T. and Gillen, E. (eds.), *Industriekultur in Berlin im 19. Jahrhundert: Die Metropole*, Munich, Beck, 1986.

Boberg, J., Fichter, T. and Gillen, E. (eds.), *Industriekultur in Berlin im 19. Jahrhundert: Exerzierfeld der Moderne*, Munich, Beck, 1984.

Bode, W. v., Die amerikanische Konkurrenz im Kunsthandel und ihre Gefahr für Europa, *Kunst und Künstler*, 1 (1903), pp. 5-12.

Bode, W. v., Die Berliner Museen und die amerikanische Konkurrenz, *Der Cicerone*, 2 (1910), pp. 81-4.

Bode, W. v., *Kunst und Kunstgewerbe am Ende des 19. Jahrhunderts*, Berlin, Cassirer, 1901.

Boime, A., Entrepreneurial patronage in nineteenth-century France, in E. C. Carter, R. Forster and J. N. Moody (eds.), *Enterprise and Entrepreneurs in Nineteenth- and Twentieth-Century France*, Baltimore and London, Johns Hopkins University Press, 1976.

Borchmeyer, D. (ed.), *Wege des Mythos in der Moderne. Richard Wagner: 'Der Ring des Nibelungen'*, Munich, dtv, 1987.

Bosl, K. (ed.), *Bayern im Umbruch. Die Revolution von 1918, ihre Voraussetzungen, ihr Verlauf und ihre Folgen*, Munich and Vienna, Oldenbourg, 1969.

Bourdieu, P., *La distinction. Critique sociale du jugement*, Paris, Éditions de minuit, 1979.

Brandes, G., *Moderne Geister. Literarische Bildnisse aus dem 19. Jahrhundert*, 4th edn., Frankfurt-on-Main, Rütten & Loening, 1901.

Brehmer, A. (ed.), *Am Hofe Kaiser Wilhelm II*, Berlin, Neuer Verlag, 1898.

Brewer, J. and Porter, R. (eds.), *Consumption and the World of Goods*, London and New York, Routledge, 1993.

Bröhan, M., *Hans Baluschek 1870-1935. Maler, Zeichner, Illustrator*, Berlin, Nicolai, 1985.

Bröhan, M., *Walter Leistikow 1865-1908. Maler der Berliner Landschaft*, Berlin, Nicolai, 1989.

Brougier, A., *Gedanken über die fernere Entwicklung Münchens als Kunst- und Industriestadt*, Munich, 1905.

Brunn, G. and Reulecke, J. (eds.), *Berlin. Blicke auf die deutsche Metropole*, Essen, Reimar Hobbing, 1989.

Bruns, V. (ed.), *Württemberg unter der Regierung König Wilhelms II*, Stuttgart, Deutsche Verlags-Anstalt, 1916.

Buddensieg, T. and Rogge, H. (eds.), *Industriekultur: Peter Behrens und die A.E.G., 1907-14*, Berlin, Mann, 1979.

Bühler, H.-P., *Anton Braith, Christian Mali: Tiermalerei der Münchener Schule*, Mainz, Philipp von Zabern, 1981.

Burns, R. (ed.), *German Cultural Studies. An Introduction*, Oxford, University Press, 1995.

Busch, W. (ed.), *Funkkolleg Kunst. Eine Geschichte der Kunst im Wandel ihrer Funktionen*, 2 vols., Munich and Zurich, Piper, 1987.

Bussmann, W., *Zwischen Preussen und Deutschland. Friedrich Wilhelm IV: Eine Biographie*, Berlin, Siedler, 1990.

Carey, F. and Griffiths, A., *The Print in Germany 1880-1933. The Age of Expressionism*, London, British Museum, 1984.

Carr, W., *A History of Germany 1815-1990*, 4th edn., London, Arnold, 1991.
Cecil, L., *Wilhelm II. Prince and Emperor, 1859-1900*, Chapel Hill and London, University of North Carolina Press, 1989.
Chadwick, W., *Women, Art, and Society*, London, Thames & Hudson, 1990.
Chapple, G. and Schulte, H. H. (eds.), *The Turn of the Century. German Literature and Art, 1890-1915*, Bonn, Bouvier, 1981.
Clarke, M., *The Tempting Prospect. A Social History of English Watercolours*, London, Colonnade, 1981.
Cleve, I., *Geschmack, Kunst und Konsum. Kulturpolitik als Wirtschaftspolitik in Frankreich und Württemberg (1805-1845)*, Kritische Studien zur Geschichtswissenschaft, Vol. 111, Göttingen, Vandenhoeck & Ruprecht, 1996.
Debschitz, W. v., Eine Methode des Kunstunterrichts, *Dekorative Kunst*, 7 (1904), pp. 209-26.
Defregger, H. P., *Defregger 1835-1921*, Rosenheim, Rosenheimer Verlag, 1983.
[Deiters, H.], *Bericht: 'Ein Dokument deutscher Kunst'. Die Ausstellung der Künstlerkolonie Darmstadt 1901. Anregung, Vorarbeiten, Finanzierung*, Darmstadt, [1900].
Deiters, H., *Geschichte der Allgemeinen Deutschen Kunstgenossenschaft*, Düsseldorf, Bagel, 1906.
Deshmukh, M. F., Max Liebermann: observations on the politics of painting in Imperial Germany, 1870-1914, *German Studies Review*, (1980), pp. 171-206.
*Deutschland als Weltmacht: vierzig Jahre Deutsches Reich . . . herausgegeben vom Kaiser-Wilhelm-Dank, Verein der Soldatenfreunde*, Berlin, Kameradschaft, 1911.
Dibbern, M., Die Hamburger Kunsthalle unter Alfred Lichtwark, 1886-1914. Entwicklungen der Sammlungen und Neubau, PhD dissertation, Hamburg, 1980.
Diem, E., *Heinrich von Zügel. Leben, Schaffen, Werk*, Recklinghausen, 1978.
Diem, E., *Johann Sperl: Ein Meister aus dem Leiblkreis*, Munich, Bruckmann, 1955.
Dijkstra, B., *Idols of Perversity. Fantasies of Feminine Evil in Fin-de-Siècle Culture*, New York and Oxford, Oxford University Press, 1986.
Distel, A., *Impressionism: The First Collectors*, trans. B. Perroud-Benson, New York, Abrams, 1990.
Doede, W. and Doede, G., *Die Berliner Secession: Berlin als Zentrum der deutschen Kunst von der Jahrhundertwende bis zum Ersten Weltkrieg*, Frankfurt-on-Main, Propyläen, [n. d.].
Doerner, M., *The Materials of the Artist and their Use in Painting, with Notes on the Techniques of the Old Masters*, rev. edn., trans. E. Neuhaus, London, Harrap, 1949.
Donath, A., *Der Kunstsammler. Psychologie des Kunstsammelns*, Bibliothek für Kunst und Antiquitätensammler, Vol. 8, 4th edn., Berlin, Schmidt, 1923.
Drey, P., Der Kunstmarkt, eine Studie über die wirtschaftliche Verwertung der Bilder, PhD dissertation, Munich, 1910.
Drey, P., *Die wirtschaftlichen Grundlagen der Malkunst. Versuch einer Kunstökonomie*, Stuttgart and Berlin, Cotta, 1910.

Dube, W.-D., *The Munich Gallery, Alte Pinakothek*, London, Thames & Hudson, 1970.

Duveneck, J. W., *Frank Duveneck, Painter–Teacher*, San Francisco, John Howell, 1970.

Eberle, M., *World War I and the Weimar Artists: Dix, Grosz, Beckmann, Schlemmer*, New Haven and London, Yale University Press, 1985.

Eberlein, K. K., *Geschichte des Kunstvereins für die Rheinlande und Westfalen, 1829–1929*, Schriften des städt. Kunstmuseums Düsseldorf, Vol. 3, Düsseldorf, 1929.

Eberlein, K. K., Idee und Entstehung der deutschen National-Museen, *Wallraff–Richartz Jahrbuch*, NS 1 (1930), pp. 269-81.

Eberlein, K. K., Vorgeschichte und Entstehung der Nationalgalerie, *Jahrbuch der preussischen Kunstsammlungen*, 50/51 (1929-30), pp. 250-61.

Eggum, A., *Munch and Photography*, trans. B. Holm, New Haven and London, Yale University Press, 1989.

Ehrismann, O., *Das Nibelungenlied in Deutschland. Studien zur Rezeption des Nibelungenlieds von der Mitte des 18. Jahrhunderts bis zum Ersten Weltkrieg*, Münchner Germanistische Beiträge, Vol. 14, Munich, Fink, 1975.

Eichner, J., *Kandinsky und Gabriele Münter. Von Ursprüngen moderner Kunst*, Munich, Bruckmann, 1957.

Einem, H. v., Peter Cornelius, *Wallraff–Richartz-Jahrbuch*, 16 (1954), pp. 104-60.

Eitelberger, R. v., Die deutsche Renaissance und die Kunstreformbestrebungen der Gegenwart, *Zeitschrift für bildende Kunst,* 11 (1876), pp. 74-85, 106-12.

Elze, R. and Schiera, P. (eds.), *Das Mittelalter. Ansichten, Stereotypen und Mythen zweier Völker im 19. Jahrhundert: Deutschland und Italien*, Berlin and Bologna, Duncker & Humblot/Il Mulino, 1988.

Engels, E., *Münchens Niedergang als Kunststadt: Eine Rundfrage*, Munich, Bruckmann, 1902.

Eschenburg, B., *Landschaft in der deutschen Malerei: vom späten Mittelalter bis heute*, Munich, Beck, 1987.

Falke, J. v., *Die Kunst im Hause. Geschichtliche und kritisch–ästhetische Studien über die Decoration und Ausstattung der Wohnung*, 4th edn., Vienna, Gerold, 1882.

*Festschrift zum 25jährigen Regierungsjubiläum S. K. H. des Grossherzogs Ernst Ludwig von Hessen und bei Rhein*, Leipzig, 1917.

*E. A. Fleischmann's Hofkunsthandlung, Jubiläumsschrift, 1871-1896*, Munich, 1896.

Förster-Hahn, F., Adolph Menzel's 'daguerrotypical' image of Frederick the Great: a liberal bourgeois interpretation of German history, *Art Bulletin*, 59 (1977), pp. 242-61.

Franke, E. A., Publikum und Malerei in Deutschland vom Biedermeier zum Expressionismus, PhD dissertation, Heidelberg, 1934.

Franz, E. G., Der erste und der letzte Grossherzog von Hessen: fürstliche Kunstförderung in Darmstadt, in K. F. Wagner (ed.), *Hof, Kultur und Politik im 19. Jahrhundert*, Pariser Historische Studien, Vol. 21, Bonn, 1985.

Frecot, H., Geist, J. F. and Kerbs, D., *Fidus, 1868-1948. Zur aesthetischen Praxis bürgerlicher Fluchtbewegungen*, Munich, Rogner & Bernhard, 1972.

Frevert, U., *Women in German History. From Bourgeois Emancipation to Sexual Liberation*, trans. S. McKinnon-Evans, New York, Oxford and Munich, Berg, 1988.

Frey, B. S. and Pommerehne, W. W., *Muses and Markets. Explorations in the Economics of the Arts*, Oxford and Cambridge, Mass., Blackwell, 1989.

Frykman, J. and Löfgren, O., *Culture Builders. A Historical Anthropology of Middle-Class Life*, trans. A. Crozier, New Brunswick and London, Rutgers University Press, 1987.

Füssli, W., *Zürich und die wichtigsten Städte am Rhein, mit Bezug auf alte und neue Werke der Architektur, Skulptur und Malerei*, 2 vols., Zurich and Winterthur, Literarisches Comptoir, 1842-43.

Gaehtgens, T. W., *Die Berliner Museumsinsel im Deutschen Kaiserreich. Zur Kulturpolitik der Museen in der wilhelminischen Epoche*, Munich, Deutscher Kunstverlag, 1992.

Gebhardt, H., *Franz Hanfstaengl. Von der Lithographie zur Photographie*, Munich, Beck, 1984.

Gebhardt, H., *Königlich Bayrische Photographie, 1838-1918*, Munich, Laterna Magica, 1978.

Gillett, P., *The Victorian Painter's World*, Gloucester, Alan Sutton, 1990.

Gilmour, P. (ed.), *Lasting Impressions. Lithography as Art*, London, Alexandria Press, 1988.

Godé, M., *Der Sturm de Herwarth Walden ou l'utopie d'un art autonome*, Nancy, Presses Universitaires, 1990.

Gordon, D. E., *Expressionism. Art and Ideal*, New Haven and London, Yale University Press, 1987.

Gordon, D. E., Kirchner in Dresden, *Art Bulletin*, 58 (1966), pp. 335-61.

Gordon, D. E., *Modern Art Exhibitions 1900-1916*, Vol. 1, Munich, Prestel, 1974.

Graul, R. (ed.), *Die vervielfältigende Kunst der Gegenwart, 3: Die Radierung*, Vienna, Ges. für vervielfältigende Kunst, 1892.

Graves, A., *Art Sales. From Early in the Eighteenth Century to Early in the Twentieth Century*, Bath, Kingsmead Reprints, 1973.

Grimm, H., *Albrecht Dürer*, Sammlung gemeinverständlicher wissenschaftlicher Vorträge, ed. R. Virchow and W. Wattenbach, Vol. 16, 2nd edn., Berlin, Lüderitz, 1873.

Grote, L., *Die romantische Entdeckung Nürnbergs*, Bibl. des Germanischen Nationalmuseums Nürnberg zur deutschen Kunst- und Kulturgeschichte, Vol. 28, Munich, Prestel, 1967.

Grundmann, G., Schlösser und Villen des 19. Jahrhunderts von Unternehmern in Schlesien, *Tradition*, 10/4 (August 1962), pp. 149-62.

Grützner, E., Von der Geburt bis zum Verkauf meines ersten Bildes, *Velhagen & Klasings Monatshefte*, 18 (1903-04), pp. 98-107.

Gutbrod, E., Die Rezeption des Impressionismus in Deutschland, 1880-1910, PhD dissertation, Munich, 1980.

Haack, F., *Die Kunst des 19. Jahrhunderts*, 3rd edn., Esslingen, Neff, 1909.

Halle, D., *Inside Culture. Art and Class in the American Home*, Chicago and London, University of Chicago Press, 1993.
Hardtwig, W., *Geschichtskultur und Wissenschaft*, Munich, dtv, 1990.
Hardtwig, W., Soziale Räume und politische Herrschaft. Leistungsverwaltung, Stadterweiterung und Architektur in München 1870 bis 1914, in W. Hardtwig and K. Tenfelde (eds.), *Soziale Räume in der Urbanisierung. Studien zur Geschichte Münchens im Vergleich 1850 bis 1933*, Munich, Oldenbourg, 1990.
Hartmann, W., *Der historische Festzug. Seine Entstehung und Entwicklung im 19. und 20. Jahrhundert*, Studien zur Kunst des 19. Jahrhunderts, Vol. 35, Munich, Prestel, 1976.
Hartmann, W., 'Historische Wahrheit - Künstlerische Weihe'. Der historische Festzug zur Einweihung des Kölner Domes 1880 und die Wandbilder im Gürzenich, *Wallraff–Richartz-Jahrbuch*, 41 (1980), pp. 223-43.
Haxthausen, C. W. and Suhr, (eds.), *Berlin. Culture and Metropolis*, Minneapolis and Oxford, University of Minnesota Press, 1990.
Heller, R., *Munch. His Life and Work*, London, John Murray, 1984.
Hentzen, A., Die Entstehung der Bildnisse des Historikers Eduard Meyer von Lovis Corinth in der Hamburger Kunsthalle, *Jahrbuch der Hamburger Kunstsammlungen*, 6 (1961), pp. 117–42.
Hepp, C., *Avantgarde. Moderne Kunst, Kulturkritik und Reformbewegungen nach der Jahrhundertwende*, Munich, dtv, 1987.
Herbert, R. L., *Impressionism. Art, Leisure and Parisian Society*, New Haven and London, Princeton University Press, 1988.
Heres, G., Gloria Dresdensis. Dresdens Ruhm in der Goethezeit, *Jahrbuch der staatlichen Kunstsammlungen Dresden*, 1976-77, pp. 7-27.
Hermand, J., *Adolph Menzel: Das Flötenkonzert von Sanssouci. Ein realistisch geträumtes Preussenbild*, Frankfurt-on-Main, Fischer, 1985.
Herrmann, G., Die 'Jugend' und ihr Künstlerkreis, *Zeitschrift für Bücherfreunde*, 4 (1900), pp. 57–70.
Hesse-Frielinghaus, H. *et al.*, *Karl Ernst Osthaus. Leben und Werk*, Recklinghausen, 1978.
Hettling, M. and Nolte, P. (eds.), *Bürgerliche Feste. Symbolische Formen politischen Handelns im 19. Jahrhundert*, Göttingen, Vandenhoeck & Rupprecht, 1993.
Heyck, E., *Hans von Bartels*, Bielefeld and Leipzig, Velhagen & Klasing, 1903.
Hiddleston, J. (ed.), *Laforgue aujourd'hui*, Paris, Corti, 1988.
Hirth, G., *Das deutsche Zimmer der Renaissance. Anregungen zu häuslicher Kunstpflege*, 2nd edn., Munich, Hirth, 1882.
Hirth, G., *Kleinere Schriften, 1: Wege zur Kunst*, 3rd edn., Munich, Knorr & Hirth, 1918.
Hochreiter, W., *Vom Musentempel zum Lernort. Zur Sozialgeschichte deutscher Museen, 1800–1914*, Darmstadt, Wissenschaftliche Buchgesellschaft, 1994.
Holt, E. G. (ed.), *The Art of all Nations, 1850-1873. The Emerging Role of Critics and Exhibitions*, New York, Anchor Press/Doubleday, 1981.

Holt, E. G. (ed.), *The Triumph of Art for the Public. A Documentary History of Art 1785 to 1848*, New York, Anchor Press/Doubleday, 1979.

Holtfrerich, C.-L., *The German Inflation 1914-23. Causes and Effects in International Perspective*, Berlin and New York, De Gruyter, 1986.

Honour, H., *Romanticism*, London, Allen Lane, 1979.

Horn, P., *Düsseldorfer Graphik in alter und neuer Zeit*, Schriften des Städt. Kunstmuseums, Vol. 2, Düsseldorf, 1928.

Howitt-Watts, A., *An Art-Student in Munich*, 2nd edn., London, de la Rue, 1880.

*100 Jahre Bruckmann. Ein Blick zurück. Den Freunden unseres Hauses gewidmet im Jubiläumsjahr 1958*, Munich, Bruckmann, 1958.

*150 Jahre Kunstverein Darmstadt*, Darmstadt, Kunstverein, 1989.

*150 Jahre Württembergischer Kunstverein Stuttgart 1827-1977*, Stuttgart, Württembergischer Kunstverein, 1977.

Huret, J., *En Allemagne. La Bavière et la Saxe*, Paris, Fasquelle, 1911.

Hutchison, J. C., *Albrecht Dürer. A Biography*, Princeton, NJ, Princeton University Press, 1990.

Hütt, W., *Die Düsseldorfer Malerschule, 1819-1869*, 2nd edn., Leipzig, Seemann, 1984.

*Im Kampf um die Kunst: Die Antwort auf den 'Protest deutscher Künstler'*, Munich, Piper, 1911. (Later reissued as *Deutsche und französische Kunst*, ed. W. Heymel.)

Imiela, H. J., *Max Slevogt: Eine Monographie*, Karlsruhe, Braun, 1968.

Immel, U., Die deutsche Genremalerei des 19. Jahrhunderts, PhD dissertation, Heidelberg, 1967.

Ishikawa-Franke, S., *Albert Weisgerber. Leben und Werk*, Saarbrücken, 1978.

Ivins, W. M., *Prints and Visual Communication*, Boston, Mass., Harvard University Press, 1953.

Jacobs, M., *The Good and Simple Life. Artist Colonies in Europe and America*, Oxford, Phaidon, 1985.

Jensen, J. C., *Adolph Menzel*, Cologne, DuMont, 1982.

Jensen, J. C. (ed.), *Polnische Malerei von 1830 bis 1914*, Cologne, Dumont, 1978.

Jensen, R., *Marketing Modernism in Fin-de-Siècle Europe*, Princeton, NJ, Princeton University Press, 1994.

Jeszenszky, S., 'Le déjeuner sur l'herbe' de Szinyei, *Bulletin de la Galerie Nationale Hongroise*, 11 (1960), pp. 5-78.

Jones, A. H. and Kingsley, K., Salome in late nineteenth-century French art and literature, *Studies in Iconography*, 9 (1983), pp. 107-27.

Junge, H. (ed.), *Avant-Garde und Publikum. Zur Rezeption avantgardistischer Kunst in Deutschland 1905-1933*, Cologne, Weimar and Vienna, Böhlau, 1992.

Justi, L., Die Landes-Kunst-Kommission, in *Im Dienste der Kunst*, Breslau, Korn, 1936.

Kaes, A. (ed.), *Kino-Debatte. Texte zum Verhältnis von Literatur und Film 1909-1929*, Munich and Tübingen, dtv/Niemeyer, 1978.

Kahn, J., *Münchens Großindustrie und Großhandel*, 2nd edn., Munich, Lindauer, 1913.

Kalkschmidt, E., *Carl Spitzweg und seine Welt*, Munich, Bruckmann, 1945.
Kandinsky, V., *Über das Geistige in der Kunst*, 6th edn., Bern-Bümpliz, 1959.
Kaufhold, E., *Bilder des Übergangs. Zur Mediengeschichte von Fotografie und Malerei in Deutschland um 1900*, Marburg, Jonas, 1986.
Keen, G., *The Sale of Works of Art. A Study Based on the Times–Sotheby Index*, London, Nelson, 1971.
Kiaulehn, W., *Berlin. Schicksal einer Weltstadt*, Munich and Berlin, 1958.
Klee, P., *Schriften, Rezensionen und Aufsätze*, ed. C. Geelhaar, Cologne, DuMont, 1976.
Knackfuss, H., *Menzel*, Bielefeld and Leipzig, Velhagen & Klasing, 1895.
Koch, A. (ed.), *Ein Dokument deutscher Kunst, Darmstadt 1901. Großherzog Ernst Ludwig und die Ausstellung der Künstler-Kolonie in Darmstadt von Mai bis Oktober 1901*, Darmstadt, Herbert, 1901.
Koch, A. and Zobel, V., *Darmstadt. Eine Stätte moderner Kunstbestrebungen*, Darmstadt, Koch, 1905.
Kocka, J. (ed.), *Bürgertum im 19. Jahrhundert. Deutschland im europäischen Vergleich*, 3 vols., Munich, dtv, 1988.
Kugler, F., *Kleine Schriften und Studien zur Kunstgeschichte*, 3 vols., Stuttgart, Ebner & Seubert, 1853-54.
Kutter, P., *Das materielle Elend der jungen Münchener Maler*, Munich, 1911.
Lackner, B. K. and Stark, G. D. (eds.), *Essays on Culture and Society in Modern Germany*, Arlington, Texas University Press, 1982.
*Jules Laforgue: Critique d'art*, ed. M. Dottin, Lille, Presses Universitaires, 1988.
Lahnstein, P., *Münter*, Ettal, 1971.
Langenstein, Y., *Der Münchener Kunstverein im 19. Jahrhundert. Ein Beitrag zur Entwicklung des Kunstmarkts und des Ausstellungswesens*, Miscellanea Bavarica Monacensia, Vol. 122, Munich, 1983.
Lankheit, K., *Franz Marc. Sein Leben und seine Kunst*, Cologne, DuMont, 1976.
Lankheit, K., Nibelungen-Illustrationen der Romantik. Zur Säkularisierung christlicher Bildformen im 19. Jahrhundert, *Zeitschrift für Kunstwissenschaft*, 7 (1953), pp. 95-112.
Lehrs, M., *Gesammeltes*, Freiburg im Breisgau, Urban, 1924.
Leiss, L., *Kunst im Konflikt. Kunst und Künstler im Widerstreit mit der 'Obrigkeit'*, Berlin and New York, De Gruyter, 1976.
Lenman, R., Art and tourism in southern Germany, 1850-1930, in A. Marwick (ed.), *The Arts, Literature and Society*, London and New York, Routledge, 1990.
Lenman, R., A community in transition: painters in Munich, 1886-1924, *Central European History*, 15/1 (1982), pp. 3-33.
Lenman, R. Der deutsche Kunstmarkt 1840-1923: Integration, Veränderung, Wachstum, in E. Mai and P. Paret (eds.), *Sammler, Stifter und Museen. Kunstförderung in Deutschland im 19. und 20. Jahrhundert*, Cologne, Weimar and Vienna, Böhlau, 1993.
Lenman, R., *Die Kunst, die Macht und das Geld. Zur Kulturgeschichte des kaiserlichen Deutschland 1871-1918*, Frankfurt-on-Main and New York, Campus, 1994.

Lenman, R., Painters, patronage and the art market in Germany, 1850-1914, *Past & Present*, 123 (1989), pp. 109-40.

Lenman, R., Politics and culture: the state and the avant-garde in Munich, 1886-1914, in R. J. Evans (ed.), *Society and Politics in Wilhelmine Germany*, London, Croom Helm, 1978.

Lepsius, M. R. (ed.), *Bildungsbürgertum im 19. Jahrhundert, Teil III: Lebensführung und ständische Vergesellschaftung*, Industrielle Welt, Vol. 47, Stuttgart, Klett–Cotta, 1992.

*Alfred Lichtwark. Eine Auswahl seiner Schriften*, ed W. Mannhardt, 2 vols., Berlin, Cassirer, 1917.

Lichtwark, A., *Aus der Praxis*, Berlin, Cassirer, 1902.

Lichtwark, A., *Drei Programme*, Berlin, Cassirer, 1902.

Lichtwark, A., *Hermann Kauffmann und die Kunst in Hamburg von 1800-1850*, Munich, Bruckmann, 1893.

Lichtwark, A., Der Sammler, *Kunst und Künstler*, 10 (1912), pp. 229-41, 281-91.

Lieb, N., *München. Die Geschichte seiner Kunst*, Munich, Oldenbourg, 1971.

Lindsay, J., *Gustave Courbet. His Life and Art*, Bath, Adams & Dart, 1973.

Lindsay, K. C., Kandinsky in 1914 New York: solving a riddle, *Art News*, 55 (1956), pp. 32-3, 58-60.

Löfgren, O., The nationalisation of culture, *Ethnologia Europaea*, 19 (1989), pp. 5-23.

Löhneysen, W. v., Paul Cassirer - Beschreibung eines Phänomens, *Imprimatur*, NS 7 (1972), pp. 153-180.

Lübke, W., *Altes und Neues. Studien und Kritiken*, Breslau, Schlesische Buchdruckerei, 1891.

Lübke, W., *Geschichte der Renaissance in Deutschland*, 2 vols., 3rd edn., rev. A. Haupt, Esslingen, Neff, 1914.

Lübke, W., Die heutige Kunst und die Kunstwissenschaft, *ZfbK*, 1 (1866), pp. 3-13.

Lübke, W., *Die moderne französische Kunst*, Stuttgart, Weise, 1872.

Lüdecke, H. and Heiland, S. (eds.), *Dürer und die Nachwelt. Urkunden, Briefe, Dichtungen und wissenschaftliche Betrachtungen aus vier Jahrhunderten*, Berlin, Rütten & Loening, 1955.

Ludwig, H., *Kunst, Geld und Politik um 1900 in München. Formen und Ziele der Kunstfinanzierung und Kunstpolitik während der Prinzregentenära (1886-1912)*, Kunst, Kultur und Politik im Kaiserreich, Vol. 8, Berlin, Mann, 1986.

Ludwig, H., *Münchner Malerei im 19. Jahrhundert*, Munich, Hirmer, 1978.

Mai, E. (ed.), *Historienmalerei in Europa. Paradigmen in Form, Funktion und Ideologie*, Mainz, Philipp von Zabern, 1990.

Mai, E., 'Unsere Düsseldorfer Schule ist und kann nichts anderes sein als eine veredelte niederländische': über die Beziehungen der Düsseldorfer Maler zur niederländischen Malerei des 17. Jahrhunderts, *Kölner Museums-Bulletin*, 1989/93, pp. 4-22.

Mai, E. and Paret, P. (eds.), *Sammler, Stifter und Museen. Kunstförderung in Deutschland im 19. und 20. Jahrhundert*, Cologne, Weimar and Vienna, Böhlau, 1993.

Mai, E., Pohl, H. and Waetzoldt, S. (eds.), *Kunstpolitik und Kunstförderung im Kaiserreich. Kunst im Wandel der Sozial- und Wirtschaftsgeschichte,* Kunst, Kultur und Politik im Kaiserreich, Vol. 2, Berlin, Mann, 1982.

Mai, E., Pohl, H. and Waetzoldt, S. (eds.), *Das Rathaus im Kaiserreich. Kunstpolitische Aspekte einer Bauaufgabe des 19. Jahrhunderts*, Kunst, Kultur und Politik im Kaiserreich, Vol. 4, Berlin, Mann, 1982.

Mai, E. and Waetzoldt, S. (eds.), *Kunstverwaltung, Bau- und Denkmalpolitik im Kaiserreich*, Kunst, Kultur und Politik im Kaiserreich, Vol. 1, Berlin, Mann, 1981.

Mai, E., Waetzoldt, S. and Wolandt, G. (eds.), *Ideengeschichte und Kunstwissenschaft. Philosophie und bildende Kunst im Kaiserreich*, Kunst, Kultur und Politik im Kaiserreich, Vol. 3, Berlin, Mann, 1983.

Makela, M., *The Munich Secession. Art and Artists in Turn-of-the Century Munich*, Princeton, NJ, Princeton University Press, 1990.

Martin, K., *Die Tschudi-Spende. Hugo von Tschudi zum Gedächtnis, 7 Februar 1851-26 November 1911*, Munich, Bay. Staatsgemäldesammlungen, 1962.

Martin, M., *Alt-Holländische Bilder*, Bibliothek für Kunst und Antiquitätensammler, Vol. 15, Berlin, Schmidt, 1918.

Martin, R., *Jahrbuch des Vermögens und Einkommens der Millionäre in Bayern*, Berlin, Martin, 1914.

Mayr, J., *Wilhelm Leibl. Sein Leben und sein Schaffen*, 4th edn., Munich, Bruckmann, 1936.

Mehl, S., *Franz von Lenbach in der Städtischen Galerie im Lenbachhaus München*, Materialien zur Kunst des 19. Jahrhunderts, Vol. 25, Munich, Prestel, 1980.

Meier-Graefe, J., Handel und Händler, *Kunst und Künstler*, 11 (1913), pp. 27-34, 104-9.

Mende, M., *Im Namen Dürers. Druckgraphische Jahresblätter des Albrecht-Dürer-Vereins in Nürnberg, 1833-1974*, Nuremberg, Hans Carl, 1992.

Mennacher, T., *Adolf Lier und sein Werk*, Munich, Piloty & Loehler, 1928.

Michel, W., Münchner 'Lehr- und Versuchateliers für angewandte und freie Kunst', *Deutsche Kunst und Dekoration*, 17 (1905-06), pp. 379-98.

Milner, J., *The Studios of Paris. The Capital of Art in the Late 19th Century*, New Haven and London, Yale University Press, 1988.

Minihan, J., *The Nationalisation of Culture. The Development of State Subsidies to the Arts in Great Britain*, London, Hamish Hamilton, 1977.

Mitchell, T. F., *Art and Science in German Landscape Painting 1770-1840*, Oxford, Clarendon Press, 1993.

Mittlmeier, W. (ed.), *Die Neue Pinakothek in München, 1843-54: Planung, Baugeschichte und Fresken*, Studien zur Kunst des 19. Jahrhunderts, Vol. 16, Munich, Prestel, 1977.

Möckl, K., Hof und Hofgesellschaft in Bayern in der Prinzregentenzeit, in K. F. Wagner (ed.), *Hof, Kultur und Politik im 19. Jahrhundert*, Pariser Historische Studien, Vol. 21, Bonn, 1985.

Möckl, K., *Die Prinzregentenzeit. Gesellschaft und Politik während der Ära des Prinzregenten Luitpold in Bayern*, Munich, Oldenbourg, 1972.

Mommsen, W. J., Stadt und Kultur im deutschen Kaiserreich, in T. Schabert (ed.), *Die Welt der Stadt*, Veröffentlichungen der Carl Friedrich von Siemens Stiftung, Vol. 4, Munich, Piper, 1990.

Moulin, R., *Le Marché de la peinture en France*, Paris, Éditions de minuit, 1967.

Moulin, R. (ed.), *Sociologie de l'art. Colloque international, Marseille 13-14 juin 1985*, Paris, La Documentation française, 1986.

Moulin, R., *L'Artiste, l'institution et le marché*, Paris, Flammarion, 1992.

Mühsam, K., *Die Kunstauktion. Licht- und Schattenseiten des Vesteigerungswesens im Kunst- und Antiquitätenhandel für Käufer und Verkäufer*, Berlin, Verlag für Kunstwissenschaft, 1923.

*München und seine Bauten*, Munich, Bay. Architekten- und Ingenieurverein, 1912.

Muther, R., *Aufsätze über bildende Kunst*, 3 vols., Berlin, Ladyschnikow, 1914.

Muther, R., *Geschichte der Malerei*, 4th edn., 3 vols., Berlin, Chryselius, 1922.

Nagel, O., *Käthe Kollwitz*, London, Studio Vista, 1971.

Needham, G., *Nineteenth Century Realist Art*, New York, Harper & Row, 1988.

Niederhauser, E., Literature and the arts in the movements of national revival among the peoples of eastern Europe in the first half of the nineteenth century, *European Studies Review*, 3 (1973), pp. 347-68.

Nipperdey, T., *Deutsche Geschichte 1800-1866. Bürgerwelt und starker Staat*, Munich, Beck, 1983.

Nipperdey, T., Kirche und Nationaldenkmal. Der Kölner Dom in den 40er Jahren, in W. Pöls (ed.), *Staat und Gesellschaft. Beiträge zur Geschichte der modernen Welt*, Stuttgart, Klett–Cotta, 1979.

Nipperdey, T., Nationalidee und Nationaldenkmal in Deutschland im 19. Jahrhundert, *Historische Zeitschrift*, 206 (1968), pp. 529-85.

Nipperdey, T., Religion und Gesellschaft: Deutschland um 1900, *Historische Zeitschrift*, 246 (1988), pp. 591-615.

Nipperdey, T., Verein als soziale Struktur in Deutschland im späten 18. und frühen 19. Jahrhundert: eine Fallstudie zur Modernisierung, in *Gesellschaft, Kultur, Theorie. Gesammelte Aufsätze zur neueren Geschichte*, Kritische Studien zur Geschichtswissenschaft, Vol. 18, Göttingen, Vandenhoeck & Rupprecht, 1976.

Nitschke, A., Ritter, G. A., Peukert, D. and vom Bruch, R. (eds.), *Jahrhundertwende. Der Aufbruch in die Moderne, 1880-1930*, 2 vols., Reinbek, Rowohlt, 1990.

Nochlin, L., *Realism*, London, Penguin, 1971.

Nochlin, L., *Women, Art and Power and Other Essays*, London, Thames & Hudson, 1989.

Oettermann, S., *Das Panorama. Die Geschichte eines Massenmediums*, Frankfurt-on-Main, Syndikat, 1980.

Osborn, M., *Berlin*, Berühmte Kunststätten, Vol. 43, 2nd edn., Leipzig, Seemann, 1926.

Osten, G. v. d., Manets Spargelbündel 'Bei Liebermann' jetzt in Köln, *Wallraff–Richartz-Jahrbuch*, 31 (1970), pp. 135-48.
Ostini, F. v., *Grützner*, Bielefeld and Leipzig, Velhagen & Klasing, 1902.
Ostini, F. v., *Hugo von Habermann*, Munich, Piper, 1912.
Ott, K., Erinnerungen an die Erwerbung des Mannheimer Manetbildes 'Die Erschiessung Kaiser Maximilians', *Kunst und Künstler*, 31 (1932), pp. 105-6.
Panofsky, E., *Albrecht Dürer*, 2 vols., 2nd rev. edn., Princeton, NJ, Princeton University Press, 1945.
Paret, P., Art and the national image: the conflict over Germany's participation in the St Louis Exposition, *Central European History*, 11 (1978), pp. 173-88.
Paret, P., *Art as History. Episodes in the Culture and Politics of Nineteenth-Century Germany*, Princeton, NJ, Princeton University Press, 1988.
Paret, P., *The Berlin Secession. Modernism and its Enemies in Imperial Germany*, Cambridge, Mass. and London, Belknap, 1980.
Paret, P., The Tschudi affair, *Journal of Modern History*, 53 (1981), pp. 589-618.
Pascal, R., *From Naturalism to Expressionism. German Literature and Society 1880-1918*, London, Weidenfeld & Nicolson, 1973.
Paul, B., Drei Sammlungen französischer impressionistischer Kunst im kaiserlichen Berlin: Bernstein, Liebermann, Arnhold, *Zeitschrift des deutschen Vereins für Kunstwissenschaft*, 42 (1988), pp. 11-15.
Paul, B., *Hugo von Tschudi und die moderne französische Kunst im deutschen Kaiserreich*, Berliner Schriften zur Kunst, Vol. 4, Mainz, Philipp von Zabern, 1993.
Paulus, A., Zwanzig Jahre Münchner Secession, 1893-1913, I: die geschichtliche Entwicklung, *Die Kunst*, 27 (1912/13), pp. 326-33.
Pecht, F., *Geschichte der Münchener Kunst im 19. Jahrhundert*, Munich, Verlagsanstalt für Kunst und Wissenschaft, 1888.
Perry, G., *Paula Modersohn-Becker. Her Life and Work*, New York and London, Harper & Row, 1979.
Peters, H., Wilhelm von Schadow, *Annalen des historischen Vereins für den Niederrhein*, 164 (1962), pp. 56-117.
Peters, U., *Stilgeschichte der Photographie in Deutschland 1839-1900*, Cologne, DuMont, 1979.
Pevsner, N., *Academies of Art: Past and Present*, Cambridge, Cambridge University Press, 1940.
Pfeiffer, G. (ed.), *Nürnberg - Geschichte einer europäischen Stadt*, Munich, Beck, 1971.
Pietsch, L., *Knaus*, Bielefeld and Leipzig, Velhagen & Klasing, 1896.
Pixis, E., *Verzeichnis der von Weiland Seiner Kgl. Hoheit dem Prinzregenten von Bayern aus privaten Mitteln erworbenen Werken der bildenden Kunst*, Munich, 1913.
Plagemann, V., Die Anfänge der Hamburger Kunstsammlungen und die erste Kunsthalle, *Jahrbuch der Hamburger Kunstsammlungen*, 11 (1966), pp. 61-88.
Poll, B., Preussen und die Rheinlande, *Zeitschrift des Aachener Geschichtsvereins*, 76 (1964), pp. 5-44.

Prinz, F. and Krauss, M. (eds.), *München - Musenstadt mit Hinterhöfen. Die Prinzregentenzeit 1886 bis 1912*, Munich, Beck, 1988.

*Ein Protest deutscher Künstler, mit Einleitung von Karl Vinnen*, Jena, Diederichs, 1911.

Przybyszewski, S., Meier-Graefe, J., Pastor, P. and Servaes, F., *Das Werk von Edvard Munch: Vier Beiträge*, Berlin, 1894.

Quast, R., Studien zur Geschichte der deutschen Kunstkritik in der zweiten Hälfte des 19. Jahrhunderts, PhD dissertation, Münster, 1936.

Rall, H. and Petzet, M., *König Ludwig II*, Munich, Schnell & Steiner, 1968.

Ranke, W., Le 'cas Böcklin'. Un épisode toujours actuel de l'art en Allemagne, *Revue de l'art*, 45 (1979), pp. 37-49.

Ranke, W., *Franz von Lenbach, der Münchner Malerfürst*, Cologne, Kippenheuer & Witsch, 1986.

Ranke, W., *Heinrich Zille. Photographien. Berlin 1890-1910*, 4th edn., Munich, Heyne, 1975.

Ranke, W., *Joseph Albert - Hofphotograph der bayerischen Könige*, Munich, Schirmer/Mosel, 1977.

Raupp, K. and Wolter, F., *Die Künstlerchronik von Frauenchiemsee*, Munich, Bruckmann, 1918.

Rave, P. O., Anfänge preussischer Kunstpflege am Rhein, *Wallraff–Richartz-Jahrbuch*, 9 (1936), pp. 181-204.

Rave, P. O., *Die Geschichte der Nationalgalerie Berlin*, Berlin, Nationalgalerie, [n. d.].

Rave, P. O., Schinkels Museum in Berlin, oder die klassiche Idee des Museums, *Museumskunde*, 29 (1960), pp. 1-21.

Reitlinger, G., *The Economics of Taste. The Rise and Fall of Picture Prices 1760-1960*, London, Barrie & Rockliff, 1961.

Reulecke, J., *Geschichte der Urbanisierung in Deutschland*, Frankfurt-on-Main, Suhrkamp, 1985.

Reverdy, A., *L'École de Barbizon: l'évolution du prix des tableaux de 1850 à 1960*, Paris and The Hague, Mouton, 1973.

Rewald, J. and Weitzenhoffer, F. (eds.), *Aspects of Monet. A Symposium on the Artist's Life and Times*, New York, Abrams, 1984.

Ribbe, W. (ed.), *Geschichte Berlins*, 2 vols., Munich, Beck, 1987.

Richter, O., *Geschichte der Stadt Dresden in den Jahren 1871 bis 1902*, Dresden, Zahn & Jaensch, 1903.

Roennefahrt, G., *Carl Spitzweg: Beschreibendes Verzeichnis seiner Gemälde, Ölstudien und Aquarelle*, Munich, 1960.

Roper, K., *German Encounters with Modernity. Novels of Imperial Berlin*, Studies in German Histories, Atlantic Highlands, NJ and London, Humanities Press International, 1991.

Rosenberg, A., *Defregger*, Bielefeld and Leipzig, Velhagen & Klasing, 1900.

Rosenberg, A., *E. v. Gebhardt*, Bielefeld and Leipzig, Velhagen & Klasing, 1899.

Rosenberg, A., *Friedrich August Kaulbach*, Bielefeld and Leipzig, Velhagen & Klasing, 1900.

Rosenberg, A., *Handbuch der Kunstgeschichte*, 3rd edn., rev. H. Rosenhagen, Bielefeld and Leipzig, Velhagen & Klasing, 1921.
Rosenberg, A., *Lenbach*, Bielefeld and Leipzig, Velhagen & Klasing, 1898.
Rosenberg, A., *Die Münchener Malerschule in ihrer Entwicklung seit 1871*, Hanover and Leipzig, Seemann, 1887.
Rosenberg, A., *Vautier*, Bielefeld and Leipzig, Velhagen & Klasing, 1897.
Rosenblum, R., *Modern Painting and the Northern Romantic Tradition. Friedrich to Rothko*, London, Thames & Hudson, 1975.
Rosenblum, R. and Janson, H. W., *Art of the Nineteenth Century. Painting and Sculpture*, London, Thames & Hudson, 1984.
Rosenhagen, H., *Kampf*, Bielefeld and Leipzig, Velhagen & Klasing, 1922.
Rössler, A., *Neu-Dachau: Ludwig Dill, Adolf Hölzel, Arthur Langhammer*, Bielefeld and Leipzig, Velhagen & Klasing, 1905.
Röthel, H. K. and Benjamin, J. K., *Kandinsky. Catalogue Raisonné of the Oil-Paintings, I: 1900–1915*, London, Sotheby, 1982.
Ruederer, J., *München*, Stuttgart and Munich, Krabbe/Müller, 1907.
Schadendorf, W. (ed.), *Beiträge zur Rezeption der Kunst des 19. und 20. Jahrhunderts*, Studien zur Kunst des 19. Jahrhunderts, Vol. 29, Munich, Prestel, 1975.
Schama, S., *Landscape and Memory*, London, HarperCollins, 1995.
Scharf, A., *Art and Photography*, rev. edn., London, Penguin, 1974.
Scheffler, K., *Adolf Menzel. Der Mensch. Das Werk*, Berlin, Cassirer, [*c.* 1915].
Scheffler, K., *Berlin. Ein Stadtschicksal*, Berlin, Reiss, 1910.
Schenda, R., Der Bilderhändler und seine Kunden im Mitteleuropa des 19. Jahrhunderts, *Ethnologia Europea*, 14 (1984), pp. 163-75.
Schiefler, G., *Die Graphik Ernst Ludwig Kirchners bis 1924, 1: bis 1916*, Berlin, Euphorion, 1926.
Schivelbusch, W., *Lichtblicke. Zur Geschichte der künstlichen Helligkeit im 19. Jahrhundert*, Munich and Vienna, Hanser, 1983.
Schmid, M., *Klinger*, 5th edn., rev. J. Vogel, Bielefeld and Leipzig, Velhagen & Klasing, 1926.
Schmidt, S., Bernhard Koehler - ein Mäzen und Sammler August Mackes und der Künstler des 'Blauen Reiter', *Zeitschrift des deutschen Vereins für Kunstwissenschaft*, 42 (1988), pp. 76-91.
Schmoll, gen. Eisenwerth, J. A., Salome 1900, *Du*, 8 (1981), pp. 45-55.
Schoch, R., Die belgischen Bilder, *Städel-Jahrbuch,* NS 7 (1979), pp. 171-86.
Schulte-Wülwer, U., *Das Nibelungenlied in der deutschen Kunst des 19. und 20. Jahrhunderts*, Kunstwissenschaftliche Untersuchungen des Ulmer Vereins, Verband für Kunst- und Kulturwissenschaften, Vol. 9, Giessen, anabas, 1980.
Schumann, P., *Dresden*, Berühmte Kunststätten, Vol. 46, Leipzig, Seemann, 1909.
Schweinitz, J. (ed.), *Prolog vor dem Film. Nachdenken über ein neues Medium*, Leipzig, Reclam, 1992.
Seidlitz, W. v., Museumsvereine, *Museumskunde*, 9 (1913), pp. 36-43.

Sengle, F., Wunschbild Land und Schreckbild Stadt: zu einem zentralen Thema der neueren deutschen Literatur, *Studium Generale*, 16 (1963), pp. 619-31.

Sheehan, J. J., Liberalism and the city in nineteenth-century Germany, *Past & Present*, 51 (1971), pp. 116-37.

Singer, H. W., *Die moderne Graphik*, Leipzig, Seemann, 1914.

Souriau, E., L'Art et la vie sociale, *Cahiers internationales de sociologie*, 5 (1948), pp. 66-96.

Spindler, M. (ed.), *Handbuch der bayerischen Geschichte, IV: Das neue Bayern, 1800-1970*, 2 part-vols., Munich, Beck, 1975.

Starzynski, J., *Aleksander Gierymski*, Warsaw, Auriga, 1971.

Stein, R., *Leo Putz. Mit einem Verzeichnis der Gemälde und bildartigen Entwürfe*, Vienna, 1974.

Stern, F., *Gold and Iron. Bismarck, Bleichroeder and the Building of the German Empire*, London, Penguin, 1987.

Strauss, M., Kandinsky and 'Der Sturm', *Art Journal*, 43 (1983), pp. 31-5.

Sutton, D., Bonnard and Vuillard in Hamburg, *Jahrbuch der Hamburger Kunstsammlungen*, 12 (1967), pp. 7-28.

Tafel, V., Paul Cassirer als Vermittler deutscher impressionistischer Malerei in Berlin. Zum Stand der Forschung, *Zeitschrift des deutschen Vereins für Kunstwissenschaft*, 42 (1988), pp. 11-15.

Taylor, R., *Tini Rupprecht: eine Zeit steht Modell*, Munich, [n. pub.], 1968.

Teeuwisse, N., *Vom Salon zur Secession. Berliner Kunstleben zwischen Tradition und Aufbruch zur Moderne 1871-1900*, Berlin, Deutscher Verlag für Kunstwissenschaft, 1986.

Teupser, W. (ed.), *Kunst und ihre Sammlung in Leipzig. Festschrift zum 100-jährigen Jubiläum des Leipziger Kunstvereins und Museums der bildenden Künste*, Leipzig, Breitkopf & Härtel, 1937.

Thausing, M., *Dürer. Geschichte seines Lebens und seiner Kunst*, 2 vols., 2nd rev. edn., Leipzig, Seemann, 1884.

Thiekötter, A., and Siepmann, E. (ed.), *Packeis und Preßglas. Von der Kunstgewerbewegung zum Deutschen Werkbund*, Werkbund-Archiv, Vol. 16, Giessen, anabas, 1987.

Thiemann-Stoedtner, O., *Dachaus Maler. Der Künstlerort Dachau 1801-1946*, Dachau, 1981.

Tietze, H., Der Blaue Reiter, *Die Kunst für Alle*, 27/23 (1 September 1912), pp. 543-50.

Timm, R. (ed.), *Die Kunst der Illustration. Deutsche Buchillustration des 19. Jahrhunderts*, Wölfenbüttel, VCH, 1986.

*Towards a New Art: Essays on the Background to Abstract Art 1910-20*, London, Tate Gallery, 1980.

Trier, E. (ed.), *Zweihundert Jahre Kunstakademie Düsseldorf*, Düsseldorf, Ernst Forberg-Stiftung, 1973.

Trier, E., and Weyres, W. (eds.), *Kunst des 19. Jahrhunderts im Rheinland, 1: Architektur I: Kultusbauten*, Düsseldorf, Schwann, 1980.

Trier, E. and Weyres, W. (eds.), *Kunst des 19. Jahrhunderts im Rheinland, 2: Architektur II: Profane Bauten und Städtebau*, Düsseldorf, Schwann, 1980.

Trier, E. and Weyres, W. (eds.), *Kunst des 19. Jahrhunderts im Rheinland, 3: Malerei*, Düsseldorf, Schwann, 1979.

*Trophäe oder Leichenstein? Kulturgeschichtliche Aspekte des Geschichtsbewusstseins in Frankfurt-on-Main im 19. Jahrhundert*, Kleine Schriften des Historischen Museums, Vol. 12, Frankfurt-on-Main, Historisches Museum, 1978.

Trübner, W., *Personalien und Prinzipien*, Berlin, Cassirer, [n. d.].

Tschudi, H. v., *Gesammelte Schriften zur neueren Kunst*, ed. E. Schwedeler-Meyer, Munich, Bruckmann, 1912.

Uechtritz, F. v., *Blicke in das Düsseldorfer Kunst- und Künstlerleben*, 2 vols., Düsseldorf, 1839.

Uhr, H., *Lovis Corinth*, Berkeley, Los Angeles and Oxford, California University Press, 1990.

*Unser Kaiser und sein Volk! Deutsche Sorgen. Von einem Schwarzseher*, Freiburg im Breisgau and Leipzig, Waetzel, 1906.

Vaughan, W., *German Romantic Painting*, New Haven and London, Yale University Press, 1980.

Venzmer, W., Adolf Hölzel, Leben und Werk, *Der Pelikan. Zeitschrift der Pelikan-Werke Günther Wagner, Hannover*, 65 (1963), pp. 4-14.

Venzmer, W., *Adolf Hölzel. Leben und Werk,* Stuttgart, Deutsche Verlags-Anstalt, 1982.

Venzmer, W., Adolf Hölzel und Hannover, *Niederdeutsche Beiträge zur Kunstgeschichte*, 5 (1966), pp. 223-44.

Verbeek, A., Das erste Wallraff–Richartz-Museum, *Wallraff–Richartz-Jahrbuch*, 23 (1961), pp. 7–36.

Vierhaus, R., Preussen und die Rheinlande, 1815-1915, *Rheinische Vierteljahresblätter*, 30 (1965), pp. 152-75.

Voss, H., *Franz von Stuck 1863-1928. Werkkatalog der Gemälde mit einer Einführung in seinen Symbolismus*, Munich, Prestel, 1973.

Vriesen, G., *August Macke*, 2nd edn., Stuttgart, 1957.

Waetzoldt, W., *Deutsche Kunsthistoriker*, 2 vols., Leipzig, Seemann, 1921, 1924.

Waetzoldt, W., *Dürer und seine Zeit*, Vienna, Phaidon, 1935.

Wagner, K. F. (ed.), *Hof, Kultur und Politik im 19. Jahrhundert*, Pariser Historische Studien, Vol. 21, Bonn, 1985.

Waldmann, E., Der Krieg und die Bilderpreise, *Kunst und Künstler*, 15 (1917), pp. 376-84.

Weber, L., *Der Gegensatz des deutschen und des französischen Volksgeistes. Zugleich ein Mahnwort zur Selbstaufraffung des deutschen Volkes*, Leipzig, 1891.

Weber, L. (ed.), *Die Wissenschaften und Künste der Gegenwart in ihrer Stellung zum biblischen Christentum*, Gütersloh, Bertelsmann, 1898.

Weigmann, O. A., *Sion Longley Wenban 1848-1897. Kritisches Verzeichnis seiner Radierungen mit einer biographischen Einführung*, Leipzig, Klinkhardt & Biermann, 1913.

Weiler, C., *Alexei von Jawlensky*, Cologne, DuMont, 1959.

Weimar, W., *Die Daguerrotypie in Hamburg 1839-1860. Ein Beitrag zur Geschichte der Photographie*, Hamburg, 1915.

Weisberg, G. P., *Beyond Impressionism. The Naturalist Impulse in European Art 1860-1905*, London, Thames & Hudson, 1992.

Weiss, P., *Kandinsky in Munich: The Formative Jugendstil Years*, Princeton, NJ, Princeton University Press, 1979.

Weitzenhoffer, F., *The Havemeyers. Impressionism Comes to America*, New York, Abrams, 1986.

Werckmeister, O. K., *The Making of Paul Klee's Career 1914-20*, Chicago and London, University of Chicago Press, 1989.

White, H. C. and White, C. A., *Canvases and Careers. Institutional Change in the French Painting World*, New York and London, Wiley, 1965.

White, N. C., *The Life and Art of J. Frank Currier*, Cambridge, Mass., Riverside Press, 1936.

Wichmann, S., *Franz von Lenbach und seine Zeit*, Cologne, DuMont, 1973.

Wichmann, S., *Meister, Schüler, Themen. Münchener Landschafter im 19. Jahrhundert*, Herrsching, Schuler, 1981.

Wichmann, S., *Realismus und Impressionismus in Deutschland. Bemerkungen zur Freilichtmalerei des 19. und beginnenden 20. Jahrhunderts*, Stuttgart, Schuler, 1964.

Wietek, G. (ed.), *Deutsche Künstlerkolonien und Künstlerorte*, Munich, Prestel, 1976.

Wilberforce, E., *Social Life in Munich*, London, W. H. Allen, 1863.

Wilke, K., Die 'Leipziger Illustrierte Zeitung' und ihre Geschichte, *Zeitschrift für Bücherfreunde*, 5 (1901/02), pp. 188-96, 228-36.

Wind, E., The revolution of history painting, *Journal of the Warburg Institute*, 2 (1938/39), pp. 116-27.

Windsor, A., *Peter Behrens: Architect and Designer 1868-1940*, London, Architectural Press, 1981.

Wingler, H. M. (ed.), *Kunstschulreform 1900-1933. Fünf Beispiele ihrer Verwirklichung*, Berlin, Mann, 1977.

With, C., Adolph von Menzel: a study in the relationship between art and politics in 19th-century Germany, PhD dissertation, University of California at Los Angeles, 1975.

With, C., The Emperor, the National Gallery, and Max Slevogt, *Zeitschrift des Deutschen Vereins für Kunstwissenschaft*, 30 (1976), pp. 1-4.

With, C., *The Prussian Landeskunstkommission 1862-1911. A Study in State Subvention of the Arts*, Kunst, Kultur und Politik im deutschen Kaiserreich, Vol. 6, Berlin, Mann, 1986.

Woermann, K., *Von Apelles bis Böcklin und weiter. Gesammelte kunstgeschichtliche Aufsätze, Vorträge und Besprechungen*, 2 vols., Esslingen, Neff, 1912.

Wolf, G. J., *Leibl und sein Kreis*, Munich, Bruckmann, 1923.
Wolf, G. J., *Münchener Künstlerfeste, Münchener Künstlerchroniken*, Munich, 1925.
Wolf, G. J., Sechzig Jahre Münchener Künstlergenossenschaft, *Das Bayerland*, 39 (1928), pp. 291-304.
Wolff, J. and Seed, J. (eds.) *The Culture of Capital. Art, Power and the Nineteenth-Century Middle Class*, Manchester, Manchester University Press, 1988.
Woltmann, A., *Holbein und seine Zeit. Des Künstlers Familie, Leben und Schaffen*, 2nd rev. edn., Leipzig, Seemann, 1874.
Zacharias, T. (ed.), *Tradition und Widerspruch. 175 Jahre Kunstakademie München*, Munich, Prestel, 1985.
Zammito, J. H., Der Streit um die Berliner Kultur 1871 bis 1930, *Jahrbuch für die Geschichte Mittel- und Ostdeutschlands*, 35 (1986), pp. 234-68.
Ziemke, H.-J., *Das Städelsche Kunstinstitut - die Geschichte einer Stiftung*, Frankfurt-on-Main, Städelsches Kunstinstitut, 1980.
Zimmermanns, K., *Friedrich August von Kaulbach 1850-1920. Monographie und Werkverzeichnis*, Materialien zur Kunst des 19. Jahrhunderts, Vol. 26, Munich, Prestel, 1980.

# Index

(Note: page numbers in *italic* type refer to illustrations)